The Fire and the Staff

THE FIRE AND THE STAFF

LUTHERAN THEOLOGY IN PRACTICE

KLEMET I. PREUS

CONCORDIA PUBLISHING HOUSE • SAINT LOUIS

Published by Concordia Publishing House
3558 S. Jefferson Ave.
St. Louis, MO 63118-3968
1-800-325-3040 • www.cph.org

Library of Congress Cataloging-in-Publication Data

The fire and the staff : Lutheran theology in practice / Klemet I. Preus.
p. cm.
Includes bibliographical references.
ISBN 0-7586-0404-1
1. Lutheran Church—Doctrines. 2. Lutheran Church—United States. I. Title.
BX8065.3.P73 2005
230'.41—dc22 2004023363

3 4 5 6 7 8 9 10 13 12 11 10 09 08 07 06

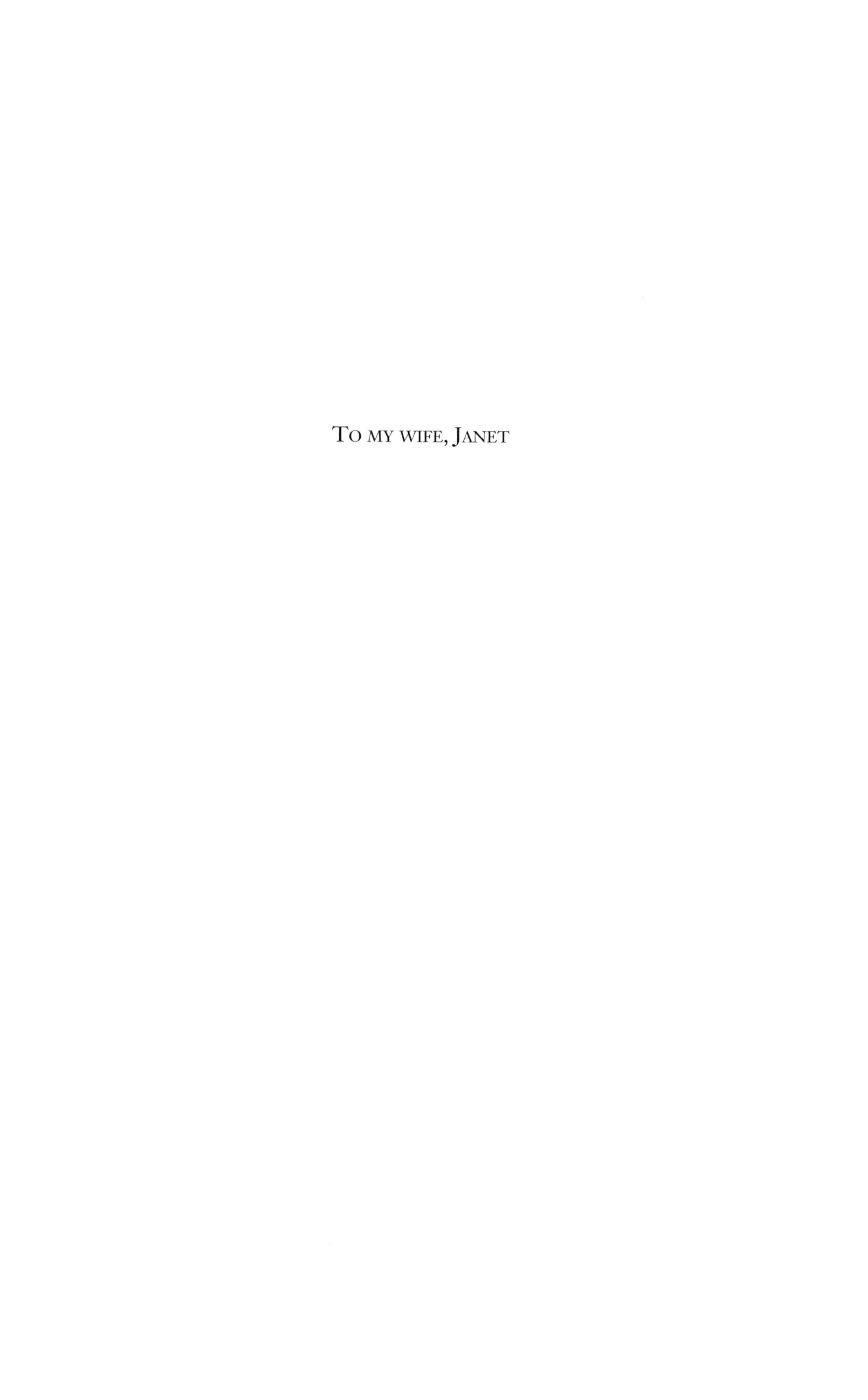

To my wife, Janet

Contents

Preface	9
Introduction	13
1. Light the Fire: Doctrine	19
2. The Heat of the Fire: Justification	55
3. The Fire Spreads: Word and Spirit	79
4. The Fire and the Staff: Doctrine and Practice	107
5. The Church's Staff: Worship in the Lutheran Church	137
6. The Christian's Staff: Good Works	185
7. The Fire Is Doused: Word and Spirit Separated	213
8. The Staff Is Bent: The Excitement of American Christianity	243
9. The Staff Is Broken: The Dynamism of American Christianity	277
10. The Staff Is Lost: American Worship Ideas	313
11. The Fire Kindled: Confessing the Faith	359
12. The Fire Stoked: Change in the Church	397
13. Conclusion: A Plea	435
Answers to Study Questions	445
Abbreviations	459
Notes	461
Bibliography	473

Preface

As a child, I used to sit in church—bored. It was not the sermons that put me to sleep. When my pastor preached, I usually listened. It was before and after the sermon that the tedium of the service would assault me, especially before I was confirmed and allowed to take Communion. When I got older, I would horse around with my brothers during services, an activity that, though less monotonous, was more dangerous. By the time I went to the seminary to become a pastor, I was a hardened Lutheran. By that I mean that I truly loved the Lutheran doctrine. I believed it with all my heart. Through sermons, catechism instruction, Bible classes, college courses, youth group conversations, private readings, and especially at home around the dinner table with family, I had come to understand that Lutheran doctrine is both biblical and overwhelmingly relieving. It presents Jesus to me as my Redeemer who, with no strings attached, forgives me through His death on the cross and endlessly offers that forgiveness to me through the Gospel. Abandoning the Lutheran doctrine or leaving the Lutheran church is not simply impossible for me, it is incomprehensible. I do not understand when others do so.

I was a hardened Lutheran in a second, less positive, way. I was hardened in my belief that Lutheranism was not that exciting. Don't get me wrong. The Lutheran doctrine is enormously exciting—if exciting means it moves people in some way. It always moved me to deeper faith and a desire for more. But if exciting means that it aroused my emotions and made me want to dance, start to cry, kiss someone, or raise my hands in the air during songs, then, I confess, it was not exciting to me. I was hardened in my antipathy for the Lutheran customs, the Lutheran traditions I did not often understand, the Lutheran style—in short, the practices of the Lutheran church. I accepted them because they were there, much as I accept the weather or a mosquito bite. I so cherished the good that I was resigned to accept the bad with it.

While preparing to be a pastor, especially after some years in the ministry, I began to realize the customs, traditions, and practices of the Lutheran church were not accidental accessories to our doctrine. I started to realize and appreciate the close relationship between our church's doctrine and her practice. Two observations strengthened this insight. First, I was always intrigued by the doctrine of other churches—living and dead. Gradually, I began to see that the practices of these churches correspond to their doctrine. If a church deviated from Lutheranism in doctrine, then that church would also deviate in practical ways. There seemed to be a correlation between doctrine and practice not only among Lutherans but also with Baptists, Roman Catholics, and Puritans. Second, I started to notice that people who joined the various churches I served would tell stories of unique, perhaps even unusual, practices at their former churches. These people would come with doctrinal quirks as well. I began to realize that the peculiarities of different doctrinal systems usually brought with them idiosyncrasies of church style. Subsequently, I become more intentional in my observations about the relationship between doctrine and practice. The more I observed people, studied theology, and learned history, the more I began to see the intricate link between the two.

A pleasant consequence from my observations was that I grew to love that which I had ignored growing up. The customs and practices of the Lutheran church are like fine vintage wine. The first time you taste wine you lean toward the sweet stuff. The subtleties and finesse that characterize a robust cabernet or a crisp pinot noir go unnoticed. You wonder why anyone would spend more money than the going rate for Boone's Farm. But as you mature and gain experience your fondness for heaven's libation increases and takes on the complexities of the fruit of the vine itself. So the more I learned about church practices, the more I loved them—whether they excited me yet or not.

In the mid-1980s I started to hear people talking about doctrine and practice as if the two were almost unrelated. It bugged me slightly. I also noticed that many of the cherished customs of the Lutheran church were not so cherished by everyone. Some customs were discarded or changed. Some customs were questioned. Uniformity among Lutheran congregations was disappearing. This troubled me a bit. But I was probably guilty of some unneeded innovation myself, so I continued to observe rather quietly. I figured there was no sense indicting myself unnecessarily. In the late 1980s I began reading books in which the style of the Evangelical Protestant churches in America was encouraged with the admonishment that we Lutherans retain our distinct doctrine. I must confess that I did not believe the premise of such books before I read them, and even less afterward. I was starting to get a bit alarmed. My alarm intensified both my studies and my parishioner watching. I also began to talk openly to members of my congregation as well as pastors about their views of the relationship between doctrine and practice. My conversations and studies led me back to those "boring" days of my childhood. Amazingly, I remembered the customs I had disdained and the practices I had misunderstood with greater clarity than I would have guessed. My memory led me to repent, if belatedly, of the impish behavior my brothers and I had substituted for them. I also repented, more seriously, of the pain I had inflicted and endured, often through my own suggestions of innovations that were neither needed nor salutary.

By the time I actually started talking about my observations and insights, be they ever so meager, The Lutheran Church—Missouri Synod was in full-fledged controversy about the very issue that had occupied my attention for so long: How do doctrine and practice relate? So, one day, I decided to write.

This book is not a theological treatise, though it is theological. It is not a primer on pastoral practice, though it is practical. Anecdotal and at times light, it, nevertheless, deals with a serious matter. It is intended for those who need to understand the "change and decay in all around I see."[1] It will also be helpful for those preparing themselves for church work. I learned many lessons through failure or stupidity. I pray that others may learn lessons less agonizingly than I did, through reading. I want people—pastors, teachers, students, administrators, anyone—to understand and value Lutheranism and specifically the Lutheran understanding of the relationship between doctrine and practice. A short study guide and discussion questions have been added to each chapter to help those who wish to explore these topics further.

The many stories and anecdotes in this book that employ the real first and last names of people are both true and factual. Other stories are true in the sense that they occurred. I have generally changed the names to protect the anonymity of those involved. Some of the stories are clearly embellished. Hyperbole is neither false nor wrong. I trust the reader to discern when it is used.

Many people helped me. I thank the Rev. Fritz Baue who started this project with me while at Concordia Publishing House; he is truly a man for all seasons and an artist as well. He trusted me and gave invaluable counsel. The Rev. Scot Kinnaman and the Rev. Mark Sell nursed the project along. They are true Israelites in whom there is not guile, friends of each other, my friends, and strong friends of the church. Editor Laura Lane is especially appreciated. I always admire people who can do so efficiently those things I do not even understand. I thank those who read the book before it was published. My son Klem is my best, if most brutal, critic. He understands the art of organization. He can turn thoughts into words and change a humdrum sentence into flowing prose. I thank the Rev. Ron Pederson who worked with expeditious zeal and still found more mistakes than I thought possible. Maxine Pierson, my former administrative assistant, deserves heartfelt thanks. She seized, with obvious relish, the opportunity to point out my flaws. Her honesty is exceeded only by her wisdom—she made especially helpful suggestions. Thank you to Kathy Hebert, my current administrative assistant, who does many efficient things without even being asked, such as proofreading the document. Finally, thanks to Donna Preus, my mother, who felt it was her duty to make sure I was doing a good job. I had forgotten how picky, and encouraging, she is. I am especially grateful to God for my infinitely patient wife, Jan. She loves me so much that she encouraged me in this project while sacrificing time with me in deference to her wifely ambitions. I also thank my wonderful mother and sainted father for teaching me to appreciate the churchly customs I did not always understand, who modeled true Christian love, and whose devotion to theology could not but be infectious.

Introduction

I had an argument with my editor about this book. I wanted to title it *A Lutheran Understanding of the Relationship between Doctrine and Practice in Light of the Influence of American Evangelicalism*. The Rev. Fred Baue, my original editor at Concordia Publishing House, said that the title was too long and unimaginative. He suggested *The Fire and the Staff*.

"But, Fritz," I countered, "how will people know that this book is about the Lutheran understanding of the relationship between doctrine and practice if they cannot read it in the title?"

Fritz reminded me that the Holy Bible did not, in its title, proclaim the theme of the saving work of Jesus. In addition, without actually reading it, one might think that the Book of Concord is a manual for transatlantic, high-speed airplane travel. People value these books, he maintained, even though they actually have to read them to know what they are about.

I was unconvinced. "What about C. F. W. Walther's *The Proper Distinction between Law and Gospel*? That title tells you what the book is about. Or think of that great book by Theodore Schmauk, *The Confessional Principle and the Confessions of the Lutheran Church: As Embodying the Evangelical Confession of the Christian Church*. We need a title like that. Those books were written when churches were churches, preachers were preachers, and books were books."

Fritz, ever patient, reminded me that these were books written by stodgy, old, German Lutheran theologians of the nineteenth century. Did I want people to think I was a stodgy, old, German Lutheran theologian from the nineteenth century?

I have to confess I agonized about that for some time. The fact is that most people who know me consider me a middle-aged, twenty-first-century, lightweight, American "wanna be" theologian. The nineteenth-century image had its attraction, but I thought the description "stodgy" might be a bit harsh.

Regardless of the title, I want people to read this book because I believe it says something important—even urgent—to the church. The relationship between church doctrine and church practice is often neither valued nor understood. Some accept the church's historic doctrine but adamantly demand the right to implement novel or different practices than Lutherans have often employed. Some correctly claim that our common doctrine unites us as a church but also claim that, in matters of practice, uniformity is neither desirable nor even possible. Others insist that the church be united in both doctrine and practice. Consequently, the church is not only confused by an overabundance of church practice options, but we cannot even agree on the function of church practice. How much should the Lutheran church strive for uniformity of practice? How crucial is unity of practice for our walk together as a church? What is the Lutheran understanding of the relationship between doctrine and practice?

We settled on the title *The Fire and the Staff* for three reasons. First, it was the editor's idea, and I have learned not to argue too much with the editor. Second, the last thing I want to be is stodgy. Third, and most important, *The Fire and the Staff* captures the relationship between doctrine and practice. Doctrine is like a fire. It lights our way and warms us. The evangelical Lutheran doctrine gives us our identity and attracts others to the Lutheran church. Practice, by which I mean the regularly accepted actions of a church body, a congregation, or an individual, is a staff that points to our doctrine and reinforces it.

Doctrine and practice are more closely related, even interdependent, than is often realized. Doctrine affects practice and practice affects doctrine. The two are so intimately woven together that when you change one, you will inevitably change the other, sometimes without realizing what has happened. The analogy of a shepherd is apt. A shepherd warms himself and his flock by the fire. With his staff he gently nudges the sheep toward the source of warmth. So God gives us doctrine, and through churchly practices He nudges us toward the biblical doctrine of Christ. What shepherd builds a fire that offers warmth and light then uses his staff to drive the sheep away from the fire? Wouldn't that be like a pastor who teaches the true doctrine but through faulty practice actually undermines his own teaching? Or think about a foolish shepherd who might gently guide his sheep with a good staff only to find that the fire is out. That would be akin to establishing good practices within the church but teaching faulty doctrine.

The first chapter, "Light the Fire," shows the importance of pure doctrine. Biblical doctrine points to Jesus Christ and saves sinners through faith in Him. Pure doctrine unifies Christians. The benchmark we measure the work of the church against is neither our own charm nor the perceptions of numerical effectiveness. Rather, we measure our church and our work as pastors and people against the pure doctrine of the cross that God has given us. Chapter 1 establishes the importance of doctrinal fire.

The second chapter proclaims the central article of Christian doctrine. It shows from the Holy Scriptures that "justification by grace through faith" is the article of doctrine upon which the church stands or falls. Salvation by grace is the central and most important teaching of the Bible. We are saved without the works of the Law and are purely passive in our salvation. Justification is often questioned today, especially by those who think that we are saved by Jesus in our heart rather than on the cross. We need an objective Savior and an objective doctrine of justification. Chapter 2, "The Heat of the Fire," shows the importance of the doctrine of the cross.

Chapter 3 deals with the Gospel of Christ and the sacraments of Baptism and the Lord's Supper. These are the instruments Christ uses to "bespeak us righteous" and to apply to us the treasures of His cross. The Holy Spirit has committed Himself to these means of grace and to no others. The Word and Sacraments alone are the power of God unto salvation. Further, they are always powerful. You neither need to search for the Holy Spirit elsewhere nor wonder whether you have Christ's Spirit wholly so long as you have Christ's promises in Word and Sacrament. God gives us neither a wordless Spirit nor a Spiritless Word. As in chapter 2, we are passive in our reception of God's grace through these means. As God extends His kingdom through the Gospel, this chapter is entitled "The Fire Spreads."

Chapter 4 analyzes the close and varied relationship between doctrine and practice. Sometimes doctrine and practice are so intimately related that they cannot be separated. Other times the two are related because of close associations during conflicts in the church, both past and present. When certain practices are forced upon the church, they should often be resisted. Frequently, the catholic nature of the church demands our acceptance of historic practices. A certain practice may teach the church so wonderfully that it must be retained for its didactic value. Chapter 4, "The Fire and the Staff," is built upon the first three chapters and lays the foundation for the rest of the book.

Chapters 5 and 6 discuss worship and good works, respectively. Chapter 5 shows that our understanding of grace alone shapes the way we hear and receive the Gospel. As we are passive in receiving salvation, so we are primarily passive in worship. And as we are one in Christ in our salvation, so we are as uniform as possible in the Divine Service. On the other hand, we are very different in the ways we serve our neighbor. We have all been given different skills and stations in life. Chapter 6 is a discussion of the uniqueness of every Christian in the various vocations God has placed upon us. It also shows the importance of the Christian confession of the faith—the greatest good work. These chapters deal more directly with the practice of the Lutheran church. Because chapter 5 addresses the church assembled, it is called "The Church's Staff." As the shepherd guides to the warmth of the fire through the staff, so the church guides to the warmth of the Gospel through the Divine Service. Chapter 6, "The Christian's Staff," moves our focus from corporate and uniform worship to individual acts of love for our neighbor. Through our vocation, works, and confession, we serve Christ and guide others to Him.

Chapter 7 changes the mood a bit. It is a presentation of the theology of American Evangelicalism, which consistently and disastrously separates the Holy Spirit from the Gospel. One result of the separation is an insatiable and unrequited quest for the assurance of salvation through exciting manifestations. A second result is a pursuit of the Holy Spirit's power in places where God has not led us. A third result is decision theology, which denies the precious Gospel of grace alone. I fear that we, living amid American Evangelicalism and its tendency to rip the Spirit from the Word, are forced to worry that "The Fire Is Doused."

The false doctrine of the Evangelical community affects its practices. When the Spirit is separated from the Gospel, then people no longer look to the Word and Sacraments of Christ for the assurance of their salvation. Doctrine is disparaged and theology is downplayed. The church no longer stresses the predictable power of the evangelical doctrine and the Sacraments. Instead, she craves excitement as the guarantee of salvation. Her style reflects this craving. Denominational distinctions are blurred as doctrine recedes and is replaced with excitement. Historic Christian practices such as sacramental examination and closed Communion are discarded while new practices are introduced. Chapter 8 shows how Lutherans who accept the practices of American Evangelicalism are in danger of accepting its doctrine as well. Church practice starts to point away from the Gospel. Hence the title, "The Staff Is Bent."

In chapter 9 we examine the second aberration of the American Evangelical separation of the Spirit from God's means of salvation: the pursuit of the Spirit's power through dynamic preachers or congregations rather than in the Gospel. Consequences in practice are obvious. Pastors are valued for their dynamism rather than their faithfulness to true doctrine. Those not perceived to be effective are often not respected. Women, provided they are demonstrably vibrant, are acceptable as pastors despite scriptural admonitions to the contrary. These practices reinforce the bad doctrine of Evangelicalism. The staff has led to a cold and artificial fire—"The Staff Is Broken."

Chapter 10 comes back to worship. This time we explore the source of worship innovations that even Lutherans have encountered and embraced recently. Most find their roots, predictably, in American Evangelicalism, especially the revivalist preachers, such as Dwight Moody. From marketing the church to altar calls, from preaching to felt needs to church hopping, the style of worship that has changed Lutheran churches with staggering speed in the last two decades is critiqued in this chapter. The Gospel of forgiveness in Christ does not often dominate. Worship no longer teaches Jesus Christ and His cross. It no longer leads to the warmth of the Gospel doctrine and "The Staff Is Lost."

Chapters 11 and 12 cast a more positive light on the future of the church. Chapter 11 presents the manner in which Christians confess the Gospel of Christ. Our talk of Christ is not merely witnessing to what God has done in our lives. Rather, we confess the saving Gospel of our Lord. This requires learning the doctrine of the faith, adorning it with a gentle Christian disposition, speaking it in various contexts, and perhaps risking the loss of face or reputation in our ambiguous age. When Christians offer the good confession of the faith, we see "The Fire Is Kindled."

Chapter 12 answers the question of how the church changes. God forbid that we would ever change the saving doctrine of Christ. That would kill the church. Sometimes a change in practice is called for. Martin Luther initiated great change in the church. In a series of sermons preached in 1522, the "Eight Wittenberg Sermons," Luther outlines for us the principles Lutherans need to follow when they contemplate a change of church practice. Luther, a truly strong yet patient leader, gives us words and examples that should be heeded by pastors and churches today. All change, even all salutary practice in the church, must serve the Gospel. Luther shows us "The Fire Stoked."

The theme of this book is that doctrine and practice have a reciprocal relationship. If you change one, you will change the other. The chapters outlined above show that this is precisely what is happening with Lutherans in America who blithely copy the practices of the Evangelical community around us.

We need to understand the influence of novel, uncritically accepted practices, subtle or not. They will gradually change our doctrine. And we should equally understand what happens when the historic practices of Lutheranism are discarded. Read on and you will, I pray, understand the relationship between doctrine and practice in the Lutheran church, especially in the face of American Evangelicalism.

STUDY QUESTIONS

1. To what does the doctrine of the Bible point?
2. What is the central article of Christian doctrine?
3. What are the Holy Spirit's means of grace?
4. What does the theme of the book hope to emphasize about doctrine and practice?

1

Light the Fire

DOCTRINE

I was ready to save the world as a young pastor. I was eager and sure I would succeed in the ministry. My first call was to start a mission church, and there was nothing to get in my way. How could anyone not absolutely love the message I was about to proclaim? All I had to do was remove any barriers to God's Gospel of grace and I would be raking in the converts.

Things did not work out exactly the way I had planned, even though I worked very hard to build up my church. I went from house to house distributing Christian pamphlets, inviting people to church, and spending long hours talking about Christ. I organized community canvasses of the neighborhoods to make people aware of our church. My sermons were Christ centered and clear—the best sermons I knew how to preach. I taught good Bible classes. Even with all of this activity, my little mission church grew only slowly and modestly. I grew discouraged.

In order to find out what else I could do to help my church, I attended seminars offered by my District or by parachurch groups. They all followed the same pattern. The leaders told the audience the five steps to successful ministry or the three principles to effective church growth or how to create a vibrant family of dynamic believers. These speakers, polished and energetic, told inspirational stories of mass conversions, of 100-percent congregational growth rate per decade, and of countless changed lives.

As I listened to the speakers' stories of success, I wondered why I had to work so hard to get families to church? Why, when I did get people into the church, were they so prone to backslide? Why did I have to spend so much time training the Sunday school teachers and elders of my fledgling church? Other churches appeared to have members who were born experts at all types of church responsibilities. Maybe I just was not cut out for the ministry. I would always go home from these seminars even more discouraged.

I figured I needed a change. After I had been in the ministry for four years, I took a call to be a pastor at a campus ministry at the University of North Dakota. I wanted another chance to succeed in the ministry. The District president was a friend of mine and wanted me to change certain practices at the campus chapel. I was to insist that all the students attending the church must understand and accept the teachings of The Lutheran Church—Missouri Synod before they could take Communion. I was to reintroduce the traditional hymns that praise songs had largely replaced. I was to teach the beliefs of my church body in terms of the role of women in the church. The District president told me that the District board of directors, which had called me, was behind me 100 percent. What a challenge! With the board of directors behind me, how could I fail?

Again, things did not work out as I had planned. Two weeks into my tenure, I was informed that the students had specifically requested of the board that I not be called. I was their tenth choice out of ten. Undaunted, I still felt assured of success. I figured the students would like me once they got to know me. Two weeks later, four people on the church council quit because they disagreed with "the direction I was taking the ministry." Two weeks after that the secretary quit along with one-fourth of the choir. After another couple of weeks I was informed that church attendance was significantly down from the previous year. About that time I was told by the District president that I would have to give a fifteen-minute presentation to all the pastors of the District on how things were progressing at the campus ministry.

I was afraid. How would I stand in front of a room full of pastors and tell them that I had totally failed? This chapel was supported with money from their churches. It was intended to serve the kids over whom they had pastoral responsibility. What should I say? "Your kids are leaving the church. Our attendance is down 25 percent over six weeks. The voices that once graced your youth choirs have fallen silent before the throne of God. The kids entrusted to my care have left, and I do not know how to get them back. I feel like Little Bo Peep who has lost someone else's sheep." How would I say these things?

Today I thank God for teaching me about discouragement early in my ministry. Otherwise, I might have really made a fool of myself. This is what I said to those pastors:

> During my whole ministry I have been listening to the glowing success stories of other pastors. I have felt intimidated by those who obviously knew an awful lot more than me about growing their churches. Out of sheer self-doubt I have shirked the daunting task of saving the world. I have felt guilty because my Gospel presentation is apparently not winsome enough. I have lost sheep and lost sleep. My joy has taken a vacation and my natural optimism has deserted me, all because I have not done what the experts said. And I refuse to tell you gentlemen how great my current ministry is. It's bad. All the numerical indicators are down. I am losing members. I am losing leaders. Confusion reigns among those who are staying. They are sad. I don't know what will happen next week much less next year. I have no five-year plan. I just barely have a five-day plan. Yet, gentlemen, despite this terrible news I still think that God is doing just fine in my church, and I think I am too. Here I stand. I cannot do otherwise. God help me.

I added that last part because I knew for sure that I would be martyred right then and there.

A strange thing happened after my speech. The pastors applauded. The applause seemed genuine and even a bit loud and prolonged. I would like to say that I was given a standing ovation, but that would not be true. A few guys did stand, but it turns out they just wanted to be first in line for lunch. That day I was redeemed. I was redeemed from the heady, arrogant attitude that insists that numerical success has much to do with being a good pastor.

Later I realized why the men applauded. I had put words to their own feelings. These pastors were faithfully serving small, rural congregations in shrinking communities. They were, demographically speaking, in the wilderness with no view of the Promised Land. But they were still faithful, even vibrant, ministers of Christ. Most of these pastors had already learned that the indicators of success in the ministry have always been the same. We call them the marks of the church.

Success in the ministry is measured by the standards the Great Minister, Jesus Christ, has given us. These standards or "marks" are (1) the Gospel of forgiveness in Christ that pronounces us right with God and absolves us, (2) Baptism that washes us of our sins through Jesus Christ, and (3) the Lord's Supper, where we receive the body and blood of Christ who carried our sins on Calvary and washed them away. These marks are employed by all faithful pastors to bring grace and new life to those for whom Christ has died.

Since my years in North Dakota, I have served God's church faithfully. Sometimes my churches grew; sometimes they did not. Life seems easier when church membership increases. People praise you and pastors tend to get more generously remunerated when the numbers swell. But all in all, as I look back on my years in the ministry, I would say that I can see the hand of God just as clearly when things did not go well, when the church did not grow, and even when I got hassled. Every pastor, every Christian, sooner or later learns with the apostle Paul: "When I am weak, then I am strong" (2 Corinthians 12:10). Above all, I learned that success in the ministry is not measured in numbers, but in faithfulness to our Lutheran doctrine and our zeal in teaching it to others.

The Great Commission

The last words Jesus spoke to His apostles were "Go therefore and make disciples of all nations, baptizing them in the name of the Father and of the Son and of the Holy Spirit, teaching them to observe all that I have commanded you" (Matthew 28:19–20). These words are known as the Great Commission. They instruct us in what Jesus wants us to do in order to make disciples. He wants His church to baptize and to teach.

Based on experience, I can tell you that baptizing is not too tough. When you baptize someone, you just speak the words of Christ from Matthew 28, "I baptize you in the name of the Father and of the Son and of the Holy Spirit," and apply water. Baptism is God's work, not the pastor's. It is simple.

Teaching, however, is difficult. You have to know what to teach, so you must study, learn, and understand the Bible in order to instruct from it carefully and faithfully. Teaching is the same thing as doctrine. Pure doctrine is extremely important. Paul tells Timothy, a young pastor, to "devote yourself to the public reading of Scripture, to exhortation, to teaching. . . . Keep a close watch on yourself and on the teaching" (1 Timothy 4:13, 16). Timothy is to give honor to "those who labor in preaching and teaching" (1 Timothy 5:17). Paul also instructs Titus, another pastor, to "give instruction in sound doctrine" (Titus 1:9) and to "teach what accords with for sound doctrine" (Titus 2:1). Martin Luther also emphasizes the importance of pure doctrine in his explanation of the first petition of the Lord's Prayer. How is God's name hallowed? "Whenever the Word of God is taught clearly and purely and we, as God's children, also live holy lives according to it."[1] Teaching the Christian doctrine purely from the Word of God is the commission of the church, the duty of pastors, and the way to hallow God's name. True church growth must come from pure doctrine.

A church's doctrine is the same as her theology. I am a Lutheran theologian because I believe that the Lutheran doctrine is biblical. You are a theologian if you are interested enough to read this book, which is about theology. And you probably hold to a certain teaching (doctrine) about Jesus and the various topics that deal with Christ. What you believe about Jesus—His life and death and their meaning to you, His gifts of Baptism and Holy Communion, the end times, about all sorts of things—this is the doctrine you hold. Clearly doctrine is important, as we will see throughout this book. My father used to tell me about an old Norwegian lady in northern Minnesota who would read the Bible and study books on Lutheran doctrine. When asked why she read so much theology, she would reply, "*Lehre er Liv.*" Doctrine is life. That sentiment, that faith, blessed this woman in this life and led her to heaven.

CAN DOCTRINE BE PURE?

When my kids were little, one of my daughters would be commissioned to call the other children to dinner. Typically, the invitation would go something like this: She would first yell as forcefully as possible at her siblings, "Time to eat!" Silence and profound inactivity were the predictable response. Next, she would go right up to her brother or one of her sisters and speak with quiet charm in their face, "Dinner time!" Her voice would be raised a couple of notes in singsong fashion, prolonging the word *time* and morphing it into a three-syllable word. She was still ignored. Finally, sacrificing any attempts to motivate by her own authority or force of personality, she spoke the magic words that brought immediate and positive results: "Mom says . . . "

The doctrine of the Gospel works in the same manner. Teachers of the church do not speak with their own force, charm, or demands. Just as the news that dinner was served was Mom's message and not that of my daughter, doctrine is God's—not ours. God's doctrine should be accepted because it is His, not because of anything in the preacher. No one understood this better than Paul, who said, "But even if we or an angel from heaven should preach to you a gospel contrary to the one we preached to you, let him be accursed" (Galatians 1:8). Such confidence characterized a man who was completely positive that his doctrine was true and faithful to God's Word. Doctrine can and must be true and clear. Luther commented, "With Paul, therefore, we boldly and confidently pronounce a curse upon any doctrine that does not agree with ours."[2] The Bible is clear enough and important enough for the teachers of the church to be able to teach it purely.

Would my children have told their sister: "Well, that is just your interpretation of what Mom is really saying. You know, there are many interpretations of the words of Mom in the world today. In America alone there are more than 200 interpretations. How can I be sure that your understanding is the correct one? Quite frankly, I think that you are acting with a bit of pride and arrogance to think that you have unequivocally understood and communicated the will of Mom in this regard." Conversations such as these do not take place when the authority, word, and blessings of Mom are under discussion. Unfortunately, many people do not offer the same respect to God.

DOES DOCTRINE DIVIDE?

Doctrine is never simply kept in your head or upon your heart. It comes from your mouth or is written on a page. Doctrine cannot be taught if merely contemplated or mulled. So, periodically, the church will summarize the biblical doctrine of Christ in written statements. The three creeds and our Lutheran Confessions are written statements that our church has accepted as being faithful to the Bible. Throughout her history, the Lutheran church has resolved doctrinal disagreements through written statements with the expectation that pastors and churches accept them. Whenever a church is divided over doctrine, the only way to heal the divisions is to do what the Holy Spirit says: "I appeal to you, brothers, by the name of our Lord Jesus Christ, that all of you agree and that there be no divisions among you, but that you be united in the same mind and the same judgment" (1 Corinthians 1:10).

I have heard people claim that insistence on true doctrine divides the church. A friend once told me that focused doctrinal statements divide the church because they force people to take sides. He claimed that some of the doctrinal statements made by various Lutheran groups in America have unintentionally divided Christians.

However, doctrinal statements actually unite the church in three ways. First, doctrinal statements show the whole church and the world what the church believes. The Nicene Creed was formed in response to the false teachings of Arius, a fourth-century heretic who denied the full deity of Christ. The creed was written so that all could unite behind a single doctrinal statement and oppose a teaching that would have destroyed the Gospel. The same action applies to the Formula of Concord, the response to various disagreements that had risen within Lutheranism after the death of Luther. The Formula of Concord shows the world and Lutherans alike what it means to be called Lutheran.

Second, doctrinal statements unite the church by exposing disunity. I had a friend in North Dakota who was a Roman Catholic priest. As we discussed theology, he said things that were contrary to the Scriptures. For example, I disagreed with him on how a person is justified before God. Our conversations allowed us to articulate and explore our differences. We actually grew to trust each other precisely because we were able to discuss these disagreements in the context of the doctrinal statements we each held to be true.

Third, doctrinal statements unite the church in its mission to proclaim the Gospel. Don't misunderstand—it is true that we might possibly be united in Christian love without doctrinal unity. We could possibly be united in speaking to the ills of society without doctrinal unity. I could certainly unite with my Catholic friend in a common protest of abortion. But we never can enjoy a joint ministry of the Gospel unless we express and agree with the same doctrine of the Gospel. Without mutually agreed upon doctrinal statements there can be no common ministry.

If we are to teach "them to observe all that I have commanded you" (Matthew 28:20), then we must agree on what the Lord has commanded before we can work toward the same goals. For example, suppose Mom and Dad tell Junior what time to be home. Junior believes that Mom has told him a different time than Dad. Mom and Dad sit down to discuss what they have said to Junior. The moment either one of them actually communicates their will regarding Junior's curfew, there is the risk that the other will disagree. But Junior needs to know. They simply cannot avoid resolving an apparent difference for fear that they will become disunited. In fact, Mom and Dad must risk disunity in order to communicate with one voice to Junior.

DOCTRINE AND LIFE

I have heard the accusation that Lutherans are acting unchristian and prideful because we say we have the true statements of doctrine. In 1966 a major Lutheran church in America passed a resolution that said in part: "The believer's best efforts to formulate a theology in terms of statements will fall short. To assume that the church can arrive at human expressions that are in every respect correct is as much a symptom of pride as to assume that the church or its members can achieve sinlessness in their daily lives."[3] I realize that synodical resolutions are often written so as to confuse even the angels in heaven, but this one is not too tough. This church body was claiming that statements about God (such as the creeds) cannot be correct and that to insist that they are correct is just as bad as if one claims to be sinless. So, according to this particular Lutheran church body, the insistence upon purity of doctrine is sinful.

Paul turned the world upside down with his doctrine. Could he have carried on his ministry if he were uncertain about his beliefs? Luther changed the world of his day with doctrine. Was he uncertain about his beliefs? Listen to what he cautions:

> Therefore, as I often warn you, doctrine must be carefully distinguished from life. Doctrine is heaven; life is earth. In life there is sin, error, uncleanness, and misery. . . . Here love should condone, tolerate, be deceived, trust, hope, and endure all things (1 Cor. 13:7); here the forgiveness of sins should have complete sway, provided that sin and error are not defended. But just as there is no error in doctrine, so there is no need for any forgiveness of sins. Therefore there is no comparison at all between doctrine and life. "One dot" of doctrine is worth more than "heaven and earth" (Matt. 5:18); therefore we do not permit the slightest offense against it. But we can be lenient toward errors of life. For we, too, err daily in our life and conduct; so do all the saints, as they earnestly confess in the Lord's Prayer and the creed. But by the grace of God our doctrine is pure; we have all the articles of faith solidly established in Sacred Scripture.[4]

As Christians, we need to repent of our sinful lives. Even our most noble deeds are tainted with sin. But doctrine is a gift of God. We should repent of doctrine no more than we repent of the creeds or the Bible or our confession of faith.

Every time I confirm a group of young people I am impressed by what they promise. They are first asked about doctrine and then asked about life.

> Do you hold all the prophetic and apostolic Scriptures to be the inspired Word of God and confess the doctrine of the Evangelical Lutheran Church, drawn from them, as you have learned to know it from the Small Catechism, to be faithful and true?
>
> *I do.*
>
> Do you intend faithfully to conform all your life to the divine Word, to be faithful in the use of God's Word and Sacraments, which are his means of grace, and in faith, word, and action to

remain true to God, Father, Son, and Holy Spirit, even unto death?

I do so intend by the grace of God.[5]

Notice that when we confess doctrine in the first question, we do not say that we intend by God's grace to be pure. We simply state, "I do." Doctrine is a gift. Its purity does not depend on our efforts. When we promise to live as Christians, however, we need to ask for God's help. As Christians, we know that at times we do not "conform our lives to the divine Word." There is a difference between doctrine and life. Martin Luther repented constantly of his sinful life, yet he was able to say about his doctrine:

> It should not be necessary for the preacher to ask God's forgiveness for the doctrine he has preached; he should rather be in a position to say: "It is God's Word and not mine, and so there can be no reason for His forgiving me; He can only confirm, praise, and crown what I have preached, saying, 'Thou hast taught correctly, for I have spoken through thee, and the Word is Mine' . . . Whoever cannot truthfully say that of his sermon should quit preaching, for he must surely be lying and blaspheming God when he preaches."[6]

Doctrine must be pure, and we must be certain of it. True and pure doctrine is based on the Word of Christ—in that there is nothing uncertain.

THE CENTRAL BIBLICAL DOCTRINE

The central and most important doctrine of the Bible is stated clearly by Martin Luther in the Schmalkald Articles.

> Here is the first and chief article:
>
> That Jesus Christ, our God and Lord, "was handed over to death for our trespasses and was raised for our justification" (Rom. 4[:25]); and he alone is "the Lamb of God, who takes away the sin of the world" (John 1[:29]) . . . furthermore, "All have sinned," and "they are now justified without merit by his grace, through the redemption that is in Christ Jesus . . . by his blood" (Rom. 3[:23–25]).

> Now because this must be believed and may not be obtained or grasped otherwise with any work, law, or merit, it is clear and certain that this faith alone justifies us, as St. Paul says in Romans 3[:28,26]: "For we hold that a person is justified by faith apart from works prescribed by the law"; and also, "that God alone is righteous and justifies the one who has faith in Jesus."[7]

This brief statement of Luther's is a summary of the Gospel of Christ, a string of Bible passages, and is called "doctrine." These three elements belong together and can never be separated—Gospel, Scriptures, doctrine. The Bible witnesses to Christ, the Gospel is the Good News of Christ, and doctrine is the teaching of Christ. Whether we speak of faithfulness to the Gospel of Christ, faithfulness to the Bible, or faithfulness to the doctrine of Christ, we speak of the same thing.

According to Luther and the Lutheran Confessions, doctrine is not plural. We do not talk about many doctrines, but about one doctrine. There is only one Christ, and true doctrine must teach that one Christ. The one doctrine has many facets—the Lutheran Confessions call them "articles of faith" or "articles of doctrine." We have one doctrine with many articles. Lutherans will talk of the article on Baptism, the article on the Lord's Supper, the article on predestination, the article on good works, or the article on justification by grace through faith.

The distinction between the one doctrine of the Gospel and the many articles of faith is extremely important. We should never talk about the articles of faith as if they are unrelated or only loosely strung together. Rather, there is one unified doctrine of Jesus. Luther compares doctrine to a golden ring, "Doctrine must be one eternal and round golden circle, in which there is no crack; if even the tiniest crack appears, the circle is no longer perfect."[8] Doctrine is not some cold, boring, academic subject full of *wherefores*, *therefores*, and *thuses*. Doctrine is the teaching about Jesus. Doctrine is life. No wonder Jesus said to make disciples by teaching (Matthew 28:20). He knows that doctrine leads to life.

Doctrine also saves us. I suppose that's a bold statement. You might, correctly, be thinking that only Jesus saves. Obviously, doctrine did not die on the cross for the sins of the world. And no pastor gets up in church on Sunday and pronounces you forgiven for the sake and by the command of doctrine. No one prays to doctrine or worships doctrine. After I die, I do not expect doctrine to come in glory and bring me to my heavenly home. Only Jesus will do these things. But there is a sense in which doctrine saves. Jesus has earned and accomplished salvation for all. God has taken that salvation, earned by Jesus, and gives it to us through the doctrine of the Gospel of Christ. The teaching of Christ bestows Christ upon us and brings the salvation of Jesus to us. Because the doctrine of Christ is the Gospel, and the Gospel saves (Romans 1:16), then doctrine saves us. Luther says that we need to look at forgiveness and salvation in two ways: "First, how it is achieved and won. Second, how it is distributed and given to us. Christ has achieved it on the cross, it is true. But he has not distributed it or given it on the cross. . . . he has distributed and given it through the Word, as also in the gospel, where it is preached."[9] When the doctrine of salvation in Christ alone is taught, then God is giving salvation to us. He is saving us. Every pastor in the Lutheran church has promised to teach what our Lutheran Confessions teach: "This article on justification by faith . . . is the 'most important of all Christian teachings,' 'without which no poor conscience can have lasting comfort or recognize properly the riches of Christ's grace.' "[10]

The dinner announcement from the mouth of my daughter was dependable because it came from Mom. It was also powerful because the statement led the kids to the table. The doctrine of the Gospel of Christ has the same power. The Word of God accomplishes what it announces. It creates the faith it requires. Robert Kolb, professor of systematic theology at Concordia Seminary, St. Louis, explained: "Christian doctrine acts. It effects what it announces and describes. For it is the living, active voice of the living, active God."[11] Christian doctrine "acts" by bringing the grace of Christ to us. It saves us because it is the evangelical doctrine—the Gospel doctrine of Jesus. And you can't be saved without it. "Everyone who goes on ahead and does not abide in the teaching of Christ, does not have God. Whoever abides in the teaching has both the Father and the Son" (2 John 9).

When Luther discovered the Bible teaching that he was saved by God's grace without having to earn it, he is reported to have said it was like taking a walk through heaven. So the early Lutherans wanted the wonderful doctrine of the Gospel to be spread all over Germany and throughout the world. They were asked to defend their doctrine before Emperor Charles V. The most powerful man in Europe at the time, Charles wanted to know why the Lutherans had started a huge controversy with their doctrine. What an opportunity this was for the upstart theologians from the little town of Wittenberg, Germany. Luther's colleague, Philip Melanchthon, wrote a document called the Augsburg Confession. This confession had a defense, or apology, added to it. In it we find these words:

> Since this controversy deals with the most important topic of Christian teaching which, rightly understood, illumines and magnifies the honor of Christ and brings the abundant consolation that devout consciences need, we ask His Imperial Majesty kindly to hear us out on this important matter. Since the opponents understand neither the forgiveness of sins, nor faith, nor grace, nor righteousness, they miserably contaminate this article, obscure the glory and benefits of Christ, and tear away from devout consciences the consolation offered in Christ.[12]

Notice what is at stake in the discussion and debate about doctrine: the honor of Christ, the consolation of consciences, the forgiveness of sins, faith, grace, righteousness, the glory and benefits of Christ. It is no wonder that Lutherans have always been concerned about doctrine. Luther summarizes the Christian view of the vital importance of doctrine: "With the utmost rigor we demand that all the articles of Christian doctrine, both large and small—although we do not regard any of them as small—be kept pure and certain. This is supremely necessary. For this doctrine is our only light, which illumines and directs us and shows us the way to heaven."[13] That old Norwegian woman in northern Minnesota was correct. *Lehre er liv*. Doctrine is life.

CATECHISM CLASS

Catechism instruction is remembered fondly by Lutherans. Well . . . perhaps not fondly, but it is remembered. The kids in my catechism classes are usually ready for a break about the middle of April, but we hold classes until the first week of May. Consequently, I hear some creative complaints about the Wednesday classes. My favorite came from Saundra. "Pastor, I don't think that we need to be spending all this time learning the catechism. I looked up the word in my concordance, and it's not even in the Bible. Where does it say that we have to learn the catechism?"

Normally, I would have simply told Saundra to quit her complaining, but her reference to the concordance indicated to me that she might have actually researched the question. So I gave her a challenge. "If you can find the word *catechism* in the Bible, I will take you out for pizza the last week of class." Of course, I did not tell Saundra that I always took the students out for pizza the last day of class.

Saundra was adamant. "Pastor, it's not in the Bible. I already checked. The assignment is impossible, and it's not fair."

I replied, "With God nothing is impossible, and with me nothing is unfair. Use any tools you want. The word is there. Find it and show it to me."

Did you ever wonder where we got the word *catechism* or what it means? It comes from the Greek word *katacheo*, which literally means "to sound from above." We get our word *echo* from the Greek root, so it could also mean "to echo from above." It is translated as either "inform" or "instruct." Luke used the word when he wrote an account of Jesus to Theophilus so that he may "have certainty concerning the things you have been taught" (Luke 1:4). Theophilus was catechized. Paul used the word to refer to the instruction the Jews received into the Law (Romans 2:18). In 1 Corinthians 14:19 Paul boldly asserts that he would rather speak five words to instruct (literally "to catechize") than ten thousand words in an unknown language. My favorite use is in Galatians 6:6 where Paul says, "One who is taught the word must share all good things with the one who teaches." Literally, he is telling those who are catechized to share their wealth with those, usually pastors, who teach the catechism. So the catechumens paid for their catechesis from the catechism. We have no idea what tools of instruction were used. The teachers probably asked questions and the students echoed back the answers. This much is certain: Catechesis was done and commanded in the Bible.

In response to the church's need of instruction and the Lord's command, Luther, and many others throughout the years, have written catechisms, little books of Christian instruction. Sometimes a book of instructions is called an "enchiridion," which means "in the heart." We use that word to show that the instruction needs to be understood and believed. The best way to teach doctrine is through catechesis. In the Lutheran church, Luther's Catechism has been referred to as "the people's Bible" because it contains the central teachings of the Bible and can be easily learned and memorized. We teach the catechism because we care about doctrine.

Saundra came back the next week and told me that she had found the word *catechism* in the Bible. She showed me Galatians 6:6. I was utterly amazed. How on earth was she able to find the word without knowing Greek? Her answer? "You said we could use any tool we wanted to, so I asked Pastor Schmidt at St. John's if the word *catechism* was in the Bible. He had a Greek dictionary and gave me the verse. Where's my pizza?"

Saundra had not only learned about the importance of the catechism and Christian instruction, she had also found one of the best tools the Christian has—your pastor. His job is to catechize.

CATECHESIS AND CHURCH GROWTH

I have a few shelves full of books in my office with titles such as *How to Grow a Church*, *How to Break the 200 Barrier*, *Leading Your Church to Growth*, *Twelve Keys to an Effective Church*, *How to Create a Successful Church*, *Ten Steps for Church Growth*, and *44 Ways to Increase Church Attendance*. All of these books, and thousands more like them, claim that success or effectiveness is measured by how many people enter your church. While they all suggest strategies for church growth, many have one glaring omission. Rarely does this body of literature contain the suggestion that the way to succeed in God's eyes is to teach the doctrine of the Gospel faithfully, along with administering Christ's gifts of Baptism and the Lord's Supper according to Jesus' institution.

I have read far too many of these books. Too often I get the impression that the teaching of the Bible, the doctrine, is just not important to some advocates of the Church Growth movement. These words are typical of the issues these books emphasize: "Perhaps the most common characteristic of the churches that are attracting increasing numbers of people today is not where the minister is on the theological spectrum or the denominational affiliation, but on what people hear and feel during the worship experience."[14] In other words, growth and theology are not particularly related. One Lutheran Church Growth advocate lists seven characteristics of today's growing churches and seven characteristics of first-century growing churches. "Faithfulness to the Word and Sacraments" did not make either list.[15] Another Church Growth guru lists the "Twelve Keys to an Effective Church." None of the keys suggest that the church should be faithful to the Gospel of Christ and His sacraments of Baptism and the Lord's Supper.[16] One writer lists the "twelve boxes that stagnate the church and stop the powerful flow of what God wants to do." His fifth box is "Focus on Doctrine." He claims doctrine stagnates the church: "People in our world who are perishing from a variety of diseases of mind, body and soul—which are all the results of being apart from God's love—do not give two hoots about cold doctrine."[17] These pundits want numerical growth without the purity of teaching that Christ expects.

A Conversation with Carl George

The indifference toward doctrine among the advocates of Church Growth was made apparent to me years ago when I had two conversations with Carl George, arguably the most influential proponent of the modern-day Church Growth movement. He is the director of the Charles E. Fuller Institute of Evangelism and Church Growth and has written many books, including his pioneering book, *Prepare Your Church for the Future.*[18] In this book George introduces the "Meta-Church" concept, a strong defense of Church Growth through small groups. I have heard Rev. George speak twice. The first time occurred in Michigan in the late 1970s. He was discussing the importance of spiritual gifts for the advancement of the church's growth. At one point in the lecture he waxed eloquent on the "gift of evangelism." This gift was defined as "the ability to witness to Christ in a way which effectively brings people to a saving relationship with Him." I was troubled at this part of his lecture because, to me, it gave the impression that the Holy Spirit works not "where and when he wills, in those who hear the Gospel,"[19] but more effectively through those who have the gift of evangelism.

I had taken a "spiritual gifts inventory" earlier in the day. This test was calculated to help me discover which gifts of the Spirit I had. I remember testing very high on the gift of "discerning the spirits" and very low on the gifts of martyrdom, celibacy, and tongues. I had also not tested particularly high on the gift of evangelism. I confess that, at the time, I was not particularly perturbed at my apparent reluctance to die for the faith or to spend the rest of married life sleeping on the sofa. Others in the crowd were intrigued by the whole notion of martyrdom as a gift of the Spirit and began to pepper the speaker with probing questions as to the various ways in which such a gift could be expressed. Happily deprived, my mind was more occupied with the mundane task of preaching the Gospel. Did my test results mean that the Holy Spirit was not working through the Gospel that I preached? I certainly did not believe so or I would have quit the ministry right then and there. Gradually, I marshaled the courage to ask, "Rev. George, how do we know who has the gift of evangelism?" He answered with an anecdote. He told of a little boy who was on fire for the Lord and witnessed every chance he could. He related how this little boy, though less than 10 years old, was always inviting people to believe in Jesus. He concluded the story by commending the little tyke as an example of the gift of evangelism. The occasion was a Lutheran conference, so all the attendees were Lutheran. I leaned over and asked my friend, "Isn't Carl George a Baptist? Would this little kid be baptized? Can you be an effective witness, possessing the gift of evangelism, without even being baptized yourself?" I quickly raised my hand again. Rev. George was about to call on me when my friend yanked my arm down. "Don't be rude. Just let the guy speak."

Years passed and I was plagued by my own reluctance to insist on posing my question earlier. As luck or providence would dictate, ten years later I attended another conference where Carl George was the speaker, this time in Hollywood, California. Pastors and church leaders from all types of churches attended. Again, an opportunity presented itself to pick the churchly brain of Rev. George. So the unasked question of a decade earlier sprang to my lips with no polite Lutheran pastors around to dissuade or constrain me. "Do you have to be baptized yourself to have the gift of evangelism?"

I thought that this was a pretty good question. Think about it. How much credibility can an evangelist have without being baptized? How can an unbaptized person carry out Christ's commission in Matthew 28, when the very first part of that commission orders us to baptize? Can you have any gift of the Spirit if your very possession of the Spirit is in doubt?

Carl George's answer? "That depends on your denominational perspective."

I am sure that Rev. George does not remember a solitary Lutheran pastor asking questions ten years apart, but his answer made an impression on me. I learned to hate that answer, which I have since heard many times. I learned even to hate the word *denomination* unless it is referring to a measure of financial currency.

Rev. George's answer was not an answer. He was saying that he would not answer my question with a clear yes or no. Try to answer other theological questions with that answer. "Is Jesus the only way to heaven?" Well, that depends on your denominational perspective. "Are you justified by faith alone without the deeds of the Law?" That depends on your denominational perspective. "Is the Bible God's inspired Word?" That depends on your denominational perspective. What if Jesus answered a theological question like that? "Who sinned, this man or his parents that he should be born blind?" Well, that depends on your denominational perspective. "May a man divorce his wife for any reason?" That depends on your denominational perspective. "Are you the Christ, the Son of the living God?" That depends on your denominational perspective? There is no confession of faith, no doctrine, no purity of theology—just a non-answer.

Lutherans who study with Carl George at Fuller Theological Seminary often talk the same way. One such Lutheran praises the Bible studies of Robert Schuller. "While one might not agree with all of the doctrinal content, depending on denominational perspective, it is easy to realize that proper attention is given to the depth of God's teaching."[20] Christ's instruction to "teach all that I have commanded," to focus on the pure doctrine, is seriously lacking in these church leaders. Success seems more important.

What is success in the church? What is effective ministry? What is an effective church? Our Lord gives us a clue in His conversation with Nicodemus. Nicodemus comes to Jesus with a curious mind and little insight. Jesus explains to him the proper Church Growth attitude: "Truly, truly, I say to you, unless one is born of water and the Spirit, he cannot enter the kingdom of God. That which is born of flesh is flesh, and that which is born of Spirit is spirit. . . . The wind blows where it wishes, and you hear its sound, but you do not know where it comes from or where it goes. So it is with everyone who is born of the Spirit" (John 3:5–8). These are not tough words to understand and apply. Jesus is saying that you become a child of God in Baptism. That's what the expression "born of water and the Spirit" means. He is also saying that you cannot become a Christian by anything you do, whether it is your decision or your good works or your common sense or your anything. That's what the expression "born of flesh" means. Jesus is stating that the Holy Spirit's effectiveness simply does not depend on us. That's what He means by the expression "The wind blows where it wishes. . . . So it is with everyone who is born of the Spirit."

The Augsburg Confession, which defines what it means to be a Gospel-centered Christian, explains: "Through the word and the sacraments as through instruments the Holy Spirit is given, who effects faith where and when it pleases God in those who hear the gospel."[21] Notice that the word *effect* is used by the Lutheran Confessions. An effective church is one in which the Spirit works through the Word and Sacraments. We cannot become more "effective" than the Spirit already is. But we can "effect" faith by the Gospel and the Sacraments.

An effective church, a successful church, is one where the Word is taught and the Sacraments administered. The results of these instruments of God are left to the Holy Spirit. Our success as ministers or as churches is measured only by whether we consistently and purely teach this Word and rightly administer Baptism and the Lord's Supper.

CHURCH GROWTH IN THE BOOK OF ACTS

The infant Christian church grew by 3,000 souls on Pentecost and to 5,000 shortly thereafter, according to Acts (chapters 2 and 3).

Luke tells us in Acts 6 that the dramatic church growth resulted in increased staff. Growth of the church continued with the conversion of many priests. Those must have been exciting times.

I have often heard Church Growth advocates use the statistics in the Book of Acts to justify their expectation for numerical growth in the church. I am impressed with the remarkable growth reported in the first six chapters of Acts. Everything seems wonderful until you read these ominous words: "And there arose on that day a great persecution against the church in Jerusalem, and they were all scattered throughout the regions of Judea and Samaria, except the apostles" (Acts 8:1). After that, the Jerusalem congregation never grew again. Is this failure? Were the apostles not following proper Church Growth principles? Had they not read about the 44 ways to increase church attendance?

The same phenomenon occurred on Paul's first missionary journey. In chapter 13 of Acts everything was going great. More and more people were coming to church. Huge crowds were gathering. All of a sudden the floor fell out. Jealous and competitive leaders from other churches hassled the Christians. Paul and Barnabas "shook off the dust from their feet" in protest and left town (Acts 13:51). Was this effective leadership? Had they not read *Leading Your Church to Growth?* God simply does not measure success or growth by numbers. The Book of Acts has far more failures than successes if you judge by numbers. God uses a different criterion for judging success. He wants us to judge by His Word.

In chapter 15 of Acts things were not going so well. Here we have the account of the first synodical convention, which, of course, was characterized by doctrinal infighting. The issue was whether one has to obey the Law, specifically the requirement of circumcision, in order to be saved.

How does the church deal with doctrinal controversy? If we listen to the Church Growth advocates, we should ignore such controversy. One growth counselor, Kent Hunter, says that even if church leaders "don't all agree on everything," as long as we can "believe of each other that we are all going to heaven," then we should never publicly disagree. To publicly disagree "confuses, divides and hands the victory to the enemy, whose strategy is to divide and conquer."[22] C. Peter Wagner, prolific Church Growth writer and the second-generation apostle of the movement, lists the "theological non-negotiables" of the Church Growth movement. Notably absent are salvation by grace alone or any mention of the Sacraments. Also missing from Wagner's list is whether you need to get circumcised and submit to the Law in order to get to heaven.[23] Yet that is exactly what Paul and Peter argued in Acts 15. It's a good thing that Hunter and Wagner were not leading the church during the council of Jerusalem because the apostolic doctrine would not have survived the first century. Back then, James and Peter were willing to risk their reputations and their credentials for the sake of the truth. They even risked splitting the fledgling church over doctrine.

The church, in fact, was irreparably split over the issue argued in Acts 15. Paul was vexed, suffered great tribulation, and had to bear the cross of Christ because he refused to compromise doctrine. Was this the action of a man interested in numerical growth? Yes, but Paul loved something loftier than growth. He loved the precious and pure Gospel of salvation without the works of the Law. The church's first convention ended with a clear resolution based on the Word of God. But, humanly speaking, the church was split right down the middle. The opponents of Paul and Peter were called Judaizers. For the rest of his ministry these men persecuted and maligned Paul, exhausted his energies, and distracted his attentions. But James, Paul, and Peter never regretted standing upon the truth, even on an apparently minor point, though the church was never the same again.

In Acts 21 Paul receives a vision from God that he will be bound by his enemies and handed over to the Gentiles if he goes to Jerusalem. Is he willing to spend the rest of his life in jail and deprive the church of one of her greatest change agents? Doesn't that go against every Church Growth principle? Thankfully, Paul goes to Jerusalem and is arrested. He never makes another missionary journey. He never establishes another congregation. Here is a man with such obvious and abundant gifts of the spirit, yet he stifles these gifts. King Agrippa, who had jurisdiction over Paul's case, made the comment, "This man could have been set free if he had not appealed to Caesar" (Acts 26:32). But Paul knew something that many today do not: When we are weak, we are strong.

In fact, strength in weakness is the theme of the Book of Acts. Through persecution, heresies, and the death of her greatest pastor and leader, the church prevailed. Samuel J. Stone, in one of the church's traditional hymns, writes:

> Though with a scornful wonder
> Men see her sore oppressed,
> By schisms rent asunder,
> By heresies distressed,
>
> Tho' there be those that hate her,
> False sons within her pale,
> Against both foe and traitor
> She ever shall prevail.[24]

THE THEOLOGY OF THE CROSS

How does the church prevail? How has she survived over all these centuries? The answer I have given thus far is "Word and Sacrament." These are the marks of Christ's church, and they are also the means of grace. Another answer to this question, from a different perspective, is "the theology of the cross."

The expression "theology of the cross" was a favorite of Martin Luther. Probably his best-known use of the phrase occurred in 1518 at the Heidelberg Disputation. Every good Lutheran knows the date October 31, 1517, when Luther placed his Ninety-five Theses on the Castle Church door of Wittenberg, Germany. Perhaps less well-known, but equally important, is the date April 26, 1518, for that is when Luther presented 28 theological statements, or theses, to his fellow monks in the German city of Heidelberg.

Under threat from his opponents, Luther's friends had advised him not to go to Heidelberg. He made the trek anyway out of obedience to his priest, Father John Staupitz. With fellow priests, he walked from Wittenberg to Heidelberg, a journey that required fourteen days of constant travel. Along the way he was treated well, thanks to letters of introduction provided by his prince and protector, Frederick the Wise. Arriving just two days before he was to speak, exhausted, scrutinized, and hesitant, Luther presented his theology.

Thesis 4, "Although the works of God are always unattractive and appear evil, they are nevertheless really eternal merits."

Thesis 18, "It is certain that man must utterly despair of his own ability before he is prepared to receive the grace of God."

Thesis 20, "He deserves to be called a theologian, however, who comprehends the visible and manifest things of God seen through suffering and the cross."

Thesis 21, "A theology of glory calls evil good and good evil. A theology of the cross calls the thing what it actually is."

Thesis 26, "The law says, 'do this,' and it is never done. Grace says, 'believe in this,' and everything is already done."[25]

These words did not immediately rock the world. Both friend and foe commented on Luther's "sweetness," his "remarkable patience," his "brief, wise answers," and the "admiration" of his hearers.[26] Obviously, Luther was on good behavior. Slowly his words penetrated the thinking and church practices of the early followers of Luther. What they mean is obvious. The theology of the cross affects the church's doctrine and practice in three ways.

First, the theology of the cross applies to the manner in which God acted in Christ. You simply cannot judge the actions of God by what you see. God's greatest work, the sacrifice of His only-begotten Son, seems harsh and appears evil. A righteous man is condemned not only by wicked earthly rulers but also by God Himself. How can that be good? Yet every Christian counts Christ's death as the greatest treasure. A good theologian "comprehends the visible and manifest things of God seen through suffering and the cross."[27] You cannot have the true and loving God without the bloody death of Christ. God will not love you without the gruesome spectacle of His Son's corpse. God cannot accept you except through the naked, bloody, dead Savior on Golgotha. That is the theology of the cross.

Second, the same basic theology applies to the Word of God and Christ's sacraments. How can little words do anything? How can water accomplish such great things? How can bread and wine really be a meal of eternal life? Because God works graciously in the lives of His people through lowly, everyday, little things: words, water, bread, wine.

Third, the theology of the cross applies to the methods we use in carrying out the Great Commission. We do not measure our success by that which is obvious and visible. Rather, success is only in the cross. So an effective church is not one that simply brings in hundreds of members or that has thousands in attendance on Sundays. Success is not in programs or budgets or the exercise of our gifts or anything else that we do. Success is in the cross. It is found in the sacrifice Christ made on the cross and the work He continues to do through the Gospel.

Paul wrote to his church in Corinth:

> For the word of the cross is folly to those who are perishing, but to us who are being saved it is the power of God. For it is written, "I will destroy the wisdom of the wise, and the discernment of the discerning I will thwart." . . . We preach Christ crucified . . . the power of God and the wisdom of God. For the foolishness of God is wiser than men, and the weakness of God is stronger than men. . . . God chose what is weak in the world to shame the strong; God chose what is low and despised in the world, even things that are not, to bring to nothing things that are. . . . Christ Jesus, whom God made our wisdom and our righteousness and sanctification and redemption. Therefore, as it is written, "Let the one who boasts, boast in the Lord. (1 Corinthians 1:18–31)

These words inspired Luther 1,500 years later. These words inspire Christians all over the world today. They instruct us to measure God's activities by His cross, by His Gospel, by His Baptism, by His Holy Supper, and by our own weakness.

Years ago I wrote a little poem based on Paul's words to express the theology of the cross.

> When Jesus came, whom did He seek?
> Was it the kings and men of pow'r?
> No, Jesus came to find the weak,
> On people lost His grace was shower'd.
>
> Christ's place of birth, man would suppose,
> Would be a castle large and bright.
> But no, our Savior simply chose
> A stable in the dead of night.

Take Jesus' twelve apostles then;
How often do we realize,
By standards known to worldly men
The words they preached weren't very wise?

Or think of Christ upon the cross;
He seems so foolish and so weak,
How could this man redeem the lost?
He's dying, tortured, hungry, meek.

If we would have to find a way
To bring salvation to the world,
We'd choose some wonderful display
Of wisdom, strength and pow'r unfurled.

Our wisdom would not choose the shame
Of humble death and foolishness;
The world would want a Christ whose fame
Lies in His strength and His success.

But God has chosen foolish shame
To fool the wise and shame the strong.
Now who will glorify Christ's name?
We foolish weaklings raise the song.

I am not powerful or wise.
I'm weak and foolish just as He.
And so it should be no surprise,
That Christ, by grace, has chosen me.

In Jesus' weakness there is might,
And in His foolishness is pride;
Now, I am wise and strong to fight,
I'm proud to boast in Him who died.

DOCTRINE AND LOVE

Some of the early Protestant settlers in North America used the expression "Deeds not Creeds." They believed that our deeds of love were more important than the faith of the Gospel expressed in the creeds. That was a terrible and wrong sentiment. Don't ever say that your love or my love is more important than God's love. God's love—His doctrine—is salvation.

Let's return to the story of my daughter inviting her siblings to dinner. One evening Mom told her to announce that dinner was served in exactly ten minutes. We would start when dinner was served whether kids were at the table or not. And if they were not washed and ready, they would go without. Apparently Mom was getting sick and tired of kids waiting until the last minute and the food getting cold. So the "Ambassador of Mom," as she was dubbed, made the appropriate announcement, "In the place and by the command of Mom . . . " She was ignored. Thereupon she grew more insistent, more strident. "Mom is serious. If you don't come now, you will not have dinner." Slowly, too slowly, her siblings began to rise from their lethargy. "Hurry or you will not eat" was her final and desperate warning, summarily shouted as she rushed to the dining room herself. Predictably, the others were late. "We had to wait for the commercial" was their pitiful excuse. They knew full well that "Mom waits for no one," and certainly for no commercial. The doors were locked, metaphorically, and the siblings, like the five foolish virgins, were left wailing and gnashing their teeth.

Negotiations immediately began between the errant children and their mother. They wanted and needed to get up to the table that had, justifiably, been closed to them. And whom did these selfish children blame for their own procrastinating behavior? Every parent reading these words knows the answer. They blamed their sister. "She yelled at us. She wasn't polite. She was impatient. She only told us three times and we were distracted." Finally, in devious desperation the children hit upon the best accusation yet: "She wasn't loving."

Do you sometimes wonder where kids pick up some of the things they say? I'll tell you. They get their silliness from bad theologians. According to Luther:

> They accuse us of offending against love . . . We are surely prepared to observe peace and love with all men, provided that they leave the doctrine of faith perfect and sound for us. If we cannot obtain this, it is useless for them to demand love from us. A curse on a love that is observed at the expense of the doctrine of faith, to which every thing must yield—love, an apostle, an angel from heaven, etc.![28]

Perhaps my daughter could have been more charming. Maybe she acted impatiently. Certainly her "love" was imperfect. But what about her message from Mom—the "doctrine" of dinner she preached? Was it her fault, her sin, her lack of love, that the others missed dinner? No. They deemed themselves unworthy. (Cf. Acts 13:46.)

Ask yourself, whom would you rather have as your preacher? Would you like a pastor who believes that nothing he says about God could be 100 percent correct? Or would you like a pastor who believes that he speaks the truth of God? I cannot imagine any Christian wanting the former. My daughter was loud and strident and insistent—perhaps even unloving. But I cannot imagine any Christian unwilling to forgive "loudness," "stridency," "insensitivity," or even occasionally "lack of love," if it means hearing the true doctrine of the Gospel.

There are two main teachings of the Bible: Law and Gospel. The Law points to what we do. The Gospel points to the cross of Jesus Christ. "The law says, 'do this,' and it is never done. Grace says, 'believe in this,' and everything is already done."[29]

The Law tells us what to do, including that we have not done what God expects. The Gospel tells us of a Savior who has done everything for us. Love is Law. The doctrine of Christ is Gospel. The Law says, "I fail." The doctrine of Christ—the Gospel—says, "I am forgiven." Our churches must never be churches of the Law. They must be churches of the Gospel.

What is the clearest expression of the Law in the Bible? That's easy. It is the Ten Commandments. They make me guilty. What is the clearest passage of love in the Bible? That's also easy. Paul tells us:

> Love is patient and kind; love does not envy or boast; it is not arrogant or rude. It does not insist on its own way; it is not irritable or resentful; it does not rejoice at wrongdoing, but rejoices with the truth. Love bears all things, believes all things, hopes all things, endures all things. Love never ends. (1 Corinthians 13:4–8)

Every time I read 1 Corinthians 13, the love chapter, I become depressed. I cannot do all that. Oh, I think it's a beautiful section of the Bible. It is inspiring. The prose is exquisite. But it makes me feel guilty, and it should. Love never fails? Love always trusts? Love is patient? That sure does not describe me. Love is Law. We need to repent. We are imperfect. God's doctrine is perfect. The lovely doctrine of Christ tells us that God loved us in such a way that in Christ He forgives us all sins, accepts us, promises us eternal life, and provides everything necessary for us to get there—all this despite our lack of love.

When people tell me that Christ's church, His ministers, or even I do not show love, I think, "Well, this is no surprise." When have we ever shown much love? That's why Christ had to die for us. But may it never be said of Christ's church or of His ministers that they did not teach the love of Jesus. With my love the world might be a little bit better, though I often doubt it. I'm more inclined to think that very little changes because of my love. But with the doctrine of the love of Christ everything changes—everything is new. Sins are forgiven, God is pleased, guilt is relieved, and heaven is opened.

A serious responsibility is placed upon pastors by the vital nature of pure doctrine. God is simply not content with servants who understand all the nuances of His grace. He desires—no, He demands—pastors who endeavor to teach it. The work of a pastor is a complex and difficult task, for it requires effort with both the Word and with people.

WORKING WITH THE WORD

Pastors in the Missouri Synod have a little inside joke. When you are visiting another pastor and happen to notice the books on the shelves in his office, you ask, "Has the circuit counselor approved these?" Our church is divided into circuits made up of about eight or ten congregations. The pastors of the congregations will gather together monthly to study the Word of God and the Lutheran Confessions. Each circuit chooses from among its pastors a circuit counselor. Back in the early days of the Synod one of the jobs of the circuit counselor was to visit each pastor to make sure that his library was adequate, hence the comments about his approval. The whole idea seems a bit presumptuous by twenty-first-century standards when many pastors have literally thousands of books available online or on disks. Nevertheless, you can tell a little bit about a pastor by the books he keeps.

I have been in pastors' studies where the only books were required texts from the seminary. I wonder whether such pastors have tried to learn anything since their school days. I have known pastors who are unable to name a single theology book they have read in the past year or any article from a theological journal. I have known pastors who presume to teach a text without even trying to analyze it much. I have to believe that such lack of work shows in both the preaching and the teaching of such pastors. What do they do with their time?

If pastors neglect the task of learning, they will also neglect the teaching of God's saving doctrine. I knew a college student, a member of my congregation, who, because he owned no car, actually walked three miles to the closest Lutheran church. The time investment on his part was two hours every Sunday—one on the way to church and one on the way home. Noticing his predicament, a kind lady of the church one Sunday offered to drive him home. In the comfort of her car the young student asked when the Bible classes of the church were scheduled.

"Oh, we don't have any Bible classes" was her happy reply.

The young student was quiet for a moment. "Not even on Sunday? What if someone wants to learn a bit more than what the pastor teaches in his sermons?"

"We go to the Baptist church down the street. You can get there just in time after services. They're a Bible church, you know."

Some months later, when the student recounted this story to me, I was outraged at the profound laziness of this pastor. He did not even care enough about his church to study the Bible and teach the Bible doctrine to his people more than the twenty minutes a sermon requires. The hearer of the Word invested more time than the called teacher of it.

People have the right to expect more of their pastor. Would you go to a lawyer who had not cracked a law book for years or who was not versed on recent legal decisions or developments? Would you trust a doctor who made no attempt to stay current in his or her field of expertise? Yet pastors sometimes blithely continue their lazy ways as if they have carte blanche for irresponsibility and no one dare gainsay them.

Working with People

More serious is the temptation for pastors to spend so much time studying theology that they ignore the sheep of Christ's flock.

Jesus was a pastor and a teacher. Under-shepherds would be wise to emulate the Good Shepherd. One day Jesus was tired and hungry and told His disciples that they should come with Him to a solitary place for some rest (Mark 6:31). When Jesus came to the place, He noticed that the crowd, anticipating His moves, had gotten there ahead of Him. Robbed of His "alone time," what did our Lord say? He did not say, "I'm sorry. Office hours are from 9:00 until 5:00." Nor did the Savior blurt out in frustration, "Can't a guy get a little rest now and then?" Jesus did not sigh in exasperation, look at His wrist-sundial, and say, "Okay, but I have a lot of work to do." He didn't tell the people that services were at 8:00 and 10:30 with Bible class at 9:15 and invite them to come hear Him then. He certainly didn't tell the people to go to the local Baptist church down the road because they were doing such a great job. The Bible says that, right then and there, Jesus had compassion on them because they were like sheep without a shepherd, and He began to teach them. Pastors are not called merely to learn theology but to learn it so as to teach it. They are not appointed by God simply to understand true doctrine but to impart it to the sheep.

Too often I have heard pastors say of their congregation, "They know my phone number. They can call me if they need me." The truth is that most parishioners probably do not know the pastor's number and will not call him when they need to, unless they are either completely desperate or have learned to trust him intimately. When they first call, most people say, "I know you're busy pastor, but . . . " At that moment the pastor better do everything possible to allay the nervousness or fear that people naturally feel. A pastor should never act too busy, indifferent, annoyed, or impatient.

Paul told Timothy, a pastor, that he was to "do the work of an evangelist" (2 Timothy 4:5). Every pastor is an evangelist. An evangelist is one who proclaims the Gospel. And every pastor better realize that he must "do the work." The apostle does not use the verb "evangelize." He does not say, "Do evangelism." Paul calls it work. The pastor's job requires energy, effort, a work ethic, and zeal. It especially requires that pastors get to know their people, love them, understand them, and do what they can to get the people to come to church and to attend Bible class. If it's worth the time of the pastor to prepare wonderful and insightful Bible classes, then it's worth the pastor's time to encourage and exhort the people to come.

I was privileged to have a father who was a pastor. When I was little, he would take me with him on his afternoon calls as he visited the farmers in northwestern Minnesota. He brought me to get me out of my mother's hair, but I loved it nonetheless. I'd play in the barns and chase the chickens. It was quite an adventure for a 6-year-old kid. The women we visited would always give us cake—huge pieces. I remember eating four pieces of chocolate cake at four different farms, all in one afternoon! I was so full of cake by the last house that I simply threw as much as I could under the table to the dog. She caught me and scolded me for being messy. Dad wondered out loud where I got such poor manners. Later, I was privileged to edit a book of my father's sermons preached to seminary students. One sermon contains a description of the heart of a pastor. No doubt he thought of those generous people in northern Minnesota when he preached to young men intent on entering the ministry.

> My dear friends, unless you love people, unless your heart reaches out in sympathy to all who are troubled and distressed, unless you simply find yourself rejoicing with them that rejoice and weeping with them that weep, like Jesus at the grave of Lazarus, then for Christ's sake don't enter the Christian ministry. There is no such thing as a perfunctory theology or a perfunctory pastoral call, just as a perfunctory love is an impossibility. No, like your Master Theologian, you must identify yourself with him whom you would seek to help. He groans at the grave of Lazarus, He weeps over Jerusalem, He feels so sorry for the crooked woman that He interrupts a sermon to heal her before she even knows what has happened. He spends a whole day theologizing with greedy, misguided Zacchaeus, because He has identified Himself with a lost man. He has compassion on a multitude that is hungry. He even makes water into

> wine because He wants people to be happy on a festive occasion. And He has so completely identified Himself with our troubles that He took our flesh and became a brother to each of us, a brother who endured temptation in our place and suffered our guilt and punishment.
>
> Now I want to tell you something: if you will enter your ministry with that same compassionate theology which we behold in our Savior, oh, how glorious and rewarding your ministry will be![30]

If doctrine is worth keeping pure, it is worth the time, the effort, and the heart to teach with tireless zeal.

Purity of Doctrine and Reaching the Lost

I have sometimes heard it said that pastors are either guardians of pure doctrine or they are blessed with a missionary zeal. These two types of pastors are presented as if you must be either guardian or missionary when, of course, any decent pastor must be both. I suspect such either/or choices are presented by those who are less than adamant about the preservation of true doctrine. Although this either/or dichotomy is neither true nor truly sensible, it seems to be believed here and there in our church as though zeal for the pure doctrine renders one also somewhat indifferent toward the work of an evangelist or insensitive to the people of God.

Because this unfair and untrue caricature is believed in the church, it is especially necessary for pastors who love the true doctrine to be doubly devoted to spreading the message of that Gospel doctrine. When a pastor who loves the true doctrine fails, it is always the doctrine that is blamed. If a pastor who loves the doctrine shows insensitivity or indifference to people, his advocacy of true doctrine is often viewed as the reason. "If you would be less of a guardian and more of a missionary, you might get along better with people." We can complain about these false accusations and scream to the heavens about a double standard. We can bemoan those "alligators in the pew" or ecclesiastical overseers who refuse to support pastors who teach true doctrine, but no such whining will adorn the true doctrine with the beauty of patient pastoral service that Christ expects. Suffer in silence, do the work, hold to the truth, smile, assert your call, and love your people all the more.

Have you ever watched a basketball game where it seems like the referees are unfair? They appear to call fouls on your team at the slightest infraction, while they look the other way when the opposing team commits the most flagrant transgressions. The truly great teams respond to any apparent unfairness in a singular manner. They play harder and grumble less. The time it takes to plead with a referee simply slows them down and they lose more. The effort it takes to complain is effort they do not spend on the game. So it is with those who love pure doctrine. They are often vilified and insulted. They are said to be bad evangelists and callous pastors. The only effective response to such accusations is to work harder at evangelism and pray more fervently for pastoral understanding. The doctrine is simply too important for its defenders to do otherwise.

FIGHTING FOR THE TRUTH

I am a big movie buff. My wife and I see about 50 movies a year either in the theaters or at home. When people ask me what the best movie I have seen in the last ten years is, I usually answer *Big Night*.

Big Night is the story of two brothers who have immigrated to the United States from Italy with the dreams of running a successful Italian restaurant. Primo is the chef and Secondo runs the business aspects. The two are constantly fighting, even though they love each other. Primo insists that there is a right way to make Italian cuisine. He will not compromise on the ingredients or the recipes that he has brought from the old country. The restaurant has a loyal, if small, clientele. Secondo is concerned about the profit margin. He needs the restaurant to be successful or it will close its doors. Secondo is drawn to a vulgar, distasteful man who is running a successful American-Italian restaurant. This man tells Secondo that he must "get with the times" and "give people what they want." Americans don't appreciate the fresh herbs, marinara, and pesto sauces made daily, or the homemade pasta. Secondo, who is having an affair with the beautiful young wife of this successful restaurateur, is a true character, a man of deep complexity. His fiancée requires faithfulness and a commitment he is unwilling to give, and his brother demands a culinary purity he is afraid to embrace. Tragically, Secondo loves his fiancée and appreciates the wonderful food his brother prepares. He just cannot have them and still be successful. Secondo becomes a tragic and truly pathetic character whose dilemma is understood by all and desired by none.

In time, Secondo settles on a plan that will resolve the conflict. He will invite a dignitary, some famous person, to the restaurant. He figures that this famous person will attract all sorts of other guests, including critics. These critics will praise the food, the little bistro will thrive, and everyone will live happily ever after. So Secondo goes to his vulgar, competitor friend who arranges for Louis Prima, the famous jazz musician, to dine at the restaurant on the given evening. Louis will arrive with his band and a complement of guests and will pay for the entire meal. Other nonpaying guests and critics are invited. Finally, the "Big Night" arrives.

What a night it is! Primo is in his element. He spends the entire day preparing a culinary experience that is pure and perfect in every way. A menu, featuring the most varied and tasty offerings, is planned. At the market Primo selects fresh spices and other ingredients. Flowers, to adorn the tables and brighten the mood, are chosen. Most of the day is spent in the kitchen carefully, lovingly, agonizingly fixing the repast. The dinner is finally ready. Louis Prima is tardy, so the meal begins without him and his contingent. Primo and Secondo serve the guests. Their enraptured expressions tell the story. Senses throb at each additional course of food. Delicate wines complement the various servings with exact precision. Such a feast had never been served before and will never be served again. Even the unscrupulous competitor is overwhelmed by the beauty he is allowed to enjoy. But, as the meal progresses, a painful truth dawns on the two brothers: Louis Prima is not coming. The successful, unscrupulous man had lied and had never intended to invite the special guest. Primo and Secondo are financially ruined.

This movie is a picture of the ongoing battle between numerical success and purity. We sympathize with Secondo. We share his agony. We deplore his faithlessness, and, somehow, we still love him. But we admire Primo. We do not really care if Louis Prima shows up. The meal, the *Big Night*, the food and wine—these have a value that truly transcends success. The profit margin doesn't matter. Numbers don't matter. We have beheld and experienced perfection. We have tasted the *Big Night*.

In a closing scene, the mutual and reciprocal frustration of the brothers, having grown and festered throughout the movie, explodes and they fight. They hit and claw and push as only brothers can who feel far more pain in their hearts than they can possibly inflict with their fists. The fight ends. Exhausted and gasping for breath, they realize something that Christ's church must also realize. Certain things cannot be compromised. Certain things are worth fighting for and worth dying for. Certain things are so precious we must even be willing to fail for them. For us, these things are a meal more valuable than that served in *Big Night* and a word more compelling than any of the conversations around the table in that charming and poignant drama. Our treasures are the Last Supper of Christ, the Gospel of our Lord, and the washing that buries and raises us with Jesus.

May God teach us to fight only for the truth of the doctrine of Christ.

CONCLUSION

The church needs to set her sights high and expect what God expects. He expects neither numerical growth in every situation nor glorious reports of how well we are doing. He expects faithfulness to the pure doctrine and the Sacraments. This faithfulness will always involve proclaiming justification by grace for Christ's sake, teaching Luther's Catechism, and teaching the theology of the cross. Faithfulness is compromised when anyone, but especially church leaders, are indifferent to doctrine or actually suggest that doctrine is harmful. Our "success" ought to be measured by the cross. Wherever true doctrine is valued and taught, the truth of the Gospel burns itself into the lives of people. Christ's church can "Light the Fire" only by teaching purely.

STUDY QUESTIONS

1. What are the marks of successful ministry?
2. How is doctrine most simply defined?
3. To whom does doctrine belong?

4. What three ways does doctrine unite the church?
5. What is the central message of the Bible?
6. Does doctrine save us?
7. What is lost if doctrine is not pure?
8. How is success in the church rightly measured?
9. What is the theology of the cross?
10. What are the two main doctrines of the Bible?

DISCUSSION QUESTIONS

1. The old Norwegian lady said, "*Lehre er Live*" or "Doctrine is life." What is the significance of that statement?
2. The author writes, "Doctrine is God's—not ours." What is the implication of this statement for a pastor? A church? A church member?
3. In the conclusion to chapter 1 we read: "The church needs to set her sights high and expect what God expects. He expects neither numerical growth in every situation nor glorious reports of how well we are doing." What then does God expect? What does this answer mean for a congregation and her leaders?

2
The Heat of the Fire

JUSTIFICATION

Doctrine is important because of the central doctrine of the Bible—the doctrine of Christ. Christian doctrine teaches Jesus.

The Bible teaching that we are justified before God because of the death of Christ through faith is the central and most important doctrine of the Bible. "This article on justification by faith . . . is the most important of all Christian teaching, without which no poor conscience can have lasting comfort or recognize properly the riches of Christ's grace."[1] Lutherans do not believe that the doctrine of justification is something that they discovered or that justification is unique to their church. This is the Gospel that has always been taught and will last until Christ comes again. Charles Porterfield Krauth, the great nineteenth-century Lutheran theologian, said that Lutheranism "professed to make no discoveries, to find no unheard-of interpretations," but took "the Scriptures in that very sense to which the greatest of her writers" had always assented.[2] Justification, Lutherans insist, is the doctrine upon which the whole Christian church on earth stands and has always stood. Luther says: "Where this single article remains pure, Christendom will remain pure, in beautiful harmony and without any schisms. But where it does not remain pure, it is impossible to repel any error or heretical spirit."[3] If a pastor or church is pure on this doctrine, everything else will fall into place. If you are wrong on this doctrine, everything else will fall apart. Chemnitz says:

> This one article above all distinguishes the Church from all other people and their superstitions. . . . this article is . . . the fortress which most excellently safeguards the entire Christian doctrine and religion. If this article is obscured or vitiated or destroyed, it is impossible to retain the pure doctrine in other articles. But when it is kept sound, all idolatrous notions, superstitions, and the corruptions in nearly all other articles will fall of themselves.[4]

Every so often I will hear someone say, "You believe in doctrine. I believe in Jesus." Such an expression may sound very pious, but the devil is behind it. We cannot believe in Jesus unless we are taught the doctrine of Jesus. You cannot separate Christ from the doctrine of Christ. Christ without doctrine is some vague, wordless, fleshless, and incomprehensible blur, unknowable and unworthy of knowing. If you can't teach it, you can't believe it. Luther says that we must do the following:

> [A]lways repeat, urge, and inculcate this doctrine of faith or Christian righteousness. . . . For by this doctrine alone and through it alone is the church built. . . . Otherwise . . . Christ will be so darkened that no one in the church will . . . be comforted . . . . Whenever you consider the doctrine of justification and wonder how or where or in what condition to find a God who justifies or accepts sinners . . . know that there is no other God than this Man Jesus Christ. . . . Take note, therefore, in the doctrine of justification or grace when we all must struggle with the Law, sin, death, and the devil, we must look at no other God than this incarnate and human God.[5]

Notice how the reformer talks of doctrine and of Christ as if the two are the same. Doctrine brings Christ. Without the pure doctrine of justification in Christ, we cannot build the church, be comforted, know God, struggle against evil, or look at Jesus our Savior.

Not surprisingly, all the major controversies throughout the pages of church history are over the proper way of understanding and teaching justification by faith. One of the fiercest controversies occurred in the middle of the sixteenth century. It was called the Osiandrian controversy. Here's how one of my congregations learned of it.

Church Constitution

No form of church work is more thankless and boring than serving on a congregational constitution committee. Even if you can enter the task with a modicum of enthusiasm, your zeal is usually depleted by the sheer tedium of the task or the listless stares of your colleagues who tried not to get roped into the job in the first place. Pastors tend to justify the constitution committee's work with pious exhortations to "do the work of the Lord" or to "carry on the ministry." Everyone else on the committee respectfully, and hypocritically, nods in agreement to these platitudes. Or maybe they are nodding back to sleep.

Our congregational constitution committee used to meet on Saturday mornings at 8:30. Our goal was to get as far as we could by 10:00 A.M. We were revising our entire church constitution, updating it, trimming it, and expanding it as needed. On one particular Saturday morning I just wanted the time to pass. We were discussing Article Three of our constitution: Doctrinal Standards. This discussion should not have taken too long. We did not need to reinvent the wheel. As a Lutheran church we accepted the Scriptures as the Word of God and the Lutheran Confessions as the correct exposition of the Word of God. I simply asserted that these matters were not really negotiable and that, at any rate, this article of our constitution was unalterable. But then George, senior member of the group, raised a question. "What are these things we are promising to go by?"

George's curiosity was greeted by impatient sighs and murmurings all around the table. "It's the way it has always been." "We don't have a choice on this article, so let's just move on." "Enough with the unnecessary questions. We have to be a little more result oriented. That is a process question. We are not here for that." I have to admit I was, at least initially, a bit annoyed with the question because it was going to slow us down.

George insisted on an answer. "I won't sign off on a constitution that I do not fully understand. It says that we bind ourselves to the Formula of Concord. I don't even know what that is."

My annoyance transitioned to embarrassment. How could one of my members not know what the Formula of Concord was? I answered: "The Formula of Concord and all the writings of the Lutheran Confessions are the documents that define us as Lutherans. They tell the world what we believe, the church what to confess, and the pastor what to teach. In a sense, these confessions protect you by keeping me from teaching anything I please." I hoped this answer would satisfy George because I really did want the committee to move along. But part of me hoped he would resist. I was not disappointed.

"Why should we need protection? And how can we be protected by something with which we are completely unfamiliar?"

I looked around the room. Something very exciting was beginning to happen. The rest of the committee members ceased from their imitation of the Stepford Wives, sat up in their chairs, poured another round of java, and leaned forward. I was being told, nonverbally, that there was a theological question on the floor that required an answer from me. I studied their faces. My hesitation fed their expectancy. "Well," I replied, "it looks like we need a Bible class. Starting with the next meeting, I think we should begin each session with 30 minutes of study about the Book of Concord."

George leaned back in his chair, "Pastor, that would be a waste of time."

I knew it. He was already backing off.

"Why," he continued, "would you want to teach us on Saturdays when you would just have to teach the whole church again on Sundays. The whole congregation is going to have to approve this constitution. It would be bad stewardship of time to have to teach it twice."

"And I suppose that you would insist that all the members must understand the theological content of the Formula of Concord before they approve this constitution?" I mused.

George only smiled.

So it came to pass that our congregation studied the Formula of Concord during Sunday morning Bible class. It is actually a pretty easy book to teach. Each of the eleven articles, except the last, is the response of the young Lutheran church to a controversy that it faced. In each article of the Formula of Concord are statements that we, as Lutherans, either affirm or reject. So every week I would present both sides of a controversy, then provide Bible passages that revealed the correct doctrinal position. I would then produce statements from the Formula itself, but I would omit the portion of the sentence that said either "We believe" or "We reject." The Bible class would have to decide which side of the controversy they thought the early Lutherans should have settled upon. My church always came out on the right side.

JESUS *IN* US OR JESUS *FOR* US.

Lesson three of the Bible class covered Article Three of the Formula of Concord, "Concerning the Righteousness of Faith before God." This lesson lasted three weeks, generating keen interest and at times heated discussion. Below is part of the lesson. Let's see how well you can do.

Read the following Bible verses:

> In His days Judah will be saved, and Israel will dwell securely. And this is the name by which He will be called: "The LORD is our righteousness." (Jeremiah 23:6)

> He is the source of your life in Christ Jesus, whom God made our wisdom and our righteousness and sanctification and redemption. (1 Corinthians 1:30)

> For our sake He made Him to be sin who knew no sin, so that in Him we might become the righteousness of God. (2 Corinthians 5:21)

Now read the following two statements. One was rejected by the Lutheran church, and one was accepted. Using the Bible passages, choose which is right and which is wrong.

> A: ____ our righteousness before God consists in this, that God forgives us our sins by sheer grace, without any works, merit, or worthiness of our own, in the past, at present, or in the future, that he gives us and reckons to us the righteousness of Christ's obedience and that, because of this righteousness, we are accepted by God into grace and regarded as righteous.[6]

> B: ____ faith should look not only to the obedience of Christ but also to his divine nature, as it dwells in us and produces results, and that through this indwelling our sins are covered.[7]

(Keep reading for the answer.)

Immediately after Martin Luther died (in 1546) a controversy arose among the Lutherans. The two key figures were Martin Chemnitz and Andreas Osiander. They debated the question of the justification of the sinner before God. Both Osiander and Chemnitz taught that a person is justified by faith without the works of the Law, but they differed in their beliefs about the basis of God's justification.

Chemnitz taught that God counts to our credit the righteousness Jesus earned through His obedient life and death for us. Chemnitz used the word *impute*. God imputes or declares us righteous. Impute is a courtroom word. God pronounces His verdict upon you: "You are not guilty. You are righteous." The righteousness is from outside of you, from Jesus. God counts to your credit the innocence and righteousness earned by Christ. You receive this verdict by faith in the life and death of Christ. "In what, then," asks Chemnitz, "does justification of man the sinner before God consist according to the statement of the Gospel?" He answers, "In this very thing, that God imputes to us the righteousness of the obedience and death of Christ . . . without our works or merits, alone by faith that apprehends the grace of God the Father and the merit of Christ."[8] To Chemnitz, justification is the pronouncement of the forgiveness of sins. So Christ's life and death have "become for us wisdom from God—that is, our righteousness, holiness and redemption" (1 Corinthians 1:30).

Osiander taught that the righteousness that counts before God is not that which Christ earned. Rather, "Christ dwelling in us by faith is our Righteousness."[9] To Osiander, one did not look exclusively to the life and death of Jesus for the basis for God's verdict of not guilty. Instead, you looked into your heart where Jesus dwells. "They are errorists," claimed Osiander, "who say . . . that the righteousness is outside of us. . . . They also teach things colder than ice [who hold] that we are regarded as righteous only on account of the forgiveness of sins, and not on account of the [essential] righteousness of Christ who dwells in us through faith."[10] Justification is not the same as forgiveness. Rather, according to Osiander, it is a process in which sin, already forgiven, is "mortified and destroyed in us."[11] Osiander taught that "Christ, living in us through faith, is our Wisdom, Righteousness, Holiness, and Redemption. 1 Cor. 1,30."[12]

Chemnitz and Osiander were asking: Are you saved because Jesus died for you or because Jesus lives in your heart?

Luther, twenty years earlier, had predicted, "This doctrine [of justification] will be obscured again after my death."[13] Who was guilty of obscuring the Gospel? Which statement above is pure doctrine and which is false doctrine?

The Osiandrian controversy produced countless meetings and theological debates. Conferences were called. For 25 years the greatest theologians of the Lutheran church fine-tuned their theology. They produced Article Three of the Formula of Concord. Amazingly, this document settled the issue, deciding completely for one side of the controversy. There was no compromise. There was no convergence—a silly word often used today. It was not a matter of "both for us and in us." It was one way and not the other.

Really, there should not have been a controversy in the first place. The Augsburg Confession, to which all the Lutherans agreed, had asserted the biblical view in 1530. The word " 'justify' is used in a judicial way to mean 'to absolve a guilty man and to pronounce him righteous,' and to do so on account of someone else's righteousness, namely, Christ's, which is communicated to us through faith."[14]

So Chemnitz is right and Osiander is wrong. If you said that statement "A" is biblical, then you answered correctly. If you answered that statement "B" is biblical, then here's another chance. It seems some of the people in my Bible class were upset at me for not teaching that you are saved because Jesus is in your heart. "Jesus may well be in your heart," I agreed, "but that does not save you." Besides, I was not certain what it meant that Jesus is in your heart. So I wrote another test.

Take the following test. Answer either A or B. It will determine whether you follow Osiander or Chemnitz.

1. A. I am righteous before God because Jesus lived for me in time.

   B. I am righteous before God because Jesus lives in my heart.
2. A. The righteousness that avails before God is inside of me.

B. The righteousness that avails before God is outside of me.

3. A. God accepts me because my attitude toward God has changed.

   B. God accepts me because God's attitude toward me has changed.

4. A. I am saved because God counts the merit and worthiness of Christ to my credit.

   B. I am saved because God pours the merit and worthiness of Christ into my heart.

5. A. The righteousness that counts before God for me is the righteousness that Jesus always possessed as the Son of God.

   B. The righteousness that counts before God for me is the righteousness that Jesus earned through His life and death.

6. A. God accepts us only because of the forgiveness of sins.

   B. God accepts us also because Jesus lives in our hearts.

7. A. Justification happened 2,000 years ago and is received by faith.

   B. Justification depends on faith and did not happen 2,000 years ago.

8. A. I know Jesus lives because I feel Him in my heart.

   B. I know Jesus lives because of the Gospel.

The correct answers are: 1. A; 2. B; 3. B; 4. A; 5. B; 6. A; 7. A; 8. B. Thankfully, by the time people took the second test, they had studied so many sections of the Bible (Romans 3–5, Galatians 2–4, 1 Peter 3, Ephesians 2, and huge sections of Jeremiah and the Psalms) that all but one person got all the answers correct. She was a pious, elderly woman whom I was forced to love by the sweetness of her disposition. To this day I'm convinced that she did poorly on the test only because she was nervous. I think she had the impression that her eternal salvation was based on her academic doctrinal prowess. I told her that her salvation does not depend on how well she performed on this test. It depends on the performance of Jesus—His obedient life and His obedient death counted to your credit. The Lutheran view is, in truth, the Bible view, the Christian view, and the view that brings eternal life.

The Formula of Concord settled this issue once and for all. Or did it?

What about Those Contemporary Songs? Part One

Today, every true Lutheran pastor must swear before God and the church to uphold the teachings of the Formula of Concord. That means that it should be virtually impossible for anyone to hear in any Lutheran church that you are saved because Christ is in your heart. You should never hear that your salvation depends on anything that happens in you at all.

But how many Lutherans have heard or sung praise songs that strongly suggest or explicitly teach that salvation comes to us because Jesus is "in your heart." One well-known song drives home the Osiandrian doctrine by repeating the phrase "heaven is in my heart" on every other line of the song.[15] Another, which I sang at various and sundry campfires when I was a kid, asserts that Christians have "the joy, joy, joy, joy" or "the peace which passes understanding" or "the love of Jesus, love of Jesus down in my heart." And in case you miss the point, the words "down in my heart" are repeated 15 times in three verses.[16] Another song that I have heard sung in Lutheran churches is an old revivalist, Homer Rodeheaver classic called "He Lives," in which the assurance of the Gospel truth of Christ's resurrection is based neither upon the Scriptures nor the witness of the church. Rather, "You ask me how I know he lives? He lives within my heart."[17] Consider the countless little Lutherans attending vacation Bible school who combine theology with spelling by asserting with joyful ambiguity that they are Christians and will live eternally since "I have Christ in my heart."[18] John Barbour, a contemporary Christian music composer of no small note, entitled one song "Make Your Presence Known." Throughout the song he calls upon God to give "assurance from above" and to "make your presence known." How? "We pray, . . . Make your presence known in our hearts."[19]

These songs point to Jesus in our hearts rather than to Jesus on the cross. Some are sufficiently unclear as to avoid the charge of false doctrine. But they are all certainly bad theology. Yet I have heard these songs sung in churches or seen them printed in church bulletins. Did Paul claim, "I have determined to know nothing among you except Jesus Christ and Him in my heart?" Did Peter pronounce, "Christ lives in your hearts for sins, the righteous for the unrighteous, that He might bring us to God"?

My heart, yours as well, is a vile place. I do not really want to look at my heart too much. To rely on my heart, my heart feelings, a heart language, a heart warmed—the thought is scary. I don't go to church to look at my heart. I am not a Christian by looking at my heart. I need to see Jesus—not in my heart but on the cross. I need a Savior who distracts me from the narcissistic examination of my own heart.

I have a crucifix in my office. It hangs right next to the door so I am forced to see it each time I leave my office. Every time I am called upon to visit the hospitalized or to commune a shut-in, every time I leave to teach or to make a call on a prospective member, every time I put on my vestments and proceed to the sanctuary to give to God's people Christ's Word and Sacrament, I see that crucifix. It tells me that my ministry as a pastor is to proclaim "God [who] imputes to us the righteousness of the obedience and death of Christ."[20]

OBJECTIVE AND SUBJECTIVE

One way to look at the doctrine of justification is to look at it objectively and subjectively. But what do the words *objective* and *subjective* mean?

The argument that has troubled Lutherans in North America for more than 150 years is the difference between objective and subjective. *Objective* means that something is analyzed and evaluated apart from its effect on you. *Subjective* means that something is analyzed and evaluated only as it affects you. Subjective always depends on objective. For example, suppose I tell you that you are absolved. You are forgiven. I can say that you are objectively absolved because Christ pronounced you righteous through His death. And I could say that you were subjectively absolved when you heard and received God's absolution by faith. Both objective absolution and subjective absolution are true. They are just two ways of looking at the same thing. But you have to be objectively absolved in order to be subjectively absolved. So when your pastor absolves you, he is not making a comment about your faith or your heart. He is making a comment about Christ and applying Christ to you. He is saying that you are objectively absolved because of Christ.

During the middle of the nineteenth century, millions of Lutherans came to North America from the old countries—Denmark, Germany, Norway, Sweden, Latvia, and Finland. With them they brought controversy. Mostly it was just the same argument repeating itself to different people in different ways. But it was always the same controversy, and we are still arguing over it today. Theologians and churches did not understand and teach the difference between objective and subjective.

The Lutheran churches in North America had a controversy over absolution in the middle of the nineteenth century. The question was this: Is absolution true, real, and valid even if a person does not have faith? The first side said, "Yes, the absolution is true and valid. It bestows forgiveness even if a person does not have faith, though it does not benefit you without faith." The other side said, "No, the absolution does not bestow forgiveness unless a person believes. You must have faith to be absolved." The first side talked of absolution in objective terms. That way it could be spoken of with certainty. The second side refused to speak in objective terms and had great difficulty speaking with certainty. The first side was correct theologically. The second was condemned.

Then there was the controversy about justification in the late nineteenth century. One side said, "All people are justified because Jesus died for all. The Gospel declares you righteous before God because God declared you righteous on Calvary." The other side said, "Only believers are justified and righteous before God. You must have faith to be justified." This same controversy reared its ugly head again in the 1970s and 1980s. The first group taught objective justification. "God has justified all people through the death of His Son." Remember that the Lutheran Confessions treated forgiveness and justification as the same. If your sins have been taken away, then you have been justified before God. So the Bible says, "Behold, the Lamb of God, who takes away the sin of the world!" (John 1:29). "In Christ God was reconciling the world to Himself" (2 Corinthians 5:19). These passages mean that all people have been justified. We are objectively justified. The other side said that unless you believe, you are not justified. Thankfully, both in the 1870s and the 1980s this controversy was settled on the basis of the Scriptures. The first side was correct theologically. The second side was rejected.

The greatest controversy to afflict Lutherans in North America occurred in the early twentieth century. It was called the predestination controversy. One side said: "God chose us from eternity to be saved in Christ. God's choice of you does not depend on faith. He chose you because of Christ and that's what causes your faith. You are objectively chosen and predestined." The other side said: "Christ chose you because He looked into the future and saw your faith. He chose you in view of your faith. You cannot be chosen unless you have faith. You must have faith to be predestined." Again, based on the Bible, the church settled the issue and decided in favor of the first side, which stressed the objective choosing of God. The second side was condemned.

Notice how each controversy is similar. Must you have faith to be absolved? Must you have faith to be justified? Must you have faith to be chosen? These were very complicated issues that exhausted the church. In each case one side said no. The other side said yes.[21] In each case the side that said yes was condemned.

In the 1970s the Lutheran churches argued about the Word of God. Most historians will tell you that we were arguing over the inerrancy of the Bible. Is the Bible really the Word of God? Is it free of error—inerrant? Of course it is. The arguments were prolonged, fierce, and sometimes not very loving. But there is another way you can look at that bitter controversy of a generation ago. It was the same old thing again. One side said that the Bible is the Word of God whether you believe it, understand it, or even know that it exists. The Bible is inspired and inerrant because that's the way God made it. He inspired the book. The other side said that the Bible becomes the Word of God when you add faith to it. You must have faith for the Bible to be God's Word.[22] It was the same old argument. Is the Bible the Word of God objectively apart from my understanding? Or is the Bible the Word of God only subjectively when I acknowledge its effect on me? Again, one side stressed the objective side of God's blessings, and the other looked at things only subjectively. And again, the church settled the issue.

The controversy can be stated in a slightly different way. Do the blessings and actions of God—absolution, justification, predestination, His Word—depend on faith? Or does faith depend on the actions of God? When you put the question like that, you can easily see that we Lutherans in North America have been arguing the same thing for more than 150 years. Sometimes people say that Lutherans just like to argue. I don't think so. It's just that the same argument never seems to get settled.

Today we are still fighting the same fight, though the focus of the argument has shifted. Today we are arguing over the liturgy, songs in church, the importance of pure doctrine, the ministry, and fellowship between churches or groups. But when you phrase the argument, it ends up being the same objective/subjective distinction.

It's time for another test. This time test yourself to see where you are on the objective/subjective continuum.

Liturgy

1. A. The most important aspect of liturgy is that it reflects the objective truths of the Gospel.

   B. The most important aspect of liturgy is that it speaks subjectively to the heart of the worshiper.

2. A. The words of the worship service should be the objective language of a gracious God, whether we always understand that language or not.

   B. The words of the worship service should be in the subjective heart language of the people, who must understand in order for the service to be meaningful.

Songs and hymns

1. A. The most important aspect of songs in church is that they reflect the objective truths of the Gospel.

   B. The most important aspect of songs in the church is that they move me subjectively to express my experience of the Gospel.

2. A. The purpose of music is to reflect the objective words of the Gospel.

   B. The purpose of music is to move the people to subjective faith.

DOCTRINE

1. A. Doctrine is vital because it teaches objectively about Jesus, whether I understand it or not.

   B. Doctrine becomes important only when I subjectively understand it.

2. A. Doctrine reflects God's objective Word.

   B. Doctrine reflects my subjective denomination.

THE MINISTRY

1. A. The pastor is to be evaluated by his faithfulness to the objective Word of God.

   B. The pastor is to be evaluated by his effectiveness in dealing with the subjective needs of people.

2. A. A man is called to the ministry when the church has objectively taught him, examined him, and issued him a call, whether he likes it or not.

   B. A man is called to the ministry because the Lord has laid on him the subjective desire to spread the Word.

FELLOWSHIP

1. A. We have fellowship with those churches that share the same doctrine based on the objective Word of God.

   B. We have fellowship with those churches that share the same subjective faith in the Gospel.

2. A. When you go into a church, you can get a sense of their fellowship only by analyzing their objective statements of doctrine.

   B. When you go into a church, you can get a sense of the closeness of their fellowship by the subjective sense of their love.

So the same old argument continues. I believe that the endless discussions in college and seminary classrooms, at pastors' conferences and voters' assemblies, in District and Synod boards and committees, at virtually every convention of our church for the last century, over countless coffee clutches where Lutherans and Christians gather to discuss the matters of the day—all the arguments center around one issue: Does the church define herself objectively or subjectively?

HIKING WITHOUT WATER

I lived in California for twelve years, seven in the shadow of Mt. Diablo, where I developed a passion for hiking. A remarkably beautiful and varied mountain, Diablo rises with majestic nonchalance above the coastal ranges about 20 miles east of San Francisco. It features breathtaking, panoramic views in virtually every direction and, at the same time, picturesque streams, meadows, and cliffs nestled, almost hidden, in the countless nooks and crannies. Manzanita, live oak, and bay trees adorn this Eden and, mingled with the wind and arid heat, simultaneously assail all your senses. It's almost as good as church. From my house I could, within 30 minutes, be transported from the midst of a sprawling urban area of six million to absolute solitude, save the ground squirrels, lizards, hawks, and occasional snakes. A good day of hiking starts at about 7:00 A.M. when the fog has barely lifted and the grass is still moist with the nightly dew.

One day I forgot my water.

I had gone only about a half a mile when I noticed that my water container was missing. "No matter," I figured. I can handle it. That same day I got a little lost. My 6.4 mile loop turned into a 9.4 mile loop. And the additional three miles were not level. I had deviated from *terra cognita* into a charming little valley. Well, it was charming, but not little. The path took me deep into a ragged gorge, dry as a lecture on medieval monasteries. The August heat had long since dispossessed this natural oven of anything resembling H_2O, and the hoped for aquatic gurgling was replaced with a tunnel of wind that howled in concert with the groaning of my empty stomach. I was beginning to realize why they had named the mountain "Diablo." It was suited only for the devil and his spawn.

Parched is a rather insipid word. Such an expression does not adequately describe my lips and mouth as the long morning dragged on. Withered, scorched, desiccated—gaping cracks void of life and moisture—such were my lips. In the hot California sun you do not really sweat because the water evaporates as quickly as you perspire. On that day, however, I know I did not sweat because there was nothing left in my prune-like body to emit. I was thirsty.

You can safely assume that, as this little volume is not published posthumously, I survived the ordeal—not without the help of God's angels. I finally got back to the car only to notice that I had not even brought water in the car. It was at least six miles to the nearest drinking establishment, and no rural Lutheran pastor has ever driven so fast. I ordered a beer. I took a drink.

Beer is objective. It has value and power apart from me. Drinking is subjective. It's the way I get the beer.

In that precious moment as I lingered, so I thought, between this life and the next and felt the happy nectar overcome my dehydrated condition, I can tell you what I did not say. I did not say, "How thankful I am for my subjective assimilation of this draught." I did not focus on how I was able to ingest the brew. I did not think about my ability to drink. I thought about the beer. Beer alone occupied my thoughts. Cold, wet, objective beer.

So it is with justification, absolution, the Word of God, and all God's blessings. Sometimes you are thirsty for forgiveness. Your conscience condemns you soundly. You know that God is justifiably outraged at you. You linger between spiritual life and spiritual death and want only to be absolved. You have stupidly neglected God's word of grace. Your "strength was dried up as by the heat of the summer" (Psalm 32:4). All you want is God's life-giving water of grace. When you receive the pardon and justification of God, you do not focus on your own faith or how you receive God's promises subjectively. Rather, you think only upon the blessings of God found in the life and death of Jesus. You think about objective absolution, objective justification, and the objective Word. Objective is foundational and certain.

Where does faith fit into the picture of justification? Simply answered: Faith receives. Christians often hear the question, "What do you have to do to get to heaven?" And we know the answer. Ya gotta have faith! But what exactly does that mean? Just as there are two ways of looking at Jesus—in us or for us—so there are two ways of looking at faith. Sometimes faith is presented in the Bible as an active thing. Faith produces things. Chapter 11 of Hebrews looks at faith this way. Often faith is looked at as a passive thing. Faith receives something. It receives Christ and the verdict "not guilty," which is ours in Christ. This is how Paul looks at faith in Romans 3–5. When Christians say "We are saved by grace alone" or "We are justified through faith alone," they are referring to faith as it is passive, not active. Faith does not add anything to the work of Christ. It only receives Christ. If faith added something to the forgiveness of sins, then Jesus would not have said, "It is finished." Instead, He would have said, "Well, except for faith, it is finished."

Trick or Treat

Faith is like trick-or-treating. "Trick or treat!" Those were great words. They still are. They are words of kids either greedy or full of trust. The words conjure memories both painful and pleasant. I suppose that a literal interpretation would be that if you do not give the kids some candy, they will push over your outhouse or throw eggs at your car. But that's not what the words mean. They simply mean: "We think that you are going to give us some candy."

When I went trick-or-treating for the first time, around the age of 7, I was green, a novice. My family had just moved to the big city of St. Louis from the country. Knowing nothing of the rules of Halloween, my ignorance showed. My costume was cumbersome. It was cold outside, so I had to wear a jacket over the skeleton outfit. The string on my mask broke after the fourth house, and I somehow felt obligated not to appear at the doorsteps of any erstwhile donors without a covering, so I held my mask in place with one hand. At the same time I had to go to the bathroom, a condition that worsened as the evening dragged on. My outfit was all one piece and I could not relieve myself without stripping down to my underwear, a process that modesty precluded. So, as little boys are wont to do, I used my second hand to hold something else. Both hands occupied, I could not offer my bag to the nice people at the doors who wanted to shower the coveted confections upon all the kids of the neighborhood. Desperate, I begged my friend, Mark, to get candy for the both of us, and he graciously complied. Unfortunately, his bag had previously been used by his mother to haul meat from the grocery store and had sprung a particularly insidious leak. The evening's efforts were largely lost.

I come from a large family and practiced "survival of the fittest" where any food not in the five main groups was concerned. So my siblings shared only enough goodies to forestall the creeping guilt often associated with enjoying themselves too much in the presence of another's pain. The evening was not at all what it was cracked up to be. The only happy note was when Mrs. Franzmann, who lived down the street, came by out of sheer pity and gave me a couple of leftover popcorn balls. I learned a very valuable lesson that night. The bag is the most important instrument in the trick-or-treater's arsenal. Without it you are dead. With it you have everything.

The next year I used a pillowcase and had enough candy to last until Thanksgiving. I stuffed my face with sweets until my belly swelled and my teeth rotted. I was the happiest guy on earth and never gave the bag a second thought.

Faith is like a trick-or-treater's bag. When you don't have it, you are lost. When you do have it, all you think about is what's in it. When a person does not have faith, we say, "They are lost. You can't get to heaven without faith. Faith is necessary." But when a person believes, you stop talking about faith and talk only about Jesus. The way to get a person to believe is not to discuss the importance of faith. Instead, you have to talk about Jesus Christ and Him crucified.

PASSIVE FAITH

Saving faith is passive faith. What do you have to do to get to heaven? "Nothing!" Yet often Christians answer the question with, "Ya gotta believe! Ya gotta have faith!" Of course, faith is necessary for salvation. But I cringe when I hear the sentence, "All you have to do to get to heaven is believe." Let me explain by analyzing three pieces of bad theology.

1. I once heard a sermon where the preacher proclaimed, "God has done His part. He has sent His Son to die for you. Now you have to do your part. You have to believe in Jesus." That is bad theology.

2. I had a professor at the seminary who wrote the following equation: "Forgiveness + Faith = Justification." That is also bad theology.
3. I tell the kids in my catechism class, "Jesus has taken away all of your sins on the cross. You are totally and 100 percent forgiven because of Jesus." Inevitably, one of them asks me, "But pastor, you have to ask for it, right?" And I always respond, "That is bad theology."

Why are these three statements bad theology? Because in each case the focus is drawn away from Jesus. Let's look at the three expressions.

1. It is false to say that God has done His part and that we must do ours. Rather, God sent His only Son into this world to do our part. Christ became flesh, not to do God's part but to do the part required of all flesh. He died, not for God, but for us. Our part has been done. If you wanted to make the sentence good theology, you would say, "God did His part and Jesus did your part." Notice the focus is on the cross and the work of Jesus.
2. To say "Forgiveness + Faith = Justification" makes it seem that forgiveness is not good enough just by itself to make us stand before God and be accepted by Him. Faith is seen as completing forgiveness. But faith does not complete the work of Jesus. Jesus did not say, "It is finished if you believe." He simply said, "It is finished." If you wanted to make the formula correct, you would say, "Forgiveness = Justification." Notice how the focus is on the cross and the forgiveness of Jesus.
3. It is wrong to say that you are not forgiven unless you ask. No one was asking Jesus for forgiveness while He died on the cross. He was earning and accomplishing our salvation all alone. "What punishment so strange is suffered yonder! The Shepherd dies for sheep that loved to wander."[23] In fact, if God had waited for someone to ask, Jesus would never have come. The statement "Jesus has taken away all your sins" needs no improvement because it focuses on the cross.

So where does faith fit in? Faith is not a condition that must be met. Faith is not what we add to the equation. Faith is not the way we get God to do something. Faith receives. Faith simply receives all the gracious promises and blessings of God. Faith is passive. It does nothing. It offers nothing. It contributes nothing. It's like the bag of the trick-or-treater. Our confessions say, "To have faith is to desire and to receive the offered promise of the forgiveness of sins and justification."[24]

C. F. W. Walther was one of the founders of The Lutheran Church—Missouri Synod and its first president. When he came to the United States during the 1840s, he was alarmed at the bad theology of those churches around him. He was especially troubled by their understanding of faith.

> Modern theologians assert that in the salvation of man two kinds of activity must be noted: in the first place, there is something that God must do. His part is the most difficult, for He must accomplish the task of redeeming men. But in the second place, something is required that man must do. For it will not do to admit persons to heaven, after they have been redeemed, without further parley. Man must do something really great—he has to believe. This teaching overthrows the Gospel completely.[25]

Then what makes faith so important? Walther quotes Adam Osiander: "Faith does not justify in so far as it is obedience in compliance with a command,—for thus viewed, it is an action, a work, and something required by Law,—but only *in so far as it receives* and is attached to justification after the manner of a passive instrument."[26] Faith is passive. Walther compares faith to the hand of a beggar who receives a dollar. In fact, it was this illustration of Walther that made me think of the bag of the trick-or-treater.

Walther learned his doctrine from Luther, Luther from the apostle Paul, and Paul from the Spirit of Christ. Luther says:

> But this most excellent righteousness, the righteousness of faith, which God imputes to us through Christ without works, is neither political nor ceremonial nor legal nor work-righteousness but is quite the opposite; it is a merely passive righteousness, while all the others, listed above, are active. For here we work nothing, render nothing to God; we only receive and permit someone else to work in us, namely, God. Therefore it is appropriate to call the righteousness of faith or Christian righteousness "passive."[27]

For this reason Lutheran theologians typically say that faith is purely passive when it comes to salvation.

ACTIVE FAITH

We are saved by faith alone, but faith is never alone. Good works always follow true saving faith. Faith is always accompanied by love and hope. We should never imagine that there is such a thing as a faith that can exist and remain alongside an evil intention to sin. So faith always produces works. Faith is always active. Luther says that faith is always "a living, busy, active, mighty thing, this faith. It is impossible for it not to be doing good works incessantly."[28]

God is not so weak that He would produce a faith in us that did not immediately start doing the things God expects of His children. And faith is not so anemic that it does not both desire and perform the things that please God. So faith is always active. Actually, to talk about active faith is the same as talking about love. Active faith is love. "Faith takes from God. Love gives to the neighbor," says Luther.[29]

But when it comes to justification and salvation, then faith is passive. Chapter 6 will discuss active faith.

PASSIVE AND ACTIVE FAITH

The most difficult task of the Christian, and the most important, is to understand the difference between passive faith and active faith. The difference can be expressed in couplets that contrast with each other.

1. Passive faith is everything when it comes to salvation.

   Active faith is nothing when it comes to salvation.

2. Passive faith is nothing when it comes to serving your neighbor.

   Active faith is everything when it comes to serving your neighbor.

3. Passive faith is always perfect because it receives from Christ.

   Active faith is always imperfect because it serves your neighbor.

4. Passive faith is in God's doctrine.

   Active faith is toward your neighbor's need.

5. Faith is passive in justification.
   Faith is active in sanctification.
6. Passive faith tolerates nothing.
   Active faith tolerates all things.
7. Passive faith saves.
   Active faith serves.
8. Passive faith belongs to heaven.
   Active faith belongs to earth.
9. Passive faith is hidden under the cross.
   Active faith is exposed to the world.
10. Active faith must be based on passive saving faith. True
    Passive saving faith must be based on active faith. False

That last sentence totally threw off the balance. Why? Because in all of this we must remember that Jesus is the center of our theology. We have Jesus by passive faith. We are never saved, even in part, because of what we do but only because of what Jesus has done. Faith saves because it is passive—it receives Jesus. When it comes to salvation, Christians learn to stop asking questions about what they can do. They have learned that it is wrong, bad, misleading, and ultimately damning to assert that faith must be active to save.

At the time of the early Lutherans there were some theologians who were concerned that all Christians needed to be encouraged to do good works. They taught that faith always produced good works. So far so good. But they went too far. They also said that "without good works (active faith) a person cannot be justified." Such statements are wrong because they add works to justification. "We are justified by faith alone without the works of the Law." So says the Holy Spirit. The Formula of Concord agrees.[30]

I used to play outfield on my church softball team. The outfielder has a tough job. He has to field the ball and throw it. One big mistake you can make as a player is to take your eyes off the ball. With many outfielders the temptation to look around before you catch is particularly acute because much of the time you are rushed. You can't begin to throw until you have the ball. You can't look over to third base or home plate until the ball is in your mitt, or you will drop it. That's the way it is with passive and active faith. Grace is like the ball. If you are thinking about what you are going to do with God's grace while you are simply receiving it, then you will lose the grace of God. You must first catch it. Only then can you do something with it. First, you must be passive—only then can you be active. Catching the ball does not depend on throwing the ball. Passive faith does not depend on active faith. Throwing the ball does depend on catching the ball. Active faith does depend on passive faith. In fact, as I will show in the next chapter, you can't even "catch the ball" by your own efforts. It's not really something "Ya gotta do." Faith is 100 percent a gift of God, for "I cannot by my own reason or strength believe in Jesus Christ, my Lord."[31]

The difference between passive faith and active faith is similar to the question all Lutherans learn in their childhood: "What are the two main teachings of the Bible?" The answer, of course, is Law and Gospel. The Gospel informs passive faith. It tells about Jesus and invites us to do nothing but trust in Him. The Law informs active faith. It tells us what to do. The Gospel saves. The Law does not.

CONCLUSION

You can stand before the throne of God's judgment knowing that God accepts you. Your assurance is based not on Jesus in your heart, but on Jesus on the cross. He counts to your credit His innocent life just as He assumed the blame for all of your sins through His sacrificial death. The wonderful, comforting, sweet verdict of "not guilty" is true. It is not merely "potential" or "possible" when and if something else happens or if some other condition is met. It is true because God has already objectively rendered the verdict on Calvary's cross. So the Gospel is objective. It is outside of you. We understand, hold, and treasure the Gospel because it is objective. You receive this verdict of "not guilty" through faith alone. Faith, as far as it saves, is always purely passive and contributes nothing. It simply receives, like the trick-or-treater's bag. If doctrine is fire, then the saving article of doctrine, justification by grace through faith, is "The Heat of the Fire." It attracts the sheep of Christ and provides safety, comfort, warmth, and life itself.

There are really two questions that must be asked whenever you are doing theology. The first question is "What does the Bible say?"

To answer this question you study the text of the Scriptures and figure out the grammar, the vocabulary, and the context. Then you arrive at what the Bible says: "For we hold that one is justified by faith apart from works of the Law" (Romans 3:28).

The second question is "How does this relate to justification?" How does Baptism relate to justification? How does Holy Communion relate to justification? How does the Great Commission relate to justification? In the next chapter we will tackle the question "How does the scriptural doctrine of the Holy Spirit relate to the doctrine of justification?"

STUDY QUESTIONS

1. What was the error of Andreas Osiander?
2. What was the response of Martin Chemnitz and Article III of the Formula of Concord to Osiander's error?
3. Define "justify."
4. Define "objective."
5. Define "subjective."
6. What is objective justification?
7. Is the Bible God's Word because you believe it to be so? Why or why not?
8. Why is faith like a trick-or-treater's bag?
9. Is saving faith passive or active?
10. What is the activity of faith?
11. What is the Gospel that has always been taught and will last until Christ comes again?

DISCUSSION QUESTIONS

1. Discuss the most difficult and important task of the Christian, understanding the difference between passive and active faith.
2. Discuss the author's statement that it is wrong, bad, misleading, and ultimately damning to ask, "Doesn't my faith have to be active to save?"
3. Why does the author state that "the devil is behind" the expression "You believe in doctrine—I believe in Jesus"?

3

The Fire Spreads

WORD AND SPIRIT

An elderly couple visited my church a while back and said they could tell that the Spirit was really active in our congregation. When I asked them how, they replied, "We just knew from the joyful looks on the people's faces." Sometime later, while visiting a young man who had come to our church a couple of times, I asked what he thought of our church. He said, "Pastor, meaning no offense, I just didn't get the impression that the Spirit was really alive in your church." Again, I asked how he could tell, to which he replied, "There just didn't seem to be the joy you would expect from a church that was really alive in the Spirit."

How do you know whether the Holy Spirit is alive and active in a church? The answer to that question is extremely simple. The Holy Spirit is active wherever the word of forgiveness in Christ is spoken. The Holy Spirit can be found only and always through the Word of Christ.

There are two ways of doing theology. Both are right. One way is to look at what the Bible says. Below I have cited a couple of verses to show that the Spirit comes to us only through the Word. The other way of doing theology is to ask how a particular article of doctrine relates to the doctrine of justification. How does the claim that the Holy Spirit works only through the Word relate to the biblical doctrine of justification?[1]

Do you remember Mrs. Franzmann, the woman who gave me a couple of popcorn balls when I lost all my Halloween candy? Her husband, Martin, wrote a few hymns. One of those hymns has this stanza:

> Thy strong Word bespeaks us righteous;
> Bright with thine own holiness.[2]

This little phrase tells us all we need to know about the relationship between the Spirit, the Word of God, and justification in Christ.

Follow this line of theological thought:

1. Jesus' death pronounces the world "not guilty." (This verdict is our justification, as chapter 2 of this book shows.)
2. The word of the cross pronounces this gracious verdict upon us. (That's what Martin Franzmann meant when he wrote, "Thy strong Word bespeaks us righteous.")
3. The Spirit testifies to Jesus through the word of the cross (John 15:26).
4. So the Spirit uses the word of the cross to testify to Jesus Christ, and when He does so, we are justified.

Other ways to say "Thy strong Word bespeaks us righteous" are to say "Thy strong Word absolves us," "Thy strong Word forgives us," "Thy strong Word pronounces us not guilty," "Thy strong Word saves us," or "Thy strong Word justifies us." You can say the same thing many different ways. Through the Word of the Gospel, the Holy Spirit is applying to our lives the death of Jesus.

When you say that a person can be forgiven through something other than the Word of Christ, then you are saying that a person can be saved without Christ. Just as God says that there is no justification outside of Christ, so He also says that there is no justification outside the Gospel of Christ. You may wonder why Martin Franzmann wrote his hymn using such unfamiliar words and such an unusual way of speaking. His answer: "Why must a hymn be easy? Whoever said it should be easy?"[3]

The Village, the Well, and the Water

Once upon a time there was a beautiful little village nestled in a valley between two mountains. In the center of the village was a well. The well provided water to all the inhabitants of the village. People came from all over the world to drink the cool, clean, crisp water that was drawn daily from the well. Countless people remained in the village and made their homes there. They loved the water.

The well was sufficient for the people of the village. No other wells graced the cobblestone streets of that mountain town. There was no need. No one ever suggested that they might like some other well more. Such a thought would be incomprehensible. The well was sufficient to satisfy all their needs, and it seemed that no matter how many people came to dwell in the mountain village there was always enough water. Water from another well? The thought was unheard of—absurd.

The well was also powerful. At the suggestion that the well might run dry some day, the people only laughed. "A waterless well?" The thought was unheard of—absurd. Whenever anyone went to the well, from the smallest child to the mayor himself, water was always there. The well was predictable, trustworthy, and always dependable. The well had power.

The people depended on only one well, and that well never let them down. The well and the water went together. You could not have one without the other. If you wanted water, you got it from that well and that well alone. If you went to the well, you always had water. There was no water without the well and no well without the water.

One day, the saddest day the town had ever known, a stranger came to the village. He tasted the water, as had every visitor before him. The visitor said, "This is good water. But I know another source that can give you water just like this well."

The people were divided. Some said, "Impossible. Water comes only from this well." Others were curious.

The visitor took another drink and said, "This is a good well. But I don't think that we can depend on the well."

The people were divided. Some said, "Impossible. Water always comes from the well." Others were curious.

So the townspeople discussed two questions. First, was it *only* the well? Was that well sufficient enough? Second, was it *always* the well? Was that well powerful enough? The stranger proposed an experiment. "Why not cover the well? I'm sure that there will be water from some other place. This well is not sufficient. Yes, let's cover the well. I don't think we can afford to rely on it forever. The well is not powerful enough."

But the people protested. "No, the well and the water belong together. If you cover the well, we will not have water."

Scornfully the stranger replied, "You are well lovers. You should love the water. Don't you think that God can give us water from anywhere He wants? Are you trying to limit God? You faithless people, you lovers of wells, God does not need a well to prosper you." That talk of "God" seemed so pious and godly. Of course the people did not want to limit the power of God. They covered up the well.

And, alas, all the people in the town died.

That has got to be the most absurd fairy tale you have ever heard. Read it again. This time change "village" to "church." Change "the well" to "the Word." Change "the water" to "the Spirit." What happened to that town has happened to countless churches throughout history. They separated the Word and the Spirit, and they ended up dead.

How do you know if the Spirit is active in a church? There is only one way. If the Gospel of Christ is proclaimed, then the Holy Spirit is active. And if the Holy Spirit is active, then there must be the proclamation of the Christ. There can be no wordless Spirit and there can be no Spiritless Word.

NO WORDLESS SPIRIT

The Holy Spirit works only through the Word of God. "Therefore we should and must insist that God does not want to deal with us human beings, except by means of his external Word and Sacrament. Everything that boasts of being from the Spirit apart from such a Word and Sacrament is of the devil," says Luther in the Schmalkald Articles.[4] Luther got his doctrine from the Holy Scriptures. "So faith comes from hearing, and hearing through the word of Christ" (Romans 10:17). "Since you have been born again, not of perishable seed but of imperishable, through the living and abiding word of God" (1 Peter 1:23). God works graciously only through the Word.

I once gave a devotional at the dorm of a Lutheran college. I said pretty much what our doctrine is. "The Holy Spirit works only through the Word." I may even have told the little parable of the village, the well, and the water.

One of the students asked, "Aren't you putting God in a box?"

That was a good question. I was tempted at first to say, "No, you should never put God in a box." Instead, I said, "Yes, I am putting God in a box. I am putting God where He wants to be for us."

"God wants you to limit Him?" was her incredulous response.

I replied: "When our Lord Jesus came into this world to save us, where did His mother place Him? In a box. It was called a little manger. Our God and our Lord is in a box. When Jesus' disciples, fearful of perishing on the stormy Sea of Galilee, cried out to God for deliverance, where did they find Him? The Bible says He was asleep in the bow of the boat. God is sleeping. God is in a box. When Jesus agreed to drink the bitter cup of His Father's angry will, where did this commitment place the Lord of the universe? Upon a cross. It was a box—a box from which He chose not to escape, a box by which the limitless God was limited. When Jesus was dragged from the cross, where was He placed? He was placed in a sealed grave. It was a box."

Clearly, God limited Himself. We call this the theology of the cross. "He deserves to be called a theologian, however, who comprehends the visible and manifest things of God seen through suffering and the cross."[5] That was Luther's great insight. God works through the cross. He limited Himself 2,000 years ago in order to earn salvation for us, and He limits Himself today in order to bestow salvation on us.

Salvation in No Other

"There is salvation in no one else, for there is no other name under heaven given among men by which we must be saved." Every Christian knows these great words from Acts 4:12. We know that God will not save us except through His Son. There is salvation in no other. I get so frustrated when I hear pastors, ostensibly Christian pastors, who can't seem to say that salvation is only in Christ. We need to say again and again that God has limited salvation to Jesus. Without Christ and without faith in Christ you can't be saved.

If we believe this so strongly—and we do—then can't we also believe that God limits His gift of salvation to the Word of Christ? God has chosen to earn salvation only by His Son's cross, and He has chosen to give salvation only through His Son's Word. The job of the Holy Spirit is to testify to Jesus. So we need to limit ourselves to the Gospel, which is the only testimony of the Spirit to Christ.

THE SACRAMENTS

What about the Sacraments? Doesn't the Holy Spirit work through them? The short answer is yes. But there is a more complete answer. Predictably, that answer centers in justification.

Most Lutherans learned in catechism classes that there are two sacraments: Baptism and the Lord's Supper. We say there are two because we define the word *sacrament* in a certain way. In *Luther's Small Catechism with Explanation*, the "blue" catechism published by Concordia Publishing House, a sacrament is defined as "a sacred act instituted by God, in which God Himself has joined His Word of promise to a visible element, and by which He offers, gives, and seals the forgiveness of sins earned by Christ."[6] The catechism goes right on to say that sometimes Holy Absolution is counted as a sacrament, even though there is no visible element connected to absolution. Probably the best thing is not to argue too much on the precise definition of the word *sacrament* or how many sacraments there are and instead to focus on the doctrine of justification as it relates to the Sacraments. The Sacraments are powerful works of the Spirit because the Word of God is always in them.

BAPTISM

Every once in a while something happens in church that you could never expect and that will never be repeated. One such unexpected event occurred at my church during a Baptism one Sunday. The young couple had three children, the youngest about a week old. A month earlier I had visited them in their home to review what the Bible teaches about Baptism. Little Johnny, about 3 years old, had listened with rapt attention as I went through a few of the many verses that tell us what "Baptism gives and profits." We had scheduled the Baptism for the Sunday after the birth no matter when the birth would happen. I was pleased that the young couple believed in baptizing their child right away and not simply when the relatives could get there. After the baby's birth, I visited the mom and was introduced to her healthy infant daughter. Everyone was excited and joyful the following Sunday when the big day arrived. The baby was dressed in a gorgeous and intricate gown, the same worn by her mother and grandmother. It was a beautiful Holy Sacrament, and we were treating it that way. Just before the service began, I was asked, "Would it be okay if we brought Johnny up to the font? He probably won't behave in the pew."

"Of course," I replied, "that way he can see exactly what is happening." I never mentioned that I was skeptical as to whether Johnny's particular location in the Lord's house would guarantee behavior significantly improved from his norm. Johnny was a little hellion.

"Oh, that would be so nice." The family beamed their pleasure. Dad held Johnny who, I concede, did appear to be interested in the sacramental goings on and seemed to squirm slightly less than usual. When the family returned to their pew, I was pleased both at the Baptism and at Johnny's uncharacteristically good behavior. Perhaps, I thought, witnessing his sister's Holy Baptism had positively affected Johnny, increasing his level of sanctification.

Then it happened. Halfway back to their pew, Dad let Johnny walk. The agile little imp quickly seized his opportunity and escaped. Before I could even turn around (I was walking back to my chair on the far side of the chancel), Johnny was standing in front of the altar, facing the congregation. I gasped. Mom and Dad gasped. The congregation smiled, less amused at Johnny's antics than at my predicament. Then Johnny spoke. It was one of those short, brilliant, and completely orthodox statements that indicates a life in the ministry. "All clean!" he shouted and summarily returned to his pew. I sighed. The parents sighed. The congregation smiled again. "Out of the mouths of babes" was the oft-repeated comment as the people exited the church that day and offered me their obligatory handshakes. I realized that Johnny had captured the purpose and meaning of Baptism perfectly and precisely. He had preached a better sermon that day than I had.

I suppose Johnny could have said, "In Baptism the justification that Jesus accomplished and pronounced from the cross has now been spoken specifically and intimately over my little sister." I think his sermon was just as clear and to the point, "All clean!"

What are the blessings of Baptism? When you were baptized:

- God pronounced you forgiven. "Repent and be baptized every one of you in the name of Jesus Christ for the forgiveness of your sins" (Acts 2:38). "I acknowledge one Baptism for the remission of sins" (Nicene Creed).
- You were washed clean of your sins. That's what the word *baptize* means. "Rise up and be baptized and wash away your sins" (Acts 22:16).
- You were made radiant in the eyes of God, without blemish—stainless, pure, and holy. "Christ loved the church and gave Himself up for her, that He might sanctify her, having cleansed her by the washing of water with the word, so that He might present the church to Himself in splendor, without spot or wrinkle or any such thing, that she might be holy and without blemish" (Ephesians 5:25–27).
- The name of God was placed upon you. "Baptizing them in the name of the Father and of the Son and of the Holy Spirit" (Matthew 28:19).
- You were born again and given faith. "Unless one is born of water and the Spirit, he cannot enter the kingdom of God" (John 3:5).
- You were "there when they crucified my Lord," laid Him in the grave, and when He rose from the dead.[7] "Do you not know that all of us who have been baptized into Christ Jesus were baptized into His death? We were buried therefore with Him by baptism into death, in order that, just as Christ was raised from the dead by the glory of the Father, we too might walk in newness of life" (Romans 6:3–4).
- You were justified by grace. "He saved us . . . by the washing of regeneration and renewal of the Holy Spirit, whom He poured out on us richly through Jesus Christ our Savior, so that being justified by His grace we might become heirs according to the hope of eternal life" (Titus 3:5–7).
- The Holy Spirit came into your life. "Repent and be baptized . . . and you will receive the gift of the Holy Spirit" (Acts 2:38).

In summary, can you think of any blessing of grace that you did not receive in your Baptism? Did the Holy Spirit withhold, defer, delay, postpone, suppress, hold back, restrict, or otherwise keep from you any of His blessings? In case you are a little hesitant in answering, Paul says, "You have been filled with Him . . . having been buried with Him in baptism" (Colossians 2:10–12).

How can water do such great things? If you have heard that question before, you can thank the pastor who instructed you in the catechism. He probably also taught you the answer. "Clearly the water does not do it, but the Word of God, which is with and alongside the water, and faith, which trusts this Word of God in the water."[8] In your Baptism the Holy Spirit was working through the Word, connecting it with water, and pronouncing you righteous. In Baptism God's strong Word bespoke you righteous. In Baptism God said, "All clean."

HOLY COMMUNION

At the time of the Reformation God gave to the church a brilliant artist by the name of Albrecht Dürer. He made dozens of woodcuts depicting biblical stories or contemporary church happenings. My favorite is a picture of Christ on the cross. Blood is streaming from the wounds in His hands and feet and especially from the deep cut in His side. Angels are hovering around the dead body of our Lord, each holding a chalice. In sacramental cups these heavenly messengers collect the blood of Christ and transport it to the countless altars where God's people drink it.

This picture powerfully teaches us what God wants us to believe about Holy Communion. "What is the Sacrament of the Altar? It is the true body and blood of our Lord Jesus Christ under the bread and wine, instituted by Christ himself for us Christians to eat and to drink."[9] Jesus did not give us a mere reminder of Himself or a symbol of His death. He did not give us a spiritual meal that mystically transports us up to heaven. He gave His true body and blood for us to eat and drink.

I had lunch with the neighborhood Pentecostal preacher one day. We had borrowed chairs from his church a few times, and I invited him to lunch to return the favor. He was a gracious man and a dedicated minister. During the lunch he told me a story about a woman in his congregation who was going through a time of spiritual doubt. While trying to raise a handful of little kids, a chronic illness drained her energies and retarded her body's healing capabilities. One night, lying in bed, half-awake, half-asleep, her eyes were suddenly drawn to the wall where the picture of Jesus had often given comfort and solace to the family members. Jesus was depicted as gazing lovingly at His children and holding His hands out, palms up, to bless them. But this time the picture took on an ethereal countenance. She was certain that it was real, but different than what she had seen on the wall previously. The hands of Jesus and His heart suddenly began to ooze blood. It streamed out of the picture and dripped to the floor, making its way slowly but inexorably toward the bed on which she lay. Flight was rendered impossible by her weakened, almost trancelike, condition and unwanted by her desire for deeper communion with the Lord. Fearful, yet hopeful, she waited until the crimson fluid had traversed the floor and began to climb the bedsheets. Eventually it covered her body. "She was bathed in the blood of the Lamb," claimed the pastor, "and awoke refreshed, physically well, and relieved of her doubts."

I have to confess that pastors are as sinful as the next person, and I was tempted to transgress my good neighbor. I wanted to "one up" him and say, "Oh yeah? Listen to this." But I couldn't. How do you beat a story like that? I didn't have anything in my repertoire that I could share. Then I was tempted to get really theological on the guy. I wanted to say, "Wow, that's like the Lord's Supper where you get to drink the blood of Christ for the forgiveness of sins. The blood that dripped from His wounds and is placed in your mouth forgives all your sins, strengthens your faith, allays your doubts, prepares you for the heavenly feast, and saves you." But it wasn't the time or the place. I was especially tempted to raise my eyebrows and ask rhetorically, "And you believe that?" I just said, "Wow, what a story." But I did not believe my new friend. I much preferred the woodcut of Albrecht Dürer to the vision of this preacher.

The Lord's Supper gives more assurance and is more consistent than such dreams. In the Lord's Supper Christ adds His Word to bread and wine and they become His body and blood. The Holy Spirit uses Christ's Sacrament to apply the forgiveness of sins to us. We can have this salvation every week. Jesus spoke 2,000 years ago, and His words have power today: "Take, eat; this is My body. . . . Drink of it, all of you, for this is My blood of the covenant, which is poured out for many for the forgiveness of sins" (Matthew 26:26–28). These Words of Institution are the Holy Spirit's testimony to the cross of Christ. His meal "bespeaks us righteous." Every time you kneel in faith to eat the body and drink the blood of Christ, you are blessed again with the verdict of righteousness before your Father in heaven. You are justified.

ABSOLUTION

Absolution is the pronouncement of forgiveness. No one explained the doctrine of absolution better than C. F. W. Walther.

> A Lutheran minister, when announcing the forgiveness of sins, or absolving a sinner, does nothing else than communicate to him the intelligence that Christ has interceded for him . . . and restored him to favor. Moreover, the Lutheran minister does this by order of Christ. . . . At absolution we say nothing but what has happened. That is the precious truth that forgiveness of sins has been acquired. If we would only truly believe in absolution, with what joy would we attend church whenever it is pronounced![10]

Absolution is the announcement of an accomplished fact—the forgiveness of Christ earned on the cross and pronounced in the resurrection. But it is more than an announcement. In Absolution, Christ's verdict of justification is bestowed, imparted, conferred, and given truly, personally, intimately, and powerfully. Luther says:

> Confession consists of two parts. One is that we confess our sins. The other is that we receive the absolution, that is, forgiveness, from the confessor as from God himself and by no means doubt but firmly believe that our sins are thereby forgiven before God in heaven.[11]

Absolution can be announced in a variety of ways. Sometimes an announcement achieves its purpose when it is made publicly and addressed to all. Sometimes it is necessary to make an announcement personally to a specific person. That is the way the Gospel works as well. Every Christian learns of forgiveness in the public Absolution, in the sermon, in the Benediction, and in many other ways. Through these general absolutions Christians learn to apply the forgiveness of sins to themselves. But in private absolution God makes it possible for you to hear the promise of grace personally and specifically. We need the private absolution.

Every year my wife and I invite our entire congregation to our house for a Christmas party. It's a gala affair. We serve smoked salmon, shrimp cocktail, cheese and crackers, those little meatballs and hotdogs that you eat with toothpicks, and mounds of Christmas cookies. The mountains flow with new wine and even some old vintage is brought forth. Beer is plentiful. Laughter and fun abound, and a good time is had by all. Most guests bring a little something to add to the feast. We always make the general announcement to the whole church in the newsletter and on two or three previous Sundays. Everyone is told to apply the announcement to themselves, and the house is always full.

But we noticed something over the years. Those members who are new to the church seldom come. Members who may have experienced some hurt feelings in the church during the previous year never come. People who are not really active often don't come. We want them to come. In some ways we want inactive members to come more than the steady members. So I have made it a habit to make a list of these people and take an evening and call each one on the phone, encouraging them privately and personally to come to the party.

So it is with absolution. Sometimes private absolution is called for. Maybe you have done some specific thing wrong that really plagues your conscience. You want to hear privately that your specific guilt is forgiven. Maybe you feel estranged from God and need to hear a word specifically to you that God accepts and loves you in Christ. Maybe there is no specific sin, but you are simply devastated by all the commands of God that do nothing but condemn and depress you. Maybe you need strength to fight a recurring temptation. Maybe you just need to hear your name in connection with forgiveness. If any of these conditions apply to you, then you need private absolution. Go to your pastor and confess your sins. Ask for the forgiveness that is found only in the wounds of the Lord and expect your pastor to speak it to you. The Holy Spirit will work through your pastor. His absolution bespeaks you righteous.

In a certain sense, all the means of God's salvation are absolution. When you hear the Gospel of redemption in Christ from the pulpit, it is absolution. When you were baptized, you were absolved. In Holy Communion you are absolved. When your father tucked you into bed at night and told you that Jesus loved you and died for you, he was absolving you, even if he may not have used or known the term. When you confided to your college roommate a certain sin, and heard from your friend's lips, "Well, you know, Jesus died for that sin too," that was an absolution. Paul Gerhardt speaks to you through the lyrics of a hymn written 350 years ago:

> A crown of thorns Thou wearest,
> My shame and scorn Thou bearest,
> That I might ransomed be.
> My Bondsman, ever willing,
> My place with patience filling,
> From sin and guilt hast made me free.[12]

This hymn is an absolution. Any time the forgiveness of Christ is applied to the sinner, absolution is taking place. Absolution, like Holy Baptism and Holy Communion, simply applies the verdict of the cross—not guilty—to sinners. In Absolution, like Holy Baptism and Holy Communion, the Holy Spirit of Christ bespeaks us righteous.

THE OFFICE OF THE MINISTRY

For the first 250 years of the Lutheran church's history those appointed to preach and teach were called "ministers" or "preachers." In the nineteenth century the term "pastor" became popular and is generally used today. It doesn't really matter what title you bestow upon your pastor as long as you know what he is supposed to be doing. The expression "office of the ministry" means the same as "pastor," "minister," and "preacher."[13] Martin Chemnitz wrote a little book about the office of the ministry called an *Enchiridion*. It contains questions and answers much like a catechism. Here is how he defines the office of the ministry.

> What, then, is the office of ministers of the church?
>
> This office, or ministry, has been committed and entrusted to them by God Himself through a legitimate call

> I. To feed the church of God with the true, pure, and salutary doctrine of the divine Word. Acts 20:28; Eph 4:11; 1 Ptr 5:2.
>
> II. To administer and dispense the sacraments of Christ according to His institution. Matt 28:19; 1 Cor 11:23.
>
> III. To administer rightly the use of the keys of the church, or of the kingdom of heaven, by either remitting or retaining sins (Mt 16:19; Jn 20:23), and to fulfill all these things and the whole ministry (as Paul says, 2 Ti 4:5) on the basis of the prescribed command, which the chief Shepherd Himself has given His ministers in His Word for instruction. Mt 28:20[14]

A few important elements in this definition of Chemnitz's are noteworthy. First, notice that the minister has tools or instruments. These are the same tools that the Holy Spirit uses to declare us righteous in Christ: the proclamation of Christ, Baptism, Holy Communion, and Absolution. The Augsburg Confession says: "So that we may obtain this faith, the ministry of teaching the Gospel and administering the sacraments was instituted. For through the Word and the sacraments as through instruments the Holy Spirit is given, who effects faith where and when it pleases God in those who hear the Gospel."[15] In chapter 1 I referred to the Word and the Sacraments as the "marks of the church." Earlier in this chapter I referred to them as the "means of grace." Lutherans also can refer to the Word and Sacraments as "the office of the ministry." We use the expression "means of grace" when we are talking about how the church is created and sustained. "Marks of the church" indicate how the church is identified. "Office of the ministry" refers to how the church is served. Pastors serve the church by giving her the Word and the Sacraments. So the ministry is nothing more or less than "bespeaking people righteous" through the Gospel and the Sacraments.

Notice, second, that applying the Word and Sacraments is the whole job of ministers. They are not to do this plus other things. Pastors are to do only this. Ministers are to preach and administer the Sacraments. That's it. It's the easiest job description in the world, though in many ways it may be the toughest job. Of course, pastors may do other things such as invite members over for Christmas parties. But these are not absolutely necessary to the ministry.

Pastors may spend hours studying the Word of God and doing things that prepare themselves to preach. They may spend hours with their people simply being friendly, knowing that such kindness will result in people coming to church more faithfully. But the job of the pastor is to preach and administer the Sacraments. There is a tendency to talk of all sorts of ministers in the church: youth ministers, music ministers, ministers of compassion, and ministers of stewardship. I knew a pastor who once told me he had a "ministry of presence" in that he was simply "there" for the people of his church. Actually, there is one ministry and one office of the ministry. That ministry is to preach Christ and to administer His Sacraments.

Notice, third, that the Great Commission is given specifically to pastors. This is consistent with what Matthew says: "Now the eleven disciples went to Galilee . . . Jesus came and said to them . . . 'Go therefore and make disciples of all nations, baptizing them . . . teaching them' " (Matthew 28:16–20). Both Chemnitz and Matthew realized that you have to ask specific people to do something if you want it done. So Jesus asks specific people—ministers—to preach, teach, and baptize.

Fourth, the ministers of Christ speak for Christ. They do not speak on their own authority, and they are not entrusted with the job of making the message credible or winsome. They simply speak what they have been given from Christ to speak. Ministers have authority, but it is only the authority to speak for Jesus.

Notice, fifth, that not everyone is a minister. Ministers and their people must know that the office has been "committed and entrusted to them by God Himself through a legitimate call."[16] When members of my congregation visit other churches, they bring me the bulletins. I have often read at the top of the bulletins words like these:

> St. John's Lutheran Church
> Pastor: John Smith
> Ministers: All the people of St. John's

Such statements are based on a book published in 1974 entitled *Everyone a Minister*.[17] Chemnitz would have been puzzled, even alarmed, by this title. The thought behind such sentiments, and it is a praiseworthy thought, is that all Christians should be encouraged to tell others about Jesus. But only confusion results when you call everyone a minister.

I was at the playground with my kids one afternoon when they were still attracted to slides and jungle gyms. Our reverie was suddenly disturbed by a scream of pain. There was no doubt that someone had been hurt and that it was pretty serious. All the moms and dads looked around to make sure it wasn't one of theirs upon whom the misfortune had fallen. Gradually, we discovered that a little girl, about 7 years old, had toppled from the teeter-totter and twisted her ankle. Regrettably, her mother was not immediately available. About six of the parents and a couple of the kids gathered around to help. The little girl's friend consoled her by stroking her hair and murmuring softly, "It's okay. You're okay. Your mom will be here soon." One of the adults kneeled beside the victim, asking where it hurt. A strong man, one of the dads, picked her up out of the sand and dirt and carried her to the grass at the edge of the sandlot, placing her gently where it was clean. Finally, the mother rushed in, alarmed at her daughter's peril and chagrined that she had left for five minutes at exactly the wrong time. This woman was Mom. She held the office of Mom. No one else was Mom. I was, frankly, quite impressed at the maternal instincts of the little friend who had functioned as the mom in her absence. And the nice man who carried her out of the dirt onto the grass was soundly thanked for his Mom-like actions. But neither of these helpers was Mom.

That's the way it is in the office of the ministry. You may teach in Sunday school. You may offer Christian words of comfort to the bereaved. You may do many things that ministers of the Gospel normally do. But you are a minister only if you have been appointed by God through the church. And if you are a minister, your job is to preach, teach, and administer the Sacraments.

There is no wordless Spirit. God decided to win salvation for us only through Christ. He has decided to give salvation to us only through the Word—Baptism, Absolution, Holy Communion, and the office of the ministry. God placed Christ in a box 2,000 years ago. He places Christ's forgiveness in a box today. We know where to find it. Forgiveness is in the Word and the Sacraments.

There is no wordless Spirit, no wordless forgiveness, and no wordless salvation.

NO SPIRITLESS WORD

Go back to the beginning of this chapter and read once more the story of the village, the water, and the well. The stranger who came into town questioned two things. He questioned whether water could come from somewhere other than the well. Was the well sufficient? Was there such a thing as well-less water? Many in the church have questioned whether the Spirit comes from places other than the Gospel and Sacraments. Are Word and Sacrament sufficient? Is there a wordless Spirit? This question has been answered above. No! There is no such thing as a Wordless Spirit. The Spirit has bound Himself to the Word. The Word is sufficient.

But there was a second question the stranger asked. He asked if the village could always depend on the well for water. Could there be a waterless well? Was the well dependable? So today in the church many have questioned whether the Word always has the Spirit connected to it. Or does the Spirit come upon the Word or anoint the Word in such a way that the Word may not always be powerful? Is there such a thing as a Spiritless Word of God? Again, the answer is no.

THREE GOOD QUESTIONS

I am not a morning person, yet I preach at 8:00 A.M. every Sunday. This combination is a real challenge to me. I set my alarm for 5:45 A.M. so I can have two hours to wake up. Sometimes I am forced to stay up too late on Saturday, and I am sleep deprived. So I drag myself to church, go through the motions, and pray that I'm intelligible. It's almost embarrassing. I am frustrated at my apparent inability to function at the high level required to lead the early service and preach. However, by 10:30 A.M. I am all warmed up. I am energized. My juices are flowing. I am dramatic from the pulpit and pastoral from the chancel. I am working.

The sermon at both services has the same words. Here's the question: Is the Word of God I preach just as powerful in the first service as it is in the second?

Here's a second good question. I was standing outside of church one sunny Sunday after services. A little baby had been baptized, and the boy's uncle sidled up to me and said, "I sure hope it took."

"What took?" I queried.

"The Baptism. I hope the Baptism took." Apparently, I had this puzzled look on my face so he explained, "I hope the Baptism took. I hope it really made this little boy into a Christian. I hope he really got Jesus into his life. I hope the Holy Spirit was working. Do you think it took?"

Can one person be baptized and have the Holy Spirit move in their lives and another be baptized without the Holy Spirit?

Here's a third good question. I used to be part of a circuit where the pastors would get together for a conference and we would begin the meeting with the Lord's Supper. Usually the pastor of the host church would put on his vestments. He would have prepared the elements of unleavened bread and wine ahead of time. The service would be respectful. When we communed, we would always bow and kneel at the altar. We would show reverence to the body and blood of Jesus we received. One of the pastors served a small congregation that rented the student union of the local university to meet in on Sundays. Unfortunately, the union was unavailable during the week when the pastors met. So he had no facility at which to host the monthly circuit Communion service. The pastor offered the use of his home. The rest of us thought the idea was both gracious and thoughtful. With great anticipation we entered the pastor's apartment the next month. What we saw I shall never forget.

Messy, *disheveled*, *cluttered*, *sloppy*, and *untidy* are all words that come to mind but are inadequate to describe the domicilic carnage before us. There were theological journals and magazines literally piled to the ceiling, blocking easy access to any part of the home. What narrow passages were discernible between the books angled strangely back and forth like some medieval labyrinth. The living area was separated from the kitchenette by a sofa whose springs had long since sprung. No one wanted to sit there for fear of trouser tears. Finally, the vicar was forced to do so because it was determined his clothes were more easily replaced. Besides, like all young pastors, he had not yet learned to say no with any real conviction. In the kitchen, chipped and dirty dishes were piled on all the counters, making entrance to the cupboards quite impossible. We doubted if there were any eating accoutrements within anyway. Opposite the kitchen, about five feet from the sofa, was the "altar." Around it were those brown folding chairs you would normally see in 1940s church basements that experienced churchgoers have learned to avoid, again because of fear of trouser tears. On the altar/coffee table was the Blessed Sacrament. The ciborium, with seven pieces of matzo carefully counted and placed within, was a bluish-green, opaque, plastic cereal bowl. The chalice was one of those transparent glasses you find in your local motel with the little outdentation about three fourths of an inch below the rim. It was filled with a chablis, whose bottle and screw cap were conveniently placed on the floor below.

"The feast is ready," he boldly and joyfully announced. "Come eat and drink for your salvation." I admired his theology. The Lord's Supper is, after all, a feast of salvation. It was his sense of aesthetics, his . . . well . . . taste that I struggled to comprehend. I could not understand how a man could live like that—much less worship like that. But he was so pleased to be hosting the affair and so effusive in his gushing words of welcome that we simply and silently assumed our places much as in a church. There we celebrated the Sacrament. This old pastor (did I mention he was single?) properly consecrated the elements, he distributed them, and we ate.

Now here's the question. Was that any less the body and blood of Jesus Christ given and shed for the forgiveness of sins than when Communion was celebrated on the altar of your church this last Sunday?

Actually, all three of these questions are the same. Can we be certain that the Holy Spirit is acting whenever and wherever the Gospel and Sacraments are given? The answer is *yes*. There is no such thing as a Spiritless Gospel.

THE THREE QUESTIONS ANALYZED

The Word is always powerful. It is objectively powerful. Its power does not depend on us, either those who speak or those who hear. Isaiah answered the first question above. "So shall My word be that goes out from My mouth; it shall not return to Me empty, but it shall accomplish that which I purpose" (Isaiah 55:11). Paul says the same: "For I am not ashamed of the gospel, for it is the power of God for salvation to everyone who believes" (Romans 1:16).

But what if the preacher is tired or competitive or not particularly dynamic? What if he is ill prepared or has distracting mannerisms? Maybe he grooms himself poorly or is obese. Perhaps the preacher has a high squeaky voice or wears those glasses with huge black rims that went out of style in 1968. What if the preacher has a thorn in the flesh? Paul says, "I was with you in weakness and in fear and much trembling, and my speech and my message were not in plausible words of wisdom, but in demonstration of the Spirit and of power, that your faith might not rest in the wisdom of men but in the power of God" (1 Corinthians 2:3–5). Paul even states that the integrity and motivation of the preacher do not affect the Gospel's power. "Some indeed preach Christ from envy and rivalry . . . not sincerely but thinking to afflict me in my imprisonment. What then? Only that in every way, whether in pretense or in truth, Christ is proclaimed, and in that I rejoice" (Philippians 1:15–18). Luther says the same: "For the word of God is the true holy object above all holy objects . . . At whatever time God's Word is taught, preached, heard, read, or pondered, there the person, the day, and the work is hallowed . . . on account of the Word that makes us all saints."[18] The Word is always powerful.

Baptism is always powerful. Paul says, "For in Christ Jesus you are all sons of God, through faith. For as many of you as were baptized into Christ have put on Christ" (Galatians 3:26–27). He does not say that *most* of you have been clothed with Christ. He does not say that those of you whose "Baptism took" have been clothed with Christ. "*All* of you," are Paul's words.

But don't some people fall away from their Baptism? Tragically, yes. That does not mean that Baptism was any less God's gracious work. Baptism is powerful even if the person later rejects it. Baptism is objective. It always works. Unfortunately, not all Lutheran pastors believe this. Larry Christenson, one of the most influential Lutheran charismatic pastors of the last century, claims that "in Baptism one is given all things that he will ever receive in Christ—potentially." He goes on to say that if a person does not live up to one's Baptism, "God's purpose in Baptism has failed of achievement," and "it would have been better if the person had not been baptized at all."[19] To Christenson, the Spirit's work in Baptism is only potential and is doubtful. Contrast that with what Martin Luther says:

> Christians always have enough to do to believe firmly what baptism promises and brings—victory over death and the devil, forgiveness of sin, God's grace, the entire Christ, and the Holy Spirit with his gifts. In short, the blessings of baptism are so boundless that if our timid nature considered them, it may well doubt whether they could all be true. Suppose there were a physician who had so much skill that people would not die, or even though they died would afterward live eternally. Just think how the world would snow and rain money upon such a person! Because of the throng of rich people crowding around, no one else would be able to get near. Now, here in baptism there is brought, free of charge to every person's door just such a treasure and medicine that swallows up death and keeps all people alive.[20]

Baptism is always powerful.

And the Lord's Supper is always powerful. Paul asked, "The cup of blessing which we bless, is it not the communion of the blood of Christ? The bread which we break, is it not the communion of the body of Christ?" (1 Corinthians 10:16 KJV). Paul does not ask, "Is it not most of the time a communion?" He does not ask, "Is it not a communion when we are devout enough or use it properly or have strong enough faith?" The Sacrament is always and objectively the body and blood of Jesus. The body and blood of our Lord always have power.

I serve a congregation with lots of noisy kids. They are a blessing, I think. During the distribution of the Sacrament, the little ones squirm and wiggle and distract their parents. I have often been asked if sins are forgiven in the Sacrament even when you are not paying attention or are distracted. I always say, "Yes. You ate the body of Jesus. You drank His blood. These were poured out for the forgiveness of sins. Do you think that God only forgives the sins of those whom He has not blessed with wiggly and distracting kids?" That's what is so great about the Lord's Supper. Even if you do not concentrate on it, you are forgiven. Sometimes the Lords' Supper is the only thing in the service that young parents can receive. It is always a forgiving meal of grace. The objective gift of grace is imparted even to distracted parents.

Absolution is, likewise, always powerful. You don't have to add something to absolution to make it a powerful work of God. It is not powerful sometimes or only if other conditions are met. True Christian absolution is unconditional and objective. All that needed to be done was done. We are absolved because of Jesus on the cross. Bad theologians are constantly tempted to add conditions to absolution as if you have to do your part. Throughout the history of the church, perhaps no blessing of Christ has been so corrupted as absolution. At the time of the Reformation and continuing to this day, the Roman Church has said that you must add "satisfaction" to God's word of forgiveness. That is the "third" part of absolution in Roman Catholic theology. The Roman Church also insisted that the absolution is valid only if spoken by a priest. So another condition was placed on God's unconditional grace. Lutherans, of course, say that confession has two parts. We confess and God absolves. The minute you add a third part, grace depends on something other than the crucifixion of our Lord.

A more subtle way of adding a condition to absolution is to say that you have to be sincere in your confession in order to be forgiven. In the last half of the seventeenth century a theologian named Jacob Spener was active. He is the father of Pietism, which influences many in the Lutheran church to this very day. He taught that you had to fulfill all sorts of requirements of true repentance before you could be certain that absolution was true. You had to (1) have hatred of sin, (2) desire to amend your life, (3) have faith in Jesus, (4) promise not to continue in your sins, (5) be sorrowful that you had offended God, (6) know that your sins have earned damnation, (7) feel shame before the heavenly Father, (8) desire the grace of Christ, (9) intend to put away all sins that you have discovered in your self-examination, (10) resolve to carry out all the demands of the rules of the Christian life, and (11) know that it is the Holy Spirit who has led you to make your resolution.[21]

All Christians would agree that these "conditions" were praiseworthy aspects of a pious Christian attitude. We should feel ashamed before God and intend to put away our sins. But such an evaluation forced upon sinners the type of heart examination that, though well intended, was actually quite harmful to Christians.

Why? First, who could possibly fulfill all eleven requirements? People started to question their salvation. Second, Absolution has always been a way in which Christians prepare for Holy Communion. With these kinds of conditions laid upon the Christian, many people simply stopped going to Holy Communion. So they lost not only the assurance of the absolution but Holy Communion as well. Third, people began to define saving faith as active faith. Remember that faith is passive as it saves and active as it serves one's neighbor. When the sinner is forced into such an active evaluation as a condition of forgiveness, then active faith and passive faith are confused. Fourth, and worst, Spener's requirements changed the theology of the church. Absolution was no longer viewed as an objective, true, powerful Word of God. Our forgiveness was no longer conditioned solely on the work of Jesus Christ already completed. No longer would we sing, "Hold Thou Thy cross before my closing eyes." Now the church began to lament, "Hold Thou my heart before my closing eyes." Spener separated the Holy Spirit from the Word. You could get Him back into the word of absolution only if you fulfilled Spener's requirements. The blessed absolution of our Savior was lost.

How much more comforting to follow the words of Jesus. When confronted by the paralytic, He simply and pointedly announced, "My son, your sins are forgiven" (Mark 2:5). It's a good thing Jesus did not follow the advice of Jacob Spener, or the poor man might have died before he actually heard the Gospel. "Come to Me, all who labor and are heavy laden, and I will give you rest," promises our Lord (Matthew 11:28). He does not promise rest on the condition that we meet a handful of requirements. Lutherans have always taught that faith is not a requirement. It is the conviction that our loving Lord has met all requirements.

Obviously, you should be sincere whether you are saying "I'm sorry" to God or to a friend. But the forgiveness of God does not depend on whether or not you truly feel sorry. I say "I'm sorry" to my wife if I have hurt her in some way. She does not respond by saying, "If you are truly sorry, then I forgive you." She certainly doesn't have an eleven-point checklist as she evaluates my confession. If she did, I would be hurt because she would be questioning my sincerity. She just says, "It's okay. I forgive you." So it is with God. He says, "I forgive you in Christ." He doesn't question your sincerity. He points you to Jesus. Jesus has fulfilled all conditions.

Have you have ever been to a church service where there was a Confession and Absolution made up by the pastor or the worship committee and printed in the bulletin? Next time you see something like that, analyze the Absolution very carefully. Too often those who put these services together have a sincere but misguided zeal. They want everyone to be really sincere in their repentance and really sorry for their sins. So they make the Absolution say something like this: "If you are truly sorry, then you are forgiven" or "If you promise to amend your sinful ways, then you are forgiven." These formulations focus on your feelings, your heart, your sorrow, and your intentions. They place conditions upon the forgiveness of sins no less than the Roman Church that Luther faced. These formulations are wrong and misguided no matter how well intentioned. If they are used, then God's people are not being served properly.

There is no such thing as a Spiritless Word. The Spirit is always in the Word because the Word is always about Jesus. And whether the Word is preached or read, whether it comes in Baptism or the Lord's Supper, whether it comes in public or private absolution, it is always true, always powerful, and always full of the Spirit.

Calvinism

In 1538 a man named John Calvin began reforming churches in Switzerland. He is the father of what are called the "Reformed Churches." Today Presbyterian, Congregational, Church of Christ, Episcopal, Baptist, even Methodist and Pentecostal churches trace their roots back to the thought and influence of John Calvin. He was a remarkably systematic thinker and writer, even though at times difficult to understand. John Calvin taught that there are two groups of people in the world: the elect and the reprobate. The elect are those whom God has chosen. The reprobate are those God has determined will not be saved. According to Calvin, the Word of God is powerful only if proclaimed to those who would be saved. When proclaimed to the reprobate, the Spirit is not working through the Word. But because the same Word was preached to both the saved and the reprobate, the people could not be assured, based on the Word alone, that they were saved. They had to find a "secret power" outside of the Word for certainty. In Holy Communion, according to Calvin, the body of Christ was present only if you believe. So Calvinists were tempted to analyze the sincerity of their faith rather than believe the words of Christ's institution.

Among Calvinists, also called Reformed, the tendency to deny the objective qualities of the Gospel crept into their thinking. The Word was not objectively powerful. Baptism was not an objective washing. The body and blood of Jesus were not objectively present in the Supper. They were present only if you believed. Over the years, Calvinism became much like a thirsty man who was about to drink a beer. But the beer would be thirst quenching only if he really believed it. So the man concentrated on his faithful drinking rather than on the beer itself.

One of the basic tenets of Calvin's theology is the thought that the Spirit of God has a secret power that transcends the mere power of the Word and the Sacrament. The "secret power" comes to us immediately, that is, without the Word and the Sacrament. Calvin says:

> So long as we are without Christ and separated from him, nothing which he suffered and died for the salvation of the human race is of the least benefit to us. And, although it is true that we obtain faith, yet, as we see that all do not indiscriminately embrace the offer of Christ which is made by the gospel, the very nature of the case teaches us to ascend higher, and to inquire into the secret power of the Spirit, through which we enjoy Christ and all his blessings.[22]

Notice that, according to Calvin, we are to seek something higher than the Word itself. We are to discover the secret power of God. Then, and only then, can we fully enjoy Christ. Calvin's followers wrote confessions of faith much like the early Lutherans wrote their confessions. One of the earliest is the Westminster Confession, a document used by all the early Reformed churches. This document teaches that the sinner is directed not simply to the Word of God and the Sacraments. He is directed instead to the inward witness of the Spirit along with the promises of God. The Spirit works in the Word, it is true, but He also works through something that is above or beyond the Word.

> The certainty (of salvation) is an infallible assurance of faith, founded upon the divine truth of the promises of salvation, the inward evidences of those graces unto which these promises are made, the testimony of the Spirit of adoption witnesses with our spirits that we are the children of God; which Spirit is the earnest of our inheritance whereby we are sealed to the day of redemption.[23]

Notice again that you cannot simply trust the "divine truth of the promises of salvation." To these promises God must add "the testimony of the Spirit." The Word is powerful only if and when God adds to it the power of the Spirit. In Calvin's thinking you cannot simply trust the promises of God. The Gospel and the Sacraments are not powerful in and of themselves. There is a secret power or an inward witness added to the Gospel. To Calvin you can actually have a Spiritless Word. You can have the word of comfort without the Comforter. The objective assurance of the Gospel is lost.

The influence of Calvin on the United States has been profound, as we shall see.

For Us and In Us

There are two ways of looking at the power of God's Word. The Gospel is powerful for us and in us. It is powerful for us by forgiving our sins. It is powerful in us by creating faith. Peter spoke of Baptism this way in Acts 2:38: "Repent and be baptized every one of you in the name of Jesus Christ for the forgiveness of your sins, and you will receive the gift of the Holy Spirit." God forgives you (He bespeaks you righteous) and He creates faith in you (you are given the Holy Spirit) through the Gospel. Whether you are talking about Baptism, the Lord's Supper, the Word preached, or private absolution, you are always talking about two blessings: forgiveness and faith. Earlier I talked about objective and subjective. Forgiveness is objective. It is there. It is earned by Christ on the cross and bestowed by Christ through the Word and Sacraments. Faith is subjective. Faith is the bag of the trick-or-treater. It receives and holds the blessing of salvation.

You cannot have faith without forgiveness. Forgiveness is the object of faith. It's what we believe in. When the Gospel "bespeaks us righteous" or gives us God's salvation, it also moves in our hearts to receive this salvation by faith. This will become extremely important when we look at what a worship service is.

Conclusion

There is no Wordless Spirit. The Holy Spirit does not come to us graciously without the Word. He always forgives through the Word, whether it is preached, spoken in absolution, or given to us through the sacraments of Baptism or the Lord's Supper. Whatever is extolled as the Spirit without the Word is really of the devil.

There is no Spiritless Word. Whenever the Word of Christ is taught, proclaimed, spoken, announced, or bestowed through the Sacraments, it is the Spirit's Word that forgives and strengthens through it. And no matter who speaks it, whether you or your pastor or your mom, as long as it is spoken purely, it is powerful.

The Lutheran teaching on the Spirit and the Word is the Bible teaching. It gives us great assurance and comfort. In contrast, Calvinism creates a sense of doubt as to where you will find the Spirit and whether or not the Word is powerful. When the church knows and believes that the Spirit of Christ works powerfully and only through the fire of the Gospel, "The Fire Spreads."

Study Questions

1. How do you know whether the Holy Spirit is active in a church?
2. Can there be a Wordless Spirit or a Spiritless Word?
3. What is the Bible verse that confesses that without Christ and without faith in Christ you can't be saved?
4. What are the blessings and benefits of Baptism?
5. What does God want you to believe about Holy Communion?
6. What is Absolution?

7. What has been committed to those who have been called to the office of the ministry of the church?
8. What are the tools, or means, of the office of the ministry?
9. Is faith a requirement for the Christian?
10. What two ways does Scripture talk about the power and the blessings God brings to us in His Word?

Discussion Questions

1. What is "the analogy of faith," and how does it form the way Lutherans read Scripture? the Confessions? (See endnote 1.)
2. Discuss the statement: "I am putting God in a box. I am putting God where He wants to be for us."
3. What is the place of, and the use of, corporate confession? private confession?

4

The Fire and the Staff

DOCTRINE AND PRACTICE

The Reformation began because a German monk was upset about a particular practice of the church. Luther disagreed with the practice of indulgences. Certificates were sold by representatives of the pope with the promise that the money would spring a soul from purgatory. This was a bad practice, and as Luther and the church began to analyze this practice, they realized that indulgences were also an attack against the doctrine of grace alone. It was bad practice that denied true doctrine. The practice was changed.

As the Reformation continued, the reformers became troubled at the practice of priests being forbidden to marry. Many of the pastors in Wittenberg (including Luther) preached against this practice. Luther's advocacy of this blessed estate led to his own marriage. As the church began to analyze the question of the marriage of priests, she also discovered the biblical doctrine of Christian vocation. The reformers learned that forced celibacy was not only unrealistic, it was a denial of Christian vocation. Bad practice had led to false doctrine, so the practice was changed.

Then there was the issue of the Canon of the Mass. The Canon of the Mass was the liturgical practice of the Roman Church at the time of Luther. The "liturgy" contained all sorts of bad practices. There were prayers for the dead and prayers to the dead. During the celebration of the Mass, certain words were spoken that indicated that the priest was offering up "an unbloody sacrifice" to God. The Words of Institution were mumbled in Latin over the elements, and the people could barely hear them. Only the host was given to the people and not the cup. Individual "private Masses" were common. These were all bad practices that indicated an underlying false doctrine. The Mass, in the Roman system, was not a gift of grace in which God gives to us His body and blood. Rather, it had become a sacrificial action of the priest that was our gift to God. So Luther vowed in 1522, "I will never again celebrate a private mass in all eternity."[1] The bad practice of the Roman Church had led to a denial of grace. The practice was changed.

Doctrine and practice go together. The correct and Lutheran doctrine was discussed in chapters 1–3. "Practice" refers to the churchly acts carried out by pastors or other leaders acting on behalf of the church.[2] Practice includes such things as the liturgies, liturgical customs, prayers, and much of the ritual that occurs during the services of the church. During Sunday services we usually stand during the Lord's Prayer or during the last stanza of a hymn if it invokes the Trinity, pastors wear robes with stoles of certain colors that correspond to seasons of the church year, and we kneel for Communion. These are church practices. Lutheran churches hold Maundy Thursday services with Holy Communion. That is a practice. Practice also includes the personal acts of piety that are encouraged by pastors or by the force of tradition in the church. Many people use Advent calendars or pray before meals based on the example of our Lord. These are individual practices of piety. Practices include both the manner and the timing in which things are done in the normal day-to-day life of a congregation, a synod, or a Christian family. Many churches confirm young people in the eighth or ninth grade. That's a practice. Some churches have congregational voters' meetings every month. In others an annual meeting seems sufficient. Both are congregational practices.

Our doctrine will always affect our practice. And practice will always influence doctrine. The two are like the husband and wife in a marriage. They always end up changing each other. Good or bad, right or wrong, sensible or weird—doctrine and practice always shape and reflect each other. If you change one, the other will change.

Church practices are not all equal in importance. Some are essential, some simply desirable, and some are wrong. There are different reasons why this or that practice might be defended or rejected.

- Sometimes a practice is essential in promoting and teaching the true doctrine.
- Sometimes a practice, either good or bad, is important within a certain context because it is intimately connected with an article of the faith in the minds of people and in the experience of the church.
- Sometimes it is critical to avoid a certain practice because others have made a rule of it where God does not.
- Sometimes a practice is significant because of the "catholicity" of the church and our desire to honor the "wholeness" of Christ's church and her universal and consistent actions.
- Sometimes a practice is extremely helpful in teaching doctrine.

PRACTICES THAT PROMOTE THE GOSPEL

Every church body and even every congregation has certain practices. Some are important; others are mere idiosyncrasies. In some churches the minister prays using the words "thee and thy," while in others the words "you and your" are employed. That really doesn't matter. In some churches babies are baptized, and in others parents wait until the children are old enough to make up their own minds. That does matter. In the case of infant Baptism most Christians, whether they agree with the practice or not, say that it matters a great deal. How can we tell the difference between a church practice that doesn't matter and a church practice that is worth arguing about? The answer is simple. If the doctrine of the Gospel is at stake, then a church's practice has significance. Some practices are so closely related to doctrine that we can't imagine one without the other. For example, the doctrine of grace alone must lead to infant Baptism.

I had a friend named Tom in my first congregation. He was raised Baptist but, upon the birth of his first daughter and the insistence of his Lutheran wife, had been instructed in the Lutheran church. When I had the honor of baptizing his baby, I had talked to him extensively about the blessings of Baptism. One day Tom stopped by the house and gave me a tree to plant in the front yard. We started talking theology. "You know, Pastor," he drawled, as he turned the posthole digger for the seedling, "I don't think it would have been possible for me to come to the true knowledge of grace if we hadn't baptized my daughter."

"How so?" I wondered.

"Well, when I looked down at that helpless little child who had never made a decision in her life, and I saw the water poured on her head and heard the words, I saw grace alone for the first time in my life. Before the Baptism I believed it, but that day I saw it. The morning of her Baptism we had to dress her and feed her. We chose her food and her clothes. We had bought her crib and painted her bedroom. We did everything for her. She did nothing. Throughout my life Baptism had been a symbol of people making decisions and doing something. Now, in the Lutheran church, well, my daughter's Baptism was a visual aid for grace alone."

Tom saw that you baptize babies because you believe that Baptism is the work of God. God brings us to faith by Himself—grace alone. But if you only baptize adults, it means that you are waiting for them to take the first step. Grace becomes something we do and indicates that God does not save us by Himself. Instead, we are saved by grace plus something else.

Tom also understood something that we all know but don't often understand. Not only does doctrine affect practice, but practice also shapes doctrine. If people see one baby after another baptized, then pretty soon they will begin to see, even if they do not fully understand, that Baptism is not a reflection of human choice. But if people never see infants baptized, and if only adults are allowed to come to the waters of salvation, then people will believe, even if they do not fully understand, that Baptism is only for those old enough to decide. Doctrine affects practice and practice affects doctrine.

Peter's Tough Lesson

There are two great facets to the Gospel. One is grace alone. Sinners are brought into the hands of a loving God by grace alone. The story of Tom and his daughter shows that the doctrine of grace alone is affected by practice. The second great facet of the Gospel is "universal grace." The Gospel applies to all people. "Universal grace" is the expression used by the church to show that Christ died for all and that Christ wants all to believe. The story of Peter, told below, shows that the doctrine of "universal grace" is affected by practice.

Universal grace is a wonderful doctrine. God sent His Son, Jesus Christ, to atone for the sins of all people. "Behold, the Lamb of God, who takes away the sin of the world!" (John 1:29). "God so loved the world, that He gave His only Son" (John 3:16). The apostle Peter had no trouble, it would seem, accepting the doctrine of universal grace. But he could not always put it into practice.

Peter understood universal grace. Jesus had commanded him and the rest of the apostles, "Go therefore and make disciples of all nations" (Matthew 28:19). He had told them that they would "be My witnesses in Jerusalem and in all Judea and Samaria, and to the ends of the earth" (Acts 1:8). Universal grace and the universal nature of the ministry of the Gospel had been made pretty clear to all of the apostles. Peter had chosen as his Pentecost sermon text the words of Joel, who promised that God would pour out His Spirit on "all flesh. . . . Everyone who calls upon the name of the Lord shall be saved" (Acts 2:17, 21). And Peter had concluded his sermon with the promise of God connected with Baptism: "The promise is for you and for your children and for all who are far off, everyone whom the Lord our God calls to Himself" (Acts 2:39). So Peter understood, believed, and preached universal grace. Furthermore, Peter was not weak in the faith. He boldly confessed Christ, suffering imprisonment, beating, and persecution at the hands of the Jewish leaders.

Yet all was not well with Peter. When persecution against the church erupted in Acts 8, the Scriptures tell us that "they were all scattered throughout the regions of Judea and Samaria, except the apostles" (Acts 8:1). So the command to "be witnesses in Samaria" was not fulfilled by those who had actually seen the risen Lord. It was carried out by someone else. Peter, despite his great sermons about universal grace, was reluctant to proclaim Christ to the Samaritans or the Gentiles.

So God had to resort to a few miracles. Keep in mind that Peter's *doctrine* was sound, but his *practice* was flawed. Acts 10 and 11 is a story of God making practice fit doctrine. God sent a vision to Peter, telling him to kill and eat unclean food. When Peter objected, God reminded him of the doctrine of universal grace. "What God has made clean, do not call common" (Acts 10:15). Obviously, God was talking of more than clean and unclean food. He was reminding Peter that all people, even Gentiles, have been cleansed in the blood of the lamb. Peter "should not call any person common or unclean" (Acts 10:28). Just then some visitors came to the door and told Peter of a message that Cornelius, an "unclean Gentile," had earlier received from an angel that he should go and talk to Peter.

Then Peter changed his practice in three ways. First, he socialized and had meal fellowship with Gentiles. He invited these Gentiles into his house and made them his guests (Acts 10:23). That is something that Jews did not do. Subsequently, Peter accompanied the Gentiles and actually entered their home. He comments on his own new practice, "You yourselves know how unlawful it is for a Jew to associate with or visit anyone of another nation" (Acts 10:28). Second, Peter preached a sermon exclusively to Gentiles. This was another new practice. Up until that time Gentiles were allowed to overhear the Gospel, but they had not had the privilege of having a sermon preached just for them. Finally, after God worked the miracle of tongues upon the Gentiles, Peter the apostle introduced a third new practice—he baptized Gentiles.

In this story we can observe a number of things about the relationship between doctrine and practice. First, God wants the two to correspond. God was so adamant that the practices of the church correspond to her doctrine that He worked three miracles—two visions and tongues—to get the church to change. He was not content for the church to practice Old Testament style with New Testament substance. God knows that practice and doctrine, style and substance, go together.

Second, practice often has a more dramatic effect upon people than doctrine does. Peter had been taught the doctrine. Yet once the practice of Gentile food and Gentile preaching had been introduced, Peter commented, "Truly I understand that God shows no partiality" (Acts 10:34). The New Testament Greek word for "realize" means "to grasp suddenly or completely"[3] Now Peter was able to perceive and understand the doctrine of universal grace in a new way. And this new realization was made possible by the church's new practice.

Third, flawed practice can undermine pure doctrine. Peter's doctrine of universal grace was pure. But as long as his practice did not change, his doctrine was not rooted firmly in the hearts and minds of the Jewish Christians. They believed the doctrine that grace was for all, but it didn't seem to occur to them that Gentiles could actually be full-fledged Christians. That's why they were "amazed, because the gift of the Holy Spirit was poured out even on the Gentiles" (Acts 10:45). If Peter's doctrine had remained separate from proper Christian practice, there is no doubt that it would have soon been lost.

In fact, that's exactly what happened a few years later in Antioch, where the Gospel had been preached and a church established. Peter had come to visit and, according to the church's newly established practice, he ate and had fellowship with the Gentiles. But pressure was exerted on him from certain Jewish Christians who wanted to retain the old Jewish style of separation. Paul complains of Peter's duplicity in Galatians 2.

> But when Cephas [Peter] came to Antioch, I opposed him to his face because he stood condemned. For before certain men came from James, he was eating with the Gentiles; but when they came he drew back and separated himself, fearing the circumcision party. And the rest of the Jews acted hypocritically along with him, so that even Barnabas was led astray by their hypocrisy. (Galatians 2:11–13)

Then Paul tells how he confronted Peter in front of them all. He never accused Peter of false doctrine. But he did say that Peter "was not in step with the truth of the gospel" (Galatians 2:14). And Paul concludes his remarks with the strong judgment that if their practice did not conform to the doctrine of universal grace, "Christ died for no purpose" (Galatians 2:21).

The minute you refuse to eat or have fellowship with someone because they are not as completely Christian as you, then you have denied the Gospel. And bad practice means "Christ died for no purpose." So the practice of discrimination between Christians on the basis of ethnicity was a denial of Christ. Bad practice meant bad doctrine.

PRACTICES THAT COMMUNICATE WITHIN A CONTEXT

Infant Baptism is a good and necessary practice that promotes true doctrine. Meal discrimination was a bad practice that promoted bad doctrine. Practice and doctrine are not always related so directly or obviously. Sometimes the practice of the church takes on significance because of church conflict. Church practice becomes extremely important when it symbolizes an underlying doctrinal issue. In these cases church practices don't particularly matter in and of themselves. But because the church is defending the truth, certain practices become intimately connected in people's minds to the doctrine they reflect. Let me provide a couple examples.

THE PRUSSIAN UNION

In the middle of the nineteenth century, five ships sailed from Germany carrying Lutherans to the New World. Unlike many of the Scandinavian Lutherans who came to the United States for a better life and the chance for land or wealth, these Germans came to North America for the religious freedom that had been snatched from them in their fatherland. They were victims of a religious/political arrangement in Germany called the Prussian Union.

Initially, the union may have been well intended. King Friedrich Wilhelm III simply wanted all Germans to unite in one expression of the Christian faith. At first the king merely requested a union, meaning that the Lutherans and the Calvinists were to put aside their differences and merge. This was not very easy for either side to do. Lutherans especially were reluctant to merge with followers of John Calvin, who denied that the body and blood of Jesus were distributed and eaten in and with the bread and wine in the Lord's Supper. In 1817 King Wilhelm, himself a devout Calvinist, began losing his patience with church bodies reluctant to compromise their doctrine. The union would mean that a common liturgy would be followed. King Wilhelm understood how important the liturgy was to the church. He ordered that a new liturgy be employed by all the churches in Prussia. In this liturgy, when the communicants received the consecrated sacramental bread, they did not hear the familiar phrase, "Take, eat; this is the true body of our Lord Jesus

Christ." Instead, the minister said, "Jesus Christ says, 'This is My body.' "

God-fearing Lutheran pastors balked at such a liturgical change. To them it sounded like communicants were free to decide for themselves exactly what Jesus might have meant when He said, "This is My body." The liturgy, which had united Lutherans in a common confession of the true presence of Christ's body in the Supper, was now used to divide people at the same altar. You could believe whatever you wanted about the Supper.

If there had been no controversy about the presence of Christ's body and blood in the bread and wine of the Sacrament, then it really would not have mattered exactly what words the minister spoke as he distributed the bread and wine. If every Christian pastor and theologian throughout the ages had simply believed Jesus when He said, "This is My body," then there would be no need for the church and for pastors to be so contentious about exactly which words are spoken during the distribution of the body and blood. Certainly no one would ever suggest that the statement, "Jesus said, 'This is My body,' " was somehow untrue. But when it was used in the liturgy to draw into question the gifts of God in the Sacrament, then Lutherans, rightly, refused to speak the words. To do so would have been a compromise of the Gospel.[4]

By 1830 the king was through making suggestions. Now he passed laws. Anyone not using his liturgy was deprived of a license to preach. So the church was purged of those pastors who, during the distribution of the sacramental elements, insisted on saying to the communicants in their churches, "Take, eat; this is the true body of our Lord Jesus Christ." Lutherans were forced to choose between the country they had loved for centuries and the Lord who had loved them forever. The religious flight, begun in the early 1830s, continued for more than a decade. In 1837 alone, two years before the five boats sailed to America, more than 2,000 people fled from Germany to North America, South America, and even Australia.[5] These people loved their doctrine more than their homes. And as the saddened residents of those five ships watched their homeland disappear beyond the horizon, you can be assured that they vowed never to sit still for any other words than those that Lutherans had heard for more than 300 years, "Take, eat; this is the true body of our Lord Jesus Christ." Their practice was precious to them because the true doctrine was precious.

Breaking the Bread

I have been to Lutheran churches where the pastor holds up a large piece of bread. He speaks the Words of Institution: "Our Lord Jesus Christ, on the night in which He was betrayed, took bread. And when He had given thanks He broke it and said . . . " And while the pastor says the words, "broke it," the minister breaks the bread. Now it certainly cannot make any difference whether the minister breaks the bread or not. No one would seriously either forbid or require this action. Or would they?

The occupants of those five fateful ships from Germany gathered for services every Sunday during the transatlantic voyage to their new homes. And one thing they steadfastly refused to tolerate aboard any ship for any service was the breaking of the bread during Communion. Why?

In 1830 King Friedrich Wilhelm not only forced the Lutherans to change the words of the liturgy, he also forced certain actions upon them. He insisted that during the consecration of the bread the minister was to break it. The Calvinists denied that Christ's body was present in the Lord's Supper. In their view you simply ate bread and drank wine. The Communion was in your heart, not at the altar. To show that they did not believe that Christ's body was present in the Sacrament, the Calvinist pastors would hold up the bread and break it. They taught their people that the sacramental bread could not be the body of Christ because the Bible says that not a bone of His was broken. "You can't break Christ's body," they said, "but look, we can certainly break the bread. So this is our way of showing that the bread is not the body."

If there had been no controversy about the presence of Christ's body and blood in the Sacrament, then it really would not have mattered whether or not the minister broke the bread during the consecration. If every Christian pastor and theologian throughout the ages had simply believed Jesus when He said, "This is My body," then there would be no need for the church and for pastors to be so contentious about what you do with the bread as long as you treat it with respect and eat it. Certainly no one would ever suggest that breaking it was wrong. It never says in the Bible that you must or that you cannot break the bread. But when the custom is introduced into the liturgy simply to draw into question the gifts of God in the Sacrament, then Lutherans, rightly, refused to break the bread. To do so would be a compromise of the Gospel.[6]

If a Lutheran minister in the twenty-first century breaks the bread while consecrating it, that does not necessarily make him a Calvinist. He is not thereby denying the faith. He is demonstrating that he is unaware of history. And he is introducing a custom that his forefathers were willing to sacrifice, suffer, and even die to avoid doing. Practice in the church does matter. It matters when that practice communicates something against the Gospel.

Someone might object: "This seems so stubborn and feisty. Why be contentious over issues that, in and of themselves, really don't matter? Why not just break the bread in Holy Communion? There are enough divisions in the church without making more. We have already admitted that breaking the bread is not wrong. Maybe we should just do it to avoid a fight." Lutherans answer: To avoid such a fight would be a denial of the Gospel. It would give the impression that we are willing to compromise, not only in our practice but also in our doctrine of the true presence of Christ's body and blood in the Sacrament. Impressions are extremely important. For the sake of Christ's Gospel and our spread of it, we cannot afford to give a wrong impression.

ADIAPHORA

When something is a matter of indifference, it is called an adiaphoron. The plural is adiaphora. Breaking the bread in Holy Communion is an adiaphoron. Whether to have red wine or white in Communion is an adiaphoron. While it is necessary for the pastor to speak the exact words of Christ while consecrating the elements, the specific words spoken during the distribution are an adiaphoron. But the minute a practice is introduced that communicates to the church something contrary to the Gospel, then that practice is no longer indifferent. It is no longer an adiaphoron.

The precise words during the distribution were changed to communicate something against the Gospel. They stopped being a matter of indifference. Breaking the bread in Communion communicated something against the Gospel. It stopped being a matter of indifference. Any time indifferent matters are employed to communicate doctrine contrary to the Gospel, they cease to be indifferent.

American History X

American History X is a provocative movie about a neo-Nazi group of youths. It is a brutal and disturbing analysis of hatred, starring Edward Norton as Derek Vinyard, an intelligent and violent youth, full of anger and eager to find an object for it. He chances upon an older man, played by actor Stacy Keach, who slowly befriends him. But the friendship has its price. Slowly Derek is caught up in conspiracy theories and crimes of hatred, mostly against Jews and African Americans. To show their loyalty to the group, the members shave their heads. Derek happily complies. To these racists, the shaved head is a badge of honor. For others, skinheads elicit fear. In time, Derek earns both a leadership role in the group and a trip to prison for his crimes against ethnic minorities. There he is befriended by a young black man. Slowly, almost grudgingly, Derek is forced to conclude that minorities can both love and be loved. His hatred subsides. He changes. In a sense, he is "born again."

After Derek serves his time, he returns home to discover that his younger brother Daniel has become involved in the same pattern of hatred that Derek wants to leave behind. So Derek collides with the same pressures he had encountered in the first part of the movie. But he has matured and cannot embrace the irrational hatred that characterized him before his "rebirth." He strives to be neutral, wanting only to mind his own business and be uninvolved with the old group. Old friendships complicate his attempts to extricate his brother Daniel from the pattern of hatred. The tension of the final scenes centers in Derek's hopeless quest for neutrality. At one point in the film, one of Derek's "old friends" asks a seemingly innocent question, "Is Derek going to shave his head again?"

Of course, in and of itself, a haircut is a completely neutral matter. There is no civil law and certainly no biblical mandate that could lead us to conclude that one type of haircut is more pleasing to God than another haircut. But Derek Vinyard knew that the decision to let his hair grow was a symbol of the most momentous decision of his life. If he left it long, he was rejecting an old and worthless way of life. If he cut it all off again, he was assuming the old attitude of anger and hatred. There was no middle ground, no neutrality. He was called upon to give a confession. Derek learned what Christians have also learned: "*In casu confessionis nihil est adiaphora*." When there is conflict, and a confession of truth is called for, then nothing is an indifferent matter.

If you want to know whether Derek shaved his head, then you will have to rent the movie. The point is that some practices in and of themselves are neutral, but within a context they lose their neutrality. They take on a profound truth-bearing significance.

In Casu Confessionis Nihil est Adiaphora

Shortly after Luther's death, a controversy arose among the Lutherans that was called the adiaphoristic controversy. Some of the Lutherans desperately wanted to discuss theology with the Roman Church. It had been less than a generation since the division with Rome had occurred. Many Lutherans still hoped that somehow the Lutherans and the Romanists could reunite under the true Gospel.

In an attempt to bring the two sides together, these Lutherans agreed to accept some of the practices of the Roman Church that they had previously abolished. Many of these practices were just plain wrong. But many were adiaphora, matters of indifference. For example, the Roman Catholics wanted the Lutherans to observe the custom of not eating meat on Fridays. Further, Lutherans were expected to confess their sins to the priests before they could be admitted to the Sacrament. All ministers had to be ordained by the bishops, according to the Roman Catholic Church. They also insisted "that henceforth the mass be observed in this country with ringing of bells, with lights and vessels, with chants, vestments, and ceremonies."[7]

Obviously, none of these practices were wrong in and of themselves. It does not matter if you eat meat on Friday. It does not matter if pastors are ordained by the bishop or not. It is actually a good thing to confess your sins to the pastor. It certainly does not matter what bells and chants and vestments are used during the celebration of Holy Communion.

Some Lutherans were willing to accept these practices. But other Lutherans smelled a rat. They did not want to give a wrong impression. Nor did they want to accept something as a law when the church was free. So they opposed the changes. They went right ahead and ate meat on Fridays. Lutherans would confess their sins to their pastor before going to Communion, but every once in a while would commune without confessing, just to show that one did not have to go to the pastor or priest first. Lutheran pastors refused to be ordained by bishops because that might give the impression that you had to be ordained that way. And the bells and vessels they had removed stayed off their altars.[8]

Were the Lutherans just being cantankerous? Their refusal to go along with the practices of the Roman Catholics did nothing to bring the two sides closer, and it only served to divide the Lutherans. If there ever was a time when Lutherans needed unity, it was right after Luther's death. Were arguments over church practices or worship style worth dividing the church? These Lutherans said yes. They were confessing their faith. Better, they were confessing Christ's Gospel. They believed, rightly so, that to accept the practices of the Roman Church would appear as though they were accepting the doctrine of the Roman Church. They understood that when there is a controversy over doctrine in the church, the controversy often shows itself in the practices of the church. They put their confession of faith into a document called the Formula of Concord. Since the adoption of the Formula of Concord in 1577, every Lutheran minister has sworn to confess his faith exactly as did those early Lutherans. "We believe, teach, and confess that in a time of persecution, when an unequivocal confession of the faith is demanded of us, we dare not yield to the opponents in indifferent matters. . . . For in such a situation it is no longer indifferent matters that are at stake. The truths of the gospel and Christian freedom are at stake."[9] Lutherans have often used an old Latin phrase to express their view, "*In casu confessionis nihil est adiaphora.*" In the case of confession, nothing is indifferent.

Practices That Are Imposed

The Gospel gives freedom, and our freedom is broad. Of course, we are free neither to sin nor to deny the Gospel doctrine. There is, however, broad latitude of option in church practice. Unfortunately, whenever someone imposes a practice not required by the Gospel, they are jeopardizing the church's freedom. If that happens, the practice must be resisted.

Paul the apostle was confronted with an imposition over the issue of circumcision. He himself taught that circumcision didn't matter. "For neither circumcision counts for anything, nor uncircumcision, but a new creation" (Galatians 6:15). In Acts 16:3 Paul willingly and freely made sure that Timothy was circumcised in order not to offend the Jews. Later, however, Paul refused to have Titus circumcised even though, like Timothy, he was a Greek. "To them we did not yield in submission even for a moment, so that the truth of the gospel might be preserved for you" (Galatians 2:5). Why did Paul refuse to do something that he had willingly done previously?

Paul took his stand because a group of false Christians was using the practice of circumcision to teach that you had to observe the Law in order to gain God's approval. They were imposing a rule upon other Christians and were saying that one had to be circumcised in order to be saved—they denied grace alone. This group, called Judaizers, was foisting on people rules from which Jesus had freed them. Paul understood that an indifferent matter can, in times of controversy, become a matter of eternal significance.

Circumcision is a matter of indifference today. You can either be circumcised or not. No one is forcing the issue. So we are free. But the minute someone within the Christian church would say that you must be circumcised in order to be a Christian, then all true Christians would refuse to do so. I suppose if someone would pass a law somewhere in Christendom forbidding people to be circumcised, then we would be equally obligated to have our little boys, and even grown men, circumcised. May the good Lord protect us from the necessity of such a confession.

Gin and Tonic in North Dakota

North Dakota summers are very beautiful. At least, that's what the residents believe when they compare them to the winters. In North Dakota you want to spend as much time outside as possible when you can. When my family lived there, our entire cul-de-sac would gather every evening in front of our house or in someone's backyard and enjoy cocktails and snacks while we watched the kids tearing around on their bikes. It was always a fitting and relaxing end to the summer workdays.

Judith lived next door and would always enjoy the festivities. More often than not I would pour her a tall gin and tonic when she joined the neighbors as they chased after the kids or threw horseshoes. We would often talk theology. People are usually pretty eager to tap the brain of a pastor as long as he doesn't act pompous or judgmental. So we would discuss matters of Baptism and the Sacrament of the Altar because Judith seemed attracted to the local "evangelical" church that accepted neither. Judith was eager both to enjoy the drink and to learn some good Lutheran theology. She even visited our church a couple of times. I never could get her to Bible class where "the real learning takes place" because she was afraid she would show her biblical ignorance. Despite my urgings she demurred. But I always got the impression she was eager for more. She never acted disinterested.

One day Judith came very close to wrecking the happy hour for the entire group, and for months after I was thanked for my redemption of the neighborhood. It seems that, despite her lack of Bible knowledge and her inexperience, Judith was offered and accepted the task of being a Bible study facilitator (she was adamant that she was not a leader, just a facilitator) at the local Evangelical Free Church. My incredulity having been tested by her announcement of the new duty, I was further challenged in my Christian patience when Judith refused my gift of the usual alcoholic concoction with the startling announcement that she had vowed to no more imbibe in public.

At first the happy group protested her characterization of our little gatherings as "public" and got bogged down in questions about how many people it took to constitute the "public." I went to the crux of the matter and asked why she would make such a vow. I followed with an explanation, drawn from the Augsburg Confession, that vows made against God's will are not binding.[10] Surely, I suggested, such a vow was not according to the will of God. But Judith was adamant. She would not drink. Finally, the entire group (public or private, it really didn't matter) insisted that she explain this abrupt and complete change in her behavior. Her answer cast a pall of quiet temperance upon the neighborhood. "As I now have a church responsibility, I have to set an example in public and not drink alcoholic beverages."

My first instinct, I confess, was to take things personally. I wondered what she thought I had been doing for the last four summers occupying the office of the holy public ministry of Word and Sacrament during the day and imbibing with the neighbors at night. I wisely left my rhetorical question unstated. Things didn't need to get personal. But what could I say? Grand Forks, North Dakota, is just across the river from Minnesota, and the people there are simply too nice to argue with a personal religious decision, no matter how harebrained or discomforting. Judith's legalistic commitment was an implicit indictment of the entire neighborhood. But we could not exclude her. That would not be nice. On the other hand, her judgmental presence made it impossible for the rest of us to enjoy our drinks with the carefree abandon that North Dakotans find so infrequently and so fleeting. I knew it was up to me because, hailing from Missouri and a member of the Missouri Synod, I was afflicted with no scruples that confined my sense of desperate candor, especially when moral freedom was under attack. "Well, I guess that just means more booze for the rest of us now, doesn't it?" And I poured another glass.

The drawn and anxious faces were again filled with the happy liberty that ought to characterize all Christians. All except Judith's. She was not happy. We had put an umbrella under her rain cloud, and the parade was moving along just fine without her. She sat for a couple of minutes, then excused herself. "You're okay with us drinking, aren't you?" asked one neighbor. "We'll stop if it really offends you," said another. But Judith had already lost her legalistic leverage. She claimed she had a roast in the oven (it was 85 degrees outside, and we knew she was fibbing), and we invited her back the next day.

I went over to her house a couple of days later when Judith absented herself from the gatherings. As we talked she revealed that she was disappointed that I had not supported her because I was a Christian pastor. She was hurt that I had dismissed her feelings. "They're not your feelings," I asserted. "They're someone else's.

And whoever has those 'feelings' does not want to help you." Then I quoted the Bible, sort of, "Those who want to make a good impression outwardly are trying to compel you to quit drinking. The only reason they do this is to boast about getting you. May I never boast except in the cross of Christ. Neither drinking nor abstinence means anything; what counts is a new creation" (cf. Galatians 6:12–15). I knew it wasn't an exact rendering of Paul's passage against legalistic imposition, but it was a faithful application to a similar situation.

THE MODE OF BAPTISM

Another example of resisting the imposition of a practice is the question regarding the mode of Baptism. When someone is baptized, should you dip, dunk, sprinkle, or pour? Lutherans have traditionally and correctly said, "It doesn't matter." The word *baptize* in the Bible means to apply water in a ceremonial washing. So you can apply it however you want. If someone has been baptized by dunking, that's okay with us, provided the proper words are used. If someone has been sprinkled with water or had the water poured, that's fine too.

Unfortunately, some churches insist that the only mode of valid Baptism is dunking. If you were to join certain Baptist or Pentecostal churches after having been baptized by sprinkling in another church, they would insist that you really have not been baptized at all. You would need to be baptized again—in effect rebaptized. Lutherans have always claimed, rightly, that the practice of rebaptism is a denial of Baptism. It draws into question the Baptism of every Lutheran, every Roman Catholic, every Episcopalian, many of the Reformed—countless Christians across the world and over the centuries. But even beside the question of rebaptism, there is something ominous about insisting that dunking is the only proper mode of Baptism. It is imposing a law where God has not. It is similar to the insistence on circumcision. We must refuse to rebaptize because it is a sacrilegious action. We should also resist the practice of Baptism by dunking because through it a certain group is imposing laws upon us that God does not impose. Incidentally, dunking should also be resisted because it is associated with false Baptistic churches, and we would give the impression that these churches might be true if we followed their customs.

Guilt by Association?

Often I have heard people say they oppose certain practices because these practices are associated with churches with which we do not wish to be confused. For example, I've heard people say, "I don't want to make the sign of the cross because it's just too Catholic." "I don't want to use a chalice during Communion because it's just too Catholic." "I don't want my pastor to wear a chasuble because it's just too Catholic." What's the difference between making the sign of the cross, which many Lutherans do, and refraining from meat on Friday?

There are two fundamental differences. First, the Roman Catholics at the time of the Reformation had made a law against meat on Friday. They were imposing a rule that God did not. Laws that are not from God must be resisted. No one was saying that you must make the sign of the cross during the Invocation or the Benediction. The Lutherans did not resist things simply because they were associated with the Roman Church. They resisted rules that were imposed on them.

Second, the sign of the cross was never considered by the Lutherans to be a uniquely Roman custom. This was a Christian custom. The sign of the cross does not identify a person as having loyalty to the pope or to the doctrine of works-righteousness. On the contrary, the practice of making the sign of the cross identifies a person as having been baptized. According to the Lutheran Rite of Holy Baptism, when a baby is baptized, the pastor says, "Receive the sign of the cross both upon your forehead and upon your heart to mark you as one redeemed by Christ the crucified."[11] This sign has been part of the baptismal liturgies of all Lutheran churches worldwide for the last 500 years.

I suppose that if the Roman Church had invented the practice of making the sign of the cross and had taught it as a way in which people could gain eternal life through their own piety and had imposed this rule on all Christians at the pain of eternal separation from God, then the Lutherans would have resisted. Thankfully, this is not the history of this Christ-centered pious custom. We do not believe in guilt by association. You will not be confused for a Roman Catholic just because you do things Catholics also do. Rather, we must avoid those practices that are made into laws and communicate a way to heaven other than through faith in our Lord Jesus Christ.

Should we say "one, holy, Christian, apostolic Church" in the Nicene Creed? Or should we say "one, holy, catholic, apostolic Church?" Lutherans have traditionally used the word *Christian* because we don't want to call ourselves *catholic*. We need to know that there is a huge difference between the words *catholic* and *Roman Catholic*. The word *catholic* means "a qualitative wholeness or integrity."[12] It also means "universal." *Roman Catholic* refers to the church that pledges loyalty to the bishop of Rome.

Something was lost when the early Lutherans, to avoid confusion, hesitated in calling the church *catholic*. It is a word that helps us understand customs and practices. Some customs and practices pervade the whole church. Christians everywhere and at every time have done them.

Sometimes church practices are like your mom's meatloaf recipe. They have been in the family so long and have been enjoyed so long that life in the family would seem joyless without them. Many liturgical customs fall into this category: pastors wearing robes; colors on the altar; Christmas celebrated on December 25; the church seasons, such as Advent, Epiphany, and Lent; services on Sunday mornings. None of these practices are mentioned in the Bible, but if I, as a pastor, tried to reschedule Christmas or to cancel Lent, I think my congregation would justifiably riot. Some customs of the church have stood the test of time and should not be tinkered with, just like you don't change your mom's meatloaf recipe.

The early Lutherans, their sacrifice of the word *catholic* notwithstanding, wanted very much to be seen as accepting those traditions and practices the whole church—the church catholic—had employed. Their only caution was that traditions never be understood as earning merit. We are saved by Christ's merit alone, and we accept those practices that do not deny Christ. "We gladly keep the ancient traditions set up in the church because they are useful and promote tranquility, and we interpret them in the best possible way, by excluding the opinion that they justify."[13] It's simple, really. If the whole church does things in a certain way, even if it is not directly drawn from the Bible, and as long as this practice doesn't go against the Gospel or isn't done for merit, then we will do it. It's the "catholic" way.

Saying the creeds is a "catholic" custom. The Apostles' Creed was written as a baptismal creed. Every baby that is baptized into Christ, from all over the world and throughout Christian times, confesses, through the mouth of godparents, parents, or the Christian congregation, conviction in the Apostles' Creed. And every Christian, when instructed in preparation for receiving the Sacrament, learns and confesses the Apostles' Creed. The liturgical rituals of the church catholic reflect this commitment. We not only believe the Apostles' Creed, the church catholic confesses the creed. It's the "catholic" way.

The same is even more obvious when it comes to the Nicene Creed. It was prepared as a response to false teachers in the third and fourth centuries who denied the full deity of Jesus Christ. For more than 1,600 years congregations all over the world have confessed the Nicene Creed just prior to receiving Communion. Through it we identify and distinguish true from false Christians. The first Lutherans were not content simply to assert their agreement with the Nicene Creed. They spelled it out in the Book of Concord. They were not content to leave it in a book used mostly by pastors. Every Lutheran liturgy of the Divine Service has contained the Nicene Creed and required Christians to speak it in anticipation of receiving the body and blood of Christ in the Sacrament. It's the "catholic" way. No true Lutheran would ever conceive of regularly omitting the creed or substituting something for it in the service. We are too catholic for that.

The Ordinaries and the Propers

Another custom is the structure of the main ingredients of the liturgy itself. Sometimes people feel bored in church. It's always the same, they declare. Actually, the service is rarely the same. In the historic liturgy, there are parts of the service that are the same each week and parts that are different each week. The parts that are the same are called "Ordinaries"—they are ordinarily done. The parts that change each week are called the "Propers"—they properly correspond to a specific season or Sunday.

The service varies week to week because of the Propers: the hymns, the readings, the prayers, and the sermon. Have you ever heard a sermon about the baby Jesus in the manger on Good Friday? That would be improper. Have you ever sung an Easter hymn in the middle of Lent? That would be improper. To do these things would not be sinful, just improper.

Ordinaries are the same each week. In the historic liturgy, the Ordinaries have been used for 1,400 years. Christians have gone to church and have sung or at least heard the following five Ordinaries: the Kyrie (Lord, have mercy), the Gloria in Excelsis (Glory, to God in the highest), the Creed (I believe), the Sanctus (Holy, Holy, Holy), and the Agnus Dei (Lamb of God). If you attend services at a congregation that follows the ancient liturgy, then you sing these same Ordinaries almost every week, depending on how often Holy Communion is served. It's the catholic way. The whole church everywhere has done it for a millennium and a half. The Lutherans did not invent the Ordinaries. They are not uniquely German or European or "classical." They are catholic. The Ordinaries have been accompanied with different musical tunes over the years and have been spoken in hundreds of languages. But they are simply too catholic to ignore or change.

If everything in the service were Ordinaries, then it would never change—same hymns, prayers, texts, and even sermon. That would get a bit tiring. If everything in the service were Propers, then nothing would be the same. You would not have any idea from week to week what to expect. The minute you got used to something, it would be different. That would be somewhat chaotic. So there is a balance.

Is there an easy way to remember the Ordinaries? There's an old mnemonic device some people have employed to help them remember the five historic ordinaries. K,G,C,S,A is Kyrie, Gloria, Creed, Sanctus, Agnus Dei = "King George cannot speak Anglais." If you ask me, it's tougher to remember the bit about King George than it is to remember the five Ordinaries.

I was casting about for an easier way to remember the historic Ordinaries, so I asked that group that always seems to give the best advice, the catechism class. I gave them the assignment to come up with a five-word sentence or phrase in which the words began with the letters K, G, C, S, A.

It was the spring of 2001. NBA basketball playoffs were in the air and in the news. One girl in the class, Jamie, was an avid fan of the Minnesota Timberwolves and their power-forward, Kevin Garnett. The T-Wolves were locked in an ultimately losing effort against the San Antonio Spurs to see who would advance in the tournament. Game two was on a Tuesday night, the night before catechism class. Propitiously, this was the only playoff game the T-Wolves would win that year, and Kevin Garnett was the star. So Jamie offered this mnemonic way of remembering the ordinaries of the Divine Service, "Kevin Garnett clobbers San Antonio" (Kyrie, Gloria, Creed, Sanctus, Agnus Dei). She received kudos for her creativity. I still think it's easiest just to remember the liturgy.

An important aspect of catholicity is that these things (the creeds and the Ordinaries) do not belong to any individual or even to the congregation. They are catholic. They belong to the entire church of all times and from all over the world.

When pastors or churches misuse, abuse, or don't use these catholic blessings, they are depriving themselves and their children of the undivided heritage that is ours by the grace and guidance of God. People lose their moorings like a boat at sea with no rudder or like children puzzled that their mother's meatloaf tastes wrong. Pastors and churches don't have the right to change what is given by the church catholic. It's tragic when they do. We will have more to say about the liturgy in the next chapter.

PRACTICES TEACH

Often the most important function of a church practice, particularly those that are repeated week after week, is to teach the church. The sign of the cross is a perfect example of a church practice teaching people. The Bible says that we are not baptized into an idea or into a denomination. We are baptized into Christ and specifically into His death. By making the sign of the cross at the name of the triune God, we are reminding ourselves—teaching ourselves—of the intimate connection between Christ's cross and our salvation in Baptism.

I can remember a number of lessons I learned from my pastor during catechism instruction simply by watching what he did. Sometimes I think I learned more by his practice than from the lessons. Let me share three examples.

Pastors wear robes. This teaches us that they have a uniform that sets them apart for the duties of their call, much as other professions are set apart through their attire. I remember asking my pastor in confirmation class why he wore the white thing over the black thing. (Later I learned that the white thing was a surplice and the black thing was a cassock.) He told me that the black thing represented sin and the white thing represented being covered with the righteousness of Jesus. So I was taught a lesson about Christ and the forgiveness of sins from the vestments of the pastor. Ever since then I paid close attention to what the pastor wore.

I was in the children's choir when I was in grade school. We had an old-fashioned church with a large nave. On either side sat the adult choir and the children's choir. One day I saw a movie where the choir sat behind the pastor in the front of the church. At the time, that seemed like a better idea to me. After all, the choir would be more easily seen and heard while facing the people from the front of the church. So I told the pastor what I had seen in the movies and asked if we could do it that way. He replied, "But are you there to sing to the people or to God?" I thought about his question for a while and reluctantly replied, "To God." "Well, then you need to face God," he replied. Again I learned a lesson about worship because of the practice of my church.

When I was a kid, every year on Reformation Sunday, at Bethel Lutheran Church, the congregation would gather outside on the front steps of the church before the service began. It would always be cold, and the pastor would wear this long, black shawl. We would watch in silence as Pastor Mundinger nailed a huge sheet of paper with words in calligraphic script to the church door. He would do so quite ceremoniously using this big old hammer and spikes that looked like the nails you imagined they must have used back in the sixteenth century. The gray stone and fortresslike appearance of our church building added to the evangelical, if somber, mood.

Then, after having pounded the last nail, Pastor Mundinger would turn and say, "Thesis one: When our Lord and Master Jesus Christ said, 'Repent' he willed the entire life of believers to be one of repentance." The first time I saw this happen, I didn't understand exactly what was being portrayed. But over the years I learned that my pastor was reenacting the fateful decision of a young monk more than 450 years earlier to post 95 theses on the church door of the Castle Church in Wittenberg. These theses challenged the practice of indulgences that the Roman Church used to burden the hapless souls of German peasants. Of course, Luther didn't post the theses on Sunday morning and certainly didn't read them out loud to a crowd of bystanders. But our ceremony in the mid-twentieth century impressed upon me that the Ninety-five Theses are still important today. I learned that today the truth of the Gospel and its defense need expression. And as Lutherans we inherited not only a doctrine but also a responsibility to teach how that doctrine was rediscovered and rearticulated back in the sixteenth century. Thankfully, all 95 theses were not read every October 31 or some of the members would have suffered hypothermia. But the practice made an impression on me. The practice taught me.

UNDERSTANDING PRACTICE

If you don't understand a practice, then just ask. Most pastors should know why things are done the way they are. And if your pastor can't answer you right off the cuff, then ask him to find an answer for you. I can remember serving a congregation in central Illinois during my seminary years. They had a custom I simply did not understand. During the Lord's Prayer, the organist would ring the outside bell of the church. It would always ring three times. What was the reason? After a couple of months my curiosity forced me to investigate, so I asked the pastor. He didn't know and was frankly puzzled himself. I asked the organist. She just did what she had been told to do twenty years earlier by the organist who taught her. I asked a couple of the old-timers at the church. They were equally ignorant of the precise reasons. "We've just always done it." That did not satisfy me, but I chalked it up as a quirky custom and ceased my quest for an explanation. About fifteen years later I was called to serve a church in California and heard those bells again during the Lord's Prayer. Now I was convinced that it was more than a Midwestern idiosyncrasy. So again I asked. Again I got dumb looks. It was as if there was some unwritten rule against understanding why we do things. Finally, I asked the right guy.

Walter was 75 years old and had been a member of the congregation for every one of those 75 years. He remembered many things. "When I was a kid, every once in a while we would have to work on Sunday either putting in the crops or harvesting them. We hated to miss church, but we had to take advantage of the good weather. Then there were those who couldn't make it to church because they were sick or shut in. The bells were for those people. They're for the people who can't make it to church." I was still a bit cloudy on what precise function the bells served, so Walter patiently explained. "When you heard the bells, you knew that the church was praying the Lord's Prayer. So you stopped whatever you were doing and prayed along. Did you know, Pastor, that in the Lord's Prayer is everything you could possibly say to God? At any rate, when you heard the first bell you started praying, then you paced yourself to be finished by the third bell."

So after fifteen years I understood a practice. Now certainly that practice is not shared by all churches and is understood by very few. It made sense once I understood it, and I was taught something. Walter had also been taught to value the Lord's Prayer, corporate prayer, and repeated prayer. Walter also learned that services were something you should not miss lightly. All this through hearing some bells.

LEX ORANDI, LEX CREDENDI

A theologian of the fifth century, Prosper of Aquitaine, is credited with having first spoken the words "*Lex Orandi, Lex Credendi.*" It's a Latin expression that means that the rule of prayer or of worship is the rule of faith. Liturgists throw around this expression. But you don't have to be familiar with fifth-century theological thought to understand what Prosper was saying. The way we worship affects the way we believe. Or, to put it another way, practice teaches doctrine.

I was never taught the posture of prayer as a young child. I just watched my parents bow their heads when they prayed. So I learned to do that. They never explained why they bowed. After 50 years of prayer I still bow my head. At some time, I suppose, I actually reflected upon the practice of my prayer posture. I figured out that I bow my head as a sign of reverence. But I was not taught first to show reverence and then to bow my head. Rather, I learned a practice, and from that I learned doctrine.

I learned to pray in the name of Jesus long before I understood the atonement and certainly before I memorized the verse, "No one cometh to the Father but by Me." From before I can remember every prayer I heard contained the words "For Jesus' sake" or "in Jesus' name." This phrase was part of the prayer practice modeled for me by my parents and Sunday school teachers. I was not first taught the doctrine of the exclusivity of Christ's claims and His once-for-all atonement and then taught to pray. Rather, I learned the practice of prayer and, from that practice, that you can't even talk to God without Jesus.

No one taught me that Sunday was the Lord's Day. I was simply brought to church on Sunday, and my dad did not go to the office as he usually did. We had no school, and we always had a big dinner. I suppose the time came when I actually reflected on the importance of the Lord's Day. I figured out that we needed a time to hear God's Word and to rest. But I was not first taught to honor the Sabbath and then to take off work and go to church. Rather, a practice was modeled for me, and from that I learned the command to honor God's Day and His Word.

I was never explicitly taught to respect the house of the Lord. I was simply given nice Sunday clothes to wear on Sundays. Others dressed up too. I was told not to run around in church or to shout and yell, and I was told to leave without tearing and weaving in and out of ambulatory traffic like we did at the baseball games. Something important was happening on Sunday mornings, and it was obvious from the change in behavior modeled for us. I was not first taught the power of the Word and then taught to act like I respected it. Rather, I was taught a practice, and from that practice I learned respect of the Gospel.

I could give hundreds of examples of how I learned doctrine from practice. And each example probably happened for you too. We know from our own experiences what Prosper of Aquitaine said fifteen hundred years ago: the rule of prayer is the rule of doctrine. *Lex Orandi, Lex Credendi*. Our practice teaches theology.

There is nothing in the Bible that says you have to bow your head in prayer, explicitly mention the name of Jesus in prayer, observe Sunday as the day of rest, wear nice clothes to church, be quiet, or don't run around. These are practices that teach. In fact, those things that we do habitually are usually the best teachers.

If the principle *Lex Orandi, Lex Credendi* applies to home devotional life, then certainly it applies more obviously and importantly to the worship life of the church. That will be the topic of the next chapter.

Conclusion

Doctrine and practice are bound together and cannot usually be separated. Sometimes a practice is necessary because the doctrine of the Gospel demands it. Such is the case with baptizing babies and with table fellowship with other believers. Sometimes practices are intended to communicate a confession in conflict with the Word of God. This can happen even when the practices are not, in and of themselves, against the Bible. Such practices should be avoided, as in the case of breaking the bread in Holy Communion and the precise words spoken during the distribution. Sometimes practices are so associated with a false doctrine that they must be avoided for the sake of our confession. Such was the case with many of the customs during the adiaphoristic controversy of the sixteenth century. Sometimes practices are unnecessarily imposed upon the church, such as circumcision at Paul's time or pietistic rules against alcohol. These practices should be disobeyed. Some practices are so universally used by the whole church over vast periods of time that their catholicity requires continued use. Just as positively, many practices teach doctrine. They do so almost without us noticing. But the lessons are so valuable that we change the practice at great peril. Doctrine and practice support and complement each other just like the "Fire and the Staff" of a shepherd.

Practices matter. To say that we are bound to hold true doctrine but can change our practice is either naïve or devious. The practice of the church is especially important in her worship.

STUDY QUESTIONS

1. How do we define "practices"? Give some examples.
2. How can we tell the difference between a church practice that doesn't matter and a church practice that is worth arguing about?
3. What are the two great facets of the Gospel identified by the author?
4. What is "adiaphora"?
5. What does "*In casu confessionis nihil est adiaphora*" mean to Lutherans?
6. What is the difference between "Roman Catholic" and "catholic"?
7. What are the five historic Ordinaries heard in the Divine Service?
8. What pupose do the Propers have in the Divine Service?
9. How is the Lutheran church's catholicity a blessing?

DISCUSSION QUESTIONS

1. Discuss how Peter's practice denied the Gospel and what was done to change this.
2. Certain practices become connected to doctrine when the church contends for the truth. Discuss two such practices and the fight for truth in the examples of the Prussian Union and the breaking of the bread.
3. Why is the Lutheran mode of Baptism a confessional statement?
4. *Lex Orandi, Lex Credendi* means the rule of prayer or of worship is the rule of faith—practice teaches doctrine. What is the significance of this for the congregation, for the pastor, and for the church when it comes to establishing or changing practice?

5

The Church's Staff

WORSHIP IN THE LUTHERAN CHURCH

In worship there are two questions that you need to have answered. First, who is doing the acting and the talking? Second, who is being acted upon and spoken to in the service?

Look Who's Talking

When I was in catechism instruction, my pastor taught the whole class a little prayer we were to say when we first came into the church service. It went like this:

> Lord Jesus, bless the pastor's word
> and bless my hearing too,
> That after all is said and heard,
> I may believe and do.

I have prayed that little prayer off and on for much of my life. It's a good prayer because it says what my job is, as a Christian, in the worship service. I am to hear. The prayer also says what my job is after the service. I am to believe and do. Paul echoes the same type of thinking when he says to the Christians in Colossae:

> We always thank God, the Father of our Lord Jesus Christ, when we pray for you, since we heard of your faith in Christ Jesus and of the love you have for all the saints, because of the hope laid up for you in heaven. Of this you have heard before in the word of truth, the gospel, which has come to you, as indeed in the whole world it is bearing fruit and growing—as it also does among you, since the day you heard it and understood the

> grace of God in truth, just as you learned it from Epaphras our beloved fellow servant. He is a faithful minister of Christ on your behalf and has made known to us your love in the Spirit. (Colossians 1:3–7)

Notice what Paul says about these Christians. He knows their faith and love. Faith is the way we respond to God, and love is what we give to our neighbor. Where did the faith and love come from? They were brought about by the Gospel the Colossians heard and learned. And from whom did they hear and learn? From Epaphras, a minister and a preacher. I suppose those first-century Christians might have prayed, "Lord Jesus, bless Epaphras's word and bless our hearing too, that after all is said and heard, we may believe and do." The job of the minister is to teach and speak. The job of the people in the pew is to hear and learn. Paul says so.

I know that Christians are anxious to do good works. The next chapter is on Christian good works and how we love others. But for now, in the worship service, the primary job is to hear and learn, just as the Colossians did many years ago.

Worship Is Receiving

Most people, when they think of the word *worship*, think of something that we do. By this way of thinking, we are active in giving God our honor and praise and God is passive in receiving our worship. Actually, the primary direction of the communication in worship is the other way. In true Christian worship we are passive and God is active. We are receiving and God is giving. We are learning and God is teaching. We are getting and God is giving. Roger Pittelko puts it this way:

> The dictionary understanding makes worship our action or response. It turns worship into an anthropocentric [human-centered] activity that is measured and normed by what we do, by what we understand God to be. The evangelical Lutheran understanding of worship is just the opposite. It is from God to us. It begins with God. It has its foundation and source with God. It is theocentric [God centered] and more specifically it is Christocentric [Christ centered].[1]

The Lutheran Confessions agree:

> Faith is that worship which receives the benefits that God offers.

> . . . God wants to be honored by faith so that we receive from him those things that he promises and offers.[2]
>
> The woman [who washed Jesus' feet] came with the conviction about Christ: that she should seek the forgiveness of sins from him. This is the highest way to worship Christ. Nothing greater could she ascribe to Christ. By seeking the forgiveness of sins from him, she truly acknowledged him as the Messiah. Now to think about Christ in this way, to worship and take hold of him in this way, is truly to believe.[3]
>
> The service and worship of the Gospel is to receive good things from God. . . . The highest worship in the Gospel is the desire to receive the forgiveness of sins, grace, and righteousness.[4]

Why is this so important? It is important because we are saved by grace alone. And if we are saved by grace alone, then, when it comes to salvation, we are passive. The worship service is the place and the occasion in which God gives to us the forgiveness of sins that Jesus won for all people on the cross. It is precisely in the worship service that He "bespeaks us righteous" through His Word and Sacrament. Because we are passive when God saves us, we are also primarily passive in worship. Almost all of the discussion and controversy about worship practices and style could be easily settled if we would just keep in mind that the direction of communication in the service is from God to us.

DIVINE SERVICE

The word *service* is also a bit unclear. When you attend the church service, are you serving God or is He serving you? Actually, there is some of both going on. But who is primarily doing the serving? God is. He is speaking to us and serving us His grace through the Word and Sacraments. Consequently, the worship service or the Sunday service are often called the Divine Service.

Here's a question: How much are we serving God in the Divine Service, and how much is He serving us?

The Divine Service is like a restaurant. My wife and I went to a fancy restaurant for our anniversary. What a place! This particular restaurant had won all sorts of awards for its menu, its service, and especially its food. Because of personal budget constraints, it is the type of place we go to infrequently.

The memory of this culinary experience is that of which legends are formed. First, we were ushered to the lounge. Immediately behind us was a bar at which you could order appetizers. The special of the day was shrimp—as big as lobsters. We decided against them as we wanted to save ourselves for the entrées. The server asked what libation we desired, and we ordered a couple of glasses of an exquisite Napa Valley cabernet and sipped while we waited for our names to be called. After a couple minutes, the host wished us happy anniversary and asked if he could escort us to the table. We wondered how he knew our names. He only smiled in response and gave us a card with our names already printed on it.

Feeling pampered and completely at ease, we were seated next to a fountain at an intimate table for two. It was as if of our needs were known and met. Complimentary shrimp (small ones, deep fried in a sweet batter with peach salsa) were brought to the table. We ordered our meals (salmon with a lemon butter sauce, fresh broccoli served al dente, complimented by wild rice pilaf with accents of saffron) and some more wine (a buttery chardonnay with a long oak finish). The servers hovered and amiably visited with us when the various courses arrived. Finally, we were given a complimentary piece of triple chocolate cake. It was a wonderful meal.

Now here's the question. Who was being served? Let's make the question really obvious. Pretend that the entire meal was free. Now who is being served?

I suppose someone might say, "But you actually had to get into the car and actively drive to the restaurant. You had to walk from the lounge to your table in the dining area. You said 'thank you' when the various courses were served. When the server came by, you asked her some questions and showed a little interest. And you praised her for the excellent service. You went Oooo and Ahhh every time you tasted something new. So, I suppose, that you could say that you were doing the serving. You were doing the acting." Well, if you would view such a meal as your service, then you can view the Divine Service as your service. Most diners, however, would not think that they were doing the work at such a restaurant. Similarly, the Divine Service is primarily God serving us.

Of course, we were not passive like stones or corpses during the meal. There were spontaneous actions in response to the generous portions of food and the delightful service. In the same way Christians do not engage in stonelike passivity during the Divine Service. We respond with thanks and praise to the generous portions of grace and the delightful service God gives us.

We call it the "Divine Service" primarily because God is serving us by giving us Word and Sacraments. We call it "Divine Service" secondarily because we return some modest service to God in our hymns, prayers, and psalms.

> The Father bears His throbbing heart of love and sends His only begotten; the Son willingly lays down His life on our behalf and victoriously takes it up again; the Spirit delivers to us Christ and all His benefits. The chief action in worship is not the meager thanks and praise that we attempt to throw God's way, but God's gift of Himself by which He imparts life and salvation.[5]

So the communication in the service is from God to us. God's best way of communicating is to teach us. That's what He says in the Great Commission: "teaching them."

LEARNING IS FRUSTRATING

Because our job in worship is primarily to hear, or as Paul says, "to learn," then the primary direction of the communication in the service is from God to us. He teaches us through the pastor. We learn from God by learning from the pastor whom He has appointed.

Learning can be frustrating. In fact, someone once said, "Frustration is the mother of learning." People who are never confused, uncertain, a bit on edge—in short, frustrated—tend not to learn. So if the worship service is to teach, then the people will be a bit frustrated at times. The less they know about God and Christ, the more they will be frustrated. If you don't believe me, then bring a friend to church. (You might want to bring a friend even if you do believe me.) People in church for the first time are universally frustrated. They haven't learned as much about God, His Son, His church, and the manner in which God communicates. They will be frustrated.

WATCHING SOAP OPERAS WITH MY BROTHER

Back in the 1980s, the primetime soap opera *Dallas* aired each week. I watched it once when I was at my brother's house for dinner. The meal was nice. We were relaxing over some coffee when suddenly shouts of alarm emitted from our hosts. "Hurry! Hurry! We'll miss the beginning. Hurry!" The table was cleared in a flash, and everyone was ushered into the family room and plopped in front of the television. It all happened so quickly I thought that one of the kids was on television. We had just been seated when the strains of the theme song afflicted our ears and the credits began to run.

"*Dallas*?" I protested. "We cut our meal short for *Dallas*?"

"Oh, you've never seen it?" my brother feigned surprise. "Well, you'll love it."

Of course, I hated it. It's not that it wasn't good, wholesome entertainment. Actually it wasn't. It's just that I didn't understand who was who. I didn't know the plot. I didn't know the context of what was happening. Every time I tried to ask a question, someone said, "Just pay attention. You'll get it," which was another lie. Finally, I took to watching the watchers. They were enraptured by the television goings-on. I could tell that they loved it. And it occurred to me that the reason I did not like the show was that I did not understand it.

That's the way the Divine Service is to many people.

I suppose it might seem sacrilegious to compare the Divine Service to a soap opera, but there are certain similarities. Both start at a certain time, and you should not be late. Both are hard to understand the first time we see them. Neither can really be explained while you're in the middle of them. Both are genuinely loved by those who understand them and despised by those who do not. And both involve sitting and receiving a message from someone else who did not consult us about what they were going to say.

When the show was over, a couple of my nephews attempted to explain it to me. They wanted me to like it and asked me to promise that I would watch it again. I promised them just to be polite. But I never bothered to watch *Dallas* again. I guess that might be another similarity between soap operas and the Divine Service: People promise to come back, but they often don't.

Soap operas are unimportant and trite. The Divine Service is the most important, urgent, and profound gift you will ever receive. We can afford to let people ignore television. People ignore the Divine Service to their eternal peril.

How do we ensure that people will return to the Divine Service a second time? The answer is Christian vocation. You'll have to wait for the next chapter for the discussion of vocation.

HYMNS AND LEARNING

The direction of communication in the Divine Service is primarily from God to us. That means that the service, which includes the sermon, the texts, the pastor, and the hymns, should teach people about Jesus Christ.

Perhaps there is no area of greater controversy in the church than the endless debate about what people should sing in church.

"Why don't we ever sing 'A Mighty Fortress' with the easy melody?"

"How come they didn't put 'In the Garden' in the hymnal?"

"Doesn't everyone sing 'Amazing Grace' at funerals?"

"What do you mean we can't sing 'Love Me Tender' in our wedding? My mom had it in her wedding and no one complained."

"Pastor, just because you like classical music doesn't mean we all do. I think we need contemporary music in church. Nobody really relates to those old German hymns anymore."

Most of these arguments could be solved if we would simply ask the question, "What does this hymn teach?" The purpose of the service is to teach. What do hymns teach?

HYMNS TEACH

Prior to the Reformation, people in the pew did not sing. Only the choirs sang, and this had been the custom in the church for almost a thousand years. Lutherans wanted the congregation to sing in order to teach about Christ through music. They understood the direction of the communication in the Divine Service. The service was God teaching us, so hymns were not written primarily to give the people a chance to praise God. Rather, the early Lutherans gave the church hymns because they believed that hymns taught doctrine. They were right.

Read Luther's hymn "Dear Christians, One and All, Rejoice."[6] It was written by Luther to teach the doctrine of salvation in verse and tune. At exactly the same time, Paul Speratus wrote a similar hymn entitled "Salvation unto Us Has Come."[7] Both of these hymns appeared in the first Lutheran hymnal, which contained eight hymns in all (seven written by either Luther or Speratus). The hymnal, commissioned by Luther, was published so the choir could "teach the young something of value," and so the congregation could learn to sing.[8] Imagine coming to church and being allowed to sing for the first time in almost a millennium. Further, imagine singing a hymn that beautifully and clearly teaches that Jesus is your Savior. Imagine that the first time you ever sang in church, you were able to sing these words:

> He spoke to His beloved Son:
> 'Tis time to have compassion.
> Then go, bright Jewel of My crown,
> And bring to man salvation;
> From sin and sorrow set him free,
> Slay bitter death for him that he
> May live with Thee forever.[9]

Years after Luther, Tileman Husshusius commented on his famous hymn:

> I do not doubt that through this one hymn of Luther many hundreds of Christians have been brought to the true faith who before could not endure the name of Luther; but the noble, precious words of the hymn have won their hearts, so that they are constrained to embrace the truth, so that in my opinion the hymns have helped the spread of the Gospel not a little.[10]

Memorizing Hymns

It was a lazy summer day. There was nothing to do. I was 12 years old. Life was dreary. "I'm bored," I said to my dad. "There's nothing to do. Besides I'm broke, and I can't even go to the ball game." His solution was one of the greatest gifts I ever received.

"Go memorize 'Salvation unto Us Has Come.' I'll give you a nickel for each verse." We had *The Lutheran Hymnal* on our bookshelf. In it the hymn had ten verses. Originally, Paul Speratus penned the hymn with 14 verses, so I found an old *Lutheran Hymnary* lying around the house, published in 1913, which contained all 14 verses.[11] That would give me 70 cents.

"Dad, it has 14 verses. Could I have a dollar if I memorized the whole thing?"

"I know it has 14 verses. I figure it is worth 70 cents, and that is why I offered a nickel a verse."

"But a ball game costs 75 cents. Could I have enough money for the ball game?"

"Okay. 75 cents." The year was 1962, candy bars were a nickel, and you really could get into a major league ball game for six bits. I figured it would be worth the time to learn the hymn, but because negotiations had exhausted me, I waited until the next day to begin.

It took longer than I had expected, but over the next two or three days I learned every stanza perfectly. When I was ready, I found my dad and proudly recited the hymn. He paid me, and I was very pleased.

And now, the rest of the story.

About three years later I was in high school arguing with a Roman Catholic friend about good works. I kept saying that you get to heaven through faith in Christ regardless of how many good works you have performed. He argued that you get to heaven by faith and good works. We went back and forth exchanging convictions and opinions when finally he posed this question: "If you get to heaven only by faith, then why would anybody do good things? Why not just live your life the way you want? You're going to heaven anyway?" I could tell in his eyes that he thought he had me. And I couldn't immediately phrase an answer to his question. Why should you do good works?

Then it came to me:

> Faith to the cross of Christ doth cling
> And rests in Him securely;
> And forth from it good works must spring
> As fruits and tokens surely;
> Still faith doth justify alone,
> Works serve thy neighbor and make known
> The faith that lives within thee.[12]

You do good works as fruits and tokens. "Works serve your neighbor and make known the faith that lives within you." So the tenth stanza of a fourteen-stanza hymn enabled me to confess my faith to my Roman Catholic friend.

Since then I have used that hymn a hundred times to help explain the relationship between faith and works. I know the difference because I was taught. Paul Speratus taught me, even though he had been dead for more than 400 years. My father and subsequent pastors taught me the doctrine of salvation by making me sing over and over again the words of that great hymn "Salvation unto Us Has Come."

I do not know if my Roman Catholic friend back in high school learned to love Luther, Speratus, or me through the hymn I quoted. But he was told the sweet Gospel. He scratched his head, knit his brow, and promised he would think about things. I learned something important back then. Hymns teach. They taught me and enabled me to confess my faith and to teach others.

CAN'T WE PRAISE GOD TOO?

Someone may say, "But hymns should praise God too. You can't just teach; you have to praise God." The greatest way to praise God is to tell everyone what He has done. The praise of God is neither in the use of verbs to describe me nor is it in the use of adjectives to describe Him. Praise of God is using verbs to tell what He did for us in Christ. Look at the Apostles' Creed: "I believe in Jesus Christ, his only Son, our Lord, who . . . " then we list eleven verbs that tell us what Jesus did for us. The creed is praise of Christ. Peter begins his first Epistle, after the greeting, with the command to praise God: "Praise be to the God and Father of our Lord Jesus Christ!" (1 Peter 1:3 NIV). Then he lists all the gifts of grace Christ gives us: mercy, new birth, living hope, inheritance that cannot fade, the shielding of God's power. These blessings became ours by the resurrection of Christ. Peter is unable to praise God without talking about what Jesus has done (1 Peter 1:3–5).

In Ephesians Paul begins the Epistle just like Peter did: "Praise be to the God and Father of our Lord Jesus Christ" (Ephesians 1:3 NIV). Paul then lists no less than 15 verbs that tell us just about everything God did for us in Christ to get us to heaven (Ephesians 1:4–15). He does the same thing, to a lesser extent, in 2 Corinthians. In Philippians 2:5–11 Paul tells the people to have the mind of Christ. He uses what many consider to be an early Christian creed to describe the mind of Christ: "Have this mind among yourselves, which is yours in Christ Jesus" (Philippians 2:5), then he lists ten verbs that describe what Jesus has done. These ten verbs have guided the church in developing her understanding of the humiliation and exaltation of Jesus Christ. They teach doctrine. The greatest praise of Christ is to list the things that He has done for our salvation. Hymns, then, will not really balance praise with the telling of the story. They will praise by telling the story of Christ. In the process of praise, doctrine is taught.

I have three daughters. Suppose a young man is dating my daughter and I'm talking to him about her. I ask, "What do you think of my daughter?"

He answers with words that describe his affections. "I just love her. I think so highly of her. I admire her. I am so taken by her."

I have to say as a father that I would not be impressed with this answer no matter how sincere. What does the guy even know about my daughter? Nothing that I can tell.

Let's try again. I ask, "What do you think of my daughter?"

He answers this time with adjectives, "What a nice young lady. What an elegant creature. What a lovely woman. She's wonderful, she's marvelous, she's beautiful, and she's fabulous."

I'm still not impressed. The young man is improving, but he still hasn't overwhelmed me with his understanding of my daughter.

I try a third time. "What do you think of my daughter?"

He answers with verbs. "I love her because she stops what she is doing to talk to you. I love her because she thinks of me and gives me presents for no reason. I love her because she works so hard and won't let anything get in the way of her goals. I love her because she loves her family and values them highly. I love her because she trusts Christ."

I would tell my daughter to marry a guy like that. He knows her. He loves her.

Our praise and love of Jesus should be the recounting of His verbs for us.

Some hymns are meatier than others. Some teach simply as though to children. Some accent the narrative features of the Gospel—they give the details of Christ's story. Others focus on a doctrinal theme taught by the various stories of Jesus. Some will interpret a text of the Bible and show how Jesus is taught by a specific passage, some will function as liturgical Ordinaries, but all good hymns will praise God by talking about what His Son has done.

WHAT ABOUT THOSE PRAISE SONGS? PART TWO

Unfortunately, the same emphasis on the teaching nature of hymns is not apparent in most contemporary song collections. The distinguishing feature of most praise songbooks is the focus on the sentiment or feelings of those doing the singing. It would be impossible to analyze the entire body of praise songs. So if you want to get a feel for praise songs, you have to choose a single collection that is most representative. I have singled out a specific collection, *The Best of the Best in Contemporary Praise and Worship*. This collection of 253 songs was published by Fellowship Ministries in 2000. It is worthy of analysis for four reasons. First, it purports to include the best songs. Second, it is compiled and edited by a Lutheran pastor and should therefore reflect Lutheran doctrine more clearly than those books published by the Evangelical community. Third, it is the sequel to *The Other Song Book*, also compiled by Lutherans. Fourth, it is popular among Lutherans.

In *The Best of the Best*, those songs that focus on my love of Jesus or use adjectives to speak of God far outnumber the songs that actually tell everyone what He has done in Christ. Less than 10 percent actually tell me what God has done for me in Christ for my salvation. If you would attempt to determine the Christian message from this praise book, you would conclude that God's central message to us is that I need to praise Him because He is so wonderful. Most of the songs say very little about Jesus or even about God.

For example, Claire Cloniger's "I Offer My Life" is an exhaustive, almost boastful, list of the things that I will give to Jesus: my regrets, claims, joy, pain, life, days, praise, and, in summary, just about everything I have.[13] Linda Duvall, in her "I Will Celebrate," is more subdued. Her commitment to God and her understanding of worship is to sing, to praise, and to celebrate.[14] Bobby Schroeder continues the emphasis on my works for Jesus with a description of worship that uses verbs such as *adore*, *praise*, and *bow*, with no information whatsoever concerning what Jesus might be giving to me.[15]

Laurie Klein's "I Love You, Lord" captures the same redundant theme of telling God how she lifts her voice and asking Him to take her joy but saying nothing about Jesus.[16] And on it goes with song after song telling Jesus of our devotion with little mention of His. Noteworthy also are the songs that use terminology usually reserved for romantic love to describe our feelings toward Jesus. One composer calls Jesus his "heart's desire,"[17] and David Graham, almost erotically, sings "a love song to Jesus." He also commends the rather novel practice, at least among Lutherans, of "lifting up my hands to the Lord," a prayer posture apparently preferred by the praise-song genre.[18]

Observe the direction of the communication in these songs. Almost none of them tell us anything about Christ. Most do not even mention His name. In *The Best of the Best*, fewer than half of the songs mention the name of Christ. They claim to praise God but don't mention the name of Jesus. One song promises God that we will "fulfill your holy mission," yet fails to mention Jesus, the Gospel, the Sacraments, forgiveness, or anything distinctively Christian.[19] When Christ's name is invoked, He is usually mentioned as the object of our affection, rather than the one who died to forgive us. And when Christ's death is stated, usually the allusion is fleeting. For example, in Jack Hayford's immensely popular song "Majesty," we are teased with a passing reference to "Jesus who died," with no explanation as to what this death might possibly mean to the world.[20]

Thomas Day, in his provocative book *Why Catholics Can't Sing: The Culture of Catholicism and the Triumph of Bad Taste*, bemoans the recent phenomena within the Roman Catholic Church that he calls, "Ego Renewal." It is the "tendency to put 'me' in the center of the liturgical landscape."[21] Mr. Day has probably not read *The Best of the Best* or he would not have limited his comments to the Church of Rome. Jesus did not give us the Word and Sacraments in the Divine Service so that we could undergo "Ego Renewal." Yet these songs promote such self-centeredness by focusing endlessly on me, my feelings, my gifts, my sacrifice, my, my, my.

It's not that these songs always contain false doctrine. Most contain no doctrine. It is not, in and of itself, a sin to sing them. But a steady diet of this type of song would never feed the thirsty soul with the forgiveness we have in Christ. So why are they used?

I have a friend in California who started a Saturday evening praise service. I asked him why. His reply: "To attract the unchurched. They can relate more to the simple praise songs. Hymns from the hymnal are too difficult to sing, and these are simpler."

I have heard this reasoning a dozen times from a dozen pastors or church leaders who prefer praise songs to the church's historic hymns. Ironically, in the vast majority of songs that are sung at the praise services, the "unchurched" are hearing nothing of value about Jesus. We think we are making it easier for them to become Christians when, in fact, we are making it almost impossible. To know Christ one must learn what He has done. This doesn't happen in most praise songs.

Someone might complain that I have chosen only the bad songs to criticize. The fact is that I did not compile these songs for publication. Another Lutheran pastor did that. In *The Other Song Book*, the predecessor to *The Best of the Best*, you find the same emphasis. Most of the songs tell us little of Christ. More than half do not mention Jesus. I suppose in five years another songbook will be published. The task of staying abreast of the rapidly growing industry of writing praise songs is quite impossible. "Over 85,000 songs are listed by the Christian Copyright Licensing Co."[22] I pray that years from now the songs will have improved. I fear they will not.

The pastor has three or four chances to choose hymns for the Sunday service. For the sake of the lost, for the sake of those saved, and for the sake of our Lord Jesus, choose carefully. If your hymn selection is made on the basis of Christ-centered saving lyrics, you will gravitate away from praise songs and toward the church's historic hymns.

MUSIC IN THE CHURCH

Songs and hymns have both words and music. It is not difficult to evaluate the words of a hymn. You simply ask questions of them. Do they teach the forgiveness of sins in Christ? Is grace alone asserted? Is the Gospel taught objectively? Do the words apply to all Christians? Are they comprehensible? The evaluation of music is much tougher. Many pastors or music committees do not choose hymns on the basis of the words. Instead, the tune, meter, beat, and rhythm become dominating factors in the song selection of many congregations.

Music is a gift from God. Luther claimed that "next to theology" music was God's greatest gift to us.[23] In the Scriptures music was used in the church (Ezra 3:10), by those who are skilled (1 Chronicles 15:22), to teach (Colossians 3:16), or to confess the truth (Psalm 145:4, 7), as well as to return our praise to God (Psalm 149:6; Psalm 98:4). Recognized as a very powerful instrument either for good or evil (2 Chronicles 5:13–14; Daniel 3:7), music should adorn the message of Christ so that Jesus and His grace are understood (1 Corinthians 14:15) and complemented.[24] The purpose of music in church is to promote Christ.

Musical theory and form may change from culture to culture and from age to age, just as instruments and even musical scales may vary. So the church should be reluctant to condemn or eschew any style of music out of hand. Some church leaders believe that music is neutral—"nothing more than an arrangement of notes and rhythm."[25] Doug Muren, for example, believes that "music—scores as opposed to lyrics—is amoral (neither moral nor immoral)."[26] Rick Warren, pastor of Saddleback Valley Community Church in Orange County, California, claims that "there is no such thing as 'Christian music' only 'Christian lyrics.' "[27] Can this really be true? No. Some music is inappropriate for use in church.

One type of music is worthy of special caution: pop music. Contemporary pop music tends to dominate wherever it goes. Everything around it, including its own lyrics, tends to disappear into the background.

In the early 1980s the popular ensemble movie *The Big Chill* hit the theaters. It was one of those movies where lots of stars get together and, with trite and tautly written clichés, talk about things that are supposed to charm the audience and make us think about the deeper affairs of life. The movie begins with the announcement of the suicide of a man named Alex and the reminiscing of his old college friends in the aftermath of the funeral. One of the first scenes is the funeral itself. Slowly and somberly the people come into the chapel while the organ oozes out its obligatory and unimaginatively sappy fare of nondescript church favorites. Never has "Rock of Ages" sounded less hopeful. Rarely has "Nearer My God to Thee" made you feel so far from God. Chords and notes are strung together with apparently as much thought as that of your typical elevator. After the Christless homily and banal eulogy, JoBeth Williams goes to the organ to play Alex's favorite song.

My attitude had not yet formed on this pedantic video sermon, so I was still earnestly trying to develop a feel for the thing. As the first chords of the hymn sounded, I heard the guy behind me in the theater start to laugh, and a split second later so did I. The musically innocuous, meaningless drivel that had characterized the service was altered. Wafting through the air of the on-screen chapel and of the theater were the chords to the great Rolling Stones classic "You Can't Always Get What You Want." Soon the characters in the movie, as well as the entire theater, got the joke. We laughed at the contrast of the Rolling Stones as background church music. We knew that the Stones did not belong at a funeral and that Mick Jagger's stylistic vocals can never be background music. Mick and a worship service cannot peacefully coexist. As the song progressed, the casket was placed into the hearse and the guests left the chapel. Initially in the background, the acoustic guitar soon began to meander boldly into the concert while the drums banged their way onto the show. The movie audience was swaying to the beat. Mick had taken over the funeral service. He had to. His music is domineering and aggressive. That's why he's so popular. For one last, brief moment the camera showed JoBeth Williams in the chapel still at the organ, playing. The place was empty. She was alone. Rock 'n' roll had usurped the service.

What does Hollywood know that we should know? Some things just don't go together. I'm not suggesting that the type of pop music used in many churches is similar to the Rolling Stones. The illustration from the movies simply shows that music is not neutral. Why?

There are at least three reasons why today's pop music is inappropriate for church. The first reason is the music's beat. Everyone remembers Baloo the bear in the animated Disney classic *The Jungle Book*. One of the most endearing film characters of all time, Baloo is supposed to guard the "man-cub," Mowgli, from the perils of the jungle. Alas, despite his best efforts, the poor kid is kidnapped by monkeys who cart the struggling and angry adolescent to the king of the orangutans. Baloo, now accompanied by a more responsible if less fun panther named Bagheera (Baggy), discovers the monkey hideout. The two contemplate their rescue of Mowgli. Every attempt by the panther to get Baloo to concentrate on the important task at hand seems to fail. Why? The monkeys are playing jazz, and the king orangutan, using the talents of Louis Prima, is singing and playing the horn. It's the music. The helpless bear is willing enough, promising to tear them limb from limb or at least to beat them. His braggadocio is unfortunately consistently waylaid by the music's beat, and he is reduced to mindless dancing accompanied by a Dick Clarkesque mantra concerning beat. Baggy implores him to stop the silly beat business, reminding him that their task requires brains and not brawn. It's all for nothing. Completely exasperated, Baggy pleads for his friend to listen. But Baloo is not able to listen to anything but the beat of the music. "Oh, yeah, yeah" is his only response as he grunts and boogies mindlessly away.

Hollywood knows something that the church should learn. The beat of music can affect you in ways you don't even know. That's why we like it.

How does beat function? Ideally, in hymns it serves the message. Walter Buzsin put it this way: "In the great hymns of the Church the element of rhythm, though always basic and present, never dominates; it is subservient and never seeks to becloud the *viva vox* [*evangelii*—the living voice of the Gospel] in order to extol itself."[28] Rhythm and beat should be like John the Baptist, "He must increase, but I must decrease" (John 3:30).

In today's pop music, the beat tends to define and dominate the music. In much of contemporary worship, "the distinguishing feature" is the "presence of a 'beat' " and particularly what is called a "backbeat."[29] "Backbeats are the beats occupying the weakest metrical position in the bar—in a 4/4 or 12/8 bar the second and fourth beats. In [music] characterized as having 'heavy backbeat' these metrical impulses are consistently stressed."[30] What does this mean for us musical laypeople? The easiest way to explain is by a quick exercise. Take your left hand and hit your left leg four beats to a measure. Now with your right hand tap out the rhythm to Martin

Franzmann's "Thy Strong Word." You will notice that your hands will hit your legs at the same time on all four beats and the first and third beats will be a little harder. Do the same for the hymn "Rock of Ages," "My Hope Is Built on Nothing Less," or "Beautiful Savior." You'll notice the same thing. The hymn tunes have predictable and regular beats. Now try the same to "I Can't Get No Satisfaction," by the Rolling Stones. Try it with the tune to Cat Stevens's "Moonshadow." Or take the praise songs "Jesus, Name above All Names" or "Shine, Jesus, Shine," especially the refrain. You will probably notice how difficult it is to maintain the regular rhythm of your left hand while tapping the meter of the song with your right. You may also notice that the strong beats are often on the second and fourth beats. That's because the stress in many of the contemporary songs, just as with rock 'n' roll, is on the offbeat or "backbeat." The effect is to interrupt your normal and predictable rhythmic patterns. You start moving your body. You will sway or shake your foot. You've seen people in the car next to you at a stoplight who are bobbing their heads while they listen to music. You don't have to guess what kind of music they are listening to. It's music with a beat, specifically a backbeat.

The backbeat always dominates. It takes over the music. The lyrics, in the nature of the case, recede into the background. They become secondary. The songs themselves inform us that we want rock 'n' roll music because it has a backbeat. Recall that the purpose of the Divine Service is to teach and proclaim the doctrine of the Gospel of Christ. Music that distracts from the teaching of that message is inappropriate. Is percussion bad? No. Are guitars, in and of themselves, wrong? Of course not. It's the beat that takes away from the message.

The second reason pop music is inadvisable for use in the Divine Service is its fleeting nature. When I suggested you tap "Thy Strong Word," I was confident that you would know the hymn. The hymn is less than one hundred years old, but I am certain that Lutherans will sing it for centuries to come because it is such a wonderful hymn both in words and in music. The same applies to hundreds of other hymns. Generation after generation knows them because the best ones last. Hymns thrive because a type of survival of the fittest, a "natural selection," takes place in which "due to artistic inferiority, bad theology or spiritual triteness" many hymns have not withstood the test of time. These hymns, like dinosaurs, are simply no longer known.[31] Very few hymns stand the test of time. Because we have 20 centuries from which to choose, however, there are plenty of great hymns in most Lutheran hymnals. If all or most of our songs come from one era, the present, then our worship will be impoverished and not "catholic."

Pop music, because of its nature, must be current and contemporary. The word *contemporary* means "with the times." Popular music changes every couple of months. The most popular songs, whether in the secular realm or played on "Christian" radio, are very short-lived in their popularity. In fact, the examples of praise songs used in this book are mostly old praise songs that have long since ceased to be popular. As you have read this book you may have said, "This guy is completely out of it. We don't sing that anymore." Pop praise songs are good only if they are current. If you travel abroad or just stop listening to the radio for a couple of months, all the songs will be different when you return.

Most of the hymns that I know I have sung my whole life. I don't wonder if "A Lamb Goes Uncomplaining Forth" is old or "out." The hymn transcends time. "Lord, Thee I Love with All My Heart" was sung by my parents and by my children and will be sung by my grandchildren and great-grandchildren. "Of the Father's Love Begotten" has been sung by Christians for 1,600 years. How long were these hymns contemporary and "popular"? Actually, they have been for centuries. They are "catholic."

Pop music, by definition, cannot be catholic. Pop songs are like the tide: in today, out tomorrow. I saw the televised performance of Simon and Garfunkel's concert in the park. They sang "59th Street Bridge Song," which contains the phrase "feelin' groovy." Even the artists laughed at the archaic words. The song was "out," even though it was only 15 years old at the time. When is the last time you sang "They'll Know We Are Christians by Our Love" in church? It's out. In twenty years 95 percent of the praise songs that you sing in church today will be greeted with the same type of polite embarrassment that you feel when you sing some of the 1970s praise songs today. The pop music heard in the churches today is liked by a certain generation. My kids laugh at the old folk songs that Boomers love. Gen Xers listen to hip-hop, which I don't understand or appreciate. Your parents didn't sing your songs, and you don't sing theirs. Fifteen years from now your kids or grandkids will sing different songs and will roll their eyes at yours. Truly good hymns transcend generations. Pop music does not. I really don't mind if my kids don't like Herman's Hermits or Paul Revere and the Raiders, two groups from the late 1960s. I don't listen to Britany Spears or Nine Inch Nails. But in the church we are "one in Christ." That means that neither your music nor mine should be featured. We must share a music. If we expect to be "one" in the church, we need to sing the same song. Generations of Christians have sung and will sing the classic Christian hymns.

The third, and most important, reason pop music is inappropriate for the Divine Service is because it is indelibly linked in our minds to something profane. We associate it with things of this world. Profane means "not connected with religion or religious matters."[32] Ball games are profane. Malls are profane. Profane isn't sinful or even bad. It's just not religious and is therefore not Christian. When a tune or a genre of music is associated in the mind of the hearers to a specific nonreligious context or purpose, then that context will be brought to mind when the tune is sung.

For example, when Hank, a wonderful Christian saint and member of my congregation, was dying, he requested that "The Star-spangled Banner" be sung at his funeral. He had served his country faithfully in the armed services during the Second World War and wanted to indicate his patriotism. I demurred, not wanting to say no but not wanting to conjure up mental pictures of rockets and bombs during a worship service. Hank was pretty adamant, and I did not know how to respond to him. One of his daughters was also concerned about her dying father's unusual request.

One day I stopped by to give Hank the Lord's Supper. It was about a month before he died, and his daughter Corinne was visiting her dad. After the private Divine Service, there in his living room, our conversation turned to the question of the national anthem at a funeral. "Dad," said Corinne, "do you really want people to think that they're at a ball game? No, Dad. People will just be confused. We are not going to allow it. And that's final." Relieved that the difficult no had been assumed by the family, I also observed how well Corinne understood music. If Francis Scott Key had composed that tune as accompaniment for a hymn, then the association it has with our country and ball games would have never been established. As it is, those connections are too strong.

Here's another example of tunes bringing with them certain baggage. My friend John understood the concept of association. One Sunday we sang the hymn "Glorious Things of You Are Spoken" to the tune *Austria*, as it is written in Lutheran Worship.[33] After church John came up to me and said, "If Grandpa had been here today, he would have gotten up and walked out of church at the singing of that tune." *Austria* is the tune for Adolph Hitler's nationalistic song, a song that had cast fear into the hearts of many a murdered Jew and not a few Allied soldiers. The associations with Hitler's terror were too strong.

Many advocates of the use of secular music in church cite Luther as their model, claiming he used tavern tunes for his hymns. Thankfully, these claims are not true. Luther never used tavern songs. He never said, "Why should the devil have all the good tunes?" as has been attributed to him. Luther, in fact, learned the hard way not to use popular tunes for hymns. When Luther wrote "From Heav'n Above," he initially "set it to a secular dance song" that was "closely associated with the Christmas wreath ceremony that was often held in a tavern."[34] Once he heard it sung he changed his mind. Wanting to avoid any association with the profane, he wrote a new tune and "indicated on the manuscript that this new melody was to be used in the Sunday service and with children."[35]

I learned the same lesson. One Lenten season I wrote a Maundy Thursday hymn to the tune of "Moonshadow" by Cat Stevens. Below is the hymn.

> Refrain:
>
> I'm gonna thank the Lord for Christ's body
> Christ's blood and His body.
> Come let us share together Christ's body
> Christ's blood and His body.
>
> Upon the night He was betrayed
> While friends as wayward sheep had strayed,

With sin and holy anger weighed,
Our Lord the Father's command obeyed.

Refrain

Oppressed with all our sin and stain
The Lamb of God is wracked with pain.
His life is lost, our life is gained.
Our Lord, the innocent Lamb, is slain.

Refrain

He is to death and hell a slave
His friends from death and hell to save,
Commits His body to the grave,
O Lord, how freely Your life You gave.

Refrain

The body's giv'n for all who grieve
Our sins and sorrows to relieve.
Come to the table and believe
O Lord, Your body we now receive.

Refrain

The blood He shed upon the tree
Has earned eternal life for me.
Come to the table thankfully.
O Lord, You poured out Your blood for me.

Refrain

My Jesus comes in bread and wine
Of hope and life the gracious sign
Forgiving sins both yours and mine.
O Lord, we come to the feast and dine.

Refrain

Christ's meal has made me strong and bold.
He's washed my sins and made me whole.
To praise His name will be my goal.
O Lord, I love You with all my soul.

Refrain

I even had the church sing this song during the service. Sing it to yourself. The tune reminds every Cat Stevens fan of the 1970s hit.

You cannot escape the association. Most of the members of my church were polite. "Very nice, Pastor." "Good words, Pastor." "Interesting idea, Pastor." Finally, Gordon exposed the emperor's lack of clothes: "That was atrocious. Don't do it again." He could have been a bit less rude, but he was correct. I did not try it again. In college I heard a group sing the Beatles' song "Help" in church by altering just a few of the words. Everyone who saw the movie *Sister Act* with Whoopi Goldberg will remember their song "My God" sung to the tune "My Girl." In both cases the audience could not escape the original association of the songs.

Tunes, when associated with the profane, are not neutral. Similarly, certain genres of music are inextricably wedded to the secular. I love the blues: Buddy Guy, Muddy Waters, Janis Joplin, B. B. King, and Stevie Ray Vaughn. Their lyrics of loss and loneliness lift my lowly spirits, and Eric Clapton's guitar gently "weeps" my cares away. But the blues are associated with smoke-filled, beer-smelling, honky-tonk drinking joints, and that connection will always exist. When I first heard the Peyton Brothers, a stark blues-singing contemporary Christian group, what did I think? I thought of losing my job or my girlfriend and coping by drowning my sorrows with the bottle—just like every other blues song suggests. Karre Ann Wakefield is a hard-rocking contemporary Christian artist who invites me to worship. I associate her sound with a dozen hard-rock groups who invite me to less wholesome fare. Even the very term "rock 'n' roll" is an implicit reference to sexual intimacy. Certain things are to be left at the front door of the church.

The music of the Divine Service must be different from the profane music we associate with ball games, drugs, booze, dancing, entertainment, and the entire gamut of human experience. It must not conjure up images of the profane. Blues, much as I love it, must be avoided. The same could be said for polka masses, hip-hop Matins services, and country-western Communion. These genres of music are associated too strongly with dancing, vulgarity, and guys with cowboy hats. Enjoy the music. But keep it out of church. Most of the praise songs that Lutherans use in church are a bit milder than the ones described above. If we become convinced that music is neutral, however, then there will be little within the music itself to prevent any and all types of music from invading the church.

When the music distracts from the message, whether because of audience association, a heavy beat, or any other feature, then that music is unsuitable for the Divine Service. Luther was concerned about the power of music. He knew that certain tunes simply moved the emotions to such a point that the attentive reasoning of the individual had been bypassed. St. Augustine, fifth-century churchman and, besides the biblical writers, probably the most influential theologian of the church for its first 1,000 years, saw the same. He loved music and knew that when it was attached to Christian words, it could have a wonderful pious effect on Christians. At the same time he knew that music had a way of "paralyzing my mind by the gratification of my senses which often leads it astray." St. Augustine struggled to "allow music some position of honor in my heart" but was also afraid at times that "I treat it with more honor than it deserves." Music, he knew, has a way of "forging ahead" of our understanding with the result that "I sometime sin in this way but am not aware of it until later."[36] Augustine both loved and feared music, always struggling to know exactly what place it should be given in his life and in the church. His caution to us: "Be extremely careful." Even apart from the lyrics of a song, the music is a powerful force.

Most pastors have seen this. On the eve of her death I visited Mollie in her home. Her body was ravaged by cancer, and she was looking forward to heaven. Mollie told me that she wanted to have the church sing "On Eagle's Wings" at her funeral. I told her that I didn't think I could reproduce the lyrics legally, which was true. She insisted that it be sung, "perhaps by a soloist." When I asked her to tell me what she liked about the words, her reply was telling, "I don't know the words, Pastor, except where it says, 'He will raise you up on eagle wings.' But the tune is so beautiful, and I want everyone to hear it at my funeral." Her answer spoke volumes. She was treating music with "more honor than it deserved."

Paul Stawn, a friend of mine, related the following story at a course he taught in Minneapolis in 2003.

> During the summer of 1996 while living in Marburg, Germany, I had the opportunity to attend a concert in Driehausen of the A cappella Choir of Concordia University, Seward, Nebraska. . . . They performed a program of standard Lutheran classical pieces

> with a few modern pieces of classical style thrown in for good measure. Needless to say the choir was warmly received, but then something strange happened. As an encore, the choir sang a spiritual—tenor in front as the lead, choir in back swaying back and forth, clapping in rhythm, and Germans eating it up. As the spiritual ended the room was filled with deafening applause and shouts at which point, the director of the choir turned around to the audience and with what can only be described as righteous anger, said firmly in halting German: "To God alone be the glory!!!" The director of the choir obviously was concerned that the audience was so taken with the music of the choir, that their thoughts had strayed from the object of the music of the choir, God Himself.[37]

Some music is so dominating that the lyrics, no matter how positive or pious, become purely secondary. The tunes are intended to tug at the heartstrings and overwhelm the hearer. Sadly, once overwhelmed, people are loathe to sacrifice the pop music and praise songs that have become the stock in trade of "contemporary worship services."

Musicologists do not always know or agree on the precise aspects of music that cause it to indulge our emotions, but they all seem to agree that it can have dramatic, unintentional, and even dangerous consequences. Donald Grout, "a giant of American musicology," asserts that "people have always generally agreed that some kinds of music, for one reason or another are simply not appropriate for use in church. Different churches, different communities, and different ages have fixed the boundary at different points, though the line is not always perfectly clear."[38] Different churches have different boundaries. The type of music that moves the body, stimulates the emotions, and paralyzes the mind would be quite suitable for any church seeking to elicit an emotional response to the message the people hear. Lutherans would avoid such music.

Preaching and Doctrine

When the service is viewed primarily as our praise and adoration of God, then the purpose of the sermon is to move the hearers to praise God. That means that the preacher must be persuasive and inspirational. He knows he has preached well if the singing is robust, the praying fervent, the praise boisterous, and the mood happy. Have you ever gone to church and gotten excited about something but weren't exactly certain what you had learned about Jesus? That preacher may have a wrong idea of the direction of the communication in the Divine Service.

If the service is primarily God speaking to us, then the purpose of the sermon is to teach the doctrine of salvation. That means that the preacher must be a student of the Bible himself and communicate the truths of God faithfully and clearly. He knows he has preached well if the people learn about Jesus. Have you ever gone to church and left without feeling particularly excited, but later you realized you learned something? That preacher may have the right idea of the direction of the communication in the Divine Service.

Preaching is teaching. Good sermons teach.

There is nothing headier for pastors than when people tell them what great sermons they preach. We just love it to no end. It's intoxicating. So susceptible to flattery are the Gospel's heralds that Satan certainly embellishes their God-given gifts so as to turn their hearts away from the rightful subject of their oratory. Aware of my own selfish frailties, one day I told my congregation, in a sermon no less, that the greatest compliment you could give a pastor for his homiletical skill was to say, "You spoke the Bible truth, preacher." That ended whatever meager flattery had been proffered for a time as the people commenced to comment on the truth-value of my sermons. Eager to elaborate, I subsequently told God's people that they could really praise me if they merely said, "Pastor, I learned something about Jesus today," as they left the church. So mini-reviews of the teaching moment ensued at the church door. It was a good thing.

Pastors need to measure their preaching by how much people learn about Jesus. So they must use the pulpit primarily to teach the doctrine of salvation.

Every pastor finds his job description in Paul's Pastoral Epistles: 1 and 2 Timothy and Titus. In these Letters written to pastors, Paul tells us the qualifications of ministers. If a pastor reads the lists in Titus 1 and 1 Timothy 3, he cannot help but be humbled. No one could seriously live up to these standards.

> Therefore an overseer must be above reproach, the husband of one wife, sober-minded, self-controlled, respectable, hospitable, able to teach, not a drunkard, not violent but gentle, not quarrelsome, not a lover of money. He must manage his own household well, with all dignity keeping his children submissive, for if someone does not know how to manage his own household, how will he care for God's church? He must not be a recent convert, or he may become puffed up with conceit and fall into the condemnation of the devil. Moreover, he must be well thought of by outsiders, so that he may not fall into disgrace, into a snare of the devil. (1 Timothy 3:2–7)

If you read the list carefully, you will also notice that Paul lists 13 or 14 words or phrases that describe the pastor's character. He uses words such as blameless, temperate, self-controlled, hospitable, and "not a drunkard." In the long list there is only one skill mentioned; "able to teach" (1 Timothy 3:2). The Bible never says that a pastor should be a good orator, counselor, fundraiser, team-player, liturgist, manager, vision-caster, conversationalist, or leader. He must be an able teacher. If he can't teach, then he can't do his job. If he can teach, he can do his job. And he must be evaluated on how clearly he teaches the Gospel of Christ. The reason you go to church is to learn about Jesus. The sermon is the primary way in which God, through the pastor, teaches you.

THE GOLDEN MOUTH

John Chrysostom, the bishop of Constantinople, was a powerful preacher in the fourth century. He was such an eloquent speaker that people would occasionally applaud his sermons. The local dignitaries, against whom he railed, so feared him that they exiled him twice for his rebuke of their wanton immorality. Chrysostom's very name is the Greek word for "golden mouth." Yet he bemoaned the fact that people evaluated preachers on their ability to entertain rather than on their ability to teach. Listen to the passion of one of the church's greatest speakers as he cautions against listening to the sermon for pleasure rather than learning:

> The majority of those who are under the preacher's charge are not minded to behave towards them as towards teachers, but disdaining the part of learning, they assume instead the attitude

> of those who sit and look on at the public games; and just as the multitude there is separated in parties, men are divided and become the partisans now of this teacher, now of that, listening to them with a view to favor or spite.[39]

Obviously, preachers must make the hearers interested. They must "preach well," as Chrysostom also said. But preachers must also cultivate "an indifference to praise," or they may be tempted to change the direction of the communication in the Divine Service.

When the preacher thinks that he must inspire or move the people, one of two bad things will happen. He might fail. Then he will believe that he must not be much of preacher and not much of a pastor. He will lose confidence in his ministry. And, most tragically, he will lose confidence in doctrine. Worse, he might succeed. Then he will believe that the essence of the ministry is to inspire. He will gather around himself a congregation that views the Divine Service as "public games" rather than the teaching of the Gospel.

Preachers teach.

The Liturgy

There are thousands of books on worship and the liturgy. Read them all and you will still be uninformed. The fundamental question regarding the liturgy is this: What is its purpose? The purpose of the liturgy is the same as the purpose of hymns and sermons. It is to teach or to show us Jesus. Of course, the liturgy moves, transforms, edifies, illuminates, and inspires God's people—but only if it teaches and shows Jesus.

What is the liturgy? The word comes from the Greek word *leiturgia*, which means "service." Actually, the word is a bit more precise. In ancient literature the wealthy had to render a liturgy or "a direct discharge of specific services to the body politic."[40] The liturgy was a kind of tax that benefited others. By New Testament times it had come to refer to the service that a priest would render in the temple with the people as beneficiaries. Zechariah was doing the liturgy (ceremonies) on behalf of the people when he saw the angel Gabriel (Luke 1:23). It is a word used to refer to helping others, not in a vague sense, but through the ceremonies of the church, such as the offering. Paul refers to the contribution or service (liturgy) of the Christians in Philippi (2:30 NIV) when he says that Epaphroditus almost died making up for the "help [literally 'liturgy'] you could not give me." The word often refers to ceremonies, such as in Hebrews 9:21 where it says that Jesus purified with His blood everything in the tabernacle used in its ceremonies (literally "liturgies"). The word *liturgy*, then, is a Bible word that refers to religious ceremonies and services rendered by God through His people to His people. A church that says that it is not a liturgical church is, in fact, saying that it is not a Bible church.

Just as there is an ambiguity connected to the words *service* and *worship*, so a similar ambiguity exists with the word *liturgy*. Are the ceremonies and services of the liturgy directed from us to God, or are these the services and ceremonies of God to us? The answer is really quite brilliant.

Liturgy is directed *from* God *to* us *through* us. In liturgy the people of God must be the beneficiaries. That's what the word means. God has given to us the gifts of His Gospel and Sacraments that are distributed through ceremonies or rituals. Again, that's what the word *liturgy* means. The ceremonies of the historic Christian liturgy are really little more than Bible verses. But they are verses that were not thrown together randomly as if some old monks were throwing darts at scrolls one day back in the Dark Ages. In fact, the liturgy was developed long before the Dark Ages.

The historic liturgy gradually evolved over the first five or six centuries of the church's life as certain scriptural passages were employed to teach the basics of the Gospel. What were these passages? Mark 10:47 is one. It's called the Kyrie Eleison, which is Latin for "Lord, have mercy." Another is Luke 2:14, called the Gloria in Excelsis, which means "Glory to God in the highest." A couple of passages form the Sanctus: Isaiah 6:3 and Matthew 21:9. Sanctus means "Holy." One more verse is John 1:29 where John says, "Behold, the Lamb of God, who takes away the sin of the world!" This verse is called the Agnus Dei, which means "Lamb of God" in Latin.

These Bible verses, along with the Nicene Creed, form the backbone of the liturgy of the Divine Service. They are called Ordinaries. Through these Bible verses, which have been translated into hundreds of languages and put to various musical settings over the years, the church has sung the Word of God's grace to herself for centuries. She has become the beneficiary of God's love through the ceremonies drawn from the Bible. She is blessed with the liturgy. In liturgy we take God's Word and return it to God by giving it to His people. That is liturgy.

In the liturgy, then, we are serving one another with the gifts of God. Whether the service is a song, a prayer, an offering, a canticle, a creed, or even a sermon, it is God serving us through the ceremonies performed by us. Every church has ceremonies. To the extent that these ceremonies are carriers of God's gifts, they are divine liturgy. But if the worship service is viewed as us serving God, then it ceases to be liturgy.

There is a rock 'n' roll song sung by U2, an Irish band, in which the lead singer starts preaching. He rebukes the television evangelists who bilk money from the poor and the widows. The last words of the brief but impassioned sermon are that the good Lord isn't short of cash. This is most certainly true. "The cattle on a thousand hills" are the Lord's, and He does not need our cash. God does not need our worship or our liturgy either. But He loves us and wants us to have worship and liturgy from Him. He wants to serve us the Gospel and the Sacraments. The Almighty does not come directly down from heaven and put cash in my checking account. Nor does He come down from heaven directly and bless me with grace. He uses means. The means He uses to get me cash are hard work and a job. The means He uses to bless me with grace are the Gospel and the Sacraments. These are contained within the liturgy of the church. They are bestowed by Christians upon Christians every time the church gathers around the Word of God to hear and speak. It's a beautiful system. It's the liturgy.

A MINISTRY OF RECONCILIATION

The worship service is more than a learning moment. It is a time in which we are forgiven of all our sins. The service teaches, but it does more than teach; it proclaims. In chapter 2 I showed that God has reconciled the world to Himself through the death of His Son. In chapter 3 I showed that God bestows His grace—He lavishes His good favor toward us—through the Word and through the Sacraments of Baptism and the Lord's Supper. The primary purpose of the worship service is for God to bestow upon us His forgiveness through the Gospel and the Sacraments. And our primary posture in the process is that we are passively receiving the blessings of God: forgiveness, life, and salvation. Because the liturgy is comprised of God's Word, it "bespeaks us righteous." In the Divine Service God proclaims the grace of Christ to us.

Sometimes experts on the liturgy or on worship will rightly say that the Divine Service has to have a balance of proclamation and teaching. Those features that impart information should be about equal with those that pronounce us righteous. When you try to distinguish teaching from proclamation in the service, you discover that the two occur at the same time. The Absolution is a perfect example. In the historic liturgy, such as Lutherans will find in *The Lutheran Hymnal* pages 16 and 48 or *Lutheran Worship* page 137, the people of the congregation confess their sins. God then absolves them through the words the pastor speaks: "Upon this your confession, I, by virtue of my office, as a called and ordained servant of the Word, announce the grace of God to all of you, and in the stead and by the command of my Lord Jesus Christ I forgive you all your sins in the name of the Father and of the Son and of the Holy Spirit."[41] Is this sentence proclamation or teaching? Christ and His forgiveness are proclaimed and pronounced nowhere more clearly and directly. The Absolution is sweetest proclamation. At the same time these words of the Absolution teach us doctrine. We are taught (1) that a man needs a call to proclaim Christ publicly in the church (I, by virtue of my office); (2) that God has given men the right to forgive sins (I forgive you all your sins); (3) that the announcement of grace entails the forgiveness of sins (announce the grace of God to all of you . . . and forgive your sins); (4) that forgiveness can only be given by and through Christ, who is our Savior (in the stead and by the command of my Lord Jesus Christ); (5) that forgiveness is bestowed upon those who are baptized (the name of the triune God recalls your Baptism); and (6) that God's grace is received by humble faith (upon this your confession). The church proclaims by teaching, and her doctrine proclaims Christ.

Every year I ask my seventh-grade catechism class why people skip church. Then we evaluate the answers. I try to show that most excuses are bad ones. Golfing, sleeping because you partied too late, brunch with the family, some sports event—these are mentioned every year. They each are an indication of our priorities. One year I got this question: "Pastor, we go to church to praise God. I know that I can't praise God very well while eating brunch or playing sports, but I can praise God other times during the week. I can sing hymns after dinner with my family. We can pray. And the Bible says 'Pray without ceasing.' Can we are pray, praise, and sing in church any better than we can at home? Why is it so wrong to skip church if you schedule your praise some other time?"

This was my answer: "You have the direction of communication wrong. You don't go to church primarily to pray, praise, and sing. You go to hear and learn and receive. Can you learn about God at home as well as from the pastor in the sermon? Can you get the Absolution at home? Can you get Communion at home?"

If the Divine Service is viewed primarily as our praising God, then you *can* do that just as well at home. In fact, once we have looked at the topic of vocation, you will see that we can serve God better in the world than in the church building. But if the service is understood as God giving us the forgiveness of sins, then you've got to be there. It is very possible that the low attendance at Sunday services seen in so many churches today is a reflection of how we define the service. If I am acting, then I can do it another time. If God is acting, I better be there.

WHO IS GOD TALKING TO?

The second question we need to answer about worship is: "Who is God talking to?" God has two messages. He speaks Law and He speaks Gospel. The Law is God's message of judgment against my sin. The Gospel is God's word of forgiveness in Christ. It is His gracious response to my guilt.

The Law differentiates. It distinguishes. It says that I have failed God and I have failed you, my brothers and sisters. You might have something against me as well. The Law forces me to measure myself against the standard of the Ten Commandments. And the Law has the nasty ability of making me better or worse than you.

The Gospel makes us all the same. When I am serving my neighbor, then I am different and unique. We will see that in the chapter on good works. But when I am being served by the Gospel, then I am just like every other sinner. I am equally as sinful as you. And I am equally as forgiven as you. We are the same. We are identical. Of course, my sins might be more profound, more heinous, and more creative than yours. But in Christ both you and I are bespoken righteous, clothed and covered in the righteousness of the heavenly Bridegroom, and cleansed in the blood of the Lamb. Sin, which makes us different and which divides, is forgiven. Good works, which distinguish and divide us, are irrelevant when it comes to salvation. So we are the same. The Divine Service reflects this.

If we are all the same, the services we attend should be pretty much the same. And if all the Christians in the world are the same, if the church is really "catholic," then the worship services throughout the world should be pretty close to the same. If the saints from age to age are the same, and they are, then the worship services from age to age reflect our oneness and sameness in Christ. To whom is God speaking in the Divine Service? He is speaking His eternal changeless word of forgiveness to His saints who are united into one holy people through that blessed Word.

But if worship is primarily me serving God, then my worship will be different than yours because we are different in our good works. Worship will then be far from uniform. If we get the direction of the communication right in worship, then we will also understand that uniformity in worship is good.

PAUL'S SOLUTION TO DIVISIONS

Paul addressed the problem of divisions in the church in his Letter to the Ephesians. In Ephesus, those who were Jewish felt that they were closer to God than the Gentiles were. The Jews had advanced in the Law and were better Christians, so they thought. What a divisive attitude. Christian people have always had the same temptations toward disunity. Today we hear the same. Some Christians are considered more advanced, more dynamic, more mature, more committed, more engaged, more vital, more something. How did God create unity according to the apostle Paul?

> For He Himself is our peace, who has made us both one and has broken down in His flesh the dividing wall of hostility by abolishing the law of commandments and ordinances, that He might

> create in Himself one new man in place of the two, so making peace, and might reconcile us both to God in one body through the cross, thereby killing the hostility. And He came and preached peace to you who were far off and peace to those who were near. For through Him we both have access in one Spirit to the Father. (Ephesians 2:14–18)

The Law makes us competitive and divisive. It makes us watch to see who is doing the best job. The Law is like a toy in the playroom of little kids. They all want it and fight over it. They make each other frustrated and angry because each wants to monopolize the toy. The Law also makes us angry and frustrated. What do parents do when kids fight over a certain toy? They take the toy away from all the kids. So when groups of people were fighting over the Law, God made peace by "abolishing the law of commandments and ordinances."

The Divine Service is God's word of peace. If it becomes an occasion for competition and fighting, then it should be taken away. The way to avoid such disunity and to reflect our unity in the Gospel is for the whole church to be uniform in her liturgy.

UNIFORMITY IN THE SERVICE: LUTHER'S EXAMPLE

"As far as possible we should observe the same rites and ceremonies, just as all Christians have the same baptism and the same sacrament [of the altar] and no one has received a special one of his own from God,"[42] said Luther. The reformer understood that we are all the same when it comes to the forgiveness of sins. So we need to receive God's gracious blessings through the same liturgy—the same service of God.

The liturgy both reflects and promotes our oneness.

When Luther published his German Mass in 1526, he was responding to a situation that had developed in the Lutheran churches. The old Roman order of service was an "abominable concoction drawn from everyone's sewer and cesspool"[43] because it contained the sacrifice of the Mass, the Eucharistic prayer, prayers to the saints, and all sorts of other bad things. All Lutherans understood the need for a service that was Gospel centered. Furthermore, there was no Divine Service in the language of the people because the Roman Church had insisted on doing the liturgy in Latin. If the liturgy was to teach Germans, it had to be chanted in the German language. Many before Luther had tried their hand at writing new liturgies. Luther, in the preface to his "Lutheran Order of Service," acknowledged as much.

> I would kindly and for God's sake request all those who see this order of service or desire to follow it: Do not make it a rigid law to bind or entangle anyone's conscience, but use it in Christian liberty. . . . For this is being published not as though we meant to lord it over anyone else, or to legislate for him, but because of the widespread demand for German masses and service and the general dissatisfaction and offense that has been caused by the variety of new masses, for everyone makes his own order of service. Some have the best intentions, but others have no more than an itch to produce something novel. . . . Where the people are perplexed and offended by these differences in liturgical usage, however, we are certainly bound to forgo our freedom and seek, if possible, to better rather than to offend them by what we do or leave undone.[44]

Luther would have been alarmed at what we see in many of the churches today—each pastor doing his own thing and producing his own service. In fact, he was alarmed when he saw exactly that type of diversity in his own day. He knew that the minute a law is made out of the proper dispensing of Word and Sacrament, then the purpose of Christ has been defeated. That is why elsewhere Luther asked for people voluntarily to "let each one surrender his own opinions and get together in a friendly way and come to a common decision about these external matters, so that there will be one uniform practice throughout your district instead of disorder—one thing being done here and another there."[45]

I have heard many pastors say that they write different worship services because Luther did. "If Luther did it, why can't we?" Luther wrote his German Mass precisely because everyone else was doing it poorly. When he saw what others produced, he complained because they "didn't sound polished or well done." The consistency between "text and notes, accent, melody, and manner of rendering" was lacking and "all of it becomes an imitation, in the manner of the apes."[46]

Luther hesitated in producing a Divine Service initially because he knew that to compose a decent liturgy requires more than a couple of afternoons in front of the word processor. When he finally did endeavor to write an order of service in the language of the people, he did so painstakingly and deliberately. Although he was an accomplished musician (he wrote the tunes to many of his own hymns, including "A Mighty Fortress"), Luther used up a couple of political favors and procured the services of the two leading musicians of the region as consultants in his composition of the chants for the service. Luther changed only those aspects of the service that were contrary to the Gospel. And he never intended a different liturgy to be used each Sunday. The result of his labors was a service so beautiful and lasting that it is sung to this very day. The immediate effect of his German Mass was that it provided a single order of service for the German people. In effect, the high quality of his German Mass pretty much ended the liturgical experimentation of his day.

THE TE DEUM: EVERYONE SINGING THE SAME THING

The thought that all believers are united and equal is taught nowhere better than in the *Te Deum Laudamus*. The Te Deum is a hymn written around A.D. 400 by a contemporary of St. Jerome. It has been used in the church for 1,600 years, primarily during the Matins service, a service sung in the morning.[47] Luther thought so highly of the Te Deum that he considered it equal with the creeds.[48]

In the Te Deum all Christians are united with those in heaven to sing the same song. Here is a list, drawn from the Te Deum, of those praising God:

- All the earth
- Angels
- The heavens and all the powers in them
- Cherubim and seraphim
- The hosts (Sabaoth)
- Heaven and earth
- The glorious company of the apostles
- The goodly fellowship of the prophets
- The noble army of martyrs
- The holy church throughout all the world

Every time you sing that song, you are promoting the belief that the church is united in our worship of Christ. Every Christian of all times and all places, the church catholic, sings the same song. The church on earth is united by the liturgy just as she is united by the creeds. And I have little doubt that we will sing the Te Deum also in heaven with the Lamb. We might as well learn it and practice it here on earth. And unlike so many pop praise songs, the Te Deum teaches the saving actions of Jesus.

LORD, LET YOUR SERVANT DEPART IN PEACE

In chapter 4 and again in this chapter there is a section explaining the Propers and the Ordinaries in the Divine Service. The Ordinaries are those parts of the service ordinarily done. They not only connect us with the church catholic, as was mentioned earlier, but also unite Christians throughout the world with each other today.

The unity of heaven and earth in the liturgy was shown to me in a touching way not long ago at the death of a friend. The Rev. Dr. Martin Taddey, longtime pastor of Trinity Lutheran Church in Palo Alto, California, was dying of cancer. It was a rather slow death, and Martin was given ample opportunity to reflect both upon Jesus' saving life and death and upon the Lord's coming again in glory.

I visited Martin exactly four days before he died. He was at his home, waiting for God's angels to come and take him home. His house was adjacent to the church, with only a narrow alley separating the two, and it seemed that you could almost reach out and touch the small house of God from Martin's bedroom window, which was always open. We talked theology for quite a while until he got tired. Then I prayed with him and for him and read to him from John 11: "I am the resurrection and the life." As I left, I couldn't resist asking my friend about the open bedroom window. The January weather, even in California, was a bit brisk. Martin replied, "I like to hear what's going on outside. I may never get there again." I smiled and said good-bye to Martin for the last time.

About a week later at the funeral I learned that Martin had entered glory during the Divine Service on Sunday morning. It seems that the windows to the church building had also been left open, at his request, and Martin had listened to the chanting of the Divine Service. He had celebrated Christmas by participating in the song of Bethlehem's angels, the Gloria in Excelsis. Palm Sunday was enjoyed during the singing of the Sanctus. Martin observed Maundy Thursday as the words of Christ's institution were chanted by the pastor in the church across the alley. Good Friday's Gospel was heard clearly as the congregation chanted the words of the Agnus Dei, "Lamb of God, you take away the sins of the world, have mercy on us." Finally, the time arrived for Martin, and the church he had served for more than 25 years, to celebrate Easter. The inspired words of the Nunc Dimitis filled the sanctuary: "Lord, now let your servant go in peace; your word has been fulfilled. My own eyes have seen the salvation which you have prepared." And at precisely that moment a small miracle occurred. Martin died.

For centuries the church has sung the Song of Simeon after taking Communion. We have sung in anticipation of leaving the Divine Service, having heard, seen, touched, and tasted the salvation of our God. And, like Simeon, we have sung the Nunc Dimitis, a song given by God, in anticipation of the heavenly feast God has prepared for His children. The angels in heaven, under orders from their Lord, brought Martin Taddey home exactly when the church on earth and saints in heaven were joined in their hymn of praise. Martin heard the entire song. It began on earth and was completed for him in heaven. At Martin's death the words of the Te Deum were also fulfilled. The holy church throughout all the world had joined the cherubim and seraphim. United by the Divine Service, heaven and earth were full of the majesty of God's glory. All of us, having sung Simeon's song on earth, will also sing it with Martin Taddey in heaven.

Why Uniformity Is Good

Uniformity in worship is desirable because it unites the saints on earth in a common Christian song. I know what is happening at St. John's Lutheran Church down the street on Sunday morning: The same thing that is happening in my church. When my people visit there, they can follow the order of service because they have learned it at my church. They, correctly, conclude that we are similar churches because our services are the same. They know that common doctrine is promoted by common practice. When I lived 7,000 miles away in France, I could follow the service pretty well. Of course, it was in French, but I could sing it with my "disgusting American accent" and know what I was saying because I knew it in English. I am united with Christians by a common order of service.

The importance of uniformity in worship is demonstrated by the following story of a young pastor.

> About three days after I was ordained, I was called in the middle of the night to a hospital I didn't know in a town I didn't know (Alton, IL), where a woman I didn't know had a rupturing gall bladder. I got lost on the back roads and in the fog, and when I arrived at the hospital at so late an hour I had a difficult time gaining entry. When I rushed to her room, she and her husband were gone. I dashed through several NO ADMITTANCE doors to the operating room, which was closed. I found her gurney parked in a small dark laundry alcove near the O. R. It was a dingy little space with nothing on the wall but a religious picture of St. Joseph and a fire extinguisher. My parishioner was disheveled and scared. Her husband said, "Thank God you are here," as if I had just landed in a jet to perform the surgery. She had large, frightened eyes, and I, three days into the ordained ministry, did not know what to say. All that came to me was the liturgy. So I said, "The Lord be with you." They replied, "And with thy spirit." I said, "Lift up your hearts," and they said, "We lift them up to the Lord." Suddenly what was disheveled and panicked regained its order, and the Lord was once again the Lord of the alcove. The presence of God among us was palpable.[49]

A conversation occurred between some people who, before that moment, had never met. It was both spontaneous and rehearsed. Meaningful, uplifting, and completely appropriate, it was the liturgy. The pastor spoke words of God and rendered a service to people in need. They were the beneficiaries. He was speaking for God.

What made this conversation possible? Everyone who has learned the liturgy knows. In countless churches for generation after generation in virtually every country of the world God's people say the same thing.

Doctrine, Practice, and the "New Measures"

Doctrine is reflected in practice. We believe in grace alone. Our worship reflects this. God does the giving in the Divine Service, and we do the receiving. He does the teaching, and we do the learning. All Christians of all times are identical when it comes to grace. So the service of God to Christians should be the same in various Christian places and throughout the ages.

When the historic liturgy of the Divine Service is changed, you should ask why. People change it for a reason, and usually the reason is doctrinal. Don't take my word for it. Learn a lesson from history. Today the Lutheran church is fighting over the form and nature of worship. It's not the first time in American history that Lutherans have been tempted to forsake the historic liturgy.

In the middle of the nineteenth century a huge controversy called the "New Measures" erupted among American Lutherans and dramatically illustrated the close relationship between doctrine and practice in the worship service. The New Measures were the worship customs that accompanied the religious revivals of American Evangelicalism.

The premier feature of the New Measures was "protracted meetings." People would travel by wagon, sometimes from more than a hundred miles, and set up camp in a designated area. Here they would worship. The services would usually last four to seven days. They would come and go as they needed to take care of the necessities of life. Dozens of sermons and preachers would be featured. While the services were never scheduled during the night hours, commonly evening meetings would extend into the morning's wee hours as the Spirit moved the people.[50]

Fiery, animated, "heart-searching" preaching was another characteristic of the revivals. The preachers would walk and run back and forth on the rostrum or stage. Occasionally the preacher would "lead a march around the grounds singing a magnificent song."[51] The preachers would not teach the catechism and certainly not preach doctrine for fear the people might think they were Anglican. Instead, they would implore the people to "Call upon the Lord while He is near," their exhortations interrupted by the encouraged responses of the congregation, "Tell it to 'em brother!" and "Amen, Glory to God, Glory Hallelujah."[52]

The revivals featured a couple of New Measures calculated to enable a person to respond favorably and immediately to the call of the preacher. One was the practice of "calling out sinners." This was an invitation for those who were not yet convinced that they were saved to come forward and receive a special prayer from the revival leader. It was the earliest form of what has become a staple of subsequent revivals, the altar call. The "mourner's bench" facilitated the desired conversions as well. Also called the "anxious seat," this was an area, usually in the front of the meeting tent, near the stage, where "seekers" could gather and receive special prayers and the attention of the leader. Usually the bench had piles of straw placed in front of it so people could lie down without significant bodily harm, which could have resulted from the shaking and jerking that often accompanied "conversions."[53]

Another new measure was the "anxious" or "inquiry" meeting. This was a meeting designed especially for the needs of those who were "inquiring" into salvation, often the spouses or children of other attendees. At any given revival there would be dozens of sermons and occasionally as many as three or four services at the same time. It was like a carnival where the crowds could choose the service that best met their needs or struck their fancy. At these "inquiry" services the preacher could preach more specifically to unbelievers in order to achieve conversions.[54]

These practices, while the stock and trade of many revivalists, were, understandably, controversial among Lutherans. Some advocated their use. Benjamin Kurtz (founding editor for 25 years of the *Lutheran Observer* and professor at Gettysburg Seminary for a third of a century), for example, adamantly defended the New Measures. He considered the anxious bench an "indispensable tool" in bringing people to Christ. "No other measure equally good could be substituted" for it, he claimed. And even "the Catechism, highly as we prize it, can never supersede the anxious bench."[55] Kurtz also tenaciously promoted the protracted meetings and the fiery new style of preaching that adorned them. People needed to hear in "a simple, direct and pointed manner with the view of promoting immediate conviction and conversion."[56]

Kurtz deflected criticism with the same relentless conviction with which he promoted the revivalist techniques. He was accused of violating the church's creeds and confessions. His response was that the creeds and confessions of the church "have been a prolific source of strife and persecution in the Christian church and are likely so to be as long as they remain in force. . . . It is impossible for all to think alike; nor is it important that they should."[57] Kurtz was no big fan of doctrinal statements or doctrinal unity. When accused of sacrificing the historic liturgy on the altar of American expedience, Kurtz wrote an article entitled "Experiential (not ritual) Religion, the One Thing Needful." In it he advocated experimenting with the liturgy "because it would increase membership and give power to families and congregations."[58] Kurtz was no big fan of the liturgy.

What do the Scriptures say of all these New Measures? It never says in the Bible that you cannot have a worship service in a tent that lasts for a week. And God's Word is silent as to whether or not Peter ran back and forth on the stage on Pentecost. We all know that there is an appeal at the end of that first Christian sermon to repent and be baptized. So who can fault the revivalist preachers for telling the people to believe? Praying for the conversion of sinners is certainly a praiseworthy thing. Who could criticize that? As for the mourner's bench, where does it say in the Bible that people can't sit in the front of church on a special bench, even laden with straw, and pray for the blessings of God? Where does it say in the Bible that the church can't have a special service for inquirers? In 1 Corinthians Paul even talks about the uninitiated, so clearly there is a place for them in church. I suppose when you look at these New Measures, in and of themselves, outside of a context, you could not say absolutely that they were wrong. Maybe Kurtz was right?

Karl Wyneken and C. F. W. Walther, both ultimately from the Missouri Synod, did not think so. Both were critical of Kurtz and the revivalist worship changes he encouraged. Wyneken, a tireless missionary pastor from Indiana, expressed "horror at the demonical power" of the revival techniques and suggested the use of liturgy instead.[59] Walther dismissed the techniques as sectarian and Methodistic. But were these practices, in and of themselves, wrong?

A NEW AUGSBURG CONFESSION?

In 1855 something happened with American Lutheranism that should for all times show that practice and doctrine always walk together. If you change your practice, you will change your doctrine. If you change your doctrine, you will change your practice. In 1855 Benjamin Kurtz and a couple of his colleagues, most notably a man named Samuel S. Schmucker, produced "The American Recension of the Augsburg Confession." The Augsburg Confession is the document more than any other that, for Lutherans, has defined what it means to be a Christian. Every true Lutheran pastor and church has sworn to uphold this confession. In The Lutheran Church—Missouri Synod, if you don't agree with the Unaltered Augsburg Confession, you cannot be part of the church. You do not mess with the Augsburg Confession. But on the 325th anniversary of the Augsburg Confession, those men who favored the New Measures presumed to improve on that document. They felt that the confession was, not to put too fine a point on it, flat out wrong.

The Augsburg Confession made five specific errors, claimed Schmucker in the "Recension." First, Schmucker and Kurtz said it was wrong when it approved the ceremonies connected with the Roman Catholic Mass. Schmucker and Kurtz felt that the liturgical ceremonies encouraged in the Augsburg Confession were bad. Second, they believed the confession was wrong when it encouraged and approved the practice of private confession and absolution. Yes, Lutherans have always encouraged Christians to confess their sins to their pastors and to "receive absolution, that is, forgiveness, from the pastor as from God Himself, not doubting, but firmly believing that by it our sins are forgiven before God in heaven,"[60] as it says in the Small Catechism. Kurtz and Schmucker denied the Absolution of the pastor. Third, they claimed the Augsburg Confession was wrong when it did not say that you had to worship God on Sunday. Lutherans, it seems, have always felt that you could go to church any day of the week. But Kurtz and Schmucker wanted to make a law that you had to have services on Sunday. Christ had done away with such laws (Colossians 2:16). Fourth, they insisted the Augsburg Confession was wrong in teaching that Baptism actually brought a person to faith. Lutherans have always believed in baptismal regeneration. If asked, any Lutheran pastor worth his salt could explain and defend baptismal regeneration in his sleep. Fifth, they maintained the Augsburg Confession was wrong when it taught that the body and blood of our Lord Jesus Christ were present in the bread and wine of the Lord's Supper.[61] Schmucker, a decade earlier, had labeled Luther's view of Christ's bodily presence as "peculiar" and claimed that it had been "abandoned long ago by the great majority of our preachers."[62]

Whew!

This was a far worse cry, it would seem, than protracted meetings, mourner's benches, or fiery preachers. What had happened?

The Lutherans who promoted the revival techniques did so because they wanted to be part of a larger group of evangelical Protestants who were also promoting the revivals. They wanted to be just one big, happy, ecumenical church. Doctrinal or "denominational loyalties" were not important to them. So they wanted to rid the Lutheran church of anything that would not gain the approval of their Methodistic neighbors. Charles Arand says that Schmucker's style of Lutheranism "was characterized by a revivalistic theology, the right of individual judgment in biblical interpretation, indifference toward doctrine, and hopes of rapprochement with an amalgamated American Protestantism."[63] Translation: We want to ignore our differences and get back together with all the Congregationalists, Presbyterians, Calvinists, and Baptists because we are all living together here in the United States. These Lutherans were more interested in being American than in being Lutheran. They did not believe you could be both, so they opted for American, even naming their particular style of Lutheranism "American Lutheranism." A competitive desire against other Americans made them crave the growth of their neighboring Evangelical churches.

Most important, their practice changed their doctrine. Style wrecked substance. Look at the five "corrections" of the Augsburg Confession again.

The first is a disapproval of the liturgy. "Mourner's benches" are for all intents and purposes an altar call. We'll look at this more fully in chapter 10. The altar call places the burden of responsibility for the new birth upon the sinner. The historic Lutheran liturgy stresses the Sacrament of the Altar, which is God's action toward us. Which is it? Is church the place where we act to get God on our side or is it the place where God acts on our behalf? You can't have it both ways. No church can have a mourner's bench and still use the liturgy. Either grace is bestowed through my answering the altar call or it is bestowed through the Word and Sacrament in the liturgy. Altar calls and liturgies cannot peacefully coexist.

The second "correction" is a rejection of Confession and Absolution. The revivalists preferred fiery, exhortational preaching calculated to elicit a decision. The way you got forgiveness in this system was to choose. So the preacher used every persuasive technique to get you to make the right choice. Lutherans believe that forgiveness does not come from a choice. Rather, God bestows it in Absolution through the pastor. Either grace is imparted by my decision in response to the preacher or it is imparted by the absolution of Christ spoken by my pastor. Preaching for a decision cannot peacefully coexist with pastoral absolution.

The third "correction" was really the imposition of a law that Christ had abolished. The revivalists wanted to insist that you worship on Sunday. The Lutherans said that we are free. You can't have it both ways. Either you are free or you are bound. The freedom we have in Christ cannot peacefully coexist with the legalistic imposition of a day of worship.

The fourth "correction" is a rejection of baptismal regeneration. You can't have "inquirer" services where non-Christians seek the Lord and still believe that God seeks us in Baptism. "Seeker services" and baptismal regeneration cannot peacefully coexist.

The fifth "correction" of the Augsburg Confession was a rejection of faith in the presence of Christ's body and blood in the Sacrament. The revivalists determined that God was present when many people were "called out in prayer." They judged by what they saw in the people. Lutherans believe that Jesus is present with His body and blood in the Sacrament of the Altar. They judge by what God says in His Word. You can't have it both ways. Either you measure grace by its observable effects or you measure it by the Word and Sacrament. Lutherans have always believed that Jesus' body and blood are present in the Holy Meal whether people get excited about it or not. Inferring the presence of Christ by the excited response of people cannot peacefully coexist with a confidence in the true presence of Christ's body and blood in the Sacrament.

Observe also that each of the New Measures focused away from the objective means of grace. Each strove to make you look at yourself, your choice, your experience, or your actions. The early Missouri Lutherans craved objective theology and objective grace.

Those New Measures were un-Lutheran practices. They were simply opposed to the Gospel. They were wrong. When Lutherans embraced them, they did so because they did not fully understand and value the Gospel. And when embraced, these New Measures hastened the decline of faith in the Gospel. Inevitably, practice affected doctrine. It always does. Bad practice led to a "recension" of the Augsburg Confession. Thankfully, God preserved the Lutheran witness in the United States, at least for a while. He did so through a heroic, brilliant, and tireless pastor named Charles Porterfield Krauth. (More on him later.)

Why would Lutherans sacrifice their doctrine? It was because their practice had changed. And why would their practice change? It changed because they wanted to be acceptable to American audiences. Read on.

Conclusion

In the Divine Service God is speaking. The direction of the communication is from God to us. While we return our thanks and praise to God, we must always remember that God serves us in the Divine Service. And God serves all of us. As we unite in Christ our differences disappear. The liturgy of God's service should reflect our unity. Uniformity in worship is a desirable thing for the church both as to time and to place. The practices of the church in her worship should reflect both the direction of the communication and the desire for uniformity. The Divine Service belongs to the church. It guides her to the true doctrine of grace. It is like the staff of a shepherd that guides the flock to the warmth of the fire. Worship is "The Church's Staff."

When the first Missouri Lutherans discovered that both the direction and the uniformity of the Divine Service were discarded by certain nineteenth-century American Lutherans, they knew that doctrinal problems were at the root of the change in practice. They knew that doctrine and practice go hand in hand.

STUDY QUESTIONS

1. The direction of communication in the Divine Service is primarily from God to us. What should be the central message and purpose of the worship service?
2. What does true praise of God entail?
3. What makes pop music inappropriate for use in the worship service?
4. What is the purpose of the sermon?
5. What is the purpose of the liturgy?
6. As used by the church, to what does the word *liturgy* refer?
7. In Holy Absolution, what is proclaimed? What is taught?
8. Why are prayers, praise, and singing in church better than doing them at home? Why is it so wrong to skip church if you schedule your praise some other time?
9. How does the Gospel unify all believers?

DISCUSSION QUESTIONS

1. Discuss the role of hymns in the worship service.
2. Discuss this statement: Praise services attract the unchurched. They can relate more to the simple praise songs. Hymns from the hymnal are too difficult to sing.
3. Discuss the purpose of music in the Divine Service. How does pop music detract from this purpose?
4. All around us, we hear those who abhor the differences among Christians and call for unity. The author suggests that unity can be found in the catholic liturgy. Discuss the implications of this argument and whether or not you think it practical in light of the truth that the liturgy teaches.

6

The Christian's Staff

GOOD WORKS

It was 3 A.M. The faintest of sounds was slowly dragging me from a deep and dream-filled sleep. Was it the babbling brook in my dream? Were nighttime visions merging with the cares of this world? I strained to hear. It assumed a shriller tone, like the raven in my dream overlooking the stream from the tree above. The dream was so nice and the sleep so needed. I struggled against the impending reality of wakefulness. Yet I could feel the happy rest slipping away. As consciousness encroached inexorably upon my carefree slumber the faint sound took on an urgent tone. Slowly, I turned and opened my eyes to peer through the crusted sleep into the unwelcome message of the alarm clock. What was that annoying noise? Then I remembered. I was a new dad. Our newborn son was in the other room, and it was time for his morning feeding. Happily, I realized that I was equipped with neither the physical accoutrements nor the maternal instincts to nurse the famished offspring, especially at such an ungodly hour. I nudged my wife. "He's awake."

Her response came so fast and so pointedly that I had to assume she'd been rehearsing it. "What's your point?"

Ever patient in such circumstances, I said, "He's hungry. I can't feed him. I have no breasts." The anatomical argument had a compelling force to it.

Again, it was as if she had thought of all this. "Well, he also has a dirty diaper, and you don't need breasts for that." Touché. She'd thrown back that anatomical thing in my face.

What should I say next? I was fully awake by now, and the realization of the conversation's import had occurred to me like a piano falling on my head from a second-story window. This was one of those "role negotiations" that psychologists talk about. If I got up now to change the baby's diapers, I would set a precedent that could actually apply for the next decade, depending on how many more kids we had. But I did not know how to answer. I have to admit that I felt a little taken advantage of. This is the type of thing that a couple should really discuss ahead of time. You've heard of the irresistible force and the immovable object. This was the irresistible force meeting the movable object. I got up.

God had blessed me with some brothers and sisters who were younger than I, so I did not lack for diaper changing experience. However, the 3 A.M. thing was new for me and, I confess, a bit troubling. It was so inconvenient as to appear suspicious. A couple of hours earlier and it would be late at night. A couple of hours later and it would be early in the morning. But 3 A.M. was perfectly planned so as to achieve the greatest discomfort. I staggered into the bedroom and looked at my precious little one. He sensed my presence and stopped his fussing. I picked him up and started to change his diaper.

Here's something for you new parents: When kids are both hungry and messed, your priorities are different than theirs. They want to eat really badly. And they don't especially care that their pants are messed. It's usually the other way around for adults. We put ourselves in their place and conclude that the diaper is the primary order of business. The kids don't agree and have a tendency to be impatient when you foist your priorities on them. Don't give in. If you feed them, they will eat and go right back to sleep. Then if you try to change them, they will wake up again and you won't be able to get them back to sleep with food. These are things you learn when you have had some experience.

At any rate, I placed my son on the changer. I took off the old diaper, scrubbed him down, and put the new one under him. Then I made a mistake. I took a couple of seconds to scratch some of the now cakey sleep from my eyes. I was fast at my job and efficient. But the kid was faster. Before I was able to attach the new diaper, I felt some fluid warming my arms and shoulder. Then I saw the narrow stream powerfully aimed at my face. I ducked. Too late. So I recommenced the process, careful this time not to give my opponent another such opening. Clean and neat, I presented the little imp to his mother for feeding. Of course, she got to snuggle and nestle him and tell him what a good boy he was. It all seemed a bit unfair.

I'm not looking for pity. Everyone who has changed a baby in the middle of the night has the same stories. I'm not looking for praise. Although a little thanks now and then would have been nice. I'm not looking for any remuneration. I was the head of the house. Who was going to pay me?

So why do I tell this story? Because it teaches everything you need to know about good works.

- Good works require action.
- Good works are done according to our vocation.
- God does not need our good works.
- Good works help other people.
- Good works are done whether we want to do them or not.
- Good works done in faith are valued by Jesus Christ.

Good Works Require Action

If we keep our doctrine of salvation straight, then our doctrine and practice of good works will be straight as well. Faith is passive when it comes to salvation. Faith is like the bag of the trick-or-treater. It is like catching the ball in the outfield. It simply receives. It gets. "Luther says that man behaves in a purely passive way in his conversion (that is, that man does not do anything toward it and that man only suffers that which God works in him)."[1]

But faith always acts. Most Lutherans learn a little saying in catechism class, "We're saved by faith alone, but faith is never alone." Faith always does things. Faith is always active. Luther is worth quoting at length.

> O, it is a living, busy, active, mighty thing, this faith. It is impossible for it not to be doing good works incessantly. It does not ask whether good works are to be done, but before the question is asked, it has already done them, and is constantly doing them. Whoever does not do such works, however, is an unbeliever, who gropes and looks around for faith and good works, but

> knows neither what faith is nor what good works are. Yet such a person talks and talks, with many words, about faith and good works. Faith is a living, daring confidence in God's grace, so sure and certain that the believer would stake life itself on it a thousand times. This knowledge of and confidence in God's grace makes people glad and bold and happy in dealing with God and with all creatures. And this is the work which the Holy Spirit performs in faith. Because of it, without compulsion, a person is ready and glad to do good to everyone, to serve everyone, to suffer everything, out of love and praise to God, who has shown this grace. Thus, it is impossible to separate works from faith, quite as impossible as to separate heat and light from fire.[2]

Good works are not an option. Nor are they, strictly speaking, a requirement. We do them spontaneously out of faith. Someone needs to make a bumper sticker that says "Good works happen." You don't have to demand them any more than you demand the sun to shine or the tide to rise. It is the nature of faith to produce good works. Yet we are saved without them.

PASSIVE AND ACTIVE FAITH

You have one faith, not two faiths. Faith is both passive and active. Christians need to be able to tell the difference between faith as it is passive and faith as it is active.

Passive Faith	**Active Faith**
Informed by the Gospel	Informed by the Law
Directed toward God	Directed toward my neighbor
Makes me identical to others	Makes me different from others
I have heaven in view	I have this world in view
Motivated by the Gospel	Motivated by the Gospel

Let's analyze these contrasting statements. I mentioned in chapter 2 the importance of knowing the difference between the Law and the Gospel. The Law tells us what to do and condemns because we don't do it. The Gospel tells what God has done for us in Christ and "bespeaks us righteous" in Him. When we talk about good works, the distinction between Law and Gospel is especially vital. What is faith based on? It is based on the Gospel as far as salvation is concerned. It tells me what I receive. By the Gospel I am directed toward God and His Son. Distinctions do not exist in the Gospel for "there is neither Jew nor Greek, there is neither slave nor free, there is neither male nor female, for you are all one in Christ Jesus" (Galatians 3:28). The Gospel tells me that we are equally redeemed from the Law and equally righteous before God through the death of Christ. Jesus is equally our Lord and our God. We are equally "bespoken" righteous. Finally, the Gospel promises both a heavenly rest and gives it in Christ. Through all this we are passively receiving from God.

I am not, however, informed how to serve my neighbor by the Gospel. I won't get that done with passive faith. Faith, when it is active, is directed toward my neighbor. When my faith is active, I am not thinking of heaven. I'm thinking of others and their needs. I'm aware of how my love is needed throughout the world. In my activities my faith is different than yours, just as it is identical to yours in what it receives. I have different abilities, gifts, inclinations, and especially a different station in life than you. So the actions of my faith will be different than the actions of your faith.

Passive faith and active faith must be distinguished, even though they can never be separated. You still have only one faith. Passive faith is foundational in two ways. First, you cannot have active faith without passive faith. Try to throw a ball before you catch it. Without asserting passive faith, you cannot even talk about active faith. But you can talk about passive faith without even thinking about good works. Paul talks about passive faith in Romans 3–6. In those chapters he says nothing about active faith. He never even uses an imperative (tells us something to do) until Romans 6:11. Christian living is presented in the later chapters of his Letter and then only because he has already discussed passive faith. Second, faith is fed by God through the Gospel. You do not make faith strong by the Law. In fact, God does not really feed active faith. He feeds passive faith, and that faith becomes active. Lots of people believe that you can strengthen your faith by doing good works. That would make active faith foundational. No, you feed active faith by forcing it to stop, rest, do nothing, and be completely passive. God is then able to feed us with His Word and Sacraments.

Passive faith lives in Christ and receives the Divine Service of Christ. Active faith lives for others and actively serves them. For six days our faith is active. We differ from one another as we live and act for one another with a view to serving one another. The world makes its claims upon us all, and within this world, under its laws, we function for one another. On the seventh day, actually the first day, we rest. We become passive. We are all the same. We think of heaven. Worship should always reflect the unity and sameness we have in Christ—never our diversity. Living for one another reflects the diversity among us—not our unity. But on the day of worship, "one does not stand *in relatione*, or meet with another human being, as one does in his vocation. . . . Before God not only does station vanish, but also every work stands as sinful and worthless."[3] When I was awakened by my son who stood in need of a diaper change, that was no time for my faith to be passive. I could have sat in bed all night thanking God for eternal life, and the poor kid would have died of starvation and diaper rash. His needs required my faith to be active.

GOOD WORKS ACCORDING TO VOCATION

I taught a Bible class on vocation and I kept misspelling the word as *vacation*, with an *a*. Because the spell check did not catch the error, some of the people got the impression that I was telling them how to behave during the holidays. The truth is that vocation never takes a holiday.

The word *vocation* is based on the Latin word for "call." So we use the word *Invocation* when we call upon the Lord. In the Bible the word *call* can have more than one referent. It can refer to God's invitation to believe: "For many are called, but few are chosen" (Matthew 22:14). Sometimes it is used when God brings you to faith. "And those whom He predestined He also called, and those whom He called He also justified, and those whom He justified He also glorified" (Romans 8:30). Sometimes the word more specifically speaks of the call of a man into the ministry. "Paul, a servant of Christ Jesus, called to be an apostle, set apart for the gospel of God" (Romans 1:1). Sometimes God uses the word to teach us of the role in life that He, through His providence, has placed upon you: "Only let each person lead the life that the Lord has assigned to him, and to which God has called him. This is my rule in all the churches" (1 Corinthians 7:17). It is this last meaning of "call" or vocation that we will discuss here.

We are called in three estates. Vocation is our place in our family: mother, father, daughter, son, brother, sister. We are called, second, to a vocation in the world or society: farmer, craftsperson, doctor, accountant, advertising agent, student, trash collector, cabbie, cop. The church is the third area in which we have a vocation: pastor, hearer, prayer, giver, singer. All these stations are jobs assigned by God. He assigns them by guiding your life, by giving you the blessings of this life, by giving you skills and abilities, and by the assignments that others in authority place upon you.

Some things that we do are done by all Christians. Forgiveness is given and received by all. All are faithful to spouses, respectful to parents, and helpful to neighbors. We all pray and are content with the things God has given us. We all confess the faith. These things are not uniquely assigned to someone in a specific vocation. On the other hand, many of our activities are dictated by vocation.

BASIC PRINCIPLES OF CHRISTIAN VOCATION

The Bible teaching of vocation is complex. You can't just develop a ten-point checklist for Christian vocation and expect everyone to feel smug and confident when every task has been checked off. Vocation is more like a cake recipe. All the ingredients blend together and the resultant whole is far greater than the parts.

VOCATION PRINCIPLE ONE: DIFFERENCE

The things I do in my vocation are different from the things you do. I got up in the middle of the night to change diapers because my vocation as father required it of me. You may not change diapers if it's not your vocation. I get up in the pulpit on Sunday mornings to preach. That is what my vocation as pastor requires of me. If you are not a pastor, you won't do that because it's not your vocation. We are different. If you are an accountant, you may balance someone's checkbook. I don't do that. We have different vocations. You may study for tests, diagnose injuries, or check the level of transmission fluid in someone's car. I don't do those things. If I refuse to change my son's diapers, I am doing a great wrong. If I refuse to preach or if I preach in a haphazard manner, I am sinning against God. That diaper needs changing, and I am the one whose vocation requires it of me. The Gospel needs preaching, and God entrusted me with the job when He called me into the vocation of pastor. But you are not doing wrong if you don't change diapers or preach. It's not your vocation.

The Bible celebrates our differences. The sections of Scripture that teach vocation most clearly are lists of the duties of the various stations in life. Ephesians 5:22–6:9, Colossians 3:18–4:1, and 1 Peter 2:13–3:7 show that husbands are different than wives, masters are different than servants, and children are different than parents. We have different duties according to our vocation. Luther's Small Catechism has an entire section called "The Table of Duties." It is simply a list of Bible passages in which the duties of various vocations are listed: pastors, hearers, government subjects, husbands, wives, parents, children, servants, masters, young persons, and widows. These diverse stations require varied duties. When the Scriptures discuss spiritual gifts, they show that people are different. First Corinthians 12 and Romans 12 indicate that in the church, as in the world or the home, we have different duties according to our different vocations. Christians even differ in their sins and in their confession of them. When we kneel before God, we are told to "consider your station."

The different duties of the various vocations at times force responsibilities on people that are not to be done by others. According to the Fifth Commandment I am not allowed to kill other people, but soldiers are called upon to kill. God says that vengeance belongs to Him (Nahum 1:2), so I am not allowed to punish criminals, yet God entrusts rulers to carry out punishment against evildoers (Romans 13:4). We are to turn the other cheek, yet fathers are not to spare the rod upon their sons (Proverbs 13:24). God tells us not to judge, yet Paul claims that he has "already pronounced judgment" against a sinner (1 Corinthians 5:1–3). So you and I have different sets of responsibilities, each according to our vocation.

There are at least four ways that we can apply this lesson to church practice. First, because we are different, we should be slow to judge. I can say that you sin if you swear or commit adultery. You can point out my sins to me if I steal or gossip. But much of what I do in my vocation may not be completely understood by others. In turn, I may not comprehend your vocation. Therefore, I should be slow to criticize. If you fall asleep in church, it could be that your vocation required you to get up four times in the night with a sick child. If you can't make bell choir rehearsal, it could be that your vocation required you to visit your stepchildren. When you skip the elders' meetings during March and April, it could be that you are an accountant and you are preparing other people's taxes. Love bears all things. Pastors and church workers should be reluctant to chide or scold anyone who does not get involved in the work of the church. Everyone has their vocation, and all are sacred to God.

A second specific application of the "difference principle" should be made when it comes to the job of the pastor. The Augsburg Confession says, "No one should teach publicly in the church or administer the sacraments unless properly called."[4] Just as you must be called as a father to care for your kid in the middle of the night or called as an accountant to audit someone's books, so you must be called by God into the ministry if you want to preach His Word. Have you ever been in a grocery store and seen a parent disciplining a kid in a manner with which you disagree? You may frown or whisper something to your spouse, but you bite your tongue. You are not called to raise someone else's kid. You are not the mother. You are not the child. You better stay out of it. So it is with the teaching and preaching of the Word and the administration of the Sacraments. If you are not the pastor, you are not called to do these things. Pray for your pastor and encourage him. Rebuke him if he clearly sins. But let him do his job and be patient. Especially, pray that God sends laborers into the harvest.

Third, the Gospel does not erase the differences between us in our vocation. Paul boldly claims that through Baptism "there is neither Jew nor Greek, there is neither slave nor free, there is neither male nor female, for you are all one in Christ Jesus" (Galatians 3:28). As we are directed to God and heaven, distinctions of sex, race, and vocation are wiped out. But as we live for our neighbor they remain. That's why Paul can say there is no difference between the sexes in Baptism where we passively receive salvation. In actively living for others, however, the huge differences between men and women remain. When God forgives us and "bespeaks us righteous" by the Gospel, He isn't telling women to act like men or parents to act like children. Today many pastors and churches advocate female pastors. We will say more about this topic in chapter 9. For now we need to know that the Bible distinguishes the sexes in its discussions of "speaking in the church," "teaching men," and "exercising authority over men" in the church (1 Timothy 2:11–14, 1 Corinthians 14:34–38). Those who blithely cite Galatians 3 as a justification for female pastors are confusing passive faith and active faith. We are identical as we receive Christ. As we live for Christ we are different. The activity of the pastor is to teach. Pastors do not get to heaven by their actions—their act of teaching. They get to heaven through faith in Jesus, just like everyone else. When it is said that the "Gospel entitles women to be pastors," then the Gospel is changed from something passively received into something that is actively done. Such an argument denies the Gospel. The question of female pastors is not trivial or indifferent. It touches the Gospel itself. When the church changes her practice to allow for women to be ordained or to carry out the duties of the pastor's vocation, then the church erodes the Gospel.

Fourth, knowing differences helps me know Jesus. Even Jesus had a unique vocation. He was called to bear the sins of the world upon His shoulders, to obey God's will perfectly in our place, and to suffer shame upon the cross as a perfect substitute for you and me. God, wisely, has not placed such a vocation upon me. Most Christians have seen those little bracelets or rings with the letters WWJD crafted upon them, which stands for "What would Jesus do?" This slogan is well intended. It asks us to use Jesus as our example when confronting various decisions in life. Unfortunately, WWJD makes Jesus into a model instead of a Savior. It ignores the Bible teaching of vocation by ignoring the unique vocation of Jesus. Suppose I want to change jobs because my skills are not being used in my current job. I ask, "What would Jesus do?" The answer is that Jesus was not allowed to change vocations. Even when He begged God in the garden, His vocation was unchangeable. He had to fulfill the Law, the Scriptures, and my atonement. I don't do those things. Suppose your son or daughter comes to you and asks if he or she should get married. What would Jesus do? He did not marry and could not have done so. Does that mean that we can't? We are not called to go immediately into the wilderness upon our Baptism. Jesus was. Suppose you are invited to a wedding reception and they have run out of wine. What would Jesus do? Don't invite me to your wedding if you expect me to do what Jesus did. We need to see Jesus as fundamentally and wonderfully different from other people. He was like us in every way as far as His nature was concerned, but His vocation is worlds apart from mine. I should emulate Jesus as He sets an example of compassion and love. And I should be like Him as a pastor, tirelessly and caringly reaching out to others. But Jesus as the Savior of the world had a unique vocation. WWJD bracelets, I am afraid, are not a good idea.

VOCATION PRINCIPLE TWO: FREEDOM

My vocation liberates me. The responsibilities of any given station in life are not always specifically mentioned in the Bible. That makes us free. The Bible does not tell me how to be an accountant except for the basic mandate to be fair and just. God does not tell police officers how to curb crime except to tell them not to extort money and not to accuse anyone falsely (Luke 3:14). God never specifies which parent is to change the messy diaper. Parents work it out in love. Even pastors, whose vocational responsibilities are spelled out with far more detail than most in the Scriptures, have great freedom. How does a Christian know how to behave in his or her vocation when the Holy Bible says so little about it? Luther tells us that each vocation has its own Bible:

> If you are a manual laborer, you find that the Bible has been put into your workshop, into your hand, into your heart. It teaches and preaches how you should treat your neighbor. Just look at your tools—at your needle or thimble, your beer barrel, your goods, your scales or yardstick or measure—and you will read this statement inscribed on them. Everywhere you look, it stares at you. Nothing that you handle every day is so tiny that it does not continually tell you this, if you will only listen. Indeed, there is no shortage of preaching. You have as many preachers as you have transactions, goods, tools, and other equipment in your house and home. All this is continually crying out to you: "Friend, use me in your relations with your neighbor just as you

would want your neighbor to use his property in his relations with you."[5]

This may be frustrating. We want to know exactly how to do our job. But it is also liberating. There are many right ways to carry out your vocation. Just act in love and do what the job requires. When asked, "What good works should you do for your neighbor," Luther responded, "They cannot be named."[6]

How does our vocational freedom affect church practice? In a couple of ways. Every so often someone comes into my office and asks my advice on a matter. Should I marry this guy? Should I take this new job? Should I go to this school? Should I ask my boss for a raise? I'm flattered at the confidence shown by the questions, but I never give a lot of direction in those matters. The person should use the wisdom God gave and exercise love. After that people are free. There is really not a Christian way to do a job search or ask for a raise. In fact, there is not a Christian way to be a plumber or an electrician except to be honest and to work hard.

A vendor called me to ask if the members of my church would like to advertise in "The Christian Yellow Pages," a list of businesses at which Christians are encouraged to shop because the proprietors of these businesses are ostensibly believers. Listed would be Christian accountants, Christian carpenters, Christian contractors, even Christian lawyers, oxymoronic as that may sound. Often the requirements of these jobs have little to do with faith in Christ. I don't want a Christian carpenter. I want a competent and honest carpenter. I declined the services of "The Christian Yellow Pages." It struck me that a "Christian Yellow Pages" was a confusing church practice. The faith of a given person is not important as far as vocation goes. Luther said, "[In external matters] whether you are preacher, ruler, spouse, teacher, disciple, there is not time to hear the gospel but the law; here you must fulfill your vocation!"[7] When it comes to vocation, even the faith of a pastor is far less important than his ability to teach the Word faithfully.

Vocation Principle Three: Heavenly Equality

God values all vocations the same. My vocation is, after all, His gift whether I am a parent, a student, a butcher, a baker, or a candlestick maker. My vocation is not more valuable to God than yours. I might achieve a nobler goal in my vocation. Or you might do a more noteworthy thing. "Has the potter no right over the clay, to make out of the same lump one vessel for honored use and another for dishonorable use?" (Romans 9:21). God simply expects both you and me to act within our vocations the way in which these vocations require. Although we are different from one another, we are all equally valued by God. Church workers, especially pastors, should never think that their vocation is more holy or more God-pleasing than any other legitimate station in life.

The application to church practice is obvious. You don't have to go into church work to be pleasing to God in your life. You don't have to put the word *ministry* in front of your vocation for it to be worthy before God. A girl dropped by my office one day and asked if I could listen as she shared with me her "ministry." I listened. She sold huge cookies that you could eat with a cup of coffee or tea in the afternoon. How was this a ministry, I wondered? "Well," she explained, "I used to go to various coffeehouses and grocery stores to see if they would sell my cookies. Some were willing and I was doing pretty well. But I always felt a little bad because I wasn't doing anything for the kingdom. Then the Lord told me that I should sell my cookies to churches. They could use them during Sunday coffee hour, or the youth could sell them at a profit for a fund-raiser. I am so much happier now that I am using my cookies to further the kingdom of God." I felt sorry for that young lady. Somewhere she got the idea that if you can bring the church into your vocation, then it must be more God-pleasing.

"You know," I assured her, "selling cookies is a good thing whether it is Christians who eat them or pagans. If that is what you do, then why not just sell them to anyone who will buy them. Do you think Paul sold his tents only to Christians?"

"But I want a Christian job."

"Every job [I could have said vocation] is a Christian job as long as you are honest and do what the job requires. Here, I'll buy one cookie. Go back to the grocery stores and coffeehouses. You'll make much more money."

"Are you sure you want a cookie? You're not buying it because you feel sorry for me, are you?"

It struck me that perhaps she needed to look for a different vocation altogether. Sadly, selling cookies was not working for her. More sadly, she had been deceived about vocation. One is no more God-pleasing than another.

VOCATION PRINCIPLE FOUR: WORLDLY INEQUALITY

The world places different values on various vocations. God makes us different but values us the same. The world sees our dissimilarities and attaches values that are different. Professional basketball players make more money than grade school teachers. CEOs are more important to the organization than the janitor. That's why people aspire to move up the corporate ladder or to get a chance at the big leagues. Different times and different places often value vocations differently. Soldiers were more highly respected in World War II than in Vietnam. Teachers were more highly respected on the moving American frontier than today.

If we accept the world's skewed values of vocation, our church practice will be grossly affected. Some vocations will never be respected by the world. The vocation of pastor is one. Yes, pastors "must be well thought of by outsiders" (1 Timothy 3:7), which refers to the pastor's moral conduct that even the world can judge. But the world will never value the real task and calling of the pastor, for the world does not esteem the proclamation of the Word, Baptism, Absolution, or the Sacrament of the Altar. Pastors will be frustrated if they expect the world to love what they do.

When the audience of a sermon or speech is primarily the people of the world, then the pastor must often choose between respect for the world and obedience to Christ. While his ego craves respect, his vocation does not allow him to seek it from the world. Every wedding and most funerals fall into this category, as do opportunities to pray in a baccalaureate observance or to speak as pastor in certain civic events. At civic events the pastor wants to get invited back. If other clerics from other religions are present, he wants to protect his "place at the table" by not being too offensive. In such cases pastors should listen to the critics. If the world comments on his eloquence, watch out. He is not called to be eloquent (1 Corinthians 2:1). If the public press talks about how nice it is for the various participants in religious-civic events to get along with one another despite their differences, then the pastor is giving an impression that is deadly to the cause of the Gospel.

I knew a priest in North Dakota who was asked to pray at the commencement exercises for the University of North Dakota in Grand Forks. The invitation came in the aftermath of a community discussion on the right to life. In his prayer he asked God to bring our nation to repentance because we treat human life in a cavalier manner. He entreated our gracious God especially to protect the lives of the unborn against the murderous knife of abortionists. The next day the local newspaper severely chastised him for his "insensitivity." He was not asked to pray again. I commended him because he had fulfilled his vocation. The next year another priest was given the same opportunity. He said nothing of the sanctity of life or of the Lord Jesus, though he tacked on to the end of his prayer the phrase "in Jesus' name." When I asked him why, he replied, "We need not offend. We need to keep our place at the table. The world will not listen to us if we carp on these issues." The media commended this priest. God does not. He had not fulfilled his vocation. God does not call men into the ministry for them to gain the approval of the world. The first priest was angry. "Now by chance a priest was going down that road, and when he saw him he passed by on the other side" (Luke 10:31). It is wrong and a denial of the pastoral vocation to refuse to speak up for life. How much worse is it when pastors speak in the forums of the world and do not identify our Lord as the only way to eternal life? Yet all of us know how often and how public such denials are.

The sermons preached at funerals are especially important. When I preach at funerals, I listen very carefully to the comments of those in the congregation, especially those who are not members of my church. If someone says, "Pastor, that was such a beautiful service," they could mean just about anything. It's usually best not to attach a lot of value to such statements. Someone might say, "That part about being certain of eternal life, I have to think about that." There you have an open mind. Maybe some good was done. Once I heard, "Why do Lutherans always mention Baptism at funerals? Don't they know that there are people here who don't believe in infant Baptism?" I knew that I had fulfilled my vocation that day. I knew because the world had judged me. Every once in a while some stranger will come up and say, "Pastor, I am a Christian. Too often I go to funerals and don't hear that Jesus is the only way to heaven. Thank you for saying He is. Everyone needs to hear about Christ. And these people may never have another chance." Through such comments I am told that I acted properly within my vocation. Shame on any pastor who is given a chance to speak to the world about Christ as the only way to heaven and does not do so.

The office of pastor is not the only office the world disdains. Any office of sacrifice and service will not be valued by the sinful world. Husbands, as they sacrifice for their wives, and wives, as they submit to their husbands—these offices are not high on the world's list of respectability. Scripture says the opposite. The Bible teaches that when I got up in the middle of the night and changed the messy diaper of my child, I was doing something God Himself esteems. We tend to value those vocations of vast influence or those vocations that do things directly for God, as if He needs it. The greatest work you do in your vocation is done for the benefit of the person closest to you. It is done when no one else even knows. Luther said:

> If you find yourself in a work by which you accomplish something good for God, or the holy, or yourself, but not for your neighbor alone, then you should know that that work is not a good work. For each one ought to live, speak, act, hear, suffer, and die in love and sacrifice for another, even one's enemies, a husband for his wife and children, a wife for her husband, children for their parents, servants for their masters, masters for their servants, rulers for their subjects and subjects for their rulers, so that one's hand, mouth, eye, foot, heart and desire is for others; these are Christian works, good in nature.[8]

God values what the world does not. Christian vocation permeates all of what we do as Christians.

VOCATION PRINCIPLE FIVE: COOPERATION WITH THE WORLD

Fifth, vocation requires you to work with others. You can't be a diaper changer without a kid messing his diaper. You can't be a sister without a sibling. If you want grandchildren, you'll have to motivate your kids to have kids of their own. You depend on others in your vocation. Lawyers need lawbreakers. Preachers need sinners.

Accountants need tax laws. Teachers need students. So your vocation requires you to ask constantly how God expects you to serve others. And your vocation requires you to live in the world with all sorts of people.

Today, many Christians view their most spiritual activity as having to do with the personal, pious things they do irrespective of their role in society. Christians often think that true spirituality means having an emotional experience or an inner feeling of the presence of God. Some think that whatever service is done in the church far transcends anything else in their lives. But God did not put us here to be involved in the church. He put us here to fulfill our vocation.

Peggy was a very nice woman, a mother of two little children, who believed very strongly that people needed to be told about Jesus. She joined the evangelism team at the church and every Wednesday night she would come to church ready to make calls on prospective members. Peggy was one of those people who was always late. She would rush in at 7:45 P.M., harried and disorganized, while the evangelism training had started at 7:30. Everyone said that her heart was in the right place. One day after a Lenten service she asked if she could talk to me privately. As soon as I closed the door to my office, tears started rolling down her face. I asked her why she was crying and what was troubling her. "I can't do evangelism anymore."

"That's okay. You can take a break from that if you want. What happened?"

"It's my husband," she sobbed. "He just doesn't care about my church. Jack knows I have to do evangelism on Wednesdays, and he went and scheduled work that night. He knows we can't afford a babysitter. So unless I bring my kids, I can't do evangelism. I signed up and gave a commitment. Now I feel guilty because he just doesn't care."

"Why do you feel guilty?"

"Pastor, you know why. Telling people about Jesus is the most important thing you can do. It's certainly more important than his work schedule. And if I don't tell them, I'm not doing the most important thing I can do. That's why I feel guilty."

I thought for a couple of seconds, then said, "Peggy, you're right. Telling people about Jesus is the most important thing. So I've got an idea. I know a way you can tell people about Jesus and still allow your husband to work the extra night." She looked skeptical. "Don't think about telling strangers about Jesus. Just take the evening and tell your kids. Read Bible stories to your kids. Which is better, Peggy, having a little influence on many people or being the single most profound and positive influence on two precious little children and the husband you love?"

"But, Pastor," she protested, "evangelism is the way that I want to be involved in church. Jack doesn't want me in church. Aren't I supposed to be involved?"

"Peggy, your involvement in church is to listen to God's Word. Be here Sunday morning and bring the kids with you. If Jack gives you grief about that, then come back and we'll talk some more. But on Wednesdays, stay home. Love your kids and tell them about Jesus. The Bible never says that you are supposed to be 'involved' in church. It says that you are to listen to God, to train your children, and to honor your husband. It sounds like you have enough pressures without feeling guilty about not doing evangelism. God does not consider you guilty."

So Peggy went home. She slowed down and smiled more. Her kids came to Sunday school. I don't know if her husband will ever become a Christian. But she is still an "evangelist." Her husband is the chief recipient of her confession of Christ.

I've heard people say that they can tell how healthy a church is by the number of cars in the parking lot at any given time. I don't agree. You want a lot of cars on Sunday morning and on Wednesday night for Bible class and services. But during the week people are busy with their vocations. They haven't always got time for church involvement.

At the time of the Reformation, monasteries and convents were extolled as God-pleasing institutions. Pilgrimages and indulgences were viewed as the greatest Christian works. Only the most pious and godly aspired to such lofty vocations. It was thought that you got into these places if you were an especially good Christian. Back then, convents were the best way to be involved in the church. But God did not put us on earth to be in monasteries, to be pious, or even to hang around the church. The Lutherans utterly rejected these institutions. Luther said that we should be like Abraham. Father Abraham followed the Word of God and lived in the world. If we were more like Abraham,

> we would never have approved of convents, pilgrimages, indulgences, and sacrifices for the dead. Every pastor would have taught the Word of God in his parish; and the church would have felt satisfied with the Word, Baptism, the Lord's Supper, absolution, and solace in death and life. Then everyone would have done his duty in his civil and household activities, whether he was a servant or a master, an officer of the state or a subject. Those monstrous papistic abominations would never have crept into the church.[9]

If our churches want to be Lutheran, they will stop laying the guilt trip when people are not particularly involved in church activities. Instead, we will encourage and expect God's people to hear His Word, receive the Sacrament, and fulfill their vocation. Our involvement with family and society will bring about far greater blessings for others than our involvement in the church.

The Lutheran insight into vocation suggests that each Christian is unique in the vocation given by God. This uniqueness allows for wonderful freedom as we serve God in this life. Although equal and identical before the throne of heaven, Christians are unequal in the eyes of the world and, therefore, work together in cooperation with both Christians and non-Christians as His instruments doing the work of God for our neighbors.

God Does Not Need Our Good Works

Someone once asked Luther what God was doing before He created the world. Luther is reported to have answered, "Creating hell for people who ask such stupid questions." God was not bored. He doesn't "do things" except to bless us. The cupboards of heaven are not stuffed with jigsaw puzzles or stamp books for the Almighty to kill time on a particularly slow millennium. The good Lord isn't sitting in heaven, wringing His hands hopefully, as He waits to see if people will show Him the proper respect. He isn't like a movie critic during the worship service, checking to see if we are doing things properly. He's God. He will be just fine whether we thank, praise, serve, and obey Him or not. Don't worry about God. When we talk about doing good works, we must never believe that God benefits from them. All talk of God is about what God does for us, not what we do for God.

What about the Ten Commandments? Don't they tell us what to do for God? The word *commandment* is unfortunate. We should call them the ten statements or the ten principles or, better, the ten descriptions of God's children. They aren't even imperative. They are descriptions of those people whom God controls. God says to His people, "You will not kill. You will not commit adultery. You will not steal." He's describing us.

Remember when you were a kid and your dad was called into the principal's office to discuss your behavior? That happened to me. I was accused of showing disrespect to a teacher. It was a false accusation. She had me confused with another guy. My father said, "My son is not disrespectful. He will not show disrespect." Grammatically, that's the same as "You will not kill." Dad did not give me an order. He described me. I suppose someone might think that this understanding of the Ten Commandments gets us off the hook. The opposite is true. What if I had, in fact, been disrespectful? Imagine if my dad's description of me were not true. I would have made him a liar. His statement would have elicited more anguished repentance than all the imperatives in the world. Imperatives don't work. Descriptions do. The Ten Commandments describe us.

Luther's Large Catechism instructs us. The Ten Commandments (I will call them the Ten Commandments because of tradition) are given so we can know how God blesses us and how He uses us to bless others. They are divided into two tables. It is often said that the first three tell how we are to love God and the next seven tell us how to serve other people. But even the first three do not have God as the beneficiary. Rather, they tell us of the manner in which God blesses us with grace for eternity. The next seven commandments tell us how God uses His children to bless others for this life.

Learn the Ten Commandments from Luther. He summarizes the first three, "Therefore you must constantly keep God's Word in your heart, on your lips, and in your ears."[10] The First Commandment is to believe, the Second to speak, and the Third to listen. So we are blessed by the commandments. In the First, God "makes no greater demand than heartfelt trust in him for every good thing, so that we walk straight ahead on the right path using all of God's gifts."[11] The Second Commandment requires that such confidence be spoken as we "honor God's name and keep it constantly upon (our) lips in all circumstances and experiences, for. . . . the lips (honor God) by confession" so others might believe.[12] The Third Commandment tells us to place the Word of God onto our ears. So we take time off on a day of rest "to attend worship services [literally 'divine service'], that is, so that they may assemble to hear and discuss God's Word and then to offer praise, song, and prayer to God."[13] The singing and praying is not for the benefit of God. It benefits others. And the learning of the Word is done not to flatter God but "for the sake of the young people" or "for the sake of the whole community" of the church.[14] When we have followed the first three commandments, God is not the beneficiary—we are, along with our children, the church, and anyone who hears our confession.

The second table of the Law tells us how to serve our neighbor in this life and for this life. We respect parents (Fourth Commandment), preserve life (Fifth Commandment), enjoy marriage (Sixth Commandment), protect property (Seventh Commandment), guard reputation (Eighth Commandment), and we do so joyfully (Ninth and Tenth Commandments). God is not benefited by our obedience to the Ten Commandments. God does not feel better when I get up and change my child in the middle of the night. He does not need the commandments. We do.

God especially does not need my good works in the area of worship. Too often we picture God as the beneficiary of our worship as if He is impressed with the quality of the musical performance in church. God is even depicted as somehow saddened if our whole hearts are not focused into the manner in which we worship. God existed from eternity without my prayers or my music. He'll do just fine. The Divine Service is intended to bless people, to bring the word of forgiveness to them, whatever roll I might play.

GOOD WORKS HELP OTHER PEOPLE

While God does not need my works, my neighbor does. God gives us the Ten Commandments to help us serve and love others. We are also blessed in the process. Every single blessing of God comes to you through someone else, acting in his or her vocation according to the Ten Commandments. God uses other people to shower His blessings on us. Count your blessings.

First Commandment: God redeemed me because Jesus fulfilled His duty as Savior in His vocation.

Second Commandment: God saved me because my parents, in their calling, brought me to the pastor who baptized me and placed the "name" of God upon me.

Third Commandment: God strengthened me and established me in His grace because pastors, parents, and teachers spoke the Word to me according to their vocation.

Fourth Commandment: God protected and nurtured me because parents and others in authority, according to their vocation, took care of me.

Fifth Commandment: God gave me life through the procreation of my parents and He preserves it through the protection of the state and the care of the medical profession. He further blesses my family with life and health through my occupation and efforts.

Sixth Commandment: God gives me intimacy through the gift of my wife and blesses society with stability through the vocation of marriage.

Seventh Commandment: God preserves my livelihood and the security of my family by providing people who, in their calling, guard my property and wealth.

Eighth Commandment: God protects my good name through people who speak well of me. He protects me from others who would take advantage of me by legitimately exposing their bad reputations.

Ninth and Tenth Commandments: God gives me contentment through a host of friends and acquaintances who are pleased with me and I with them.

The Ten Commandments, far from tedious and oppressive laws, are really descriptions of the manner in which God blesses me through other people. When I changed my son's diaper in the middle of the night, he was helped and I was following the Fourth and Ninth Commandments. All true good works serve your neighbor.

GOD USES MY VOCATION

You don't usually picture God as changing diapers. It's a pretty menial task. In fact, every time some sleepless parent has staggered through the diaper changing motions, God is the one doing it. He gave me my vocation, placed children under my care, and blessed me with the energy and skill to change diapers. He is the potter and I am the clay. He is the master diaper changer, and I am his humble instrument. If I look at diaper changing in this way, it takes on a rather sacred value. God wants us to look at everything we do as though He were doing it.

When a preacher proclaims Christ or baptizes into Christ, we would never say that he saves. Or can we? It is Christ that saves, of this there is no doubt. Paul, however, says that he saves, that "I might save some" (1 Corinthians 9:22). Obviously, Paul means that he is God's instrument. God uses His Word, which Paul preaches, to save others. We can say the same in matters of this life. God feeds by the farmer, the butcher, the grocer, the cook, and the one who sets the table. God heals by the doctor, the nurse, and a host of medical professionals. God dresses us by the farmers, the weavers, the sewers, the merchants, and the wardrobe consultants. God uses means to get us to heaven and to bless us on earth. So while God Himself does not need our good works, He has managed things so He uses our good works to do some very nice things for others. What a lofty honor God pays us in our vocation. Whatever good we do is actually the work of God Himself blessing others through us. We become His hand of help, His mouth of praise, and His heart of mercy.

Amazingly, even if we don't want to do anything nice, God still uses us. In our vocation we will bless others even if we don't want to, simply because that's the way God has ordered things. I did not want to get up and change my son's diapers. I tried to get out of it. I was forced to do it. Despite my poor motives God blessed my son with an excellent diaper change. In time I enjoyed my vocation, but even if my joy were incomplete, the kid would still be changed.

God has created a system in which the self-interests of someone can actually be used to bless others. For example, Isaiah the prophet tells us that God used Cyrus, king of Persia, to bring about the freedom of His people. "For the sake of My servant Jacob, and Israel My chosen, I call you by your name, I name you, though you do not know Me" (Isaiah 45:4). Consider also the parable of the importunate widow, who incessantly nagged the unjust judge who "neither feared God nor cared about men." He was forced to act, purely out of self-preservation and to get some sleep, in a way that benefited the widow because, in God's order of things, his vocation required it. So the widow was blessed by the means of a very bad man (Luke 8:1–8). Even the kingdom of God can be blessed by unscrupulous ministers who "preach Christ from envy and rivalry" (Philippians 1:15). Good results can come from poor motives because God wants to bless us and uses the means of sinful humans to accomplish His great goals. Marriage can be a blessing both when the husband and wife are loving and when their motives are anything but pure. Gustaf Wingren says:

> The human being is self-willed, desiring that whatever happens shall be to his own advantage. When husband and wife, in marriage, serve one another and their children, this is not due to the heart's spontaneous and undisturbed expression of love, every day and hour. Rather, in marriage as an institution something compels the husband's selfish desires to yield and likewise inhibits the ego-centricity of the wife's heart. At work in marriage is a power which compels self-giving to spouse and children. So it is the "station" itself which is the ethical agent, for it is God who is active through the law on earth.[15]

Church practice is profoundly affected by this understanding of vocation. First, even when we fail or we are grouchy, God is accomplishing great things for our neighbor. The church should remind us of our importance in family and society even when our heart is not in it. Second, we should thank God for the incredibly complex systems of this world through which amazing blessings are poured out on people, even though they do not know God. And we should thank God for people, even unbelievers, who are used by God to bless us. Third, and most important, we should "urge" all to "stay and do their duty" as the catechism says. Everyone sins within their vocation. Where else are you going to sin? That's why we pray the Lord's Prayer. But sin is no reason for leaving a vocation, and neither is your heart. A pastor should never be encouraged to quit simply because he is inadequate or a husband to desert his family even if he is tired of his duties. No teacher should leave his class or a doctor her patients simply because their heart is not in it. God never tells us to follow our dreams. He tells us that the world needs us in our vocation. Find your vocation. In it you will be more fruitful and more God pleasing than all the dreams you have ever had.

GOOD WORKS DONE IN FAITH ARE VALUED BY JESUS

God places us in our vocation; describes us and directs us on how to live in the Ten Commandments; blesses others through what we do, even if we have bad motives; purifies our motives through the gift of eternal life; and then to cap it off, He praises us publicly for all the things we do.

One thing I know about diaper changing: Kids rarely thank their father or mother for it. They fight you all the way while you're doing it to serve them, then they look at you like you hurt them in some way when you are the one who did all the disgusting work. Children thank their parents when they send them college money, buy them a car, or pay for their wedding. Sometimes kids will thank parents for good advice or for raising them as Christians. Kids do not thank parents for diaper changes. That is why Christ does.

When Jesus comes at the end of time on the clouds of glory with the angels and the sound of the trumpet, He will separate the sheep from the goats. He will say to the sheep, "Come, you are blessed by My Father from eternity, for I was hungry and you fed Me. I was a stranger and you took Me in. I messed My diapers in the middle of the night and you changed Me."

Noble works—giving all your money to the church or preaching before thousands—these have their thanks already. The professional singer who "knocks 'em dead" in the service has her reward. The famous church deeds written up in *The Lutheran Witness* or recognized at the church conventions—God has praised them already through the means of the press or the organized church. God values the mundane, lowly, unassuming, disgusting, unspeakable, and unspoken good works of His children, and He will not allow the parousia to come and go without their mention.

The difference between the works done by unbelievers and those done by Christians is often undetectable in this life. I'd like to think that Christians are more noticeably good, but I'm not sure. We may sing in that notorious campfire song that "They'll know we are Christians by our love," but Paul says that "your life is hidden with Christ in God" (Colossians 3:3). The things we do as Christians are simply not particularly apparent to others. So we wait. "When Christ who is your life appears, then you also will appear with Him in glory" (v. 4). Do not be too disappointed if the world does not recognize all the love that you show to others. Besides, as Christians we are usually so focused on others that we don't think of getting thanks. If we are hoping for thanks, it's usually an indication of original sin and our self-centeredness. It all seems a bit unfair, kind of like changing diapers. Jesus knows this. He is, after all, the one who invented the theology of the cross.

> Thesis 4, "Although the works of God are always unattractive and appear evil, they are nevertheless really eternal merits."
>
> Thesis 18, "It is certain that man must utterly despair of his own ability before he is prepared to receive the grace of Christ.
>
> Thesis 20, "He deserves to be called a theologian, however, who comprehends the visible and manifest things of God seen through suffering and the cross."[16]

The things we do, whether changing diapers, confessing the faith, helping the downtrodden, visiting the needy, all these things are "unattractive works of God" without worth in this life yet "eternal" in the mind of God. That is why we will be surprised when Jesus comes again and points out all the things that His brothers and sisters have done.

In the church we should thank people when they help. When your pastor takes a call to another church, there should be a party thanking him—not for leaving but for serving God while he stayed. People need to be thanked. But our greatest successes are usually unnoticed, even by the church.

When I served as a campus pastor in North Dakota as recounted in chapter 1, I was not thanked too often by those young people who left my chapel. They were angry with me because I was faithful. My greatest motivation during those lonely times was the knowledge that I was doing right, even if others did not notice or understand. God was pleased. Whatever public vindication I would get would have to wait. Ironically, it turns out that by the time Christ comes I really won't care that much about being right and working hard. Christ will mention all my menial little deeds nonetheless, and yours as well. Every little act of mercy that every Christian has done for the millennia of this world's existence will be mentioned. When Christ comes to you, He will mention things long forgotten or never noticed. Then the entire human race of all times will hear what you did in Christ.

What is the lesson of all this? Don't crave success. Jesus will do what He intends. He will point out the little things to the world. Leave it to Him. Just be faithful.

CONCLUSION

The proper doctrine and understanding of good works is both important and urgent in our churches. Many congregations have naively introduced many bad practices that either undermine the proper understanding of good works or teach false doctrine. According to the Bible and our Lutheran teachings we can say:

- Good works require action.
- Good works are done according to our vocation.
- God does not need our good works.
- Good works help other people.
- Good works are done whether we want to do them or not.
- Good works done in faith are valued by Jesus Christ.

This doctrine both requires proper practice and promotes it.

The doctrine of the Gospel is a fire. As Christians, we serve our neighbor in our vocations. These works of individual Christians are like a staff guiding others to the Gospel. Good works in our vocation are "The Christian's Staff."

The greatest good work that a Christian can do is to talk about Jesus: Confess the Gospel. This we will discuss in chapter 11. Before that we must analyze more closely American Evangelical Protestantism and the effect this movement has had upon our country and our church.

Study Questions

1. What are the six things one needs to know about good works?
2. How does your passive faith save you?
3. What or who is the focus of active faith?
4. What are the two ways passive faith is foundational to active faith?
5. Each believer lives out vocation in three estates: the family, the world, and the church. To what position, or job, have you been called in each of these estates?
6. How does your vocation give you freedom?
7. For whom do we do our good works?
8. What does the author tell us the Ten Commandments are?
9. How do God's blessings come to us?
10. True or false: The only good works Jesus values are those I do purposefully and with a cheerful heart.

Discussion questions

1. Discuss how a proper doctrine of salvation puts good works in proper perspective.
2. Discuss the fundamental differences between passive and active faith.
3. Discuss the principles of vocation and how they affect the call each Christian has: difference, freedom, heavenly equality, wordly equality, cooperation with the world.
4. Examine the difference between understanding the Ten Commandments as imperatives or as descriptive statements.

7

The Fire Is Doused

WORD AND SPIRIT SEPARATED

Amazingly, with all the wonderful promises connected to the Gospel and Sacraments, there are still Christian groups that insist on trying to find the blessings of the Holy Spirit somewhere else. Books are written and theologies are developed that postulate that one can find more of the Spirit outside of the Word. Luther labeled such theologians "Schwaermer" because those who held such views were like bees "swarming" and making lots of noise but never really listening. He says, "Therefore we should and must insist that God does not want to deal with us human beings, except by means of his external Word and sacrament. Everything that boasts of being from the Spirit apart from such a Word and sacrament is of the devil."[1]

Luther understood the dire consequences of teaching people to find the Holy Spirit elsewhere than in His testimony to Christ through the Word and Sacraments. What are some of these consequences?

First, when people say that they have found the Spirit outside of the Gospel of Jesus, it always involves some kind of experience. Experience replaces faith. According to Lutheran doctrine, the proclamation of Christ requires the hearers to look outside of themselves at the Word. We believe what we hear. But if the Holy Spirit comes without the Word, then you need some feeling or experience to be sure that it's Him. He becomes unpredictable. He is often perceived as more exciting. In Eden Satan claimed that there would be blessings apart from God's Word. Adam and Eve were excited when they ate the fruit. Our first parents were enticed. "This is all the old devil and old snake, who also turned Adam and Eve into enthusiasts and led them from the external Word of God to 'spirituality' and their own presumption—although he even accomplished this by means of other, external words. . . . In short: enthusiasm clings to Adam and his children from the beginning to the end of the world—fed and spread among them as poison by the old dragon. It is the source, power, and might of all heresies. . . . "[2] Experience—giddy, appealing, enticing, exciting, and ultimately deadly—had replaced faith in the Word.

Second, when people say they have found the Spirit outside of the Gospel of Jesus, then uncertainty results. There is no benchmark. Doctrine no longer rules because experience has replaced it as the mark of the church. The problem is that people start to think "my experience is just as good as yours." With diminished authority, objectivity breaks down in the church. The distinctions between speaker and hearer, pastor and people, even true and false often are blurred. One cannot say for certain, "Here is the Spirit of Christ" or "We can find the Spirit in Christ's Word." Instead, the Holy Spirit becomes a "vague oblong blur."[3]

Third, when people say that they have found the Spirit outside of the Gospel of Jesus, divisions occur. Uncertainty often leads to friction. People argue about where to find the Spirit. Some people are said to have more of the Spirit than others, to have been blessed more dynamically or to have been lifted to a higher spiritual plane. Those without the full measure of the Spirit feel spiritually inadequate. Resentment results and competition develops.

Fourth, and most important, when people say they have found the Spirit outside of the Gospel of Jesus, then Christ Himself ends up taking a backseat. Remember, it is through the Gospel that the Spirit "bespeaks you righteous." If God is said to be working through something other than the Gospel, then something else is taking the Gospel's place and Jesus' place. Jesus is diminished. Someone once said, "Whenever something else becomes more, justification becomes mere."

A look at some of the movements that separate the Word from the Spirit will show that these four things usually happen.

HISTORY

History is not boring if you are interested in the topic. The Gospel accounts are history. The Book of Acts is history. Much of the Old Testament is history. The history of Christianity is not only important, it is fascinating. So I beg your indulgence as I dash across three centuries of Christian thought. This race across the ages will show that within American Protestantism there has always been a tendency to separate the Spirit from the Word.

JOHN WESLEY

John Wesley, born in 1703, was arguably the most influential churchman in the history of England and possibly even North America. Wesley was such a powerful preacher it is reported that he preached to 100,000 people at once before the days of electricity and public address systems. While at Oxford University in his younger years, Wesley was frustrated because he thought that the love of many of his classmates and countrymen had grown cold. He wished and prayed for a change in the hearts of the religious leaders of his day. One day a powerful religious experience led him to claim, "My heart was strangely warmed."[4] Subsequently, Wesley developed a "method" of spiritual discipline that could be employed to change people's lives. Therefore, his followers were called Methodists.

Wesley believed that the Word of God had no power of its own but that God added His power to it whenever He decided. You will remember that John Calvin also said that the Holy Spirit had to add a "secret power" to the Word of God. The work of the Spirit became rather unpredictable in Wesley's system of theology.

> Whosoever . . . imagines there is any intrinsic power in any means whatsoever, does greatly err, not knowing the Scriptures, neither the power of God. We know that there is no inherent power in the . . . letter of Scripture read, the sound thereof heard or the bread and wine received in the Lord's supper; but that it is God alone who is the Giver of every good gift, the Author of all grace; that the whole power is of Him whereby, through any of these, there is any blessing conveyed to our souls.

> We know likewise, that God is able to give the same grace though there were no means on the face of the earth. In this sense we affirm that with regard to God there is no such thing as means; seeing he is equally able to work whatsoever pleaseth him, by any, or by none at all.[5]

Remember the story of the village, the water, and the well in chapter 3? Wesley is just like the man who came in and covered the well, claiming that God can do what He wants without the well. Whenever the Word of the Gospel becomes dispensable or disposable, so does the forgiveness of sins and justification. Wesley says:

> If God should send man a Redeemer, what must that Redeemer do for him? . . . Shall He be the fountain of an imputed righteousness and procure the tenderest favor to all his followers? This is not enough. . . . Must not our Redeemer be . . . one that 'baptiseth with the Holy Ghost'—the Fountain and Restorer of that to mankind, whereby they are restored to their first estate, and the enjoyment of God?[6]

Wesley introduced the notion of a "two-stage" Christianity to an unwary church. To him it is not enough to be forgiven and to be justified before God. You must also be restored to the way things were in the Garden of Eden, your "first estate." How do you achieve that estate? You must experience complete holiness, a type of sinlessness in your life. According to Wesley:

> Nor does anything under heaven more quicken the desires of those who are justified, than to converse with those whom they believe to have experienced a still higher salvation. This places that salvation full in their view and increases their hunger and thirst after it.[7]

Wesley's "heartwarming" encounter of the Holy Spirit occurred in a home on Aldersgate in London and is labeled his "Aldersgate experience." Ironically, this "spiritual baptism" happened while he was reading Luther's commentary on the Book of Romans.

Wesley's theology has been inherited by most of those involved in American revivalism, Pentecostalism, the Charismatic Movement, Campus Crusade for Christ, Promise Keepers, and the Church Growth Movement. In Wesley you can clearly see the first consequence of finding the Spirit outside of the Word: Experience has replaced faith in the Gospel.

CHARLES FINNEY AND REVIVALISM

About 100 years after Wesley, the "second great awakening" occurred in America. Charles Grandison Finney and other itinerant revivalists traveled throughout the young nation encouraging the people to "vote for Jesus" in their spiritual lives. Finney, trained in law and politics, claimed that doctrine, including the teaching that one is justified by grace, is sterile. Instead, the Spirit offered a more assuring proof of God's love. Finney took the doctrine of Wesley and added to it an exciting, experiential feature:

> Almost all the religion in the world has been produced by revivals. God has found it necessary to take advantage of the excitability there is in mankind, to produce powerful excitements among them, before he can lead them to obey. Men are so sluggish, there are so many things to lead their minds off from religion and to oppose the influence of the gospel, that it is necessary to raise an excitement among them, till the tide rises so high as to sweep away the opposing obstacles. They must be so excited that they will break over these counteracting influences, before they will obey God.[8]

The special working of the Spirit had to be felt in rather dramatic ways. Although raised as a Presbyterian, Finney's own conversion experience provided his assurance of salvation. In his *Memoirs* he shares:

> The Holy Spirit descended upon me in a manner that seemed to go through me, body and soul. I could feel the impression, like a wave of electricity, going through and through me. Indeed, it seemed like the very breath of God. I can recollect distinctly that it seemed to fan me like immense wings. . . . I wept aloud with joy and love; and I do not know but I should say, I literally bellowed out the unutterable gushings of my heart. These waves came over me, and over me, and over me, one after the other, until I recollect I cried out, "Lord, I cannot bear anymore."[9]

Touted as indispensable, Finney's dramatic experience became the inalienable right of every Christian. In Charles Finney you can see again the first negative consequence of finding the Spirit outside of the Word—experience replaces faith.

PENTECOSTALISM

Not long after the death of Finney, Pentecostalism arose in the United States. Disciples of Wesley and Finney had experienced both conversion and the "heart strangely warmed." Some even claimed a third, fourth, or fifth blessing. But they were frustrated because no one could agree exactly on how to know that one had received the second blessing that Wesley had introduced. On January 1, 1901, in Topeka, Kansas, a young preacher named Charles Parham linked the second experience with the practice of speaking in tongues. He claimed that you could know you had been Spirit-baptized if you spoke in tongues. In 1906, this teaching, called Pentecostalism, found its way to California at the famous Azuza Street Revival. Pentecostalism subsequently spread throughout the nation like a wildfire. Its distinctive contribution was the novel doctrine that the Christian's unique experience of the Spirit was evidenced by tongues. Typical is the following resolution, adopted by the Pentecostal Holiness Church in 1908:

> The Scriptures teach us that after we are cleansed with the blood we then need to receive the filling of the Spirit, the baptism with the Holy Ghost, the abiding Comforter, that which was promised by John the Baptist and corroborated by Jesus Christ that on receiving the baptism with the Holy Ghost we have the same evidence that followed Acts 2, . . . to wit, the speaking with other tongues as the Spirit gave utterance.[10]

Pentecostalism was constantly plagued by the fleeting nature of tongues. Sometimes speakers would "backslide," even suffer excommunication, without losing the ability to speak in tongues. Other people could be induced to speak in tongues by Pentecostal leaders who taught them religious tongue twisters that so confused the people that they began speaking gibberish.[11] Pious and dedicated Christian people were often unable to speak in tongues. Could these people really be carnal? Within fifty years many Pentecostal preachers were forced almost to nag their people to speak in tongues. The third consequence of separating the Spirit from the Word had occurred. Uncertainty prevailed.

THE CHARISMATIC MOVEMENT

In the early 1960s the doctrine of Pentecostalism invaded the mainline churches. Millions of Protestants, including Lutherans, and even Roman Catholics, including many pastors and priests, claimed the Pentecostal experience. The Charismatic Movement was born. Typical is the testimony of the Rev. Rodney Lensch, a Lutheran Church—Missouri Synod pastor in 1972:

> I lived under a yoke of condemnation because I never felt able to measure up to all that my church, my calling and my conscience demanded of me. To be perfectly frank, I didn't feel loved of God although intellectually I could say, "yes, but God's Word says you are even if you don't feel it." But when the Holy Spirit flooded my soul with love I felt it. There was no need to keep quoting the bible passages. The Holy Spirit was now ministering that love within my heart and not just through my intellect.[12]

An unfortunate outgrowth of the Charismatic Movement was conflict. Within many congregations a group of the members claimed to speak in tongues while others did not. Some claimed to have had the second experience while others did not. Churches and denominations were often divided into the "haves" and the "have-nots." This is the fourth consequence of placing a wedge between Spirit and Word—divisions.

I remember a young woman named Patty who came into my office when I was a campus pastor. She had been attending a Bible study group at a nearby church. They had taught her that she needed to speak in tongues before she could be a truly complete, Spirit-filled Christian. She asked me to pray with her that she could learn to speak in tongues. Instead, I quoted Colossians where it says that in Christ you have been made complete in Baptism (2:10–12). She started to cry. When I asked her the source of her tears, feelings gushed out that had obviously been trying to escape for weeks. "I know I'm already complete, and I know that I am going to heaven because of Jesus. And I do believe in Him so much. But I just want to speak in tongues because all my friends do it, and I feel so left out. They have left me behind. I'm excluded just because I can't do what they do. So you have to help me. I have to speak in tongues."

I stared at her and said, "No, you don't." I felt terribly sad for her. She had a good faith but misguided friends. They were forcing her to choose between the two. The doctrine of tongues was dividing Christians.

She sat quietly for at least thirty seconds, then, suddenly, stood up and blurted, "Heck with them, Pastor. You're right. I don't." After that she came to church regularly, but I never saw her friends. She made new ones. I was happy for her. But I remembered her sadness. The church of Christ should never be divided between "haves" and "have-nots." In Christ we are all "haves."

The quotations on the last couple of pages come from theologians who are spread over three centuries and two hemispheres. But they have one thing in common. They all teach that you can have the Spirit of God without the Word of Christ. Notice how they become more and more radical as the centuries progress. They all have the same feature in common: There is something more than the Word.

In all these movements you can discern three bad consequences. (1) Experience replaces faith. (2) Uncertainty reigns. (3) Divisions ensue.

Two-Stage Christianity

In North America the cleavage between Word and Spirit has taken on one rather unique form. Many churches claim that there are two stages of Christianity. The first stage is the salvation stage. The second stage is called "Baptism in the Spirit" or being "Spirit-filled." In the first stage you are redeemed and justified, but you are lacking Christian power or lacking some of the Spirit's blessings. In the second stage you are given power. First-stage Christianity finds you "living in the enemy's war camp," whereas in stage two you "go straight up to victory." You might be saved in first-stage Christianity, but you are still carnal. In the second stage you are no longer carnal, but spiritual. Forgiveness is found in the first stage, but you are ineffective. In the second stage you are powerful and dynamic. In the first stage you are passively receiving, but in the second stage you are making a contribution. The idea of a two-stage Christianity was introduced by John Wesley, popularized by Charles Finney, given an experience by Pentecostalism, and made respectable by the Charismatic Movement.

In many Protestant and even some Lutheran churches two-stage Christianity has replaced the central teaching of the Christian faith. You recall that for Luther justification by grace through faith was paramount. The doctrine that Luther discovered almost 500 years ago, and 200 years before Wesley ever entered a pulpit, was the article of faith upon which the church stands or falls. But in two-tiered Christianity there is a different central teaching. First-level Christianity is being justified; second-level is much better than the first, so it becomes the central teaching. For Wesley it was his warmed heart and his commitment. For Finney the central teaching was his decision and experience of Christ. For Pentecostalism the chief doctrine is the Baptism of the Spirit and speaking in tongues. For the charismatic, the central teaching is Christian renewal, usually through tongues. But in each of these movements, justification takes a backseat.

MOM LOVED ME BEST

My wife grew up in a fairly large family. Her parents were blessed with five children, all daughters. Jan tells me that she was always a little embarrassed growing up because it was so obvious that her mother favored her above the other girls. Of course, there was no doubt that Mom loved all her kids, but, said Jan, "Mothers do have favorites." Whenever her mother did something special for her, Jan would not talk about it too much for fear that the other, less fortunate, daughters might get their feelings hurt. At Christmas Jan received gifts that were, at least in her mind, just a cut above the gifts received by her sisters. And the lunches she shared with her mom just seemed to be at the better restaurants, the kind where you could linger over your meal a little longer and enjoy your mother's company a little more. Jan treasured her mother and their relationship. She felt bad that her sisters did not have the same closeness with their mom.

Then one day, after Mom, through faith in Jesus Christ, had been brought by the angels to heaven, the five girls were sharing their memories about their mother. In the course of the conversation, Jan's eldest sister said that she had something to share with her siblings. With obvious hesitation and even a little pain, she confided that she felt sad and even a little guilty that her mother had shown such clear favoritism to *her* throughout her life. "She always gave me the best Christmas gifts. She always bought me the nicest clothes. I had so many advantages. I just hope that you, my sisters whom I love, do not have any bitterness toward me because of mother's affections toward me."

At that the youngest sister laughed. "I know that you're just saying that so that *I* won't feel bad. Actually, I'm sure you noticed that mom always showed me the most attention. She spent more time helping me and guiding me. I was certain that you resented me." One by one the five sisters shared a common belief. Each one believed that their mother had loved her most. Each was reluctant to talk about it because each had no wish to hurt the feelings of her sisters.

In the course of the conversation they all came to feel ashamed of their previous convictions. They were not loved more than the others as they thought. Rather, their mother had loved each of them as much as any mother could love. She had made each daughter feel so loved that each believed her mother loved her most. But to believe Mom loved one daughter less than the others, that Mom favored one daughter less, such a view was actually an insult to Mom.

So it is with the love of God. I am convinced that there is no way that God could shower more love, lavish more blessings, or provide more favor than He has given to me. Every Christian thinks that way. It is one thing to thank God every night for all of His grace. All Christians offer such prayers. It is altogether something different to believe that one Christian has received less than another or that one Christian is not fully blessed. God does not love you less. He loves us all infinitely in Christ.

The trend in Protestantism that suggests that God blesses some in Christ more than others is very dangerous.

WHAT ABOUT THOSE CONTEMPORARY PRAISE SONGS? PART THREE

Wesleyan, Pentecostal, or charismatic praise songs will encourage being "filled with the Spirit," a "spiritual revival," or having the

Spirit fall upon us in a special manner. They give the impression that you have to enjoy a special blessing from God in order to be complete. Anguished prayer and intimate personal contact usually precipitate the blessing, not the Word and Sacraments. Those who enjoy the experience, in good Wesleyan theology, are pretty near perfect.

Around the campfires in the old Walther League we used to sing a song entitled "He's Everything to Me." It says that the news of Christmas (Nativity) and the news of incarnation just aren't enough. "What is that to me?" asks the songwriter. But when we meet God "face to face," clearly not through the nativity, then He becomes everything. The objective story of the Savior is insignificant compared to the emotional experience of faith.[13]

Consider also the song "Come, Holy Spirit," which is a four-stanza poetic opinion of the Holy Spirit's evangelistic efforts for the last two thousand years. Stanza 1 recounts Pentecost, stanza 2 tells of the third-century martyrs, stanza 3 relates the Reformation discovery of justification. Stanza 4 glowingly extols the "great revivals" that provided the holy flame to meet today's challenges. The obvious lesson of this song, which I have heard sung a half a dozen times in Lutheran churches, is that the revivals of Wesley, Finney, and the Pentecostals are about the best thing since the Reformation and certainly something we should crave.[14]

Some of the songs describe the worship service. They claim that you can be certain of the Spirit's presence either by feelings or by the faces around you. One suggests that we can know the Spirit's presence, not by the preaching of the Word or the administration of the Sacrament, but because "in each heart he lights a flame."[15] Another begins with the claim that "I can feel you flowin' through me" and asks the Holy Spirit to "Come and Fill me up."[16] Yet another identifies the presence of the Spirit by the "hands raised up to receive your love," claiming a type of Christian clairvoyance in which "I can see you [the Spirit] on each face."[17] Imagine if you took the lyrics of this song seriously and yelled at your kids on the way to church, something every Christian parent has done. You might actually conclude that the surly looks on the countenance of your offspring had prevented the presence of the Spirit of God in the Divine Service. Thankfully, the Holy Spirit comes through Word and Sacrament regardless of whether your children or you are particularly "glowing" on a given Sunday.

Finally, there is that old favorite "Blessed Assurance." The first time I sang this song in church was in 1974 during an evening Lenten service at one of the Lutheran churches in Springfield, Illinois, while I was in my second year at the seminary. I looked at the faces of my fellow worshipers as we based our eternal salvation upon our own "perfect submission," our "perfect delight," and our "visions of rapture." I scrutinized the flock as we, during this season of penitence, claimed "perfect submission, perfect delight"[18] before the awful throne of God. Many of the people were singing with their eyes closed and their worship folders on the seats. They knew the words by heart. This song was not new to the church. The people loved it. It occurred to me, as the congregation of Jesus Christ sang, that something profoundly blasphemous was happening. We were bragging before God of our experience. And we were actually smug about the whole sordid affair. Later, when I had read John Wesley's *A Plain Account of Christian Perfection*, I realized that we were just behaving like the revivalists around us. It was still blasphemous. After the service I asked an acquaintance if he had every really analyzed the words to "Blessed Assurance." His negative reply gave me slight consolation. Perhaps the people weren't really paying much attention and didn't care what they were saying. How ironic that the Lord in His mercy had created a stupor of indifference to protect His flock from the songs chosen by the pastor or worship committee.

Remember when you were a kid and your dad asked you, "Are you listening to the lyrics of that song?" Maybe you said yes. Maybe you said no. Today, if you listen to this type of music, pay attention to the lyrics. You will find that they tend to be Pentecostal. They make us think that (1) Christ is mere, (2) that experience transcends faith, (3) that God's grace is uncertain or unpredictable, and (4) that there are different levels of Christianity.

In church we need to stick to the good Lutheran hymns. The songs around church campfires, at vacation Bible school, and on Christian radio stations ought to be faithful to the true Gospel as well.

SYNERGISM

At the beginning of this chapter I mentioned four dire consequences that occur when people say they have found the Spirit outside of the Gospel of Jesus. There is a fifth consequence, arguably more destructive than the other four. When people separate the Spirit from the Gospel, a certain false doctrine called synergism inevitably results. Synergism literally means "work together." It is the notion that we cooperate with the Holy Spirit in our own conversion.

MY FIRST BAPTISM

In chapter 4 I mentioned a man named Tom who learned about infant Baptism from the Baptism of his own daughter. Here's the beginning of that story. Tom's wife was Lutheran and strongly believed that little babies should be baptized. Tom had been raised in a Baptist church and steadfastly refused to believe that Baptism was appropriate for children until they had reached a certain age. The two had been pleasantly arguing the issue for years. But one day God blessed them with a baby, and as the little one grew in her mother's womb the argument grew heated in the parents' hearts. I entered the scene in the seventh month. Out of the blue the mom called me and introduced herself with tears. The child was due in less than two months, and the parents were no closer to resolution than the day they had married. She desperately wanted the issue settled before the birth of the baby. "Could you come over and convince my husband?" was her anguished plea. I talked on the phone to her husband, Tom, who agreed to visit with me but said that he would talk about anything except Baptism. He was finished talking about Baptism, he complained. Discussion on Baptism, in his mind, led to anger and harsh words. We both agreed that God had not given us Baptism so we could have something to fight about. So I was able to visit with Tom but had been forced to promise not to broach the subject of Baptism. With my theological hands thus tied, I entered the lion's den.

Tom was one of the nicest men I had ever met. He was tall and wiry. Mildness covered his face and a quiet charm his personage. Soft-spoken and fast-thinking, Tom was as devout a father and husband as I could imagine. He was even more devout and serious about his beliefs. These beliefs included a strong conviction that the Bible was God's Word and an equally strong belief that infant Baptism was a superstitious and wrong practice.

We talked about the weather for a while. We talked even longer about their impending bundle of joy. And then we spent three hours drinking iced tea and talking theology. I wanted to convince Tom that children needed Baptism without ever mentioning the Sacrament itself. I had a strategy. First, I would convince him that children were sinful. That wouldn't be so difficult. I'd quote those standard passages such as Psalm 51:5, where the psalmist says, "Behold, I was brought forth in iniquity, and in sin did my mother conceive me." Then I would convince Tom that children, by the power of the Word, were able to believe in Jesus. I would use those standard passages every Lutheran has learned. "[W]hoever causes one of these little ones who believe in Me to sin . . . " (Matthew 18:6). "And He took them in His arms and blessed them, laying His hands on them" (Mark 10:16). "Out of the mouth of infants and nursing babies You have prepared praise" (Matthew 21:16). This would be easy. Tom listened patiently and politely as I quoted to him the Bible. And he nodded as if to say that while he agreed with the Bible he didn't necessarily agree with the guy who was quoting it. Finally, I broached the topic of human choice and grace alone. And at this Tom responded with surprising aggression.

I had asserted with a rather benign tone that salvation is not a matter of our choice. We do not choose God, rather He chooses us. But before I had finished uttering the words, Tom—mild-mannered and low-keyed Tom—rose in his chair and virtually glared at me. "How can you say that we can be saved without faith?" I had said no such thing, but my mind raced to try to ascertain why he thought I had. "Of course you have to choose," he answered my unarticulated question. "That's what faith is. It is our choice. That's why you can't baptize babies. Because in salvation they have to choose."

It occurred to me that, for Tom, the words *choose* and *faith* were synonymous. When I denied choice, he thought I was denying faith. Tom was willing, intellectually, to listen as God told him that babies could believe and were guilty of sin. But take away the notion of human free will and human choice and Tom became very agitated. I believed that I had discovered his false god. The name of his god was "choice."

As we continued to talk I realized that the entire question of Baptism was a question of faith. If faith was a decision or choice we made, then you shouldn't baptize babies until they were old enough to choose. But if faith is a gift of God, then we need to give it to our children. I quoted John 1:12–13: "But to all who did receive Him, who believed in His name, He gave the right to become children of God, who were born, not of blood nor of the will of the flesh nor of the will of man, but of God." Tom was still resistant. I cited Romans 9:15–16: "For He says to Moses, 'I will have mercy on whom I have mercy, and I will have compassion on whom I have compassion. So then it depends not on human will or exertion, but on God, who has mercy.' " Still there was resistance. Then I remembered that old standard, Ephesians 2:8–10. "By grace you have been saved through faith. . . . It is the gift of God."

"Faith is a gift," I said, "a wonderful gift. It is not something we have come to or decided upon. It is a gift. And if God can give the gift to you, sinful and stubborn though you are, He can give it to your kid no matter how young." I took a chance on calling him sinful and stubborn, but I figured him to be an honest man. I didn't think he would argue over my adjectives. Then I saw a miracle occur.

He sat and thought. He stared at me, then at the wall. When I began to speak again, he held up his hand as if to say, "Be quiet. I'm thinking." And after about three or four minutes he looked back at me. "Pastor, I'm ready," he said. "Let's schedule the Baptism."

Like a fool, I objected. "But are you sure you're convinced?"

His composed countenance was a picture of patience. "Are you in the habit of questioning even the decisions with which you agree?" Then I stayed quiet.

It turns out that Tom had been convinced of a very important article of Christian doctrine. We call it grace alone. God saves us, not by anything we have done. He creates faith apart from our choice, our will, our inclinations, our decisions, our seeking, our praying, or anything else we do. He gives us faith simply, freely by grace.

Synergism Analyzed

Follow this argument:

- The Word of the Gospel does not always have the power of God in it. It lacks something, and it cannot do all the things necessary for my salvation.
- It is necessary for me to add my own decision, free will, or choice to the Word of God.
- Therefore I have some of the responsibility and some of the credit for my own salvation.

This reasoning is the way most Evangelicals in America think. They have inherited their theology from Wesley, Finney, Dwight Moody, Billy Graham, Bill Bright, and others. They are synergists.

The argument above may seem logical, but it begins with a false premise, a statement totally against the Bible and the Reformation principle of grace alone. The Scriptures teach that God brings us to faith not by our own act of the will, or our own decision, but because of His own grace in the Gospel. The Scriptures do not teach, nor have Lutherans ever believed in, free will when it comes to matters of faith and salvation. The Formula of Concord puts it this way: "Therefore, Scripture denies to the natural human mind, heart, and will every ability, aptitude, capability, and capacity to think anything good or proper in spiritual matters by themselves, or to understand, begin, will, undertake, do, accomplish, or cooperate in them."[19] Lutherans have a pretty impressive and exhaustive list of things that we cannot do.

But most Evangelical Protestants in North America are totally and wrongly convinced that somehow salvation is partially the responsibility of the individual.

The American Idol

I am convinced that most Americans worship two false gods: football and choice. Football only lasts about five months and does not necessarily have to replace Jesus as our number one interest even during those months. But choice and the right to choose have become not only the right of every citizen but also the obligation. Choice is our god.

We choose our beer, our fast food, our careers, and the football team we like. We choose our spouses, our friends, our television stations, our music, and the classes we want to take in high school and college. We choose to purchase this car over that car because it has more options. If we get in trouble, then people say that we have made some poor choices. Just about everything conceivable is our choice. The greatest moral evil in our culture, it seems, is to deprive a person of choice. But certain things we cannot choose.

When I was a kid, my family used to drive from St. Louis through Iowa up to a lake in Minnesota every summer. Because the interstate had not been built we were forced to take Highway 218, which meandered through almost every town and city in the state. Often on the outside of a town we could read a sign that listed all the various churches in that town. The sign would say, "Worship at the church of your choice." God says that we should worship at the church of His choice. Churches are not our choice.

Abortion was very unpopular in the United States even after the infamous *Roe v. Wade* Supreme Court decision of 1973 that legalized abortion in most cases. In the late 1970s the pro-abortionists settled on a slogan that, within a decade, turned the majority of Americans toward their point of view: "A woman has the right to choose." God says that pre-born babies are His gift to us. He has chosen to give them. It is not a moral option whether or not to kill them.

I asked a Bible class whether those who do not know Jesus are lost. One of the ladies answered, "That depends." I wondered what it depends on. She was quick to explain. "It depends on whether or not that person has heard about Jesus. If they have not heard, then it would be unfair for God to send them to hell. But if they have heard, then they have a choice." The Bible, however, never says that people are lost simply because they have not had a choice. Heaven is not our choice.

I suppose that we can choose a particular ecclesiastical organization, but that does not make it a church, a good church, or the right church. I suppose that we can choose to kill our babies, but that doesn't make them any less God's gifts. It certainly doesn't make it morally right. And we can deceive ourselves into thinking that heaven is our choice. But it is not. Jesus is not our choice. Grace is not our choice. Faith is not our choice.

We dare not take credit for what God has done. Go back to chapter 2 and read again the section on active and passive faith. Choosing is active. Faith, when it comes to salvation, is passive. "I believe that by my own understanding or strength I cannot believe in Jesus Christ my Lord or come to him, but instead the Holy Spirit has called me through the Gospel, enlightened me with his gifts, made me holy and kept me in the true faith."[20] Every Lutheran has memorized these words from the catechism. Years ago Protestant Evangelicals used to put bumper stickers on their cars that read, "I have found it." Contrast that with the words of the father who welcomes home his prodigal son, "For this my son was dead, and is alive again; he was lost, and is found" (Luke 16:24). A popular praise song is entitled "I Have Decided to Follow Jesus." Contrast that with this hymn:

> Lord, 'tis not that I did choose Thee;
> That, I know, could never be;
> For this heart would still refuse Thee
> Had Thy grace not chosen me.[21]

My friend Tom initially insisted that his little baby had to choose in order to be saved. Contrast this to the Gospel. Tom came to believe that God would choose his little baby through the Gospel of grace in Baptism.

Giving God His Due

It was a cold autumn afternoon in St. Louis. My father's birthday had arrived, and all the children in the family were generating the appropriate gifts. What should I give? Homemade cards with pictures of Dad, painted handsomely, of course, were always appreciated. These, however, required some skill, so my deliberations continued. I had long since discovered that Dad was not enamored with those precious outdoor treasures little boys chance upon in their travels: rocks, reptile skeletons, uniquely shaped cigar butts. He always feigned delight, but we had learned to read his expressions, and he didn't really like that kind of stuff. My older brother had been working on some object of art for a couple of weeks. If only I had developed the talent of planning, I could be in such an enviable position. What should I give? I asked my mom, but not in such a way that she would actually produce the coveted offering. Her suggestion was brilliant in its simplicity. It seems I could wash some windows, for which I would receive certain remuneration. Thereupon I would use my income to purchase something for Dad. Hmm, what would Dad like? Again, Mom produced the solution: candy.

So I went to work. I slaved for at least an hour washing a couple of storm windows, which had attracted that wicked combination of dust and sunlight. I used Windex and clean rags, washing, buffing, and polishing until the sunlight exposed nothing but clean transparent glass. Dirty, sweaty, and spent, I triumphantly displayed my work to Mom, whose normal perfectionism was suspended in deference to my desperation. "It is finished," she announced and awarded me the 50 cents needed for the candy. "Turtles" are chocolate and caramel covered pecans. I loved them and knew my father would as well. Riding my two-speed 24-inch racer like the wind down to Citron's drugstore, I found a pack of six for 50 cents.

"Taxes? I never heard of taxes," was my desperate plea to the proprietor as he informed me of my shortage. Graciously, he covered the 2 cents I lacked, for which I nodded in humble appreciation and rode home with my prize.

That was my first lesson in capitalism, the Protestant work ethic, profit margins, labor negotiations, and government intervention. It was also my first taste of synergism.

It seems my little brother was even less prepared than I. So he made me an offer I should have refused. "How would you like it if I wrapped the present for you?" What was the downside of this I wondered, as, like a fool, I turned over the precious cargo to the devious imp.

The wrapping ended up looking as awful as I would have expected. The good news is that the candy remained both undamaged and uneaten. The bad news is that it had been far more presentable when it was still in the bag from the drugstore. But I took it with the same charm and apparent happiness that my mother had demonstrated to me earlier in the afternoon.

The party began. Cards, songs, cakes, and candles were displayed all around. Dad was in rare form, blowing out all the candles on the first try. Then came the opening of the gifts. He ooed and ahhed with each offering while I waited with ill-hidden excitement for the moment of truth. At last he came to mine. Here was the first gift I had ever purchased. Purchased with all my money and my only money, it was, without a doubt, the best gift I had ever given and, arguably, the best gift I would ever give. I knew he would like it. I wanted to see his face light up and watch his tongue and lips glisten in anticipation of the sweet treasure. He read the words that had been scribbled on the wrapping paper (did I mention that my brother had wrapped it in newspaper?) They said, "To Dad from 'so and so' and Klemet." What a thief my brother was. He hadn't even mentioned my name first.

How did I feel?

How was I supposed to feel? How would you feel? Someone else had shared the credit for the gift that I alone had given. Someone was seeking to share the thanks and praise that were due me. I had earned money without my brother's help. I had purchased the gift without my brother's help. I had given the gift without my brother's help. I was cheated, deceived, violated. I was being synergized. I felt the way God feels every time someone synergizes Him, every time someone says the reason they are saved is because of something in them. They have made a decision, contributed their free will, chosen salvation, invited Jesus, or prayed the proper petition. Synergism robs God. It is wrong.

SYNERGISM IN AMERICAN HISTORY

Let me walk you through 300 years of history again. You will see that the major spokesmen for Evangelicalism in North America have all denied grace alone. They almost always believe that faith comes about by the free will and free decision of the sinner.

Listen to John Wesley: "It is true, we receive salvation by simple faith; but God does not, will not, give that faith unless we seek it with all diligence, in the way which He has ordained." "God hardly gives His Spirit even to those whom He has established in grace if they do not pray for it on all occasions, not only once, but many times. God does nothing but in answer to prayer."[22] According to Wesley, you have to ask and pray and seek faith or you will be lost.

Listen to Finney: "As, therefore, God requires men to make to themselves a new heart on the pain of eternal death, it is the strongest possible evidence that they are able to do it."[23] Translation: Because God tells you that you must have a new heart, that proves that you are able to get one on your own. Finney also claims that you need to make a decision for Christ "similar to voting in a democratic election."[24] According to Finney, faith is like choosing between candidates.

Listen to the early Pentecostals: "Conversion is produced by the cooperation of Divine and human activities."[25] "Salvation is received quite freely through grace alone; yet for a man to accept it rests on a conscious and free decision of his will."[26]

Listen to the earliest charismatics: "The beautiful thing about God and His love is that He never removes from you the privilege of exercising our own will. By our free choice we can will to follow Him or we can WILL to follow the devil. He never forces Himself upon us, but gives us our own free choice."[27] Lutheran charismatics agree:

> On occasion, for instance, we find it helpful to "coach" a person in regard to conversion. The person genuinely wants to accept Christ, but cannot seem to put it into words. So we pray a simple prayer of repentance and faith, inviting him to repeat it after us. He does and we accept this as a genuine beginning. The proof of course must be that he goes on from that point to believe and live as a real Christian.[28]

According to Pentecostals and their descendents in the Charismatic Movement, salvation does not and cannot happen without the sinner choosing it.

These quotations do not come from fringe members of radical religious groups. They are representative of mainstream American Protestantism. Listen to a few more from Evangelical Protestant religious leaders.

Bill Bright, founder of Campus Crusade for Christ, the largest ministry in the United States directed toward university students:

> Someone may say, "I believe that Jesus Christ is the Son of God. I believe that He died for my sins. Why I have believed this all my life. Am I not a Christian?" Not if that person has refused to

> yield his will to Him. . . . At this moment, if you have not already received Christ as your Savior and Lord, Jesus is knocking at the door of your heart. Will you, in the quiet of this moment surrender your will to Him? Invite Him to come into your life to live His life in you, to pardon your sin, to give purpose to your life, to give you His peace and power."[29]

Notice how Bill Bright makes you question your faith if you merely believe that Jesus is the Son of God and that He died for your sins. According to Bright, Jesus is not enough unless you have also yielded. Jesus does His part, and you have to do yours. You are cooperating with God. Grace alone is completely denied.

Billy Graham, who has preached to more people than anyone else in the history of the world, says this of faith:

> Faith is first of all belief—belief that Christ was who He said He was. Second, faith is belief that He can do what He claimed He could do—He can forgive me and come into my life. Third, faith is trust, an act of commitment, in which I open the door of my heart to Him. In the New Testament the words "faith," "belief," and "believe," are translations of similar Greek words so they are interchangeable. Placing your faith in Christ meant that first you must make a choice. The Scripture says, "Whoever believes in Jesus is not condemned, but whoever does not believe stands condemned already because he has not believed in the name of God's one and only Son" (John 3:18). The person who believes is not condemned; the person who has not believed is condemned. In order not to be condemned you must make a choice—you must choose to believe.[30]

Notice how Billy Graham uses the words *believe* and *choose* as if they were the same thing. Observe also that the passage he sites (John 3:18) says nothing at all about choosing but says everything about faith. Billy Graham made the mistake of thinking that faith and choice were the same. Not surprisingly, yet very tragically, Billy Graham never taught infant Baptism and never came to teach grace alone.

CAN SYNERGISTS BE SAVED?

There is a risk in criticizing the theology of others. Someone will draw the conclusion that you think everyone who makes a theological mistake is going to hell. That simply is not the case. It is not for me to judge the eternal souls of John Wesley, Charles Finney, Larry Christenson, Bill Bright, Billy Graham, or anyone else. But there is a particularly nasty and evil dilemma floating around out there that must be exposed.

If I say that Billy Graham and others are going to hell, then I am being sinful in judging them.

If I say that Billy Graham and others are not going to hell, then I am being sinful for making a big deal over a theology that does not necessarily damn a person.

Either way I am being sinful, so I guess I should say nothing.

I have no choice but to point out bad theology. God called me to do so when I became a pastor. "He must hold firm to the trustworthy word as taught, so that he may be able to give instruction in sound doctrine and also to rebuke those who contradict it" (Titus 1:9). So God requires that I, and all pastors, refute synergists.

But can synergists be saved? They deny grace alone. They deprive the Holy Spirit of His rightful due. God expects to get 100 percent of the credit for our salvation. This is taken away from Him with all the talk of human free will, choice, invitation, seeking, and yielding. Can a person be saved who is guilty of this?

Actually, that is exactly the wrong question. It's the question that the devil wants us to ask. He wants us to reduce all theology to this simple, sometimes unknowable, question. Can so and so be saved? Can you be saved if you believe in the blood of Jesus but never were baptized? Yes? Then Baptism must be unnecessary. Can you be saved if you died before you are instructed and are able to receive the Lord's Supper? Yes? Then instruction into the faith and Holy Communion must not be too important. Can you be saved if you simply hear the story of the forgiveness of the cross and die before you ever hear of the Holy Spirit or the Trinity or that Jesus will come again or the church or anything else? Yes? Then I guess the Trinity does not matter or Christ's second coming or the church or anything else but that one simple sentence "Jesus died for me."

We are saved by the simple sentence, "Christ Jesus came to save sinners of whom I am chief." But that does not entitle us to throw away everything else that the Scriptures teach.

We need to change the question. This is the right question: Should you believe what synergists teach? Should you believe Billy Graham? Let's leave Billy Graham's salvation to God. Billy Graham may have a simple childlike faith despite his refusal to give that faith to children in Baptism. He may have clung to the blood and righteousness of Christ, even though he denied them in the Lord's Supper. He may have trusted in God's grace, even though he taught that this grace needed human will to supplement it. Let's not get personal about Billy Graham or me or John Wesley. Let's get personal with you. Does God want you and your children to believe that your salvation depends on grace alone? If you can say yes to that, and you must say yes, then you will agree that synergists have seriously deceived and harmed the church. If you open your hearts to their teaching, then you seriously endanger your soul. If you send your children to hear them, you are feeding them spiritual poison as surely as putting arsenic in Cheerios. And if the children somehow, by God's grace, manage to survive, that does not make the poison any less lethal.

THE GOSPEL AND EVANGELISM

But what about those evangelism programs where we encourage people to invite Jesus into their lives? Shouldn't we encourage people to believe? The word *evangelism* comes from two Greek words. The first is *Eu*, which means "good." The second is *Angel*, which means "message." So the *evangel* is the good message or the Good News. We usually translate the Greek word *euangel* as "Gospel." Evangelism, then, is any time or occasion in which the Gospel is proclaimed or taught. Your church service is evangelism if the Gospel is contained in the liturgy and if the pastor preaches Christ. The Lord's Supper is the *evangel.* Any time the Word or Sacraments are given, evangelism is being carried out. Your Sunday morning Bible class is evangelism if the pastor teaches about Christ. To tell others of the truth of the Gospel of Christ, or to declare the riches of God in Christ to others, that is evangelism. Many churches have evangelism programs. People are trained to go out into the homes of the community and tell others about Jesus. As long as the message of Christ is spoken, then evangelism is being done. The best evangelism Christians can do is to tell their loved ones, whether family or friends, of the love of God in Christ and do what we can to get them to a church that teaches the Word of God purely and administers Baptism and the Lord's Supper as Christ intended. Unfortunately, the word *evangelism* is often understood to mean going into someone else's house and giving them a planned presentation of Jesus. In reality, most planned evangelism is done in the worship services. One-on-one evangelism is more spontaneous. You simply talk about Christ when you can.

When I was in college, I was taught how to be part of an "evangelism team." I was told how to present Jesus in a clear and simple way to someone else. Actually, parts of the training were very good. But I was always a bit uncomfortable with the manner of presentation I was told to give. It was not that it seemed a bit contrived. I understood that sometimes things are forced before they are spontaneous. It was not that I was talking to strangers. I understood that someone has to tell strangers about Christ. It was not that I was a novice. I knew that you had to start somewhere.

I was troubled because we were told to invite the person to believe in Jesus right there in their living room. Again, you might say, "But a person has to believe, don't they?" Yes, but that does not mean that we have to invite them or ask them or encourage them or even inform them about the necessity of faith. C. F. W. Walther says:

> A preacher must be able to preach a sermon on faith without ever using the term *faith*. It is not important that he din the word *faith* in the ears of his audience, but it is necessary for him to frame his address so as to arouse in every poor sinner the desire to lay the burden of his sins at the feet of the Lord Jesus Christ and say to Him: "Thou art mine, and I am Thine."[31]

Walther's words apply equally to every Christian who tells others about Jesus. You don't need to mention faith much less tell the person that they have to believe. Just speak of Jesus. The Gospel has a power within it to create faith. You don't need to add an invitation to it.

Of course, in the Bible, there are many examples of people who are told to believe. The jailor of Philippi is a good example. But in these cases faith is never presented as a prerequisite that the person has to add. It is presented as the absence of work, the absence of hopelessness, the absence of credit. "And to the one who does not work but trusts him who justifies the ungodly, his faith is counted as righteousness," says Paul (Romans 4:5).

Throwing Kids into the Air

I can remember when my daughter Rachel was about 2 years old. She was a very cute and tiny little girl. And she was fearless. One day we were wrestling and roughhousing as fathers do with their kids. Suddenly, almost impulsively, I picked her up and threw her into the air. She was thrilled with the near-death experience. I did it again. Higher and higher she flew, like a small missile, with hair, arms, and legs flying every which way as she giggled with delight. It turned into a game. Sometimes I would throw her straight up into the air. Other times I would grab her under her arms and rock her back and forth and suddenly twirl her around almost like a huge yo-yo. Then I'd let her go and watch her twirl in the air. Every once in a while I would catch her but then feign dropping her only to grab her again just before she would hit the ground. In all of this she was in "little kid heaven." Every evening, when I would come home for dinner, there she was, nagging and pleading for me to do my faltering imitation of some trapeze artist. And I craved the astonishing trust that only little children can place in their fathers.

My son would always watch with studied apprehension. You could tell that he wanted a part of the action. But he was reluctant. Caution ruled. I wanted to coax him. But what should I say? "C'mon, I won't drop you." That would stress my reliability. "C'mon, you'll love it." That would stress the benefits of being thrown wildly into the air. "C'mon, I wouldn't let you fall." That would stress the safety of the venture. I could have said, "You gotta trust me," but it wasn't necessary. I just wanted him to see the fun. I thought better of using the word *trust*. His problem was that he was afraid. He did not fully trust. I did not want him to start thinking about his own trust. Instead, I wanted him to think about the blessing of the activity.

I suppose that it took me about three or four weeks to convince my son that he could trust me. I demonstrated my trustworthiness by throwing his sister with apparent control. And I was always careful not to drop her. I encouraged him by speaking words to his sister. "Oh, this is fun. Whew, that was a good one." Rachel's launchings themselves became the greatest testimony and encouragement to her brother. I never said, "You have to have faith." I surely did not say, "If only you will decide by an act of faith, then you can enjoy this too." It was obvious that he had to trust me if I was going to throw him into the air. And it was equally obvious that I didn't need to tell him to trust me.

Finally, with painful deliberation he held out his arms. So I grabbed him and threw him into the air. He liked it too. It took him a bit longer to really enjoy the experience, but he did. He was even a little sad when we were called to dinner.

That's the way true evangelism is. You picture Jesus. You talk about the Savior. You don't picture Him as fun but as loving, gracious, and forgiving. You don't have to say, "You gotta believe." If you say the right things about Jesus and His forgiveness, then it ought to be obvious that people should trust in Him.

When we demand or require faith too strenuously, then, even though we are well intended, we give the impression that faith is our doing. We may even give the impression that faith somehow adds to Christ's salvation. Both impressions are synergism. They are a denial of grace alone.

A REALLY BAD TRACT

About 20 years ago I was given a tract from The Lutheran Church—Missouri Synod Department of Evangelism entitled "Do You Know the Four Steps to Success?" It told you how to get to heaven. The first step was to believe that you could be happy. The second step was to believe that you sinned. The third step was to believe that Christ offers peace with God. The fourth step said:

> We must accept Jesus into our lives as our personal savior by permitting Him to make peace between God and us, by following His way of life as our way of life. Jesus is ready now to restore the full life to you. Are you ready now? Then ask Him to come into your life and personally accept Him. The next step is yours. Accepting Christ and finding the successful life in Him can be beautifully simple! Just admit to Him that life is incomplete, ask for His forgiveness, and request Him to begin a new life in you. You may speak to Him RIGHT NOW, for He is present and hears. Talk to Him in your own words, or use this

> prayer: "Lord Jesus Christ, I ask for your help. Forgive my sins and give me peace with God. Then, dear Jesus, I ask that You make Your way of life become my way of life. Thank You for the new peace and happiness that You give me. Amen"[32]

Notice how salvation occurs here. God does not choose us, bring us to life through the Gospel, create faith, or enlighten us with His gifts of Baptism and the Lord's Supper. He sits and waits while we do things. Count the things we must do. Accept. Permit. Follow His way of life. Be ready. Ask Him to come into our lives. Personally accept Him. Admit to Him. Ask for forgiveness. Request Him to begin a our lives. Talk to Him. Whew! If salvation were that complicated and difficult, I, for one, would not be saved. Neither would you. All these demands are made of people who, according to God, are dead.

This tract demanded faith as if faith were something that we accomplish. According to the Bible, faith is a gift of God. He creates it through the Gospel. The track was guilty of synergism.

CONCLUSION

You cannot separate the Holy Spirit from the Word without falling into serious theological mischief. Such a separation brings difficulties that threaten and even deny the Gospel.

- Experience replaces faith and the Holy Spirit becomes unpredictable.
- Uncertainties divide the church.
- Christ is minimized as the teaching of grace alone is questioned or denied.

We will analyze these aspects of American Evangelical Protestantism in chapters 8, 9, and 10. Chapter 8 will show that today's churches are tempted to replace doctrine with excitement. Chapter 9 will analyze the church's divisive tendency to demand that people or congregations be dynamic rather than trust the dynamic Word that God has given us in Christ. Chapter 10 will show the synergism and other flaws that are built into American Evangelical worship. In these next three chapters we will see that the principles of "American Christianity" are fostered and perpetuated through the various church practices of American Evangelicalism. We will also see that

Lutheranism in America often uncritically accepts the bad practices of Evangelicalism.

The true doctrine of justification by grace through faith attracts and warms Christ's sheep. In the theology of American Evangelicalism, justification is replaced by a quest for experience, denied by claims of "two-stage" Christianity, and destroyed by synergism. In the theology of American Evangelicalism, "The Fire Is Doused."

STUDY QUESTIONS

1. What are the uncertainties that are faced when one begins to look for the Holy Spirit outside the Word and Sacraments?
2. According to John Wesley, when and where did God work?
3. Describe Wesley's "two-stage Christianity."
4. What was Charles Finney's vehicle for his experiential Christianity?
5. What innovation did Charles Parham and Pentecostalism say would confirm that a person had received the second blessing of the Holy Spirit?
6. When Pentecostalism invaded mainline churches, what was it called?
7. What is the doctrine upon which the church stands or falls?
8. With experiential Christianity in mind, what does the author point to as a weakness of praise songs used in some churches?
9. What is the error of synergism?
10. To review, who alone is responsible for your salvation?
11. What is evangelism?

DISCUSSION QUESTIONS

1. Discuss how two-stage Christianity destroys the assurance of justification by grace through faith in Jesus Christ.
2. How does synergism violate the Christian doctrine of grace alone? How does infant Baptism confess grace alone?
3. Consider and discuss the proper use of our right and freedom of choice in our active and passive faith.

8
The Staff Is Bent

THE EXCITEMENT OF AMERICAN CHRISTIANITY

In chapter 7 I showed the distinctive features of conservative Evangelical American Christianity. They are:

- Excitement and experience have replaced faith and doctrine—uncertainty prevails.
- Dynamism is extolled—a divisive two-tiered understanding of the church is seen in which some are considered more Spirit-filled or dynamic than others.
- Christ is diminished through synergism—salvation becomes my choice rather than God's.

These principles are quite doctrinal in nature. They are assumed and practiced to varying degrees in most North American denominations. Woe to that church or congregation that tries to buck them. I will analyze the first principle in this chapter, showing the harmful practices we have learned by depending on experience and excitement. In chapter 9 I will look at the principle of dynamic people. In chapter 10 I will look at the worship of American Evangelicalism and show, among other things, its synergism.

Because these principles are in conflict with historic Lutheran doctrine, their acceptance is not always obvious or even conscious among Lutherans. Instead, slowly, even naively, Lutherans change their practice so it begins to teach the questionable and false doctrine of American Evangelicalism. We borrow practices of churches around us without recognizing their effects. The borrowed habitual practices of alien churches have an authority connected to them whether they are desirable or not. So, slowly, we take on the appearance of those churches around us. We are like a kid unknowingly playing wrong notes on a piano.

PLAYING WRONG NOTES ON THE PIANO

My parents loved me so much they gave me piano lessons as a child. At least, I think it was love.

I had been playing for a few years when I concluded that I did not have a lot of raw musical talent. I was good enough to understand how bad I was. Real musicians, you see, do not just play notes. They interpret the composer. Living within the confines of the musical score, they breathe, move, and express in such a way that the angels in heaven smile. To real musicians there is an unselfconscious genius that guides the music and makes it serene, ethereal, and artful. Whenever I deluded myself into thinking I possessed such genius, the facts of the music itself condemned me to the apprehension of my own mediocrity.

Once I asked Mrs. Buszin, my teacher, if she could get me the theme song to the opera "Lucia di Lammermoor." I wanted to learn it. Actually, it's quite a beautiful melody, and Mrs. Buszin was impressed at my taste, if not my abilities. It took her two months, but she tracked down a piano version of the piece that corresponded to my level of expertise and assigned it to me. I ran home with greater zeal than the kid from *A Christmas Story* who had just received his Red Ryder BB gun. I was determined to learn this classic piece of music.

Hours a day were spent at the piano. I would show my teacher, and the world, that I was worthy of such music. I devoured the notes, the harmony, the color, and the composition of the melody. I was in the groove one day, playing the beautiful opera in a world of music and beauty that far transcended mere space when something happened that dissuaded me from a musical career once and for all.

My father was in his study, a room adjacent to the hallway that housed the piano. He was usually a pretty good sport about trying to work while we practiced. We would use the muffler pedal to keep the music low, and he would basically leave us alone. But on this particular afternoon he kept yelling at me from the other room. I'd play along, enraptured by my own beauty, and he would yell, "No!" from the other room. At first I thought he was simply correcting tests and was frustrated at his errant students. But such was not the case. Then it occurred to me that I might be playing too loudly. I toned it down, transgressing my own free spirit in deference to his sensitivities. The no's from the other room grew louder and took on an exasperated tone. He was getting frustrated, and so was I. He just did not appreciate my brilliance. Finally, Dad burst through the door, strode to the piano, and said, "No! Can't you hear what you're playing? It's not a D sharp. It's a D natural. You hit the same wrong note every time you play the one section." Then, to add insult to injury, he hit the D natural and said, "Ah, that's better." Immediately, and with little fanfare, he turned on his heels and disappeared with the same abruptness that had characterized his entrance. Who did he think he was, Mozart?

I studied the musical score. I knew he was in error. He had to be. How could I have played the same wrong note for weeks? Desperately I searched for the spot of the alleged infraction. But even before I found it, I knew. For more than a month I had played the same note incorrectly. All my enraptured enthusiasm did not change what was written on the page. I had grown so accustomed to playing a note amiss that it actually began to sound right to me. In fact, when I corrected myself and played the true note, it had a dissonant ring to it.

That's the way it is with many of the practices of the church. We do the same thing so often and so uncritically that pretty soon the things we do just seem good, right, and salutary even if they are not. Our Evangelical neighbors, who do the same, just reinforce our faulty church practices. If we change these practices, even correct them, the changes themselves seem wrong. Habitual church practices not only teach doctrine, as we learned in chapter 4, they actually establish in our minds what we think is normal.

Some church practices are so ingrained in the spirit of Evangelical Protestantism that they are uncritically accepted. They are part of our culture. How that culture affects us is an interesting story.

Our Culture Craves Excitement: Revivalism

According to one Lutheran Church Growth advocate, our Lutheran congregations should be part of the "broad movement among conservative Protestants," which features "camplike revivals" similar to those employed by Charles Finney, Dwight Moody, and more recently, Billy Graham.[1] What are revivals or revivalism? William McLoughlin defines it:

> Revivalism is the Protestant ritual (at first spontaneous, but, since 1830, routinized) in which charismatic evangelists convey "the Word" of God to large masses of people who, under this influence, experience what Protestants call conversion, salvation, regeneration, or spiritual rebirth.[2]

McLoughlin's definition is pretty good. Another notable characteristic of revivals is the belief that one can tell that the Holy Spirit is present by the excitement of the crowd and the dynamism of the speaker. David Gustafson has described revivals similarly:

> Revivals, or, as they were called, the "new Measures," were an integral part of American Protestantism in the mid nineteenth century. The phenomenon crossed denominational lines. The emphasis was on a concrete personal conversion experience, and the revival was the means employed to bring about the experience. Revival preaching was highly emotional, aimed at reaching the lost sinner. . . . The purpose of the revival was to bring people to the point where they would come forward and accept Jesus.[3]

"The dominant theme in America from 1800 to 1860 is the invincible persistence of the revival technique,"[4] says another historian, who also claims that "revivals marked the beginning of the attempt to build a new Christian community united by intense feeling."[5] William Warren Sweet, "the most industrious and tireless fact-finding historian of churches in early America," claims that two types of Protestant churches existed in Europe at the time of the great emigrations to the United States. He calls them "right-wing churches," which were the established churches in the Old World and "left-wing churches," which were not. While both types of churches crossed the Atlantic, it was the "left-wing" churches that "made the greatest contribution of thought and life to the New World." According to Sweet, the influential "left-wing churches" stressed the "inner, personal character of religion, played down the church's institutional character and placed much less stress upon creeds and sacraments."[6] This is significant. Never do revivalists claim that the Spirit is present because the Word is taught or confessed in its truth and purity or because the Sacraments are administered according to Christ's institution. Instead, the churches of the new frontier preferred intense inner feelings to creeds and sacraments. If they had believed in Word and Sacraments, they would not have been revivalists and would have been open to Lutheranism.

Basically, the revivalists were Osiandrian. Osiander, if you remember from chapter 2, was a theologian in the sixteenth century who deviated from the biblical doctrine of justification by grace. The Lutherans believed that the sinner's justification before God was based on the innocent life of Christ and His sacrificial death for us. These were counted to the credit of the sinner. Consequently, the Lutherans taught Christ. They wanted people to understand and believe the Gospel that, in their preaching and teaching, bestowed the righteousness of Christ. Lutherans believed that God "bespeaks us righteous" through Word and Sacrament. Osiander believed that it was Jesus in your heart that made you righteous and acceptable before God. Eventually this doctrine led men such as John Wesley and almost all of American Protestantism to devise ways in which you could be certain that Jesus was in your heart. You had to feel Him. The revivals made you feel. And revivals were everywhere.

I LOVE ROCK 'N' ROLL

If you want to know what a revival was like, then go to a rock concert.

I am a rock 'n' roll fan. My wife gave me a t-shirt when I turned 50 that said, "I can't be 50 if I still like rock 'n' roll." My kids saw it and rejoined, "You must be 50 if you still like rock 'n' roll." Rock 'n' roll concerts are like "camp revivals." I saw U2 (an Irish rock group) back in 1989 in Oakland, California. The concert was scheduled to start at 8 P.M., but when we arrived at 7:30 the music had been playing for more than an hour. There were two warm-up bands. One was The Pretenders, which left the stage at 8:30, and we were told that U2 would be out soon. "Soon" we discovered was an eschatological term. It basically meant "No one knew the hour," even though we were somewhat certain as to the day. We waited and waited. No one seemed to mind. A disc jockey was playing some tunes. There was no assigned seating, so we just got as close as we could without being trampled and watched the people.

What a motley audience: young and old, gray hairs and toddlers, every race and socioeconomic strata. Little kids were sleeping on the outfield grass with trusting mothers casually dancing nearby. Venders were hawking their wares, whether treats, trinkets, or t-shirts. Some guys were throwing a football; others were playing hackie sack. No one seemed anxious, but everyone was anxiously waiting. Finally, the lights dimmed, and with that came the ubiquitous laughter, whistling, and shouting. The music began slowly and rhythmically, and the crowd started to sway back and forth. A bass guitar softly plucked the beat as the crowd grew more and more eager. The band was right on time, which was an hour late, and we loved it. Finally, the sonorous voice of Bono, the lead singer, wailed throughout the stadium as he ran out onto the stage. At this the crowd roared its approval, the decibel level skyrocketed, and the serious music commenced. We were graciously offered some pot by a couple of kids but politely refused. I did not think we needed drugs to achieve an altered mental state. The entire concert was doing exactly that for us. We grew increasingly excited as we listened to the band play song after song. No one just sat. The crowd lived and moved with each person doing exactly what they wanted. Some just listened. Some danced. Some chatted. Some ran around. It was programmed bedlam, and Bono worked the crowd better than Charles Finney, Elmer Gantry, or even Billy Sunday.

If you want to know what the revivals were like, just go to a rock concert. Revivals were exciting quarterly camp meetings. There would be many preachers, much like the many warm-up bands. The headline preacher would make the audience wait for hours. This had the effect of creating a fevered expectancy. I have never been to a concert where the band started playing on time. The revivals were characterized by loud rhythmic music, and people would participate by clapping, swaying back and forth with arms uplifted, or dancing. At the revivals people would leave and return hours, even days, later. If you ever attended a Grateful Dead concert, you saw pretty much the same thing. Rock stars take on almost divine qualities, much like the revival preachers. I can even remember driving home on the date of Jerry Garcia's death. I saw a "Honk if you loved Jerry" sign hanging out of a car window. I honked. He was like a religious figure. Take away the drugs, and you have all the accoutrements of your typical nineteenth-century revival. I remember once leaving a Three Dog Night concert back in 1974. It was Saturday night. I heard this kid who looked about 16 talking to a friend: "I gotta get up early tomorrow. My parents told me I could go to this concert if I promised to get up and go to church. Why can't the music in church be more like this music? Then I would like it. It wouldn't be such a drag." Little did he know what was about to happen to countless American congregations.

Oddly enough, I attended a session of the "Courageous Churches" Conference in Minneapolis in the summer of 2001. It's a conference for pastors of The Lutheran Church—Missouri Synod who want to learn the principles of the Church Growth Movement. In the session that I visited, the leader played a videotape of Bono, lead singer for U2, as an example of what preachers might be like if they wanted to "connect with" their audiences.

VILLAGE AND CAMP

David Luecke has provided a helpful analysis of the differences between what he calls a "village church" and a "camp church." The village church is the old-style church that has stability, traditions, creeds, trained pastors, and church buildings. It's the kind of church that he grew up in, that I grew up in, and that most Lutherans know and understand. The camp church, which Luecke advocates, more closely resembles the revivals. It's more like a rock concert. There are profound differences between the two churches.

- The village church recognizes parish boundaries. The camp church has boundaries determined by the members who have a "self-professed personal relationship with Jesus" and a "born again" experience.
- The village church looks to its creeds and theology for guidance, confident that these reflect the teachings of the Bible. The camp church uses only the Bible, and the people "make up their identity as they go along."

- The village church has members who are born into it and who "belong before consciously believing." The camp church expects its members to have a "consciousness of that life-transforming event" that is their "only reliable basis for initiating fellowship in Christ."
- The village church emphasizes the Baptism of infants as the way in which people become part of the church community. The camp church emphasizes initiation through "intense religious experiences."
- The village church expects the Holy Spirit to come through God's Word and Sacraments "predictably." The camp church expects the Spirit to come through the Word, but unpredictably, "quickly and decisively and right now."
- The village church stresses instruction and confirmation. The camp church stresses the importance of people being "ready to open up their feelings for Him to move them in spontaneous ways to unexpected decisions."
- The village church expects God to work through "prescribed liturgies, lessons, and authorized leaders." The camp church has little use for these "customs."[7]

In chapter 1 I showed that God works through doctrine. He loves creeds and expects His church to teach and confess doctrine. God wants us to instruct our children in the catechism and ourselves with the Gospel doctrine. His desire is that we are confident of our doctrine and look to it for our identity. Our heavenly Father does not want us to make up our identity as we go along. In chapter 2 I showed that the Word and Sacraments of Christ "bespeak us righteous" whether we are particularly conscious of God's grace or not. In chapter 3 I showed that the Holy Spirit is predictable. He works through Baptism, Holy Communion, and the Word of the Gospel. He establishes the office of the ministry because He wants to work through "authorized leaders." In chapter 4 I showed that reliance on feelings or experience is always a rather dangerous thing both for the unity of the church and for a person's faith.

God much prefers the village church.

Clearly there are irreconcilable differences between the village church and the camp church. Yet David Luecke says: "Is there anything inherently wrong with a camp church? I think not. Which is the right view? I believe the Scripture allows both ways. Which is the right view? They both can be."[8] The Church Growth Movement prefers the camp church. The goal of the movement is to turn Lutherans into revivalists.

MY CAMPFIRE EXPERIENCE

When I was in high school, our congregation had Walther League meetings twice a month where we would study the Bible, talk theology, eat junk food, bowl, or play volleyball. Once a year we would go on a weeklong retreat with the Walther Leagues from other churches. We would go to the Lake of the Ozarks or some resort in southern Missouri. It was fun. Often in the evenings we would gather around various campfires in groups of about twenty and sing songs such as "Kum Ba Yah" or "Michael, Row the Boat Ashore." At such meetings we would always be asked to share that moment in our lives when we were especially close to God.

I liked the retreats, but I hated those sharing times. It's not just that I am a guy and need help getting in touch with my own feelings. Nor was my reticence the result of having been the product of a village church and a concurrent inability to articulate my personal consciousness of God. It's just that I like to choose my own intimates. And a group of twenty kids, three-fourths of whom were relative strangers, was not, in my mind, the ideal outlet for my spiritual or moral musings. But I would always take my turn, embellishing some mundane event so as to give it more import than was rightly due. My only justification was that everyone else was doing the same thing.

In my junior year in high school I was redeemed from those torturous and embarrassing affairs.

There was a guy named Bill from one of the other churches. He was one of those noisy, raucous guys who acted like he did not care about anything but sports. Underneath that shallow, if attractive, veneer you got the feeling there might be an original thought or two. The question was the same as we had every year. "Name an experience when you were particularly close to God." Bill, cool and suave, said, "Well, I don't really remember it, but when I got baptized at the age of 10 days I was particularly close to God." Of course, such an answer was against the implicit rules of the sharing session. If you couldn't remember it, how could you talk about it? The youth counselor was not slow in correcting Bill. Normally, that would be the end of it. We've all seen it a thousand times. Some kid makes a wisecrack, gets chided by an adult, and the group proceeds on its inevitable course. But Bill was not about to be derailed. "I was serious. I was particularly close to God when I was baptized." Either he was unpracticed in defiance or trying to make a theological point. The other kids watched in hushed anxiety to discern which it was. "I learned in the catechism that when I was baptized, I was forgiven of my sins, delivered from death and the devil, and given eternal salvation, as the words and promises of God declare." I was convinced that adding the bit about the "words and promises of God" was going to land Bill some place outside of the campfire circle, which, it occurred to me, might be his desire.

Instead, the counselor asked, "What are these words and promises of God?" At this all of us smiled as Bill recited Mark 16:16 back to the counselor. "Whoever believes and is baptized will be saved, but whoever does not believe will be condemned."

Bill continued, "I don't think that we are closer to God just when we feel it. I don't remember my Baptism. It was an experience I suppose, but I can't tell you how I felt. I don't remember how I felt or even if I felt anything. But, you know, it says in the Bible that we were born again when we were baptized. I don't remember when I was born from my mom or how I felt. But it must have been an important event or I wouldn't be here. I think I was particularly close to my mom at that time, and I think I was also particularly close to God when I was born again in Baptism." The counselor smiled and commended Bill for his insight. I thought he was pretty smart, too, for a high school kid.

What happened next was a village church guy's Walther League fantasy. The next kid to share was a friend from my church. He knit his brow in feigned if agonizing thought and said, "I was particularly close to God when I was baptized too." I was next and repeated exactly the same thing. A couple of the kids sighed at us. It seems we were wrecking their fun. This was not like the campfire meeting was supposed to be. Around the campfire it went. Most of us said the same thing. We all claimed our Baptism as an experience when we were particularly close to God. Soon the sharing was over, the counselor smiled and left, and a few of the guys started some serious sharing. We talked about girls, sports, teachers, parents, siblings, and even Christianity. After a couple of hours we wondered what tomorrow's campfire would bring. We figured that bit about Baptism would only work once. Bill had the answer: "Tomorrow let's all share the last time we went to the Lord's Supper."

But we were criticized. We were accused of not taking the retreat seriously, of being "typical guys," and of "being afraid to share." It was still the best Walther League retreat I ever went to.

Usually, we would come home from the retreats and some of the kids would ask, "Why can't church be more like the retreats?" That year, when we left, Bill reversed the question, "Every year we share our experiences at the campfire, something we don't do in church. We sing songs that we don't sing in church. We talk about being close to God, which we don't do in church. Why can't our talk about God be more like church? Why can't we just have church?" It was a heretical thought if you favored camp churches, but I liked it.

WHAT'S WRONG WITH BORING?

Rock 'n' roll concerts, campfire experiences, and camp churches are strangely exciting. Most people who grew up in the church, even the Lutheran church, have gone to retreats. At them we were encouraged to share our experiences, expect the Holy Spirit to act "decisively and now," feel the excitement, and basically be different than we are. Baptism and the Lord's Supper were usually not the experiences that we were to share. We were expected to be emotional. Sometimes things happened that were unpredictable. And often we went home wondering why our churches couldn't be more like those retreats.

Bill was right. We should have brought our village churches with us to the camps. Perhaps inadvertently, he had exposed a tendency of revivalism, even the revivalism of those church retreats that does not stress doctrine, creeds, the catechism, or the Sacraments. These standard Lutheran treasures are foreign to a movement secure in "its subjectivism, its anti-intellectualism, its disinclination for philosophical clarity, its disinterest in historical tradition, and its depreciation of catechetics and the sacraments."[9] Translation: Please don't make us think clearly about what the church is all about; instead, let me feel.

Christianity is not supposed to be exciting. The word *exciting* does not occur in the Bible. The Gospel is not unpredictable, and neither is the Holy Spirit. God "places Himself in a box" so we can know where to find Him. The Gospel is not supposed to be "fun" or "dramatic." It is consoling, comforting, saving, powerful, clear, and utterly predictable. Americans crave excitement. And our churches have been forced to reflect this craving.

Despite our rich doctrinal heritage as Lutherans, I receive phone calls regularly from new people in the community asking if we have "praise services," "contemporary services," or "blended" worship. I am constantly asked if our services are "exciting" enough for new members. I have even been asked by a "church shopper" if I considered my church to be "fun." These are wrong questions. They reflect a change in our priorities and our practice. We are encouraging the "uninitiated" to look for the wrong things. And when we stress doctrine—well, that leaves people pretty cold.

The practices of our churches have been changed, but subtly. We did not pass convention resolutions that stated we would entice people to our churches by excitement rather than doctrine. Lutherans never woke up in the night with the incredible insight that faith simply should be replaced by experience. Rather, our culture has made us crave excitement both in our entertainment and in our churches. Our practice has changed and with it our expectations. Doctrine always follows practice.

Emotion in Christianity is not wrong and it is neither possible nor desirable to avoid it. I can't imagine a Christian who does not feel emotion about our Lord Jesus. Every Christian feels sad over sin, perplexed over failure, fear over the just and awesome God, joyful over forgiveness, relieved at the sight of the cross, exhilarated over new insight into the Scriptures, and a sense of incredible excitement over the positive hope of heaven in the arms of Jesus. Emotion is normal. You can no more make a law about it than you can make laws about rain or sunshine. But emotion cannot be prescribed and the intensity of it cannot be a barometer for faith. Richard Resch, music professor at Concordia Theological Seminary, explained the difference between the role of emotion in the

Bible and role of emotion in the revivals during one class lecture: "In the Scriptures faith leads to emotion. In the revivals emotion leads to faith."

OUR CULTURE CRAVES EXCITEMENT: DOCTRINAL INDIFFERENCE

The advocates for a camp church, are often proponents of the Church Growth Movement. Like their revivalistic forefathers, camp church advocates find the Holy Spirit somewhere outside the Word of God. In historic Lutheranism, doctrine is always predictable. And it requires time both to teach and to learn. But when the Holy Spirit is described as unpredictable and as "acting quickly and decisively and right now," then doctrine will not do. The camp church belittles doctrine because it cannot lead to the excitement that is craved. There is another reason for the disparagement of doctrine in the Church Growth Movement. Caring about doctrine requires Christians to engage in the difficult and painful task of making distinctions between church bodies.

The differences between the various churches were blurred and often denied as the nation moved west. The new nation was impatient with the theological distinctions between the various churches. Alexis de Tocqueville, a traveling Frenchman in the first half of the nineteenth century, observed that among Americans "there are no traditions, or common habits, to forge links between their minds."[10] The new nation was cut off from old traditions in state, home, and church. Westward moving Christians were "building roofs" based on the belief in the Bible, "but they lacked the ecclesiastical walls of liturgy, governance, theology, and instruction that are normative in a given church tradition." Consequently, "people veered from one church to another" without knowing or caring about the difference.[11] Whitney Cross, a historian who analyzed the revivals of upstate New York in the first half of the nineteenth century, described the typical young man of the area.

> The lad who emigrated from these neighborhoods could hardly have escaped at least one revival. . . . He was perhaps not himself a convert. Though he had always gone to church and had scarcely considered doing otherwise. He awaited the day when

> the Holy Spirit would marvelously elect him to church membership. In the new country he might temporarily violate the Sabbath, swear, or drink too heartily, but he always expected another revival to change his ways. His adolescent mind readily lent itself to religious excitement. . . . It mattered little whether he was nominally Congregational, Baptist, or Methodist. He might in the young country change affiliation several times as one sect or another held services nearby, or seemed to enjoy particular manifestation of heaven-born agitation.[12]

The early Americans did not distinguish between various church bodies or doctrines. Denominational loyalty was seriously lax at the revivals.

Whatever Happened to Denominational Loyalty?

In chapter 1 I bemoaned the doctrinal indifference demonstrated by many in the Church Growth Movement. Now we can see historically where this indifference came from. It happened because of a disdain for distinctions between church bodies. If that disdain continues, then doctrinal indifference will grow.

It is virtually impossible to read any literature by Church Growth advocates without also hearing about the current decreased denominational loyalty. Typical is Alan Klaas's *In Search of the Unchurched*. Klaas observes that in our current society, "most members do not know or care about their congregation's denomination." And they are not interested either. Even lay leaders don't care. Consequently, when these people feel that "the activities of their congregation no longer meet their needs, . . . they move to another congregation. . . . The denomination of the new congregation is not important."[13] How should the church respond to this type of indifference? The standard suggestion of Church Growth advocates is simply to accept the erosion of denominational loyalty. Usually that means developing strategies of reaching out to others who, in principle, don't have denominational loyalty and don't want it.

Some Church Growth advocates say that the church should not even mention publicly the doctrinal differences between the various churches. They compare church leaders who publicly disagree with other churches to "a group of generals" with "different opinions" "going public before the foot soldiers."[14] Others have complained about doctrinal purity at the expense of the mission of the church. Such concerns, however well intended, do not lead to a confession of faith in which the distinctive doctrines of the Lutheran church are clear.

Our practice has changed. Christians flit from church to church without particularly considering the doctrine of a church. Pastors accept members of other churches without making certain that they understand and accept the doctrine of the Lutheran church. We give Communion to people who have not been instructed or who do not accept the doctrine of the Gospel. These practices all reflect ambivalence about purity of doctrine. And if people were not concerned about doctrine before these changes in church practice, then the changes themselves will lead to indifference. Our practice forces us to behave as if doctrine doesn't matter.

Troy was a member of a Lutheran congregation and wanted to become a pastor. He liked people and wanted to help them get to heaven. But he didn't want to go to the seminary. Was there a way to become a pastor without having to study theology at the seminary? His pastor tried to convince him to go to the seminary, but Troy resisted. He was very bright, so he would have had no trouble academically. He was young with no children, so there were no serious family or financial obstacles. One day, completely exasperated, his pastor asked him why he was so reluctant to learn more about being a pastor. His response, "They will try to make a Lutheran out of me. And I don't want that." Such is the denominational and doctrinal disloyalty our church faces.

We don't treat our husbands or wives this way. "I will be loyal as long as you meet my needs." We don't treat our children this way. "I will nurture you as long as there are no others more worthy of my nurturing." We don't treat our parents this way. "I will respect you as long as you provide activities for me that are helpful to me." We don't even treat our dogs this way. But we treat our churches this way. And such disloyalty is accepted as the norm. In fact, we are treating Christ our Lord with disloyalty. To flit from church to church without thinking about what the church teaches is a denial of Christ. It was He who said, "Teaching them to observe all things whatsoever I have commanded you."

When huge numbers of Lutherans came to the New World and settled in the Midwest in the middle third of the nineteenth century, they discovered a situation just like ours. Few Americans back then had any denominational loyalty. Instead, they "veered from one church to another." But most of the early Missouri Synod Lutherans were convinced of their doctrine. They didn't throw their hands into the air and say, "Oh well, denominational loyalty is a thing of the past." Instead, they taught their doctrine. And none of those heroic Lutherans of long ago was ever heard saying, "I guess that depends on your denominational perspective."

Closed Communion

The blurring of doctrinal distinctions has led many pastors and congregations to question and discontinue a particular historic church practice: closed Communion. A brief analysis of the practice of closed Communion will show the close relationship between doctrine and practice.

The expression "closed Communion" comes from the practice of the earliest Christians. In the first centuries of the church's life "firm boundaries were drawn around participation in the divine service."[15] There were two parts of the Divine Service. The Service of the Word was made up of the Scripture readings, the hymns, the sermon, and the prayers. The Service of the Sacrament was the serving of the Lord's Supper and the liturgy surrounding it. People who were not members of the church were allowed to be "hearers" and could attend the Service of the Word as long as they assured the church that they had "serious intention" of actually hearing the Word of God. But before the Service of the Sacrament began, "the 'hearers' had to leave the assembly, and not only they but also the catechumens, even though they were already being solidly instructed toward reception."[16] So holy was the Sacrament to these early Christians that they would not allow the uninitiated even to witness the Communion service much less receive the Sacrament. Instead, the doors were closed and the deacons guarded them. So the expression "closed Communion" came about by the practice of closing the doors and "restricting participation to full members of the congregation."[17]

Closed Communion was practiced in the early church not just in regard to those who were not fully instructed. It was also practiced with those who came from different church bodies. If a church held to a doctrine that went against the Bible or the creeds, specifically and primarily the Nicene Creed, then that church was considered "heterodox." *Hetero* is a Greek word that means "different," hence the word *heterosexual*, which means to be intimate with a member of the different or opposite sex. *Doxa* is the Greek word for glory, praise, or opinion, hence the word *doxology*, which is a word of praise. Or think of the word *paradox*, two opinions standing next to each other. So a heterodox church holds opinions about God or glorifies and praises God in a manner different from the pure or "orthodox" church. The opposite of "heterodox" was "orthodox." *Ortho* is the Greek word for "straight or proper," hence the word *orthodontist*. Orthodox churches believe and worship in the proper manner. One of the most important collections of ancient liturgical rules comes to us in the Apostolic Constitutions, written about A.D. 380. In that document the deacon who presides over the Sacrament orders: "Let none of the catechumens, let none of the hearers, let none of the unbelievers, let none of the heterodox stay here."[18]

In the early church, heterodoxy always broke the fellowship. A congregation not only refused to commune those who were not instructed, it refused to commune those who came from churches whose false teachings had broken fellowship with the true church. Members of an orthodox church would also never commune at the altar of a heterodox church. Such an action would have been considered a participation in the sins and false doctrine of others. The only remedy to heterodoxy was for that church to return to the truth. For "where church fellowship is broken by heterodoxy, it can only be restored by the achievement of doctrinal unity. Doctrinal unity is part and parcel of orthodoxy."[19]

The practice of closed Communion, then, was based upon the belief that true doctrine is something the church can have and can confess. If true doctrine were impossible, then it would have been unreasonable for the church to expect it, sinful for her to practice it, and uncharitable for her to refuse Communion to those who did not hold to the accepted doctrine.

The Nicene Creed was written so the church could be confident that her members confessed the true doctrine. It was no accident that the churches that held to the Nicene Creed expected such a confession of the true doctrine of Christ to be spoken in the Divine Service immediately before partaking of the Lord's Supper. The whole congregation believed and confessed the true doctrine together. But if doctrinal purity and unity were impossible, then the entire enterprise of developing creeds and confessions and expecting the church to teach them was flawed.

Closed Communion was not a legalistic practice. Nor was it a test of denominational loyalty. The early church never heard of the expression "denominational loyalty." Rather, closed Communion communicated the importance of true doctrine and the importance of a common confession of that doctrine as a prerequisite for communing together.

Doctrine and Practice Hand in Hand

Closed Communion is also taught in the New Testament. When Paul wrote to the Corinthians, he was justifiably miffed at their divisions. They followed different theologies (1 Corinthians 1:11–12) and needed encouragement "that all of you agree and that there be no divisions among you, but that you be united in the same mind and the same judgment" (v. 10). When Paul introduced the topic of the Lord's Supper to this church, he said, "I do not commend you . . . When you come together, it is not the Lord's supper that you eat" (1 Corinthians 11:17–20). Paul's caution in Romans 16:17 further indicates the New Testament practice of closed Communion: "Watch out for those who cause divisions and create obstacles contrary to the doctrine that you have been taught; avoid them." The word for "divisions" means to stand in two places. When those who confess false doctrine commune alongside those who confess Christ purely, then the church stands in two places. In today's idiom we would say "straddle the fence." Both purity and unity of doctrine force the church to stand in one place. To enjoy this unity and purity the church needs to avoid both false teachers and false churches.

PRACTICES SURROUNDING CLOSED COMMUNION

The practice of closed Communion led to at least four other salutary church practices. The first was the practice of saying the Nicene Creed in the Divine Service. This has already been discussed.

The second practice was the introduction of letters of transfer or certificates of introduction. Because churches wanted to know that all who communed held to the same doctrine and had been instructed in that doctrine, the early church developed a type of transfer policy. If they were relocating or on a journey, travelers were asked to produce "Letters of Fellowship" (also called "Letters of Peace") when they desired to commune at a church. This assured both the church and the letter bearers of each other's orthodoxy. The Synod of Antioch (A.D. 341) declared that "no stranger is to be received without a Letter of Peace."[20] And the Council of Carthage (A.D. 348) directed that "no person, clerical or lay, may commune in another congregation 'without a letter from his bishop.' "[21] The current custom of sending a letter that transfers membership from one congregation to another is derived from this early church custom. If the church had not practiced closed Communion, such letters would have been meaningless. The same is true today. There is little spiritual and responsible justification for congregational transfers if membership in an orthodox congregation is not a prerequisite for Communion.

The third practice that grew out of the practice of closed Communion in the early church was declaring church fellowship with other synods. Once the Nicene Creed was accepted, it became the standard by which fellowship was declared between churches. Those who dissented from the Nicene Creed were denied fellowship by the orthodox. The same basic principle holds today. A church body or synod will declare fellowship with another based on mutual acceptance of creeds and confessions. Such a declaration means that the members of each church body will be welcomed to the altars of the other. Tragically, fellowship is sometimes broken because a church refuses to accept the same doctrinal statements or confessions as another. It means that no members of either church will be welcomed to the other's altar.

In 1969 The Lutheran Church—Missouri Synod declared altar and pulpit fellowship with the American Lutheran Church (ALC). The declaration, a topic of intense and heated discussion for the decades before and after, meant something. It meant that doctrinal unity between the synods was recognized and that there should be Communion between the members of the two churches. Later, when the ALC dissolved into the ELCA, no formal fellowship was declared. The lack of declared fellowship meant something too. It meant that there were differences between the theologies of the LCMS and the ELCA. Consequently, there should not be Communion between the members of the two churches. If we did not believe and practice closed Communion, neither a declaration of fellowship nor a lack of declared fellowship would have any meaning. Why declare fellowship if you intend on communing people from a different church regardless of whether you are in fellowship with them?

A fourth practice that grew out of closed Communion is the practice of pastors examining those who wish to commune. Such was the practice throughout the history of the church. In the early church it was the bishop who would welcome the catechumens to the altar for the first time because it was important that a person's readiness for the Sacrament was known beyond even the local parish. At the time of Luther the pastors would examine those who had been instructed into the teachings of the church to ascertain their preparedness. It was never left to the communicant himself to decide his readiness for Communion. Rather, pastors were "stewards of the mysteries of God," as St. Paul says (1 Corinthians 4:1). The Augsburg Confession says that people in the Lutheran church were allowed to commune "after they have been examined and absolved."[22]

One of the great events in the life of those confirmed in the Lutheran church is the examination prior to the reception of the Sacrament for the first time. The year was 1965 at Bethel Lutheran Church of University City, Missouri, and the catechumens were ready. Back then we were called confirmands because we didn't know any better. *Catechumen* is a better word because it stresses the instruction and the learning rather than a ritual that isn't even mentioned in the Bible. The whole point is to learn the doctrine of

Christ. At any rate, back in 1965 we gathered, huddled and anxious, in the classroom adjacent to the church basement, much like first-century martyrs before they were pushed into the coliseum. Fear was etched on each adolescent face. Eyes, swollen both from sleepless nights of catechetical studies and from groanings too deep for words, peered furtively out into the gathering crowd of elders, parents, godparents, grandparents, and siblings as they assembled to witness. We were reminded by Pastor Mundinger that Lutherans do not believe in penance. It was a necessary reminder. We were not to interpret the impending disaster as either our own meager payment for guilt or the fulfillment of some pre-sacramental requirement, like a rosary or the enumeration of sins. We had our doubts. It all seemed too painful to be completely unrelated to our own spiritual foibles.

Slowly, like lambs to the slaughter, we were ushered into the fellowship hall and the torturous process began. Questions of admittedly eternal import were asked and answered. Bible verses, painstakingly practiced and perfectly rehearsed, were falteringly confessed. It was always so frustrating to know something so well in the confines of your comfortable home and to appear ill-prepared in front of witnesses. I was asked to recite Luther's explanation of the Third Article. It struck me as a little ironic that I could not by my own reason or strength believe in Jesus Christ my Lord or come to Him, but I was expected to recite, by my own memory and strength, those words that only later did I fully love. We all "passed," and no one passed out. Again, the pastor reminded us that Holy Communion was not something we earned by our studies or memory. Confirmation is not something you "pass." Another silent observance I made at the time was that Pastor Mundinger kept saying that we do not get grace through memory work only because it seemed like we did. But his harping worked. I was not proud that evening, even though everyone dutifully piled accolades upon us all. I was not pleased with my performance. I was not happy to have done so well. Rather, sharing an ancient tradition, I was examined. At the time I had no idea of the nature of this tradition. I had witnessed my brother's examination a couple of years earlier and had heard my father and mother share stories of theirs. Comparing notes with the kids from Luther Memorial Lutheran Church down the street,

I had concluded that we all did the same thing. But the vastness, the catholicity, the fact that we shared a practice with over a millennia of Christians, this we neither knew or understood at the time of our questioning. Those ten scared kids at Bethel Lutheran Church simply knew that they had been examined and that they had confessed the saving Christian faith.

To this day I have confessed my faith on hundreds of occasions both planned and spontaneous. Every so often I thank God for the examination my pastor gave. It forced me to learn, to know, to speak, and to confess. Examination, done by the pastor and therefore public, is a tradition that has been passed on since the beginnings of the Christian church.

Creeds, letters of transfer, declarations of fellowship, and examinations by the pastor—all are common church practices that grew out of the practice of closed Communion. Unless closed Communion is a good church practice, they are all, at best, inexplicable and, at worse, legalistic. All are practices of historic Christianity and historic Lutheranism.

Coming to North America

The church throughout the ages has always practiced closed Communion. When the Lutherans who ultimately made up The Lutheran Church—Missouri Synod came to North America in the late 1830s, they practiced closed Communion in at least two directions. First, they were leaving an ecclesiastical relationship (the Prussian Union mentioned in chapter 4). Those who favored a union between the Reformed and the Lutherans were called "Unionists." The Lutherans who came to the United States were against the union. They referred to the practice of communing with the Reformed as "unionism." The first constitution of the LCMS says that the Synod is opposed to all forms of unionism and syncretism. That means that we opposed joint worship and sharing the Sacrament with those who were part of the new Union church.

When "all forms of unionism" were rejected by the early Missourians, it was because unionism came in more than one form. There was a second threat to the true unity of the church against which Walther and other Missourians had warned. The early Missourians soon became aware of the influence of John Wesley,

Charles Finney, and others upon American religious thinking. These pious Lutherans were shocked that even many Lutherans were caught up in the "New Measures" or "revivalism." The Missouri Synod refused to have fellowship with other Lutherans, such as the General Synod, who adopted the "New Measures" of revivalism. They realized, wisely, that such a difference in practice, even among Lutherans, indicated doctrinal differences as well. If you remember chapter 5, you will recall that those early Missourians were absolutely correct.

BUT CLOSED COMMUNION IS SO DIFFICULT

The practice of closed Communion is extremely unpopular. It goes against the American notion of inclusivity, as well as our craving of excitement. Consequently, some pastors are tempted not to practice it. The reasons offered for giving up the practice of closed Communion are poor.

1. Some say that we should commune people if they accept most of the doctrine we teach because it's unrealistic to expect someone to accept all the Lutheran doctrine.

Luther was confronted with this one. He understood that if you were heterodox on one article of the faith, you would be wrong on all points. He debated a pastor named Ulrich Zwingli, who taught that Christ's body was merely represented in the Sacrament. However, Zwingli still claimed to hold all the other articles of the Gospel. They debated for three long days. At the end Luther and Zwingli had not come to an agreement on the doctrine of the presence of Christ's body and blood in the Sacrament. Because no concord was in sight, one of Zwingli's allies, Martin Bucer, asked if Luther could at least say that the other side was orthodox on other doctrines such as the Trinity, Baptism, the person of Christ, and justification.

> Luther replied, "No, I cannot do that . . . You reject me as well as my doctrine."
>
> Frantically, Bucer then asked, "Will you recognize me as a brother?"
>
> Again he received no satisfaction from Luther, "Your spirit and our spirit cannot go together. Indeed, it is quite obvious that we

> do not have the same spirit. For there cannot be one and the same spirit where, on the one side, the words of Christ are accepted in sincere faith, and, on the other side, this faith is criticized, attacked, denied, and spoken of with frivolous blasphemies. Therefore, as I have told you, we commend you to the judgment of God."[23]

Notice that Luther did not say he was glad about how much the two parties agreed. Instead, he recognized that the other side had broken fellowship by its heterodoxy. Luther's conclusion was based on the deviance of Zwingli on one point of doctrine. So we must not commune with people from churches that may seem to agree on some points of doctrine but not all.

Later, in his Galatians commentary Luther said, "If you deny God in one article of faith, you have denied Him in all; for God is not divided into many articles of faith, but He is everything in each article and He is one in all the articles of faith."[24] In the first chapter of this book I made the point that doctrine is not plural but singular. We hold to one doctrine with many articles. If you deny one article of faith, you will end up questioning or denying all. People who claim to believe in most of the doctrine simply do not understand how all doctrine holds together.

2. Some insist that you should not judge people by the denomination to which they belong. Instead, for example, Roman Catholics or Reformed should be allowed to commune as long as they agree with the Lutheran doctrine.

This is the argument used to justify communing former Lutherans who have joined a different church through marriage. "Oh, Pastor, can't you give Suzie Communion? She's really a Missouri Synod Lutheran in her heart. She just joined a different church when she got married in order for there to be peace in the family."

Whenever I am asked to do that, I make it a point, if possible, to go and talk to Suzie. I once talked to a "Suzie" who had married and had joined a Lutheran synod not in fellowship with the Missouri Synod.

"Suzie, do you believe what your new church holds, or do you believe what your old church, the Missouri Synod, holds?"

"Pastor, I think the two are the same. I can't tell the difference."

"Okay, Suzie. Let me ask you three questions. A. Does the Bible have errors? B. Should women be pastors? C. Is Jesus the only way to heaven?"

Her answers were quick and short. "No. No. Yes."

"Okay, good," I said. "Now go and ask your current pastor the same questions."

The next time she visited, she said, "I asked my pastor the questions you told me to. You know, I once thought that the answers to those questions were pretty clear. But now I see that there may be more than one way to look at things. And who are we to say that we are the only right ones? I think that the Missouri Synod is pretty self-righteous."

I sadly realized that Suzie was not a Lutheran anymore. Her parents were sad too. And they stopped asking if she could commune. They knew it would be a lie to take Communion with their own daughter.

Closed Communion forces disillusionment on us. Disillusionment is always painful. It hurts us to face the truth that sons and daughters, parents and grandparents, husbands or wives, people we love and even admire do not hold the wonderful Gospel truth that unites us as Christians. We are tempted to accept or downplay the differences between the churches, especially if family is involved. But denial does not make the pain more bearable, denial never won anyone back, and denial does not change the truth. If it is worth living and dying and contending for the truth of the Lutheran doctrine, then it is worth speaking a word of caution to those who would leave it. This word of caution is the practice of closed Communion.

3. Some insist that as long as the person who wants to commune believes in the bodily presence of Jesus in the Sacrament they should be allowed to commune.[25]

All pastors have had the frustrating experience of instructing someone in the faith who refuses subsequently to join the church. It happened to me with Marie. She seemed to soak up the Lutheran doctrine like a sponge, asking intelligent and thoughtful questions. She was eager to join and take Communion. When the class was over I visited her, as was my custom when I catechized adults. "Is there any point of doctrine which you cannot accept?" I asked.

She hesitated and then responded. "I believe everything you have taught, except I can't accept original sin." This was odd to me because she had said nothing both when we discussed sin and when we looked at infant Baptism. Furthermore, Marie was raised Roman Catholic, so she was taught original sin from the time she was little. We discussed the matter, and the more we talked the worse it got. It turns out she actually didn't really believe that Baptism forgives sins either. How could she if children aren't sinful? She believed that Baptism was an anticipatory symbol of the washing that kids got when they were older. Come to think of it, the Lord's Supper turned out, for Marie, to be only a symbol of a washing. In fact, the Gospel, to Marie, was not a powerful absolution. It did not "bespeak us righteous." When we got done talking, I realized that Marie did not believe much of anything that the church teaches. Her unbelief was discovered only because she questioned one article of doctrine. Remarkably, when I told her that she should not commune until she could accept all these articles of the faith, she replied, "But I want to take Communion. My husband takes it, and it means so much to him. I do believe that it is really Christ's body and blood."

Marie continued to come to church, sporadically. One day I asked her if she was still disappointed that she was not allowed to commune. She said, "You know, I just wanted to go with Jim. I don't really think that the wine is literally Christ's blood. That's impossible." It turns out that she didn't even believe that.

4. Some say we are judging the hearts of others when we don't commune them.

This is completely false. If people are not fully catechized or examined, they are not ready to commune. No pastor is judging a person's heart just because he refuses to commune them. Lutheran pastors regularly tell the children in their churches that they must wait to commune until they are instructed. Certainly, no one accuses these pastors of judging the hearts of the young. It is not the hearts that are judged when Communion is refused to those of heterodox churches. Rather, it is the heterodox church that is condemned and rightly so.

5. Some say that we should leave the decision about whether a person should commune with each person who attends. Church Growth advocates suggest that it is simply a matter of style whether communicants are examined by the pastor or whether the church should "let the decision about meeting [conditions] for communion rest with each interested participant."[26]

But is it really "style" to violate the Bible and Lutheran Confessions? When God told pastors to be "stewards of His mysteries," it was His desire that they dispense the Sacraments with great diligence and intention. Pastors answer to God. Called by God through the church, pastors are to ensure that the Sacrament is administered properly. This task may not be abrogated or placed upon others. They simply may not choose to deprive people of the pastoral examination God's people are entitled to and communicants have received since the time of Jesus.

6. Some say that we are turning people off when we refuse to commune them. It comes across as unloving. We should try to attract them rather than repulse them.

This is what all the other arguments come down to. We don't want to turn people off. And Lutherans would be foolish to think that they can practice closed Communion without turning people off. Of course it turns people off. It turns off every member of every heterodox church. Closed Communion makes the heterodox angry, and they often say so. Consequently, Lutherans have been defending themselves against this charge of "intolerance" for almost 500 years. Luther said, "The sectarians who deny the bodily presence of Christ in the Lord's Supper accuse us today of being quarrelsome, harsh, and intractable, because, as they say, we shatter love and harmony among the churches on account of the single doctrine about the Sacrament."[27]

The same charge was leveled against the early Missouri Synod Lutherans. When the Missouri Synod refused fellowship with the General Synod, an article appeared in the journal of the General Synod, *The Lutheran Observer*, which labeled the LCMS: "presumptuous," "selfish," "a class of spiritual Ishmaelites" whose "appropriate place is in the Church of Rome" because they do not believe "what the Bible and the Holy Ghost teach them," "an inanimate congregation of wax or clay," "extremists," "men who have imbibed with their mother's milk their prejudices, who have been cradled in their superstition," "abusive," and of course the eternal and ubiquitous epithet, "intolerant."[28] (*The Lutheran Observer*, you may recall from chapter 5, was the journal of the General Synod, edited by Benjamin Kurtz who adamantly defended the revivalistic "New Measures," which early Missourians strenuously opposed.)

Every pastor who practices closed Communion has heard similar words of disapproval. "Pastor, you are so intolerant, so legalistic, so unloving, so judgmental. How can you expect people to join our church when you treat them this way?" If Luther and Walther were so vilified, why should we, certainly lesser lights than these noble church fathers, expect any less?

Why is closed Communion met with such harsh and strident judgment? Because doctrine and practice go hand in hand. When people are outraged at our practice, it is because they are outraged at our doctrine. Behind the practice of closed Communion are a number of strong doctrinal convictions. First, those who practice closed Communion believe that it is possible to know the truth unequivocally. Second, those who practice closed Communion believe that their confessions and creeds contain the truth without any doubt. Third, those who practice closed Communion believe that certain confessions and doctrinal statements of other churches are false and unbiblical. Fourth, those who practice closed Communion believe that your church's doctrine is your doctrine. Fifth, those who practice closed Communion believe that their confession and the confession of their church is a matter more urgent than life itself. Sixth, those who practice closed Communion believe indifference about their confession and their church is a sin against God. In short, denominational disloyalty is a sin. It should not be encouraged.

When you forbid someone Communion because they belong to a church not in fellowship with yours, you are saying, "Your church is heterodox. It is false. You are in spiritual danger in that church. I must caution you against that church. God wants you to hold to the true doctrine as taught by the Lutheran church." Make no mistake. That is what is being said when closed Communion is practiced. A congregation that cannot say that should not practice closed Communion, and a pastor who cannot clearly state this should not be a Lutheran pastor.

Don't Kiss My Sister

Often people expect to receive Communion from churches they visit even when they are not in fellowship or don't understand and accept the Christian doctrine. If your pastor says no or wait to these people, he will suffer for it.

When I was a teenager, I dated a girl named Val. She was a very sweet young lady. One day she told me that her brother Peter was coming to town for a visit and he would like to go out with us. That sounded fun. Val wondered if my sister would like to come along. It would not really be a double date. It would be a foursome. My sister agreed. It would be a foursome.

The evening was pleasant. We went out and showed Peter the town. He was appreciative. Then we walked home. It happened that Val and I were walking a bit more slowly than Peter and my sister. They were about a half a block ahead of us when they reached Val's home, where Peter was also staying.

Then an amazing thing happened. Peter went to kiss my sister.

It's not as if he was a repulsive guy. He had been somewhat pleasant and engaging during the evening. And he was tolerably nice looking. It's just that the attempted smooch came out of nowhere. It was wholly unexpected and even less desired, but he tried nonetheless.

I have to confess that, until that moment, I was unaware of my sister's quick reflexes. She'd never impressed me as the athletic type, yet she responded like a goaltender in the NHL. Her head turn aside and her hand went up. Not since Sigourney Weaver killed the monster in *Alien* has an unwanted predator been so thoroughly rebuffed. Twice he tried. No three times. It was altogether pathetic. He was reduced to an adolescent beggar, unable to take no for an answer and, apparently, unable to stop himself from foisting his unwanted advances.

From a distance Val and I observed like kids watching silent movies. We heard nothing, but everything was overstated and painfully obvious. I didn't know whether I should laugh or cry or punch the bum. And then, mercifully, it ended. In exasperation he sighed (*that* we heard) and went inside. Vicariously embarrassed at her brother's gauche machinations, Val grunted a "thank you" in my direction and went inside herself. The abruptness of the evening's end was both stupefying and a bit frustrating for me because I actually had anticipated, more deservedly than Peter, some type of amorous conclusion to the night's festivities. But my loss was ultimately my gain. Kisses are a dime a dozen. But my sister and I have had many conversations about the one kiss that never happened. We laughed all the way home and laugh to this day. Our conclusions regarding the episode are in the form of questions. What gave Peter the idea that he could expect a kiss? Why, with no commitment, no discussion of the matter, no hint of anticipation, did he simply expect to be given something that most people consider intimate? What was he thinking?

Later, when I saw Val, she apologized for her brother's behavior. I asked, "What was your brother thinking?"

"He kisses every girl he goes out with. He expects it. He has never encountered any girl who wouldn't let him kiss her until he met your sister."

"Well, what does he think of my sister?" I had to ask because I was so proud of her.

"Well, if you really want to know, he thinks that she is a prude and stuck up."

"And, Val, what do *you* think of my sister?"

"He had it coming. It's about time. Sometimes no is the best thing that can happen to you. Tell your sister 'Thanks.' "

I have thought about the little incident many times when I tell people no or wait as they desire Communion. "Sometimes no is the best thing that can happen." I also have thought of Peter's assessment of my sister. "She's a prude and stuck up." That's roughly equivalent to "selfish" and "intolerant."

Pluralism

What made my sister's rebuff so galling to Peter was the fact that he had kissed every other girl. That is the sign of our age. Some people feel that all girls are the same. You can kiss them all. More than that, you have the right to kiss them all. And if one won't cooperate, she suffers the lonely labels of "prude" and "stuck up."

To the modern world all religions are the same. You can commune with them all. More than that, you have the right to commune with them all. If one won't cooperate, she suffers the lonely labels of "selfish" and "intolerant."

We live in a pluralistic age in which the greatest sin is "intolerance," born from the conviction that truth is exclusive. Our world hates "binary" language that states that some things are right or wrong, good or bad, true or false, acceptable or unacceptable. Especially disdained by our "tolerant" world are the exclusive doctrines of grace. There is only one God. He saves only through His Son. His Spirit works only through His Gospel. Excluded from His fellowship are those who will not accept His exclusive claims. Our world works with the following bit of reasoning:

Closed Communion excludes.

Exclusion is wrong.

Therefore, closed Communion is wrong.

But exclusion is not wrong. It is not wrong when it comes to kissing unsolicited Lotharios, and it is not wrong when it comes to giving Communion to those whose church and confession are heterodox.

EXPECT SOMETHING

What are a church and a pastor to do? I have talked to many pastors who really do want to practice closed Communion. The pressures are too strong against them. They simply tire of saying no or wait and of suffering the unpleasant consequences. But the price of saying yes is even greater. It leads to denominational and doctrinal ambivalence and to indifference to the Gospel. The church becomes uncatechized and easy prey for the winds of false doctrine. David Wells, in his brilliant book *God in the Wasteland*, offers this assessment of today's disloyal churchgoers:

> There is a hunger for religious experience but an aversion to theological definition of that experience. There is a hunger for God but a disengagement with dogma or doctrine. And their characteristic abandonment of boundaries—boundaries between God and the self and between one religion and another—typically results in a smorgasbord of spirituality for which the only acceptable criterion of truth is the pragmatic one of what seems to work personally.[29]

People simply do not want to commit to a doctrine and to a commonly held confession of a church. Kissing the girl is all they want. They want "spirituality without theology," as Wells says. In other words, they want the Holy Spirit without the Word, yet He promises to come in no other way. People who want to "abandon the boundaries between one religion and another" must be challenged to want more. Closed Communion forces this challenge.

This challenge is especially important because scarcely anyone else is doing it. The challenge to commit to doctrine is vital precisely because it goes against our culture. The church must insist on instruction and confession as a prerequisite for Communion even if and especially if the world is shocked and even outraged. People don't want to commit. God says they must. Again, Wells offers some counsel:

> Many churches have not learned the lessons that most parents stumble on sooner or later. Churches imagine that the less they ask or expect of believers, the more popular they will become and the more contented the worshipers will be. The reverse is true. Those who ask little find that the little they ask is resented or resisted; those who ask much find that they are given much and strengthened by the giving.[30]

We need to become confident and comfortable asking all who would commune at the altars of our congregations to confess the truth of the Gospel in all of its articles.

CONCLUSION

Because of a desire for excitement and an acceptance of revivalism as a legitimate Christian expression, many churches in the United States, including Lutheran congregations, have fallen into the old heresy of Osiander and are helpless to correct themselves. The overweening preference for excitement rather than doctrine has led the church to accept a camp church understanding, which makes instruction into the doctrine of the Gospel at best difficult and at worst pointless or even wrong. The indifference to doctrine leads the church to discontinue the practice of closed Communion. Once that happens belief in the crucial importance of doctrine is even more difficult to maintain. The practices of the church no longer guide the sheep to the warmth of Christ's Gospel. "The Staff Is Bent."

Study Questions

1. According to George Marsden, what was to be the unity upon which the revivals attempted to build a new Christian community?
2. What was the error of Osiander?
3. What are some of the fundamental differences between the village church and the revivalistic camp church?
4. What is the Lutheran practice of closed Communion?
5. Define a heterodox church.
6. Define what it means to be an orthodox church.
7. What creed became part of the Divine Service as a way to assure doctrinal unity among the communicants?
8. What is the standard used for fellowship between church bodies?
9. What is the purpose of the public examination of confirmands?
10. The first constitution of the LCMS says that the Synod is opposed to all forms of unionism and syncretism. What does this mean?
11. List the six doctrinal convictions behind the practice of closed Communion.

Discussion Questions

1. How did the reality of frontier America affect denominational loyalty? What are the enduring ramifications for today's church in the United States?
2. What was the need and value of "Letters of Fellowship," and what is the equivalent today?
3. In the section "But Closed Communion Is So Difficult," the six reasons why some congregations and pastors will have open Communion are discussed. Why is maintaining the doctrine so difficult?

9

The Staff Is Broken

THE DYNAMISM OF AMERICAN CHRISTIANITY

The second characteristic of American Christianity, with its separation of the Word and the Spirit, is the belief that some people or some churches are more dynamic than others. Four hundred years ago John Calvin claimed there was some secret power the Spirit had. Many churches today seek to harness that "secret power." Evangelical Protestants need more than the Gospel. They need dynamic people. They need to "ascend higher."

I saw a cartoon in *Leadership Magazine* in the early 1990s. There are two pastors sitting across from each other sharing a cup of coffee. The first says to the second, "I'll trade you one middle-aged couple who tithes for a young exciting couple who can lead the youth group." The cartoon was funny because it says out loud what pastors privately think. They want active members in their churches. Without active members almost nothing gets done. Sunday school, church music, Sunday bulletins, visitation groups, elders, people who give money—nothing can be done in the church without members who are, to varying degrees, active. Yet faith is not valuable because it is active.

Passive and active faith were discussed in chapters 2, 5, and 6. We are Christians because God has given us grace and forgiveness. We have received it passively. We are not Christians because of our activities or our involvement. The health of a church—if there is such a thing—is determined, paradoxically, by the passivity of faith. Our health is in what we receive.

DYNAMISM IN THE CHURCH

If we forget the important distinction between active faith and passive faith, we will fall into the second error that Evangelical American Christianity has inherited from American culture. While Christianity says that people are valued by what they receive, American culture tells us that people are to be valued by their accomplishments. American culture seeks dynamic people and organizations. Christianity says that we are to find power in the Gospel alone.

One of the basic principles of revivalistic Protestantism and the Church Growth Movement is that you can determine the health and effectiveness of the church by the number of people who become active members in the church. "One characteristic of healthy churches is that they grow," says C. Peter Wagner. Consequently, "the fruit [that] the Church Growth Movement has selected as the validating criterion for discipleship is responsible church membership."[1]

C. Peter Wagner became the executive director of the Evangelistic Association of Fuller Theological Seminary in 1971. A former missionary, he is arguably the second most significant proponent of the Church Growth theory after Donald McGavern. In the back-cover biography of his book *Strategies for Church Growth*, Wagner is called "the leading thinker, speaker and author on Church Growth" and a "pioneer of the Church Growth movement" equal in stature to Martin Luther and indispensable for disciples of the movement. C. Peter Wagner is important.

Wagner defines "responsible church membership" in terms that are consistent with the American expectation of two-level Christianity.

> First, I believe it is most helpful to look at Pentecostalism not as a well-established set of doctrines, but rather as a particular Christian life style. It is more a dynamic mood than a crystallized theology. You can tell Pentecostals more by what they do than by what they teach. Not all Pentecostals speak in tongues, but none forbid speaking in tongues. Not all Pentecostals believe in the Holy Spirit as a separate person in the Trinity, but

> all claim the power and authority of the Holy Spirit as a real person.
>
> As we will see later, Pentecostals can even be members of non-Pentecostal churches. As a matter of fact, and this is highly important, it might be easier than we think for non-Pentecostal churches to "Pentecostalize" themselves without doctrinal compromise. In other words, non-Pentecostals might do well seriously to consider the possibility of behaving more like Pentecostals, even if they do not choose to believe like them.
>
> God delights to use Christian men and women to accomplish His purpose in the world. But none of us can do it alone. In the twentieth century, just like the first, we will be effective only to the degree that we are "endued with power from on high." (Lk. 24:49)[2]

Claiming a "style," not a "theology," Wagner is so indifferent to doctrine that he can refer to those who deny the Trinity as "powerful Christians." To him, Christians should "Pentecostalize" themselves by expecting the Holy Spirit to give an experience that lifts them to a higher level of Christianity. Wagner, who is very sympathetic to the claims and experiences of Pentecostalism, says what countless other Pentecostals and charismatics were saying back in the '60s and '70s. God values us not because of what Christ has done for us, but because we have been raised to a higher level of Christianity and have become more responsible or, as Wagner puts it, "endued with power from on high." We need to understand these Pentecostals.

Pentecostals divide Christians into two categories: those who are regular old Christians and those who are Spirit-filled. If a church is to thrive, then it has to be loaded with the second kind of Christian. "We understand from the preaching of the evangelists that we needed to be filled with the Spirit in order to have the power to win souls."[3] Sometimes this "filling" is called an "anointing." If enough "Protestant churches have the same anointing that the Apostles had, the world will be won for Christ in less than a generation."[4] Other times the second level is attained by a "quickening" or a "baptism in the Spirit" without which the church suffers a "powerlessness of life and witness."[5] "Responsible Christians" have something that "puts one spiritually on to a higher place with regard to assurance, prayer, Bible study, fruits of the Spirit, guidance, help and comfort."[6]

Notice that, to Pentecostals, the power of the individual or the church does not depend upon the Gospel or the Sacraments. It depends on people being "filled," "anointed," "quickened," "endued with power," or "lifted to a higher place." Notice also that without this special anointing the church cannot function very well. So Wagner's idea of "Christian responsibility" is that we accept the two-tiered understanding of Christianity and attempt to find ourselves in the higher level. Obviously, not all proponents of the Church Growth Movement are Pentecostals or charismatics. Not all practice speaking in tongues or even encourage it. But the thread that connects Pentecostalism and the Church Growth Movement is the belief that there are two levels of Christianity.

DYNAMIC CHURCHES

Over the years C. Peter Wagner adjusted his understanding of two-level Christianity. Instead of focusing upon individual Christians, he, and the entire Church Growth Movement with him, began to talk about "vibrant" Christian congregations. C. Peter Wagner's contribution to the theology of the Church Growth Movement is the teaching not necessarily that there are two types of Christian people, but that there are two types of Christian congregations. The first is a congregation that merely proclaims the Gospel and administers the Sacrament. These are the village churches. They are first-level churches that unfortunately "describe the mission of the church as proclaiming the Word and administering the Sacraments."[7] According to Church Growth experts, these regrettable congregations must assume the "mission paradigm" if they are to become the type of second-level congregations that God wants them to be. The second-level churches are camp churches. The very life of the church depends on rising to the next level and becoming a camp church. "Any local congregation that does not take on a mission posture within the next 10 years will be nonexistent as a local church within 50 years."[8] What is this "mission posture" that congregations must assume or die? Kent Hunter, chief advocate and spokesman for the Church Growth Movement among Lutherans, says:

> The primary purpose of the church is to make disciples, according to the Great Commission. It is to share the forgiveness of sins in Jesus' name. It is to be witnesses to the ends of the earth. There are many means toward accomplishing that end. One is to maintain a clear confession of faith. Another is to help people discover their spiritual gifts. Another is to equip people for the work of the ministry. Another is to provide worship services in the heart-language of the people you are trying to reach. Another is meeting the felt needs of people in your community. All of these and many more are means to the greater end, which reflects the primary purpose of the church.[9]

And where will we discover how to do all these things? Hunter answers, "I believe that God has raised up the modern Church Growth Movement to restore the church to the biblical priorities which He intended."[10] So churches must not only confess the faith and make sure that the Word is taught and the Sacraments are given. Now the people of the church must "discover their spiritual gifts," "provide worship services in the heart-language of the people you are trying to reach," and "meet the felt needs of the people in your community." If your congregation simply expects to continue proclaiming the Gospel and administering the Sacraments with people confessing their faith, then your church will be dead in 50 years. It will remain a village church.

Go back and read the section in chapter 8 where David Luecke talks about two kinds of churches—the village church and the camp church. Luecke devotes an entire section of his book *Evangelical Style and Lutheran Substance* to developing "new skills for post-village times." He is convinced that the village church will not survive. Instead, we need to be prepared for the Holy Spirit, "of whom it cannot be predicted where He is coming from or where He is going."[11] He anticipates the camp church, the revival church, as a new type of church where participants "recognize Him [the Spirit] more readily."[12] Other advocates of the Church Growth Movement have written books about how your congregation can become "courageous" or "dynamic."[13]

In short, according to the Church Growth Movement, churches must become dynamic or they will die. They become dynamic by expecting the Spirit to come upon them in new and unpredictable ways. Preaching the Gospel and administering the Sacraments will not suffice. Teaching the pure doctrine is not enough. In fact, doctrine itself is not what matters. Instead, we must become a dynamic people of God.

WHO OR WHAT IS DYNAMIC IN THE CHURCH?

I have a close friend, a pastor named Steve, who shared with me a conversation he had with another minister. They were talking shop as pastors do, sharing with each other what their congregations were doing, how their services were conducted, the various challenges they faced, and so on. In the course of the conversation the other pastor said to Steve, "It is so important to get the Word of God into the hands of dynamic people."

Steve answered, "You mean, don't you, that it is important to get the dynamic Word into the hands of people."

The other pastor smiled wryly and said, "Yeah, I guess that's it."

Think back to sixth grade when you were learning about adjectives, words that modify nouns. Take the sentence "The Word is in the hands of people." Now add the adjective "dynamic" to the sentence. The difference between Evangelical American Protestantism and the Church Growth Movement, on the one hand, and the teachings of the Scriptures and the Lutheran church, on the other, is this: Which noun does the adjective modify? Do we say that the church thrives because dynamic people speak the Word? Or do we say that the church thrives because people speak the dynamic Word? Evangelicalism and the Church Growth Movement say the former. The Scriptures and the Lutheran church say the latter.

Church Growth advocates claim that "the means of grace are given to a dynamic group of people who are sent to the world."[14] But what about people like you and me who are not particularly dynamic? Does God need dynamic people to spread His forgiveness? Can He use ordinary, hapless, unimaginative, sinful people like me? Or must I be dynamic? Can He work through "clay vessels"? Can He work through "things that are not," as Paul says in 1 Corinthians?

The word *dynamic* comes from the Greek word *dynamis*, which is usually translated "power." What a word this is. It is usually used to describe God. God has power. In the Book of Revelation, Jesus is often described through hymns, for example, "Now the salvation and the power and the kingdom of our God and the authority of His Christ have come" (Revelation 12:8). Very often the word *dynamic* is used to refer to miracles or acts of power whether done by our Lord, by His apostles, or by those on whom the apostles had laid hands (1 Corinthians 12:10, 28, 29; 2 Corinthians 12:12). Every once in a while the word is used to describe wicked things such as the beast in Revelation 13:2 or the forces of this world in Romans 8:38.

An important use of the word *power* in the New Testament is when it is used to describe God's Word. Read the following passages:

> For I am not ashamed of the gospel, for it is the power of God for salvation to everyone who believes, to the Jew first and also to the Greek. (Romans 1:16)

> For the word of the cross is folly to those who are perishing, but to us who are being saved it is the power of God. (1 Corinthians 1:18)

> And my speech and my message were not in plausible words of wisdom, but in demonstration of the Spirit and of power, that your faith might not rest in the wisdom of men but in the power of God. (1 Corinthians 2:4–5)

> But we have this treasure in jars of clay, to show that the surpassing power belongs to God and not to us. (2 Corinthians 4:7)

> Three times I pleaded with the Lord about this, that it should leave me. But He said to me, "My grace is sufficient for you, for My power is made perfect in weakness." Therefore I will boast all the more gladly of my weaknesses, so that the power of Christ may rest upon me. (2 Corinthians 12:8–9)

Notice that the *Gospel* is dynamic, not the one who speaks it. The *Word* is dynamic, not the one to whom it is spoken. The *message* is dynamic, not the congregation that authorizes its spread. The power of the Word is contrasted with the power of those who spread it. In fact, if we were to describe those who shared the Word, we would call them anything but dynamic. They were weak, clay vessels and things that "are not" (1 Corinthians 1:28).

The word *power* occurs 118 times in the New Testament. Never are the people of God called dynamic or powerful, except when they are weak. God never calls His church "successful." God's people are referred to as humble, lowly children who depend on the power of another. We depend on the power of the Gospel. The Gospel does not depend on our power.

There is one, and only one, verse in the Bible where the word *power* (*dynamis*) is used to describe the Christian congregation. In chapters 2 and 3 of the Book of Revelation, John speaks the Word of God to the seven churches of Asia Minor. John comforts these churches and challenges them. Some are rebuked harshly. Some are encouraged. To some he promises judgment, to some affliction. One church stands out. The Lord clearly has a soft spot in His heart for the church in Philadelphia. He writes these words to this wonderful Christian church.

> And to the angel of the church in Philadelphia write: "The words of the holy one, the true one, who has the key of David, who opens and no one will shut, who shuts and no one opens. I know your works. Behold, I have set before you an open door, which no one is able to shut. I know that you have but little power [the Greek word is *dynamis*], and yet you have kept My word and have not denied My name." (Revelation 3:7–8)

There is no such thing as a dynamic congregation. The greatest church in the New Testament had "little power." And this church was not commended for its "heart-language services," its "response to felt needs," or its use of spiritual gifts. The Lord of the church commends the Christians of Philadelphia because they have "kept God's Word." Perhaps this church was dead in 50 years. But at the time John wrote his letters, it was the most God-pleasing congregation on the face of the earth.

The Christians in Philadelphia believed that God's power was to be found only in His Word. They anticipated Luther:

> The second sending is that by which the Holy Spirit, through the Word, is sent into the hearts of believers. . . . This happens without a visible form, namely, when through the spoken Word

> we receive fire and light, by which we are made new and different, and by which a new judgment, new sensations, and new drives arise in us. This change and new judgment are not the work of human reason or power; they are the gift and accomplishment of the Holy Spirit, who comes with the preached Word.[15]

The power is not in us, but in the Word of God.

God is testing us. The trial He places before us is Protestant Evangelicalism and the Church Growth Movement. He wants us to know that we have little strength. He challenges us to confess that we are not dynamic. He demands us to trust the power of His Word alone. God expects us to affirm the Heidelberg theses Luther defended back in 1518.

> 18. It is certain that man must utterly despair of his own ability before he is prepared to receive the grace of Christ.
>
> 20. He deserves to be called a theologian, however, who comprehends the visible and manifest things of God seen through suffering and the cross.[16]

John Wesley and Charles Finney diminished Christ by insisting that after forgiveness you should expect a second blessing, one that transcends forgiveness. Similarly, to the Church Growth Movement, justification has become mere and something else is more. The Word and Sacrament no longer have the power of the Spirit within themselves. You need a special blessing beyond that which the Spirit gives in Christ. To Church Growth advocates, those churches that engage in Word and Sacrament ministry are mere. These advocates look for something more. They look for a dynamic people rather than a dynamic Gospel. In all these manifestations of American Protestantism, forgiveness, justification—Jesus Christ Himself—have been diminished.

Most Lutheran congregations do not accept the false doctrine advocated by Church Growth pundits. But too many accept the practices of the Church Growth Movement. We criticize our people to get to the next level. We praise the churches that act like camp churches rather than village. We encourage pastors to attend workshops and conferences that will help them learn to be more dynamic. Our practice is changing. Doctrine will follow.

DYNAMIC PASTORS

When pastors are expected to be dynamic, mischief occurs.

The American understanding of the pastoral ministry changed as the nation moved west. Christianity grew and changed with the fledgling nation, and Christ's religion "was effectively reshaped by common people who molded it in their own image."[17] As mentioned above, the revivals—quarterly camp meetings—became the central unifying events of both the religious and social spheres of the new nation. East of the Appalachians, these revivals were dubbed "quarterly Sacramental meetings" even when the Sacraments were not offered.[18] They gave rise to what has been called "folk Religion." [19]

"Folk religion," as it defines preachers, has three characteristics. First, people skills replace the call from God through the church. The ability for a pastor to be social transcends both training and the call into the ministry. "Folksiness" excels mere traditions. Effectiveness surpasses doctrinal purity. Revivals did not need trained, called, and ordained pastors. They needed preachers who could bring the people together and inspire them. "They measured the progress of religion by the numbers who flocked to their standards."[20] Alexis de Tocqueville exclaimed, "Where I expect to find a priest, I find a politician."[21] Preachers were evaluated on how effectively they could move people. The differences between pulpit and pew were obscured and even erased. America was being reshaped.

The second characteristic of folk religion is a sense of equality that led to contempt for the established clergy. This reshaping of Christianity was characterized by a number of strong sentiments. The foremost sentiment in the reshaped American Christianity was the belief that the individual conscience and sense of faith were more reliable than any other authority. Nathan Hatch claims that as the country moved west, "the deepest spiritual impulses" of people could not be subjected "to the scrutiny of orthodox doctrine and the frown of respectable clergymen."[22] Translation: You can't tell me what to believe about God and doctrine. I'm in charge of my own faith. As the nation expanded, respect for the clergy shrank. Preachers had responsibilities no different than anyone else, and they had nothing more to say. Every Christian was a minister and was thought to be inspired by God to preach. Itinerant and often fiery preachers defied the established clergy and preached with neither call nor ordination. One such self-appointed preacher accused pastors of practicing "priestcraft." Others were even less flattering:

> Hirelings; Caterpillars; Letter-Learned Pharisees; Men of the craft of foxes, and the Cruelty of Wolves; plastered Hypocrites: Varlets; seed of the Serpent; foolish Builders, whom the Devil drives into the Ministry; dry Nurses; dead dogs that cannot bark; blind Men; dead Men; Men possessed of the Devil; Rebels and enemies of God; Guides that are Stone-blind and Stone-deaf; children of Satan.[23]

Another claimed, "I see no gospel law that authorizes any man, or set of men, to forbid, or put up bars to hinder or stop any man from preaching the gospel."[24] The early Americans were loathe to distinguish between pastor and people.

A third characteristic of folk religion is the expectation placed on the sermons of preachers. Before the rise of revivalism, pastors (whether Calvinist, Anglican, or Lutheran) were evaluated according to their knowledge of the Scriptures and church doctrine. The preaching task was to "explicate the text" of the Bible. Language, analytical, and rhetorical skills were required and, consequently, training. With the advent of the revivals, people were treated to a different and more exciting type of preaching. Preachers were to "affect salvation dynamically and now." The form of the sermon became more dramatic and more exhortational—in short, preachers had to get the job done today. The "desk theology" of the village church preacher was no longer desirable. The changed style of acceptable preaching in the early nineteenth century added to the growing distrust of the clergy.

The genesis of revivals, a desire for "folk religion," altered expectations, and resistance to traditional authority all made pastors justifiably nervous.

What to Expect from Your Pastor

The change in the popular understanding of the pastoral office, not surprisingly, continues to this day. When the procuring of dynamic people becomes necessary for the survival of the church, then all sorts of changes occur. Salvation will no longer be viewed as passive.

The Divine Service will no longer be seen primarily as the place in which forgiveness is imparted. And the work of the ministry will begin to require pastors who are first and foremost dynamic. In American Revivalism the service becomes a "staging ground, an equipping area to prepare God's people for the real work of ministry."[25] Pastors are no longer given the luxury of simply being clay vessels for the distribution of the mysteries of God. Instead, they must be motivators, "vision casters," "inspirers," or "leaders" of God's people. Pastors will not just "forgive you in the place and by the command of Jesus Christ." They will "equip, train, and encourage." And their effectiveness will be scrutinized accordingly. If they fail, watch out.

The new understanding of our doctrine of the pastoral ministry inevitably changes our practice. If pastors are valued by the church for their dynamism rather than their divine call, then two historic practices of the Lutheran church will undergo change. The first is our reluctance to dismiss a pastor. The second is our opposition to women pastors. These two practices, virtually unheard of in past years, are now receiving a favorable hearing in Missouri Synod circles today.

The Tenure of Pastors

The egalitarian belief that all people are ministers places the ministry and salvation of souls squarely in the hands of each Christian, not in the hands of God, who works through pastors. Pastors become expendable. Add the idea that the minister must be personally dynamic and the pastor is endangered.

What happens if a pastor is not dynamic, "sociable," or a master of American "folk religion"? The church may be dissatisfied or frustrated. Lutherans, however, have historically not tried to figure out ways in which they can dismiss their pastor. The historic position of the Lutheran church is that congregations may dismiss their pastors only for certain reasons. If a pastor is openly and scandalously immoral, he should be dismissed. If a pastor is unable or refuses to teach the true doctrine, he should be dismissed. When you think about it, this makes sense. The pastor's job is to teach. If he refuses to teach or teaches false doctrine, then he can't do his job. But you can't just fire your pastor like you could an NFL coach simply because he has had a couple of unsuccessful seasons or because there may be some friction on the church team.

WHO'S IN CHARGE?

As long as there is sin, pastors and people will have conflict. I've heard of conflict my whole ministry. I knew a pastor in North Dakota who was in hot water with his congregation over the question of whose job it was to choose the Sunday morning hymns. Another acquaintance argued with his elders because a couple of them thought that when he communed the shut-ins, he should not refer to them as "poor miserable sinners" as the liturgy of Confession and Absolution says. A pastor close to me, in defiance of his congregation, insisted that he had the right to determine the schedule of the services. One pastor told me that his elders had instructed him not to wear his collar except on Sundays. Another pastor's elders pleaded with him to wear his collar every day. In each of these "controversies" both sides of the disagreement buttressed their position with the words "Who's in charge around here?"

"Who's in charge here?" needs the same answer every time it is asked. God is in charge. He speaks to our culture. He challenges us within the culture. He indicts and condemns the culture. But He doesn't change His message to meet the needs of our culture.

Of course, we all know that God is in charge, but that doesn't stop both pastor and people from trying to push each other around at times. In America there is a distinct and unchristian answer that is often given to the question of who is in charge. It's the answer we believe deep down in our primal American souls every time we ask it. I believe that the question "Who's in charge around here?" is a question that has defined the American experience, affected every church within her boundaries or influence, and been answered long ago. The answer to the question of who's in charge is: I am.

"I'm in charge" is a noble response for those fighting kings and princes of the world, especially King George. It is the proud American answer born on July 4, 1776, in Philadelphia, weaned at Lexington and Concord, and walking at Gettysburg fourscore and seven years later. The retort grew with the suffragettes in the early years of the last century and matured through the dreams of heroic

African American men and women who understood its import for their people. It is an answer every red-blooded, apple-pie-eating, baseball-playing American has always known. Who's in charge around here? We are.

And we will fit God into our culture if it's the last thing we ever do.

Most of the pastors I know survived their little disagreements. They learned either to soften their expectations or to be more patient in them. Other pastors are not so fortunate. That's because Lutherans have changed their practice with regard to dealing with pastors they don't like. Pastors are called by God through the congregation. But at times we are tempted to refuse to let God talk to us through the man He has chosen. Instead, we want to be the master of our church and subject our pastor either to job performance reviews based on criteria that are not God's or even to let the pastor go if he isn't working out. This was not always the way of Lutherans in North America.

Trial Ministries in the Lutheran Church?

When the LCMS was formed, the revivalistic sectarian churches surrounding Lutheran congregations of the Synod were in the habit of issuing "preaching licenses." These preaching licenses allowed the congregation to depose its pastor at will without cause and due process. The Missouri Synod, in its founding constitution, rightly rejected this practice. "Licenses to preach which are customary in this country are not granted by Synod because they are contrary to Scripture and to the practice of the Church."[26] The Synod's rejection of temporary calls echoed C. F. W. Walther's reasoned conviction. He considered such licensing "unbiblical, unconscionable and soul destroying" because, among other reasons, it places a pastor into the office "on a trial basis."[27] Reasons for this rejection were articulated by Francis Pieper, a Lutheran theologian of the early twentieth century:

> The essence of the temporary call does not consist in this that a call is limited as to time, but in this that human beings arbitrarily limit a call as to time, that is, that they want to determine how long a pastor is to be active at a certain place. This is indeed contrary to the divinity of the call to the ministry. The ministry

> is divine not only in this sense that God has ordained it for all time, but also in this sense that unto the end of time God places the persons, who are to serve Him in the ministry, at the various places and determines the time during which they are to be active at a place. Congregations are merely the instruments of divine placing and transfer.[28]

John Fritz, whose *Pastoral Theology* was standard fare for all seminarians, echoes the same thoughts. He says: "Some non-Lutheran congregations have the custom of calling ministers temporarily, so that, whenever it pleases them, they may again dismiss him. A congregation is not justified in extending such a call, not even if it be specified that the call, after a certain time, may be renewed; nor should any preacher accept such a call, since before God it is neither valid nor legitimate."[29] Fritz gives four reasons why such a call is wrong. First, it conflicts "with the divinity of the call, Acts 20:28; Eph. 4:11; 1 Cor. 12:28; Is. 41:27." Second, it "conflicts with the relation which should exist between a pastor and his congregation. . . . for if the church members may extend a 'temporary' call to their pastor, they may also, whenever they so chose, refuse him that honor and the obedience which God Himself demands." Third, it "conflicts with the continued faithfulness and steadfastness which God asks of His servants in the ministry, 1 Pet. 5:1–4; 1 Tim. 4:16; 1 Cor. 4:1 ff." Fourth, it "is contrary to the practice of the Apostles."[30]

Recently, other Missouri Synod theologians have criticized the "temporary call." Robert Preus says:

> *A "temporary call" is a violation of the divinity of the call to the ministry of the Word.* Such an action is an oxymoron. Although a divine call and letter of call is indeed a legal contract, it is much more, as we have seen. It is God's own placement in the ministry of the word. A "contract call" for two or three years, an idea contemplated here and there in our Synod, is equally pernicious.[31]

Kurt Marquart echoes:

> It is in this context [the divinity of the call] that the so-called "temporary call" must be seen for what it is: a "call" with built-in dismissal on unbiblical grounds. No one can without self-

> contradiction say to a minister: "God wishes you here for now, but wants you gone by Jan. 1 three years hence unless we are pleased to keep you another three years." . . . So strong was the early Missouri Synod's conviction on this point that the original constitution expressly ruled out "temporary calls" as contrary to AC XIV. Equally abhorrent to Missouri's founders was the system, then popular in other synods of granting provisional, temporary "licenses" to preachers to see how they would turn out.[32]

The rejection of "temporary calls" by the Missouri Synod is in contrast to other Lutherans in the United States. James Pragman relates a story about Henry Melchior Muhlenberg, who was the leading Lutheran theologian in America about a century before the Saxons came from Germany to form the Missouri Synod. It seems that a Lutheran Congregation in Raritan, New Jersey, was served by a certain Pastor Wolf from Germany. He conducted himself in a shameful manner and was determined by the church to have committed adultery. After painful and protracted negotiations, he relinquished his call in return for some money. The congregation, justifiably distrustful of ministers, issued its next call with the stipulation that it "be limited to three or four years, during which time the pastor would demonstrate his character and the congregation would be able to evaluate his performance." Muhlenberg advised in favor of this arrangement. Pragman concludes that Muhlenberg's normally "high view of the call was in need of adaptation to the different conditions of the new world. Since it was difficult in the new world to know the character of the persons coming from Europe in response to a call issued by American congregations," the solution seemed to be calls for a limited period of time—or "temporary" calls.[33] So we changed our practice.

By the time Walther and the Missourians came to the United States, the custom of issuing temporary preaching licenses was rampant among Lutherans. Although the Missouri Synod has historically opposed them, the sentiment behind this practice has returned to the Synod 150 years later.

Dismissing Your Pastor

Pastor Joe went to church one Sunday and saw the elders huddled together in the corner of the narthex, ominously whispering in hushed tones, their furtive glances betraying their unfortunate intentions. Joe had sensed some frustration in the congregation for some time.

One of the families was upset with Pastor Joe because he had balked at giving Communion to their daughter, who had joined the Roman Catholic Church years earlier upon her marriage. Joe's predecessor had always communed her. "She's still a Lutheran in her heart" was his facile justification. Another family was upset with Joe because he chose hymns that were difficult to sing. He didn't seem to understand which hymns the church liked and which they didn't like. In their minds, he didn't care. A third family was upset with Joe because he had criticized from the pulpit those churches that do not baptize babies. This family felt it was poor public relations to "bad-mouth" someone else's church. Besides, they said, "those people from other churches are just as good Christians as we are. They shouldn't be criticized." A fourth family had felt slighted by Joe. When he thanked the various helpers at the Sunday school picnic, he had forgotten their daughter who organized the egg toss. "Either thank everyone or thank no one," they insisted. Many other families were simply the objects of the complaining and frustration that was spilling over into every group and subgroup of the church. Lots of people really liked Joe. But they saw their church being divided into the pro-pastor and anti-pastor factions. Joe, of course, was mostly ignorant of all the unrest, even though it had been going on for three or four months.

The unhappy elders approached Joe and asked to talk with him after services. In the privacy of his study the pastor learned of the church's unrest. He was "probably not totally responsible," the elders conceded, but he had become a "lightning rod" for all the frustration in the church. Forgetting Luther's explanation to the Tenth Commandment to "urge him to stay and do his duty," the elders asked the opposite. For the sake of peace in the congregation, wouldn't it be better if he would resign? He had been serving the church for 18 months, and the elders were willing to give him a three-month severance package, which, they felt, was generous. It would be best for the congregation. The head elder concluded the conversation, "Pastor, we feel that you have used up your capital of goodwill. You are scaring the sheep. You have lost your effectiveness. You just don't fit in. We don't want to have to call a voters' meeting and bring this to a vote. That would be even more divisive. We simply think that you should resign."

Every once in a while pastors are dismissed from their congregations. It's always tragic. Pastor Joe had not done anything immoral. He was neither unable nor unwilling to teach the true doctrine. "What was happening?" he asked himself.

If Pastor Joe had read his history books a little more closely, he would know exactly what was happening. The Lutheran church is becoming more like the revivalistic churches of the nineteenth century. Pastors are not always valued because they teach the true doctrine and administer the Sacraments. According to the standards of revivalism, pastors are to be valued if they inspire the people with their charisma.

Pastor Joe didn't do anything wrong. He was simply working with Lutheran principles in a congregation that had accepted the practices of American Evangelicalism and the Church Growth Movement. He was a village pastor in a camp church.

If Pastor Joe wanted peace, I suppose he could simply take his severance and leave. Corporate America would expect as much. But Joe had a call from God. To leave his charge under pressure would be no more godly than the request of the elders. At the same time, Pastor Joe should listen very carefully, mend fences where possible, act patiently and with strength, be slow to anger, and teach the people.

I knew a pastor in Wisconsin who had been dismissed by his congregation without cause and without due process. When I queried as to the reasons, he replied, "I was a brown-shoe guy in a tuxedo church." He understood.

Our expectations of pastors have changed, and God is not pleased. Wrong expectations change our practice of procuring and dismissing pastors that further blurs the distinctions between pastors and hearers. The change is reflected even in our clothes.

THE UNIFORM

I have always hated and resisted clerical collars. They are uncomfortable. They force pastors to lose their ability to choose a decent tie. And the first time he wears one, the pastor inevitably puts those little tabs on backward so his Adam's apple is sore and concave by the end of the day. In my office I have a picture of a dog wearing a clerical collar with the inscription "Dog Collar." They are nasty.

But clerical collars are necessary and important not just because it's the thing for pastors to do. Collars are especially vital in America today because we have lost the ability to distinguish between pastor and people. Americans simply don't like the idea that God has chosen one man to speak for Him. Americans don't relate to God having a spokesman. Americans must be taught, and the doctrine should be pictured by the collar.

I knew a pastor who decided that he wanted to be among the people. He took off his collar. He took off his robes—no alb, no cassock, no surplice, no stoles—nothing that would distinguish him as a pastor. He came out of the pulpit and preached in the chancel, walking back and forth. You couldn't tell he was a pastor.

That pastor was making a mistake. He was changing his practice so it conformed to a false doctrine. One of the best ways to teach people to see and understand the office of the ministry is for pastors to teach God's Word in uniform. Help the people see that the pastor is to be distinguished from them. He is different, not because he is more dynamic, more effective, less sinful, closer to God, or possessing a different character. He is different because God has called him through the church to speak on His behalf and forgive sins.

Sometimes police officers take off their uniforms. Wanting to remain anonymous, these "plainclothes" cops need to mislead and trick criminals into drawing a false conclusion as to their identify. Plainclothes police officers don't take off their uniforms because of honest, law-abiding citizens. If there were no criminals, there would be no plainclothes cops. It's the same in the church. Taking off the uniform is a sign of distrust. We don't trust God's people to respect and accept their pastor simply because he is their pastor. Distrust is justifiable when dealing with criminals, but it destroys the church. May it never be that we, in the Lutheran church, have plainclothes pastors.

MEN AND WOMEN

The preachers were not always men on the American frontier. When the role of the pastor changed in the last century, the reasons for excluding women from the ministry were eroded as well.

The functions of men and women, often somewhat rigid in the old country, were at times almost indistinguishable on the American frontier. Both sexes cleared the land, raised the kids, fought the Indians, and attended the revivals. The strictures of the old world were cast aside, and women found themselves in church leadership roles next to men, speaking in the assembly, offering the public prayers, and ultimately preaching. In the early nineteenth century, women pastors drew large crowds in New England.[34] With the advent of Pentecostalism in 1900, the practice of female pastors expanded greatly. John Nichols claims:

> Further evidence of their democratization is that very early in their history the Pentecostals recognized the vital role that women could play in spiritual awakening. They utilized them as pastors, evangelists, and missionaries. Perhaps this accounts for the multitudes of women who were won to Pentecostalism in those early years.[35]

Early Pentecostal advocates for women pastors claimed that they were a good antidote to the creeds and traditions of mainline churches and "all spiritual awakenings featured women preachers" who would not "cut off their hair, put on bloomers or rompers, but just prophesy and pray as a woman."[36] Among the early American revivalists a clear tendency not to distinguish between the sexes was developing.

The development is predictable. With the change in the pastor's job description, it's only natural that women should seek and gain the pulpit. If the primary qualification for being a pastor is the ability to motivate and inspire, then anyone could do the job regardless of sex. And women, if they are demonstrably as effective as men, should never be denied.

WHAT DOES GOD SAY ABOUT WOMEN PREACHERS?

Just as the American doctrine of dynamism has resulted in blurring the distinctions between pastor and people, it has also blurred the distinctions between men and women. Just as Americans resist arguments that say that pastors should be distinguished from their people, so we resist arguments that say that women and men are different in the church.

Please indulge me a few comments on the issue of female pastors. No one will ever exhaust the subject, and no mere human will ever say the last word on the topic. The question of female teachers in the church or women's ordination is so politically charged that I broach it at great risk. It's like the old story from ancient Greece in which a young lawyer is deliberating as to whether he should become a judge. His mother tries to dissuade him. "If you do what is right, men will hate you. If you do what is wrong, the gods will hate you. Either way you will be hated." A discussion of women pastors is similar. If I say it is wrong, then some women will hate me. If I say it is right, then God will hate me. Either way I will be hated. There are, however, questions of doctrine and practice that beg for analysis.

Paul excludes women from preaching and teaching because of something that happened long ago—original sin (1 Timothy 2:14). The original sin was questioning God's Word in the Garden of Eden. That first sin has consequences for all of us, which remain to this very day. First, original sin condemns us. We are all guilty of the original sin, even though we may not have been there when Adam and Eve ate from the tree, just as we are all righteous with the innocence of Christ, even though we may not have been there when they nailed Him to the tree (Romans 5:18–19). Second, original sin means that "from birth [we] are full of evil lust and inclination and cannot by nature possess true fear of God and true faith in God."[37] In other words, we have no free will to choose or believe. Third, original sin means that we will die even if we have never committed an actual sin (Romans 5:14). Fourth, original sin means that we must rely 100 percent on the grace of God both for our redemption and for our new birth (John 3:1–6). Fifth, original sin means that women may not teach men or speak in the church, as Paul says (1 Timothy 2:11–14; 1 Corinthians 14:34–38).

Listen to the words of the Holy Spirit: "I do not permit a woman to teach or to exercise authority over a man; rather, she is to remain quiet. For Adam was formed first, then Eve" (1 Timothy 2:12–13).

Paul is saying, among other things, that the woman, in her conversation with the snake, made it seem as though she was speaking for God. "Did God say?" was the question. "God says . . . " was her answer (Genesis 3:1–3). So Eve spoke "in the place and by the command" of God, even though she had not been authorized to do so. And she did a poor job of it. When the devil outfoxed her, she simply ignored God and ate the fruit. Adam, on the other hand, was not out playing golf. He didn't come home from a fishing trip and discover what his hapless wife had done. He "was with her" (v. 6), and he ate the fruit along with her. The first man was so quiet you would hardly notice him, even though he was the one, having been created first and having been instructed by God on dietary matters (Genesis 2:16) before Eve was even formed (Genesis 2:18), who should have done the talking. So Eve talked when she should have been quiet and Adam was quiet when he should have talked. The woman's action and the man's inaction combined to form the first—the original—sin.

How should God punish men and women for this terrible sin? When it comes to speaking "in the place and by the command of God," He tells the men that they must speak and He tells the women that they must not speak. That is what Paul means when he says, "For Adam was formed first, then Eve; and Adam was not deceived, but the the woman was deceived and became a transgressor" (1 Timothy 2:13–14).

I was talking to a mother of two daughters about a decade ago. She was outraged that our church would not allow her daughters to be pastors "just because they don't have the same body parts as a man." My answer, which I'm afraid fell on deaf ears, was that the church does not make up the rules about who may be a pastor, it was God. Further, God did not make His decision based on possession or nonpossession of this or that anatomical part.

"It's all Eve's fault," I said. "Talk to her when you get to heaven. See if she feels the same way you do."

"You're always blaming Eve," was her reply. "Eve has nothing to do with this." She was wrong, as we have seen.

Of course, the male of the human species has often sinfully claimed that women can't be pastors because they are incapable. "They don't have the necessary talents or emotional stabilities.

They simply aren't fit for the job." The fact is that many women are clearly more capable than most men. God does not exclude women from being pastors because they are ineffective. Effectiveness does not depend on the preacher but on the Word of God the preacher proclaims. Women are capable of faithfulness to the true doctrine as much as men. Such unfounded reasons aggravate many women who resent being considered incapable and ineffective. God excludes women because He wants to teach original sin. He reminds both sexes that original sin still affects us. The argument that women are excluded from the ministry because they are somehow unfit also undermines God's command. This command is not based on current empirical perceptions, but upon an historical fact recorded in the Bible.

WHY ARE WOMEN GIVEN THE PULPIT?

What happens, however, when a church or pastor questions the doctrine of original sin? Such churches or pastors will deny that infants are sinful, teach free will in conversion, deny both objective condemnation and objective justification, and sooner or later they will ordain women into the pastoral ministry or at least allow them to preach and teach.

In the United States no article of the faith has suffered greater neglect and outright animosity than the biblical and Lutheran doctrine of original sin. Leading American churchmen—Charles Finney, the Pentecostals, Billy Graham, proponents of the Church Growth Movement, and virtually all of American Evangelical Protestantism down to the present—deny or question the devastating effects of original sin. All assert the freedom of the will in spiritual matters or the "role of the human will" in conversion. It should be no surprise, then, that these churchmen have a strong tendency to lighten the effects of that first and horrible sin. Practices of the church—such as excluding women from the pulpit—based on the doctrine of original sin are typically reduced to archaic old practices, sexism, or intolerance.

In the early 1970s a poll was taken of pastors in the various Lutheran synods. Respondents were to express agreement or disagreement with the sentence: "Man plays no part whatsoever in his own salvation or conversion." In the American Lutheran Church

(ALC) only one third agreed with that statement.[38] That same year the ALC approved the practice of ordaining women into the pastoral ministry.

A similar study at the same time asked certain questions of laymen in the various synods. One series of questions presented a list of sentences. The respondents were instructed to indicate whether the sentence was in the Bible or not. One sentence read, "The women should keep silent in the churches. For they are not permitted to speak." Although, that sentence is a direct quote of 1 Corinthians 14:34, yet 72 percent of the respondents said that the statement was not in the Bible.[39] What does all this mean? It means that the vast majority of the people who decided to approve women's ordination in the ALC did not know that the Bible had specific statements against it. They were asked to make a decision on a matter of practice using only a flawed theology to support such a decision. The full impact of the doctrine of original sin had been discarded by the church. They no longer believed in total depravity or that Adam and Eve did something with lasting effects. It was easy to approve the practice of women pastors. Leaders of The Lutheran Church—Missouri Synod expressed concern that the ALC was changing its practice by doing something contrary to the Bible. The criticism was certainly true. But the ALC changed its practice in order to be consistent, simply bringing its practice into conformity with its doctrine. If the doctrine of original sin is denied, there is no reason to deny women the pulpit. Doctrine always affects practice.

In The Lutheran Church—Missouri Synod today, our practice is similarly changing. Women are invited to assume the responsibilities traditionally assumed by pastors—reading the Scriptures in the Divine Service, distributing the Sacrament, leading the service, addressing the congregation during the service, preaching. These practices reflect the American inclination to blur distinctions. They also are a symptom that we don't take original sin seriously. We resent having to suffer the consequences of an action that took place at a tree in a garden millennia before we were even born. I fear that Lutherans may soon be loathe to bask in the benefits of Christ's saving actions on Calvary's tree, even though it occurred long before we were born.

Most seriously, these practices ignore the deep relationship between doctrine and practice. If we continue on the path of encouraging the involvement of women in pastoral tasks, two things will happen. Doctrinally, we will continue to undermine the doctrine of original sin among us. Practically, we will teach ourselves that there is nothing wrong with women pastors. We may still know the passages, but they will not affect us. Our practice will teach us more effectively than our doctrine or even the Bible. Everyone will become so used to seeing women leading the services and speaking in the church that the time will come when someone actually ordains a woman into the ministry. When it happens, our church will not be shocked. We will have been taught by our own bad practice, which is based on a bad doctrine of sin.

Someone might say, "But it is not, strictly speaking, against the Bible for a woman to read the Scriptures in the church service. It is not against our Lutheran doctrine for a woman to distribute the Lord's Supper." Never mind that Paul specifically gives to the pastor the job of "publicly reading the scriptures," along with preaching and teaching (1 Timothy 4:13). And never mind that Article XIV of the Augsburg Confession explicitly gives to the pastor the job of distributing the Sacrament. Even if there were no direct prohibitions against women being given these tasks, it should still not be done. When the entire world denies original sin and the biblical consequences of it, including the biblical distinctions between men and women, then we must assert them all the more. *In statu confessionis nihil est adiaphora*. Remember that phrase? In times of controversy nothing is indifferent. We face a great controversy not only with the unbelieving world but also with other Christian churches over the difference between men and women. We must, in this controversy, do nothing that would give the impression that we are capitulating or "coming over" to the worldly view. Practice reflects doctrine. If we want to teach our doctrine, then we must be concerned about our practice.

BLURRING DISTINCTIONS

Americans often blur important distinctions—between churches, between pastors and people, between the sexes. Inability to distinguish leads to a sacrifice of historic and important practices and eventually biblical doctrine. I saw an example of this during a visit to a church one Sunday. I'd been told about an "exciting" church near my home, a congregation of The Lutheran Church—Missouri Synod that was "following Church Growth principles" and "really doing some new dramatic things." I had the Sunday off, so I went to this "dramatic" church with a friend.

We made our way into the church and were greeted by friendly people eager to make us comfortable. They gave us some worship folders, showed us where to sit, and helped us get situated. So far everything was pretty normal for me. During the service I started looking around and made a couple of observations.

First, I noticed the congregation's policy regarding who could commune. Communion was not offered on this particular Sunday, but I had found a bulletin from the previous Sunday and was reading it during the offering. It said, "We invite to Communion all who believe in their hearts that Jesus is Lord and who believe that Christ is present in the Lord's Supper." This is different from what is officially practiced in Missouri Synod churches. Officially, churches of the Missouri Synod commune only those people who are members of Missouri Synod congregations or churches that are in fellowship with the Missouri Synod.

Second, I couldn't find the pastor. The opening liturgy was led by a man who was wearing a suit. I didn't think he was the pastor, but I was not certain. The Scriptures were read from the pews: the Old Testament lesson by an elderly woman, the Epistle lesson by a teenage girl, and the Gospel by a man from the front pew. They had each situated themselves on outer aisles so they could face the entire congregation. A children's sermon was preached by a woman who invited all the children up to the chancel and had them face the congregation while she showed them a trick with some balloons. Through it all I could not see a pastor. A band was playing music just to the right of the chancel, and when it came time for the sermon the drummer boldly stepped forward into the pulpit. Only then did I notice the white-on-white clerical collar I had mistaken for a turtleneck. He was wearing it under a white linen sports coat. The minister preached the sermon and did nothing else except play the drums in the band.

After the service a couple of greeters came up to us and invited us to stay for coffee and fruit. We were chatting pleasantly, so I decided to ask these people some questions. "I noticed that you give Communion to people of other church bodies as long as they say they believe in Jesus and accept that He is present in the Sacrament. You seem to leave it up to the individual. Do the people have to ask the pastor first? Are they expected to be instructed before they commune?"

Their answer was clear. "We have found that there is not much denominational loyalty these days. We are not comfortable giving the Lord's Supper to people simply based on the church they happen to be in. We feel that people need to decide for themselves when they are ready to commune. We don't want to say no when people want the Lord's Supper."

The answer indicated to me that the congregation did not distinguish between membership in churches faithful to the Gospel and membership in churches that are not.

My second question was, "I noticed that laypeople lead the worship service. They read the lessons, lead in the liturgical portions, and preach the children's sermon. In our church the pastor does that. (I didn't tell them that I was a pastor.) Why do laypeople do it here?"

Their answer was clear. "We have found that if we get people involved in the ministry, then they will be more excited about the church. We don't think that the pastor is the only minister. We are all ministers. That's what it means to be the 'priesthood of all believers.' We don't want to say no when people want to be involved."

The answer indicated to me that the congregation did not distinguish between pastor and people.

I asked my third question: "I noticed that women seem to do everything that men do in this church. They read the lessons and gave the children's sermon and, I assume, lead some of the Bible studies. Do you limit the involvement of women? Could a woman preach?"

Their answer was clear. "We have found that women are just as capable as men and just as much called by God to do these things. We feel that we should follow Paul when he says, 'There is neither male nor female.' Our pastor is not a woman, and the pastor is the one who usually preaches. I am not sure if our congregation is ready for a women pastor, and our denomination does not allow it, so for now, women do not preach."

The answer indicated to me that the congregation did not distinguish between men and women.

Each of the answers I received from those greeters indicated reluctance on the part of this congregation to make the distinctions God makes in the Bible. Why? This congregation was a camp church and had lost the ability to distinguish between true churches and false, between pastor and people, and between men and women.

It occurred to me that this Lutheran congregation had made the same cultural changes to their thinking that the early post-revolutionary revivalists had made 170 years earlier. What they did may have been "exciting," "dynamic," or even "dramatic," but it certainly was not new. Adapting to the culture, the congregation had changed its practices. No doubt doctrine would follow.

George and Martha Go Church Shopping

The Church Growth Movement falls into many theological errors because it changes the church's practices to fit the cultural norms of America.

Here's why the Church Growth Movement "succeeds."

George and Martha Churchgoer from Normaltown, America, visit a church to see what it is like. If they are comfortable at this church, they might join. George and Martha, because they are Americans, have some expectations about what truth is and what any decent church should be like. They want something emotionally satisfying. It must be a bit unpredictable and somewhat geared to their emotions. George and Martha are pretty vague in their distinctions. They don't see a big difference between various "denominations," between pastors and people, and even between men and women. They're Americans, and this is what they believe. George and Martha have learned to admire dynamic people and dynamic organizations. They are "can do" kind of people, and they want this same attitude in any organization with which they affiliate. George and Martha believe that faith, like voting and most other good things in life, is a decision they must make. If there's anything George and Martha hate, it's the idea that there is no free will.

So George and Martha visit First Lutheran Church. What do they see? First, they notice that Pastor Henry Smith does not try to persuade them through emotion. In fact, the whole service seems very rote and predictable. It is not "exciting." Then they notice that Lutheran pastors put on robes so as to distinguish themselves from the people. They notice that Lutherans tend to call themselves "Lutheran." They are proud of their church and of its name. Pastor Smith may even, on occasion, speak against the false teachings of certain denominations. Lutherans don't even really use the word *denomination* and much prefer the designation "church." George and Martha notice that only the men may serve as pastors and only male elders help lead the services. George and Martha, successful entrepreneurs themselves, notice that in the Lutheran church there is no effort to inspire the congregation with a sense of their own abilities. The people are not encouraged to "take it to the next level." In fact, the people rarely talk about themselves during the services. Finally, George and Martha are not given an opportunity to make a decision. They may even be told that decisions are not necessary or possible. George and Martha go home puzzled and frustrated. This church was not to their liking. It seemed so un-American.

Pastor Henry Smith at First Lutheran watches George and Martha come and go. He sees hundreds of Georges and Marthas come through the doors of his church like sports fans through the gates at a baseball game. And he figures that if he wants them to stay, then the church has got to change. It has to "cross the bridge" into the American culture and adapt. So Pastor Hank makes a few changes in the church's practice. He hires a music team to make the music more exciting and the service less predictable. The Sunday happenings are rendered unpredictable. Next, Pastor Hank takes off his robes. Laymen and laywomen are invited to lead the service. The congregation is renamed—First Community Church. Those old distinctions aren't meaningful, he figures. Pastor Hank begins to challenge his people. They need to succeed, "bring it to the next level," and win. Finally, Hank starts talking about the importance of decision making. He begins a "seeker" service. He introduces a modified "altar call." Now, he figures, his church will succeed. It has become a courageous church with a mission posture.

George and Martha visit the church again and what happens? They decide to join because "this is what a church should be like." Pretty soon First Community has grown and Hank is considered a success. But Hank did not make George and Martha into Lutherans. George and Martha, in fact, have not been changed by the church at all. Instead, the church has been changed by George and Martha. In response to "market-driven trends," Hank has turned the Lutheran church into something that is just like George and Martha.

The Merging of Faith and Culture

As Christians we love George and Martha. We want them in heaven. But we must never change our message just to make them feel comfortable. Our culture and the expectations it brings at times need to be confronted.

Jesus said, "You are not of the world" (John 15:19), but we live in a world that will always affect us. Our culture will influence us either negatively or positively, just as culture affects all people. And the church is not immune to the influences of culture. The church is, after all, people who hear the voice of the Shepherd. Unfortunately, His is not the only voice we hear.

The church influences culture. Usually the influence of Christians upon culture is very positive. We can thank Christians and Christian churches for our educational system, hospitals, orphanages, patterns of thinking, music, literature, economic theories, and a host of other cultural manifestations. We can also thank Christians for the Crusades, which devastated Europe and facilitated the rise of Islam, and for the Inquisition, which stifled theological development and killed innocent people. Over all, however, Christianity has no reason to hang its head for its beneficial effects on culture.

The United States has often been called a Christian nation. I'm not exactly sure what that means, but there is certainly no doubt that the American culture has been strongly influenced by many Christian groups, not the least of which is American Evangelicalism. Because Evangelicalism is both a major contributor to our culture and a recipient of our culture there is a type of symbiotic relationship between American Evangelical Christianity and American culture. What does this mean? It means that Wesley, Finney, Dwight Moody, Billy Graham, Pentecostalism, and a host of others not only were the products of our culture, they also formed our culture. George Marsden claims that throughout American history "a broad coalition of theologically conservative Protestants" was continuously "reestablishing its role as a shaper of culture."[40] When these men, and their twenty-first century heirs, speak to the culture, they are, to a large extent, talking to themselves.

Where does that place Lutherans?

The huge immigrations of Lutherans to the United States occurred in the middle of the nineteenth century, two hundred years after other Christian groups sought freedom on our shores and half a century after the most defining event in the history of the American continent—the American Revolution. Unlike the Methodists, Baptists, Congregationalists, and "Revivalists," Lutherans did not contribute to the early formation of a uniquely American culture. Ours was a different church, which did not fit so easily into American culture. When Lutherans reach out to American people, even if they are not Christian, they will think that our church is a bit odd. They will come to our church with expectations deeply rooted in the American culture. And we will disappoint them. Our music, our liturgy, our vestments, our priorities, our heroes, and especially our doctrine will sound foreign to Americans. What's a church to do?

Lutheran churches, consequently, have a choice, keeping in mind that even the suggestion of "choice" is a distinctively American idea. Should we expect Americans to become Lutheran or should we expect Lutherans to become American? The question has less to do with the nationality of church members than it does with what Lutherans actually believe. What's a church to do?

THE PRINCIPLE OF CULTURAL BRIDGES

Today, one of the most formidable expressions of the type of religion advocated by Wesley, Finney, and the Pentecostals is the Church Growth Movement. The movement traces its beginnings to a Methodist missionary from India named Donald McGavran who wrote a book in 1955 entitled *The Bridges of God.*[41] In it and subsequent volumes, especially *Understanding Church Growth*,[42] he presented the basic principles of the movement. McGavran bemoaned the fact that the church of his day had lost its zeal for reaching out to the lost. He made some suggestions on how the churches might better do so. Much of what McGavran said was praiseworthy. Wanting the church to carry out Christ's Great Commission, he noticed that many mission churches stagnated because they found themselves bogged down in things that had little to do with Christ and the Gospel. McGavran, rightly, concluded that they stagnated because they did not proclaim Christ. Based on his experiences, he developed some principles of Church Growth. McGavran brought these principles back to the United States with him when he founded the Church Growth Institute at Fuller Theological Seminary in Pasadena, California, in 1965.

Church Growth advocates claim to have identified literally hundreds of principles that will help make churches grow. All these principles stem from the first and central teaching of the Church Growth Movement. The primary and fundamental principle of Church Growth is what McGavran called "bridges." The idea sounds simple. You don't cross a river by swimming across it. You take the bridge. So you find the human bridges that allow you to communicate the Gospel with people of other cultures. People are more likely to listen to those who care about them or at least understand them than they are to strangers. People are more likely to respond when a person from their own family or from their own culture speaks to them or if the Gospel is presented in a manner that is comprehensible and understandable. When people are distracted from the Gospel by the church itself, they will not be able to hear or believe.[43]

McGavran, who relied heavily on the theories and research of his colleague George Hunter, suggested that mission work can be more effective if churches reach out to those of their own or a similar culture. Hunter theorized a "sevenfold typology of evangelism" in which he attempted to identify the varying cultural distances between people and the wisdom of sending missionaries who actually shared the culture to any "new mission field."[44] Common sense, of course, suggests that people are not only more likely to speak to those whom they perceive are similar to them, but they are also more likely to be understood. Within The Lutheran Church—Missouri Synod such wisdom has been employed even by detractors of the Church Growth Movement. Consider, for example, the practice of Concordia Theological Seminary in Fort Wayne, Indiana, and its Russian Project. Rather than sending American pastors to Russia, Latvia, and Africa, the seminary has attempted to recruit Russians, Latvians, and Africans for seminary training with the expectation that these men can return to their homelands. Consequently, McGavran's "bridges" are crossed.

For three decades the Church Growth Institute at Fuller Seminary has been "applying Church Growth to America." This means that "crossing cultural bridges" is a strategy being employed to reach out to subcultures within our own nation. That sounds pretty good too. After all, pastors who come from North Dakota are found to function at a higher level and longer in North Dakota than pastors from southern California who serve North Dakota congregations. I can tell you from personal experience that when a pastor moves from North Dakota to California, there is a significant and often unexpected adjustment that must be made. He has entered a new culture.

But crossing bridges in America means more to Church Growth advocates. It means that the churches of America today must accept the prevailing culture created by Protestant Evangelicalism. In effect, it means that Lutherans must change and become Evangelicals.

How Many Lutherans Does It Take to Change a Light Bulb?

Lutherans? Change?

Lutherans don't want to change. We especially don't want to change our doctrine. We resist change. At the same time, Lutherans want to reach out with the Gospel and bring people to heaven. We believe that the Gospel is the power of God unto salvation. So we don't change our doctrine of the Gospel. But in order to be more effective in reaching out with the Gospel, we are tempted to change our style and our techniques. In response to the advice of the Evangelical community, we adapt our practice to our culture.

Many Protestant voices today will commend us if we adapt to the culture. But it's a culture they have largely created. Evangelicals often claim that the Gospel must be made relevant to American culture itself and must be carried by those who share the values of this culture. This means "packaging" or "marketing" the Gospel—"stylizing" the Gospel—to American beliefs and values. For Lutherans it means becoming part of the "large coalition of Protestants." Ultimately, it means a new and different Gospel. When we proclaim the Gospel to Americans, it often becomes an Americanized Gospel.

What are some of the elements of American culture to which American Evangelicalism is adapting and changing the Gospel? The American Gospel, which the Church Growth Movement shares, stresses the two American ideals mentioned here and in chapter 8:

1. We need excitement.
2. We need dynamic people.

These values are taught by Evangelicalism and by the Church Growth Movement. Among Lutherans the teaching often takes place through practices Lutherans uncritically take from their Protestant neighbors—open Communion, firing of pastors, women pastors.

Conclusion

In summary, the Christianity of the new republic changed as it moved west. Questioning the power of the Gospel, Christian congregations substituted the power and dynamism of the preacher or the congregation. The result was a two-tiered understanding of Christianity and the weakening of the doctrine of justification in favor of second-level Christianity. Exhortations to reach the next level forced American Protestantism to value pastors, not for their faithfulness to doctrine but for their dynamism. Old World distinctions between pastors and people, and between men and women, were subsequently abandoned. American revivalism exchanged the authority of God, who chooses His pastors, for the authority of dynamic people and organizations. Changes in the church's practice both reflect our culture and fail to point anxious sinners to the powerful Word of God. Lutherans are often unaware of the manner in which, subconsciously and through seemingly benign changes in practice, we change our message. Salutary church practices become essentially nonfunctional. They are no longer the staff that leads to the powerful fire of the Gospel. Instead, church practice points to the power of people. "The Staff Is Broken."

This is especially true in the area of worship, as we shall see in the next chapter.

STUDY QUESTIONS

1. According to Church Growth advocates, what does it mean to become "dynamic"?
2. When congregations strive to be dynamic and stress the involvement of dynamic people, what is lost?
3. Historically, under what conditions may a Lutheran congregation dismiss their pastor?
4. What does the wearing of a clerical collar by the pastor teach?
5. What are the consequences of original sin for all people?
6. What can be lost when a pastor or congregation denies the lasting consequence of original sin?

DISCUSSION QUESTIONS

1. Rightfully, the word *dynamic* is used of God and His Word. How does ascribing "power" to the people instead of to God turn our theology on its head?
2. Discuss the overall effect that the movement toward American folk religion had upon the role and place of the clergy. (The three characteristics discussed in the text were people skills replace the call from God through the church, a sense of equality that led to contempt for an established clergy, and the expectation placed on the sermons of preachers.)
3. How is it that original sin precludes a woman from the office of the public ministry?
4. Should the church be "making" Lutherans or should the needs and desires of the culture and society transform the church? What are the results of each approach?
5. The author contends that the Lutheran church is not an American church. What are your reactions to this statement? How can this be useful information?

10

The Staff Is Lost

AMERICAN WORSHIP IDEAS

In chapter 4 I showed that true doctrine leads to sound practice and sound practice supports the true doctrine. The same applies with bad practice. A perfect example of the relationship between bad doctrine and bad practice is Dwight Moody, one of the most popular revivalists of all time. He developed or perfected six bad worship practices.

When Practice Attacks Doctrine: Dwight Moody

The westward moving American nation was eager for a new form of religious meeting in the early 1800s. Quarterly revival meetings provided the spiritual, social, and cultural experience popular in rural America. "Conversions" had to occur quickly because people would have to wait three months until the next camp meeting. Fiery speakers found success at these meetings. Effectiveness was measured by emotional excesses, such as rolling on the ground, shaking, or even "barking" like dogs—hence the label "holy rollers." "But the frontier period in any given locale was relatively brief."[1] Soon, where forests or plains had marked the horizon, towns and cities sprouted and grew. These attracted small businessmen, lawyers, doctors, teachers, other professionals, and ultimately industry. Industry attracted more people, and before you knew it, urban areas emerged. With cities came congregations, stationary buildings, and established clergy. These new congregations in the western urban areas were not always like the East-coast establishments.

Sophisticated, educated, professional city folks were not going to be attracted to camp meetings where people barked like dogs. They wanted things a bit more subdued. At the same time, they were Americans and believed that each individual was responsible for making a decision regardless of salvation. The decision was an intimate wrestling with God, not literally on the floor, as with participants of camp meetings, but inwardly through prayer and self-reflection. Preachers facilitated the wrestling, the decision, and the salvation. The most effective urban evangelist of the nineteenth century was a man named Dwight Moody, who introduced a handful of religious novelties to the urban American church that have since become the stock and trade of most Evangelical American churches. Born in 1837, Moody had become a wealthy and successful Chicago shoe manufacturer by the age of 25. All that changed when, because of his involvement in the Young Men's Christian Association (YMCA), he began to apply his business expertise to the religious realm. What were some of these business applications?

First, Moody believed that a successful revival depended on the way in which the event was promoted. He was the first preacher to advocate "marketing" the Gospel.

In teamlike fashion everything was planned in advance, with committees organized for prayer, Bible study, home visitations, publicity, tickets, ushering, and finance. All of this was supervised efficiently and methodically by an overarching executive committee. No advertising device was neglected, and huge sums of money were spent on posters and newspaper notices. Cities were systematically divided into districts, in which homes were visited by "squads" of recruiters. Celebrities were found to sit with the evangelist on the platform while Ira D. Stankey, the popular composer of sentimental Gospel songs, led the "massed choirs." Religion here may have been old-fashioned in content, but it was communicated by the use of very new techniques.[2]

Second, Moody was not about to spend all that money and effort without closing the sale. So he invented and popularized the "altar call." At a certain point in the sermon the audience was invited to come to the front of the church and go to the "prayer room," where they were encouraged to "make a decision for Jesus." "Counselors" in the room would assist the people in making a decision. The "faith" that impelled a person to answer the altar call was not the same as believing the doctrine of the Gospel or accepting the creed. "Faith is in a person, and that person is Jesus Christ. It isn't a creed about Him but it is Him."[3] Moody was unconcerned "about doctrine and form," preferring a doctrineless and formless Jesus. In fact, Moody taught that faith was different than belief. He claimed belief was in doctrine. But "faith means participation in the object of one's concern, totally and completely."[4] The "altar call," then, was not based on teaching, creeds, or doctrine, and it required not passive faith, but active faith, "totally and complete." The implications of this for American Christianity were profound.

Third, like any good entrepreneur, Moody understood that he needed to be able to measure the effectiveness of his attempts in order to improve them. "Conversion decisions" were the desired effect of the revival, so he introduced the "decision card." The card, filled out by those who answered the altar call, had a threefold purpose. First, you could give it to the local pastors who supported the campaign. Only pastors who jumped on Moody's bandwagon would receive the coveted decision cards. Second, the cards helped the "converts" make the decision. Chares Finney had encouraged the people to "vote for Jesus." Moody had now given them the ballot. Third, and most important, the decision cards allowed Moody to quantify the results of the revival. The effectiveness of the camp meetings held in rural areas had been measured by the size of the crowds, by how unusual the manifestations of the "new birth" were (such as howling or fainting, which the city dwellers disdained), and by how enraptured the people became. Moody now had a quantifiable measuring tool.

Fourth, Moody preached to the specific earthly needs of a narrowly defined group. Certainly, he wanted to save souls. Moody once likened the world to a wrecked naval vessel: "God has given me a lifeboat and said to me, 'Moody, save all you can.' "[5] Remarkably, "conversions" were not the result of Moody's revivals. Instead, he found himself speaking increasingly to the unemployed urban middle-class workers of his day who found themselves complaining of their disillusionment. There were 50,000 unemployed people in

New York in 1875. Moody's job was to encourage and help these people in their earthly life. So Moody's preaching was often an exhortation to the Protestant work ethic and advice to those who could not easily attain it. He preached to a certain social group and responded to their felt needs. "In the end Moody had to admit that the revivals did not reach the poor in the cities. His audiences were essentially middle-class, rural-born native Americans [people of European extraction but who had been born in America] who had come to the city to make their fortunes; they believed that he spoke God's truth in extolling hard work and free enterprise."[6]

Fifth, Moody preached exhortational, not doctrinal, sermons. He was not a trained theologian but a businessman and a layman. His authority was derived from neither his call nor his teaching expertise. Consequently, his preaching was not teaching. Moody did not particularly value creeds or doctrine anyway. His role was not as the spokesman for God. Rather, like some of the revivalists before him, Moody viewed himself as one of the people, persuading others to change their minds about God and thereby change God's mind about them. He preached sermons that "virtually abandoned all pretense of following conventional forms of explicating a text and were closer to 'laymen exhortation' filled with touching anecdotes with an emotional impact comparable to that of personal testimony."[7] Moody's sermons were motivational, intended to produce a decision.

Sixth, the result of this "preaching to the needs" of the people was the exclusion of anyone who did not have those needs. Moody himself knew that he preached to the better class of people. He did not reach out to the foreigners or Roman Catholics who were flooding America's cities at an astronomical rate in the second half of the nineteenth century. Richard Quebedeaux claims that Moody's preaching "did not appeal to the unchurched of whatever social class. Rather, the function of Moody's revival meetings was to lift the morale and religious enthusiasm of the already churchgoing segment of Protestant America. It popularized Christianity among them substantially."[8] Moody did "convert" people from creedal churches who already confessed Christ through doctrinal assertions about Him. He "saved" plenty of Lutherans. But Christian converts were not really made.

So here are Moody's innovations:

1. Marketing the Gospel.
2. The altar call.
3. Measuring and quantifying success.
4. Preaching God's providential care in response to the people's felt needs.
5. Exhortational and motivational preaching.
6. Reaching out for "conversions" to the already churched.

These are practices. These are style. They were new and very effective at Moody's time. Today they are practiced by increasing numbers of congregations influenced by the Evangelical revivalism of the Church Growth Movement. Let's analyze them.

1. Marketing the Gospel

What does it mean to "market the Gospel"? One author put it this way: "A marketing-oriented church, having identified the spiritual and emotional needs of its members and/or the target group it hopes to attract, must then develop an appropriate marketing mix to most effectively satisfy those needs and wants."[9] According to many church consultants, your church's worship service is the "ministry" that offers the target group the easiest way to see what your church is like. Worship "attracts" the public, so the worship service needs to be analyzed and altered if you are to effectively "market" Christ.

I once visited an elderly woman who lamented all the changes in her church during the last ten years. "First, they got women to help distribute the Lord's Supper; then they started these contemporary services with rock 'n' roll music; now guess what they've done. They had a dance at church." That part about the dance really made her mad. I tried not to get into a big discussion about dancing at church, so I asked her to elaborate on the first two complaints. She did. I felt sad for her as I listened. She was lost. They had taken away her church, and she knew not where to find it. Finally, she concluded her lament, "I know they need to do these things to bring in the young people, but I'm an old lady. Couldn't they have waited until I died?"

That woman understood the incredible forces that are at work in the churches today. Changes in church practices are being introduced. Their intent is to reach out to those who have been disillusioned, disinherited, or just flat-out ignored by the church. Laymen and laywomen are asked to participate in those actions traditionally reserved for the ministers. A worship style is advocated and practiced that is intended to speak to the hearts of a generation of the lost who cannot relate to "traditional hymns and liturgies." Advocates invoke the apostle Paul, who had "become all things to all people, that by all means I might save some" (1 Corinthians 9:22).

But the changes in practice are simply not neutral. They lead inevitably to changes in doctrine. And they themselves are the result of doctrinal winds that blow in unfamiliar and ominous patterns. Let's look at some of the changes.

Reengineering the Worship Service

Most Church Growth advocates admit that unchurched people do not initially hear of Christ through friends and family. Nor is their initial contact through the small-group ministries formed in many congregations in the 1950s and 1960s. Rather, "corporate dynamic worship becomes an increasingly important avenue through which people are reached on behalf of Christ."[10] So conscientious pastors will adapt and change the service to bring about growth. George Barna, prolific church pollster and analyst, stresses the importance of the worship service in bringing people to Christ. But he warns that "half of all regular church-going adults admit that they have not experienced God's presence at any time during the past year."[11] This lack, it is claimed, can be remedied when people are "moved physically, emotionally or intellectually by the worship experience and when they encounter God and have an undeniable sense of his presence."[12]

So what can a church do to make sure that the worship services effectively move people to encounter God? Barna answers: "The people who attend a worship service should be ushered into His presence through an intentional effort to make God's presence palpable. For highly effective churches this has meant a reengineering of how the worship service is designed, carried out and evaluated."[13] Changes must be made to the service.

What are these changes? One of the most significant is the practice of singing praise songs for about 20 minutes at the beginning of the service.[14] Easy-listening music allows people "to find a means of expression to God without having that flow disturbed by other forms of activity." "It is a mistake to assume that people are ready and prepared to worship when they first arrive on Sunday morning. Usually, they need to 'wake up' first. We believe you wake up the Body by waking up the bodies! So we intentionally choose a song with a strong fast beat and a bright melody that people can move to."[15] Once the worship leader "reads the congregation" and surmises that the people are integrated into worship, he or she then "transitions from the music to the next part of the worship experience."[16] If you attend a church that begins with a medley of praise songs, characterized often by a strong beat, then your congregation has begun the process of reengineering the worship service.

Another change is that the language of the service must be in the "heart language" of the people who are there. Traditional church language is to be avoided because those who are estranged from the church, often called "dechurched," and those who have never been in a church will hardly know the Christian jargon. One pundit explains: "To bring the Gospel to Americans on their level, the communication path will have to take the form of the country-western culture, including country-western songs with Christian content."[17] Because surveys show that almost 70 percent of Americans enjoy soft rock or country music, the worship service should employ this style of music. The theory is that if you want to convert Willie Nelson, you've got to get Willie to listen, and that means playing Willie's music. If you are part of a church where the musical style features a band that plays soft rock or folk tunes, then your congregation has continued the process of reengineering the worship service.

A third and related change is to remove or downplay those features of the worship service that require a previous commitment on the part of the worshiper. For example, formal creeds require people to have learned and understood some theology. Those who are visiting or are uninitiated in the service will not understand, speak, or recite these creeds with any conviction. Creeds could easily become the occasion of division in the worshiping or celebrating community, so a congregation that wants to welcome guests will use formal statements of faith sparingly. The same would apply to the ritualized liturgy, the use of formalized prayers, and the singing of musically complex or lyrically challenging hymns, as these require a bit of practice. Even when the people do participate in the liturgy with some comprehension, it is still not considered an effective tool unless it creates the proper mood. According to Barna, "the number of people who appeared to be singing during the congregational hymns and choruses or the number of people who recited the congregational response during liturgy response times" is *not* an indicator of effective worship.[18] If you are part of a church that has removed or decreased the use of formal creeds, prayers, liturgies, and hymns, then your congregation has continued the process of reengineering the worship service.

A fourth change is the tendency to involve as many people in worship service leadership roles as is possible. Because, to worship "engineers," "worship is our focusing on God, not God focusing on us,"[19] it only makes sense to involve as many people in worship roles as possible. "Courageous" Lutheran congregations will find things for people to do, such as make announcements, read Scripture, offer prayers, "write all the prayers for Sunday morning,"[20] and occasionally do the children's message. People want to participate and be involved, so the church needs to involve them in as many ways as possible. Visitors need to see and believe that they can fit in. If you are part of a church that has involved an increasing number of laypeople in leadership roles during the service, then your congregation has continued the process of reengineering the worship service.

A fifth change is the Communion attendance practice of the congregation. If there is a visitor in church on Sunday, the congregation wants that person to return and to make the church a part of their life. What if that visitor wants to take Communion? Traditionally Lutheran churches have said, "We ask you to wait to commune with us until you understand and accept the teachings of the Scriptures as confessed by our church. We want you to be certain that our doctrine is the true doctrine." Such a standoffish answer will no longer do. No one wants to be told no. Many congregations have slowly changed their Communion practices. They have told people that as long as they believe in Jesus or believe that He is somehow present in the Lord's Supper, then they can commune. One Church Growth advocate said, "Excluding guests will turn them off. It destroys the welcoming environment that the Church tried to create."[21] If you are part of a church that has adopted a more open Communion practice, then your congregation has continued the process of reengineering the worship service.

These five changes have occurred in hundreds of congregations throughout almost every Lutheran church or synod in America. They are:

- The use of music to affect the people and ready them for worship.
- The use of popular music styles to be relevant to the visitor.
- The decreased use of historic liturgies, creeds, and rituals.
- The increased involvement of laypeople in worship leadership roles.
- The practice of open Communion.

These changes are borrowed from the revivalists of the nineteenth and early twentieth centuries and perpetuated by the Pentecostals and charismatics of this century. Despite the good intentions of those who make them, they are all very bad changes.

These changes are advocated and initiated because the service is defined primarily as the activity of people rather than the action of God. Consequently, people have to be made more active. The church activates people by affecting their mood through music that is easy, likable, and familiar. When people can play a role, they are further activated. Conversely, worshipers are not activated when their participation is limited at the most significant moment of the service or when they are asked to participate in things they do not understand or do not like. If your number one goal is to get people to be activated in and through the worship service, then, yes, it needs to be reengineered.

But what if the service is recognized primarily and rightly as the actions of God?

Then the people would need to be more passive. When God is saving us, as He does through the Word and Sacraments of the Divine Service, then we must be passive. God's daily service to our neighbor through our vocation requires more activity. In chapter 5 we established that the Sunday service is God's service to us. God Himself echoes this understanding of the Divine Service: "Six days you shall labor, and do all your work, but the seventh day is a Sabbath to the LORD your God. On it you shall not do any work" (Exodus 20:9–10). In other words, you are actively serving your neighbor for six days every week. But on the seventh day you are to be passive. On that seventh day (or first day of the week for most Christians) God wants to serve you with His gifts of salvation. The less you "do" in the service the more clearly you will see that, when it comes to your salvation, God is "doing" everything. God comes to us.

God has wonderfully blessed the world with the doctrine of salvation by grace alone without the works of the Law. When we change our practice, we endanger that blessed doctrine. Here's what happens.

John and Martha believe that they must do something in order to be saved. They are typical people. Self-righteousness clings to us all. So John and Martha visit your typical "traditional" Lutheran service. The hymns are hard—they can't participate. The liturgy is boring to them—they are not moved. The music is unfamiliar—they are frustrated. Only the pastor is involved, at least when it comes to leading the service—they wonder whether they could be involved. Finally, they are told they cannot commune—they are angry. Everything that has happened has forced John and Martha to be passive, and they don't like being passive.

The next week John and Martha go to a Lutheran church in which the service has been "reengineered." Now they are active. They can sing the songs. They are moved. They can visualize their involvement by seeing the involvement of others. They get to commune. They are active, which is what they want.

Then, after a few weeks, John and Martha start listening to the sermons. The pastor says, "You are not saved by what you do. You are not saved by your activity, your involvement, or your actions. You are saved by being passive. You are saved through faith in what Jesus has done for you." John and Martha are now confused. What does the pastor want, activity or passivity? They ask him to visit them. When he comes by, they ask, "Why do we go to church?" His answer is the most important thing they will ever hear.

He says, "At our church we try to do exciting things on Sunday. It's important for us to get people involved. We want your Sunday experience to be memorable. I think that if you would join our church, you would find a place where you could be active." John and Martha now are happy. The Sunday morning worship is a way in which they can be active. They must have misunderstood that part about being passive.

The pastor did not change his doctrine. He changed his practice. His new practice, probably unbeknownst to the pastor himself, conflicts with the doctrine. The people believe and behave based on the practice, not the doctrine. They are learning from the practice. All the people who join the church will be attracted to activity. They will not want passivity.

By changing the service the church is in terrible danger of losing the Gospel of grace alone.

2. THE ALTAR CALL

In chapter 3 we saw that salvation is by grace alone, not by our will or decision. A couple of Bible verses will restate and reinforce this important Gospel truth.

> But to all who did receive Him, who believed in His name, He gave the right to become children of God, who were born, not of blood nor of the will of the flesh nor of the will of man, but of God. (John 1:12–13)

> What then? Are we Jews any better off? No, not at all. For we have already charged that all, both Jews and Greeks, are under sin, as it is written: "None is righteous, no, not one; no one understands; no one seeks for God. All have turned aside; together they have become worthless; no one does good, not even one." (Romans 3:9–12)

> But God, being rich in mercy, because of the great love with which He loved us, even when we were dead in our trespasses, made us alive together with Christ—by grace you have been saved. (Ephesians 2:4–5)

The doctrine that we as sinners, dead in sins and opposed to God's mercy, can somehow choose God or open our hearts to Him is false. It is synergistic. Synergism, the idea that the sinner works with God and cooperates in his or her own conversion, is wrong because it robs God of the full credit of our salvation and it claims that we can do something we can't.

Altar calls are synergistic. They are invented to get sinners to do something that God says they cannot; they stress the decision of the sinner instead of the grace of God. Billy Graham's altar call is a good example of "decision theology." I tuned in to Billy Graham's Fresno 2002 crusade because I knew someone who sang in the mass choir, and I was hoping to see her when the camera panned on the singing group. Instead, I heard Billy invite people to the altar to invite the Lord into their hearts. He insisted that even if you were baptized, but did not feel close to Jesus, you had to come down and give yourself to Him.

Observe how this view of salvation involves you doing something and how it is contrasted to Baptism as if the gracious work of God in the Sacrament were insufficient. Notice, again, the Osiandristic request for Jesus to come into your heart. Such altar calls, which are a staple of revivalistic preachers in America from Moody until the present, are a terrible insult to God and His Spirit.

The American continent was not always a breeding ground for synergistic systems of salvation. Some of the first and most lasting American Protestants were the Puritans. They were the ones who came to the new world on the *Mayflower*. Puritans, the single most dominant religious force in America prior to 1750, believed strongly that human beings do not have a free will when it comes to accepting God's grace. Like the Lutherans they believed in the total sinfulness and inability of unbelievers to choose God. Our wills were bound in sin apart from grace. The Puritans believed God when He said, "No one seeks God." Whatever their flaws might have been, Puritans were not synergists. But once the winds of freedom wafted into America and Wesleyan revivalistic worship services replaced the staid services of these Calvinists, everything changed. Practice changed doctrine. Within a generation after the Revolutionary War, the influence of Puritanism had virtually died. Instead, the emerging culture had led American Christianity to accept the notion that every person is a free agent able to choose God, "like voting in an election," as Charles Finney had put it. Culture changed the church. And it threatens to change the Lutheran church as well.

Today's Church Growth Movement originates from that long line of Evangelical Protestants who deny grace alone by insisting that salvation is a result of my action, my decision, or my choice. McGavran does not define saving faith as receiving the blessings of God's grace. Rather, he says, "to believe in the Name of Jesus Christ means at least three acts. First, intellectual acceptance. Second . . . I submit my entire life to him. I obey him in every command he gives me. . . . A third meaning of belief is that I must share the good news with others."[22] Notice that faith does not save because it receives. It saves because it does something. Faith is no longer the bag of the trick-or-treater as explained in chapter 2. It saves because it acts. Could Lutherans ever accept these changes and promote such bad theology?

Thankfully, you won't see many Billy Graham-type altar calls in Lutheran churches. That is because such altar calls are not in the Bible, are overtly works-righteous, and are too radical a change for even the most "progressive" Lutherans to accept. So perhaps it's not worth spending any time cautioning against altar calls. A word of caution is, unfortunately, necessary. Today, Lutheran pastors and congregations, often affected by the Church Growth Movement, are accepting worship principles and practices that promote the theology of altar calls.

One principle of the Church Growth Movement is the notion that the church should find individuals or groups of people who are more receptive to the Gospel—seekers. "Churches grow because the gospel is preached to a clearly receptive segment of the population where people are ready to hear it and ready to decide."[23] "That's the principle. Look for people already inclined."[24]

Tragically, but not surprisingly, Church Growth advocates among Lutherans also teach a clearly synergistic doctrine. David Luecke, in his groundbreaking *Evangelical Style and Lutheran Substance*, maintains that the substance of a church cannot change. But the style can. Style, to him, is an adiaphoron,[25] something that is a matter of indifference. One of the congregational styles of the

Evangelicals that Luecke praises is "the decision orientation."[26] He says:

> One other ingredient (which formed Evangelicalism) was in the blend that shaped Evangelical style. . . . Decision orientation is a good name for this style. Its distinctive flavor goes back to Dwight Moody, the dominant late-19th century influence in American Evangelicalism. . . . Billy Graham epitomizes this orientation today, and he is known by many as Mr. Evangelical. His message is simple and basic, yet told in a way that engages the attention of millions a year. The style is focused on putting salvation within reach of those who can be moved to make a decision for Christ. The decision orientation is distinctly modern American. Graham keeps his approach centered on it by featuring the term in his "Hour of Decision" broadcast and *Decision* magazine.[27]

Notice that Billy Graham is commended at exactly the point where he deviates from the Word of God and denies grace alone. Yet Luecke endorses his decision theology by the benign label "Evangelical style." Others make the same error. The notion of receptivity is rampant: "Church growth advocates even identify unchurched people as being in certain stages of receptivity . . . they clearly adhere to the truth that while the Holy Spirit is the one who brings a person to faith, the receptivity of the person can be stronger or weaker at any particular point."[28]

Synergism is further promoted among Lutherans by accepting the term "seeker service" from the evangelical community.[29] I routinely ask the members of my congregation to bring home the service bulletins from other Lutheran churches they have attended. Frequently, they return bulletins with the label "Seeker Service" printed on the top of the folder. These services are usually characterized by the reengineering described above. The theory behind the service is that there are certain people who are more receptive. These people are treated, in the Seeker Service, to a style of worship that is more likely to move the people to "make a decision for Christ." The apparently uncritical acceptance of the term "seeker service," with all of its implied synergism, is a testimony to the tragic effects that the practices of revivalistic Evangelicals have had on the doctrine of Lutherans.

Because doctrine and practice shape each other, you would expect Lutherans to introduce the altar call into the service. Thankfully, the practice is not common. While Lutherans are often loathe to have their own altar calls, some are not so reluctant to promote those of neighboring Baptists or Pentecostals. When the crusades of certain evangelists, such as Billy Graham, come to the major cities of America, hundreds of busses, many carrying Lutherans, eagerly deposit their cargo at the doors of the crusade. Promise Keepers, a quasi-Pentecostal men's group, enjoys the presence of many Lutherans at its rallies because Lutheran congregational leaders will encourage the men to go. Promise Keepers rallies feature altar calls. Often the youth of a congregation are encouraged to attend concerts of contemporary Christian musicians, many of whom employ altar calls. Implicit in the encouragement of these non-Lutheran events is the endorsement of their practice of altar calls and the theology that justifies them.

I can't imagine a Lutheran pastor telling his people to go to the Baptist church on Sunday morning. We want the people in our churches. But pastors and youth leaders will encourage their members to attend the same baptistic services on Saturday night at the evangelistic crusade or the contemporary Christian music concert. There Lutherans cannot only hear preachers and entertainers who urge the baptistic synergism, which usually characterizes these events, they can often answer the altar call to boot. I was once at a pastoral circuit meeting a while back and saw a poster advertising the coming Promise Keepers crusade in Minneapolis in 2000. One of the pastors of the circuit mildly asked the host pastor, who was promoting the crusade, if he was aware of the bad doctrine of Promise Keepers and their synergistic altar call. His response indicated the susceptibility of pastors to synergistic influences: "I think the good far outweighs the bad. And where does it say in the Bible that altar calls are bad?" He's right. The Bible doesn't even mention altar calls. So it doesn't explicitly condemn them. They are simply a practice whose only purpose is to teach that we must decide to be Christians. And if they are legitimized by their promotion, then their theology will be as well.

Baptist, Pentecostal, and Evangelical church members hold to a theology that is perfectly consistent with the promotion of the altar call. These churches are synergistic. But when Lutherans begin to feel "at home" in churches that practice the altar call, then this "stylistic change" will inevitably change their doctrine as well. When Lutherans adopt the practices of our evangelical neighbors, the result "will involve softening our commitment to the core Lutheran doctrine of justification in favor of a doctrine that allows a place for free choice . . . in deciding a person's favor before God."[30]

3. COUNTING THE SAVED

The services were over and I was tired and ready for lunch. I had gone back to the sanctuary to retrieve a book I had left in the pulpit. My head elder approached me with something in his hand. He showed me an offering envelope. It was the kind many churches use, with a number on the outside indicating, anonymously, who had made the offering. Then there was a place where the giver could indicate the size of the monetary gift. On this particular envelope someone had written $50. The elder turned over the envelope and showed me where there was a little note. It read: "To the pastor—keep politics out of the pulpit." My elder informed me that the $50 had been removed from the envelope before it was placed into the offering plate. He concluded that someone had come to church intending to make an offering, but having heard the sermon that person had decided not to support the church that day.

I asked the elder if he thought I had said anything wrong in the sermon. He smiled and said, "Unfortunately not, Pastor."

It happens that I had preached against the sin of abortion on the anniversary of the infamous *Roe v. Wade* decision of the Supreme Court that allowed for abortion on demand in our country. I had said that regardless of whether abortion was a crime, it was still a sin. I had also said that killing your unborn baby was no less murder than killing your neighbor in a fit of rage. I replied to my elder, "Do you think that I should tone down the rhetoric?"

Again, he replied in the negative, "No, but I think that our offerings will decrease if you don't. I think that attendance may go down as well."

These were sobering judgments on his part. I actually had never thought about whether people would leave the church or withhold their offerings if I preached against abortion. I preach against abortion, at least in passing, a couple times a year simply to remind people of this terrible sin of our society. Almost every January I make reference to the *Roe v. Wade* decision. Now I was told that such references could hurt the numbers of the church.

I haven't stopped preaching against abortion. I still teach the kids in catechism class that it is wrong. I mention it at least twice a year from the pulpit and often in Bible class. I write newsletter articles against it. But something has changed. Now, I brace myself a bit. I expect to receive some criticism. I wonder if our church is losing members or money because of what I say. And I believe, if you measure strictly by numbers, that every time I speak against the greatest social ill in the history of our nation, it hurts us. The majority of Americans, judging by the polls, would not return to my church if they felt that we condemned abortion.

The same thing could happen if I preached against homosexuality or if I indicted couples living together before marriage. And these are just moral issues. If a pastor preaches against synergism, decision theology, or free will, he is preaching against the cherished, but wrong, theological beliefs of the culture. In fact, any rebuke of false doctrine transgresses the spiritual sensitivities of our pluralistic age. Whenever a pastor preaches against anything that is popular in our world, he risks losing members, money, and support. The converse is also true. Any time a pastor preaches for something that is unpopular in the world, then he risks losing members.

How do you determine the effectiveness of the message or church program? If the bottom line for any church is membership, attendance, resources to support programs—in short, what marketing experts would use as measuring rods—then the preacher should avoid anything that could turn people away. And every pastor is tempted to do just that.

Dwight Moody was successful because he figured out how to get a lot of people to come to his revivalistic campaigns. First, he measured the number of positive responses to his message. He would then compare them against those who responded negatively.

He would also compare the various sermons he would preach at any given city to see which ones were the most popular. When he went to the next city for his revival, he would preach the popular sermons.

Moody had the luxury of preaching the same sermons over and over again because he traveled from one city to another. He found that his sermon against drinking was his most popular. So he would preach that particular sermon at each revival. The newspapers would advertise both the revival and this particular sermon. He would never tell the audience which day they would hear the sermon against alcohol. People would have to come every day so as not to miss this sermon. The numbers indicated that he was a huge success.

The problem with Moody's approach of measuring success by numbers is that the promise of success based on numbers is too tempting for many pastors and congregations to resist. What congregation doesn't want the pews filled each Sunday? What pastor doesn't want the praise and popularity that accompany an ever-growing church? When growth is the result of soft-peddling the distinctive doctrines of the church, then the price is too heavy. The temptation to measure success in terms of numbers is great.

WHAT WOULD JESUS DO?

There's an even greater danger to measuring the success of a congregation by the number of people who attend services. It usually results in a theology of glory, as presented in chapter 1. When you measure success by large numbers, you are not measuring by suffering and the cross.

Look at Jesus. He was an immensely popular teacher. Five thousand people were listening to Him preach one day. That is a larger congregation than 99.9 percent of the churches in America today. Jesus was successful. Following the sermon and the miraculous feeding of the 5,000, as told in John 6, people were confessing that Jesus was the prophet who was to come into the world. Then Jesus gave a little homily that permanently destroyed His successful ministry. In each of the four parts of His sermon, Jesus said something that, if you measure by the numbers, eroded His ministry.

First, Jesus claimed that He was the only way to salvation. "For this is the will of My Father, that everyone who looks on the Son and believes in Him should have eternal life, and I will raise him up on the last day" (John 6:40). Jesus denied the all-inclusive doctrine of American Christianity. Second, He said that no one could come to faith except by the grace of His Father. "No one can come to Me unless the Father who sent Me draws him" (John 6:43). He denied the synergistic doctrine of American Christianity. Third, He made it clear that eternal life comes only through His sacrificial death. "Truly, truly, I say to you, unless you eat the flesh of the Son of Man and drink His blood, you have no life in you" (John 6:53). He denied the American notion of experiential religion. Finally, He insulted the audience. "This is the bread that came down from heaven, not as the fathers ate and died. Whoever feeds on this bread will live forever" (John 6:58). He denied the implicit rule of American Christianity that you not criticize another religion. If Jesus had preached the same sermon today as He preached in John 6, the results would have been the same. "After this many of His disciples turned back and no longer walked with Him" (John 6:66). Would you say that Jesus' sermon was a success? Should He have preached it?

Whenever a pastor is tempted to soft-peddle his preaching, he should ask, "What would Jesus do?" Jesus would insist on saying the unpopular thing if it were true. We need to insist that Jesus is the only way to heaven, that you get there only because God draws you, that faith in the flesh and blood is indispensable, that other religions don't get you there. Jesus preached the theology of the cross, and He suffered for it. Thankfully, our Lord did not measure the effectiveness of His ministry by how many people stayed in His church or by how His messages were received. He was called to proclaim the truth. The result, for Him, was the cross. The result for us is the same.

Counting Sheep

Despite the example of Christ's ministry, many churchmen today insist that the best indicator of success in the ministry is numbers. Some say that church bodies should support only those congregations that grow.[31] Others seem to equate quality and quantity as if lack of growth indicates a poor quality of ministry.[32] Still others seem to equate "effectiveness" with growth, as if the Gospel's power can be asserted only when visible effects are seen.

Through it all the church is tempted to diminish or deny the cross. The crassest example that I ever heard of changing the Gospel in deference to the sensitivities of our culture occurred at one of the largest congregations in America: Willow Creek Community Church. In 1991 the Religious News Service published a description of this congregation's typical Sunday service. The writer of the article was impressed with the traffic directors in the parking lot, the information booths and shops in the narthex, and especially the orchestra. He described the meticulous planning, the child-care system, and the pastor, the Rev. Bill Hybels. But the sanctuary, where people gathered for worship, was unnerving. The author of the RNS article said:

> The church building itself resembles a corporate office park, complete with a pond, a fountain and a flock of geese. But it has no Christian symbols whatsoever—no cross, no icons—so as not to frighten or intimidate visitors. The minister refers to their overall programs as a "product." I find the slick contrived professionalism of Willow Creek discomforting. . . . For 12,000 upwardly mobile suburbanites, however, the formula works. If success is reckoned by numbers, evangelicals have shown once again that they can package the message to meet the demands of the marketplace.[33]

After Jesus told His disciples that He must die on the cross, Peter tried to dissuade Him. Jesus had some harsh words that would apply to any minister, such as Bill Hybels, who, for the sake of numbers, would detract from the cross. " 'Get behind Me, Satan! You are a hindrance to Me. For you are not setting your mind on the things of God, but on the things of man.' Then Jesus told His disciples, 'If anyone would come after Me, let him deny himself and take up his cross and follow Me' " (Matthew 16:23–24). Pastors and churches are tempted to use "the arithmetic of men" rather than the "arithmetic of God."[34] We are tempted to apply criteria by which Jesus' ministry would be found seriously wanting. Numbers are only one very small indicator of the work of God.

Practice changes doctrine. Moody would not preach certain sermons when their effectiveness, measured by numbers, was questionable. His practice was to soft-peddle unpopular sermons or unpopular topics. The practice led to a bad habit in the church. You can see where it leads by looking at Willow Creek Community Church, which, for the sake of numbers, has removed the cross with its offense. The more alien the Christian message becomes to an increasingly unbelieving culture, the greater will be the temptation not to say the things our culture needs to hear.

Christian congregations want people in heaven. We measure our membership, our weekly attendance, our Communion attendance, and our Bible class attendance at regular intervals. And we want more members, not simply because it makes us look good or justifies our building programs but because we want more people in heaven. Teaching the doctrine of the Gospel and administering the Sacraments gets people into heaven. We should never change that doctrine simply because it does not bear the quick fruit we would like.

ECCLESIASTICAL DARWINISM

When numbers are interpreted as the mark of success, then heavy pressure is placed on the churches. Churches are burdened in two ways. First, you need to grow if you want to attract the increased demands of a finicky market. Large churches can, presumably, have more and better programs. Second, you need to grow to believe that you are being blessed by God. If God's providential care of a church is a sign of His blessing, then that providential care needs to be apparent. The result is a type of ecclesiastical Darwinism in which large churches, either by intent or not, harm smaller congregations.

I love those nature shows on television where lions chow down on poor hapless wildebeests. It's not that I'm particularly sadistic. It's just that there is a certain elegance to the whole process, and it is really God's way of keeping both species strong. The strong and fast lions, capable of catching prey, stay strong and fast. Weak, slow lions end up dying because they can't catch the prey. The wildebeest herd stays strong because it is the weakest that end up being devoured. God's way through nature is the survival of the fittest. But He doesn't run the church that way.

Sometimes when a church seems weakest, it is in fact very strong. Congregations and individuals often learn about Christian repentance and forgiveness when they are most vulnerable. William Chadwick tells a startling story of serving a congregation that went through a time of suffering.

> In 1987 the little church I was pastoring suffered an agonizing split. In its wake I invested time in trying to heal wounds and reestablish relationships with the people who had left. This was undoubtedly the single most important growth period of my pastoral development. During this time I was confronted by my nature, the nature of all human beings and the grace of God, particularly the depth of his love. The depths of my theology and Christian character were forged on the anvil of this experience.
>
> Many of the people from whom I had become estranged had been for the past several weeks attending another church. The pastor of this church was a brother with whom I had spent several hours in various ministry-related events. I invited him over to talk about the importance of repentance, forgiveness and reconciliation. Acknowledging that these are the very essence of the gospel of Jesus Christ I explained that now was a "learning moment" for me and the estranged people to find healing in the work of the cross. I needed my fellow pastor's support and understanding so that I could pastor in this difficult situation. Specifically, I asked him not to support transfer growth from our church to his, but instead turn people back to enter a healing process.
>
> His response stunned me. "When they walk through the door of my church, they become my sheep," he replied. "Whoever steps through that door, I become their pastor."
>
> I briefly protested that such a position would cause great damage to our church. He simply smiled, got up and walked out of my life. His view of the situation, I assume, was that my ministry was not producing fruit at the moment and needed to be pruned; his ministry was the people's salvation.

> Years later I saw this man receive a regional award acknowledging his church's growth and contribution to evangelistic efforts in our area. Numerical growth is often the measure by which our peers judge our ministry.[35]

The possibility that God could actually use suffering to help His people apparently never occurred to this pastor. Ecclesiastical Darwinism was in play with a "strong" church devouring the weak one.

The "practice" of measuring the effectiveness of a congregation by its numbers leads pastors and churches to accept a flawed doctrine. The pure Gospel and faithfulness to its teaching cease to be the measure by which we evaluate the church. Instead, we tend to judge by growth and churches are pressured to grow even if it means harming someone else.

4. Preaching God's Providential Care in Response to the People's Felt Needs

According to Evangelicalism and because we live in America, we must be sensitive to the needs and expectations of Americans, identify these needs, and try to meet them. What does the American market expect? What are the typical needs of our "target group"? I'm afraid that America wants faith without Jesus. Today, the definition of faith in the United States is a Christless definition.

In the Bible, faith is receiving and holding to the promises of God in Christ. True faith without Christ does not exist. When Jesus said, "O woman, great is your faith," it was because the Canaanite woman knew He was the Christ. When Jesus chided the apostles for their lack of faith, it was because they simply could not seem to identify Him as the promised Savior. Faith takes hold of Jesus.

"Faith," in our culture, is usually defined as the ability to get things done with the help of God. It's an optimistic attitude, the conviction that God is on our side, and that our plans will be rewarded with success. In America, "faith" is the belief that we shall overcome someday or that we can rebuild the twin towers. In short, for much of America, faith is confidence in God's ongoing providential care. What the marketplace wants is a Christless faith. I was paging through the *TV Guide* while waiting to buy my groceries one day. In it movie actor Martin Sheen was called "a man of great faith," even though the article made no mention of Christ. On the way home, I heard a song by George Michael entitled "Faith." Again, there was no mention of Jesus. I picked up the paper and read an article about the post-9/11 patriotism that swept the nation, turning our country to faith. Again, Jesus was not named. America wants faith without Christ.

The best definition of American faith is offered by the most successful pastor in America, Robert Schuller, as reported by C. Peter Wagner.

Possibility thinking boils down basically to a synonym of what the Bible calls "faith." Schuller's definition of possibility thinking is "the maximum utilization of the God-given powers of imagination exercised in dreaming up possible ways by which a desired objective can be attained." He is convinced that "the greatest power in the world is the power of possibility thinking." "If your dream is from God," he adds, "then you need only to exercise this miracle working power, and you can reach the seemingly unattainable goal!"[36]

C. Peter Wagner embellishes this definition of faith. He says that there are four "levels of faith." The first level is saving faith. The second level is sanctifying faith. The third level is Schuller's "possibility thinking faith." The fourth level is "the faith which trusts God for supernatural signs and wonders."[37]

When the object of faith, at its highest level, is God's dramatic, even miraculous, daily care, rather than Jesus Christ and the forgiveness of sins, then the purpose of the church changes. Instead of "bespeaking" people righteous in Christ, the church now is in business to convince people that God is taking care of them. And when God's daily care is determined by how well things are going in this life, then the church has a stake in helping people know that God is making things good for us.

Providence or Grace

No one ever gets to heaven by believing that God is taking care of us. That is simply a true statement. God is taking care of us, of course. He provides when He showers prosperity upon us and when He sends incredible hardships. He prospers us when our kids are born and when they die in our arms. He takes care of us when we are promoted in our careers and when we lose our jobs. Every

Christian believes in God's providential care. He takes care of us, but that is not what gets us to heaven.

What's God Doing in Your Church?

Every day I drive by a church on the way to work. Every three or four months there is a sign in the churchyard that proclaims something like: "25 more members. Isn't God great?" Once it said, "Record Easter Attendance. Isn't God cool?" I believe that God is great. I think I even believe that He is cool too. But His greatness is not known because He takes care of a congregation by adding members. He is not cool because the church has lots of people on Easter. In these cases the message of the cross has been replaced by the message that God is taking care of our church by making it grow. Providence has replaced grace.

I have a gripe about those lead articles that pastors write and place in their congregational newsletters. Should the pastor teach theology in his article, or should he tell what's going on in the church? Should he tell you about what Christ did 2,000 years ago and how Christ gives His forgiveness today through the Word and Sacraments as promised in the Bible, or should he report about how great things are going in the church? Too often I hear pastors report the stewardship successes, building programs, youth retreats, all the various programs, and blah, blah, blah. God wants those articles to teach about Jesus. He is much more interested in people learning of Christ's life and death, of His story and His grace, than in everything happening in your church. Take the last four articles that have been the lead articles in your church's newsletter. Did they teach about God's grace in Christ, or did they teach about what's happening in the church? Then go talk to your pastor and say, "Pastor, we would see Jesus."

Felt Needs and Preaching Providence

Preaching to the perceived "felt needs" of the people in our community is an example of preaching providence rather than grace. According to Church Growth experts, preachers are to be practical. They are to help people make it through the week. People will return to a church if they "expect to get something they can use—messages that apply to their lives."[38] Pastors should preach "down to earth, how-to messages that tell us this God stuff is real and is meant for everyday life." People think that "there may be eternal life, but right now, Monday through Friday is enough eternity for me."[39] According to one Church Growth advocate, the church is answering a question that the unchurched are not asking. "Unchurched people are not asking, 'What must I do to be saved?' Rather, they ask, 'How can I make my life work?' In effect, people in the church are providing an answer to a question that unchurched people do not ask."[40] So according to many Church Growth experts, the church needs to respond to the needs people feel every day. The expression "felt needs" has become a watchword for the idea that God's providential care is the dominant doctrine of the church.

What are the felt needs of the typical unchurched person in America today? Some say that the greatest need is loneliness.[41] Others say it is the need for an answer to the question, "How can I make my life work?"[42] Still others insist the need for physical safety ranks near the top of the list.[43] These are all serious needs. And Christian people, characterized by love, will do what they can to answer these needs. Even non-Christians will respond to such human need. Love and service for those in need will always be in the form of God's providential care. His care comes through your vocation. To the extent that the church defines her ministry as responding to felt needs, she will be ministering God's providential care. The problem is that no one ever gets to heaven by providence. We get there by grace.

I have one great need. I know what it is. I need forgiveness. I've been a Christian my whole life, and forgiveness is still my greatest need. I'm so sinful I don't even know how much I need the forgiveness of sins in Christ. I'm so sinful I don't often feel my sin. Luther said somewhere that if he hadn't read it in the Bible, he would simply not believe how sinful he was. Sin, particularly original sin, is not often felt.

My felt needs are different. They are almost impossible to know. They change every day. Some of them are rather benign. Some of them are not particularly godly. Some are sinful.

Should the church respond to my one great need whether I know it and feel it or not? That would be a ministry of grace. It would require Word and Sacraments. Or should the church determine the felt needs of its target audience and respond to these needs. That would be a ministry of providential care. It would require an incredibly complicated and ever-changing marketing strategy. There are differences between felt needs and the one thing needful.

Dwight Moody responded to the felt needs of the unemployed of New York during the tough economic times of the late nineteenth century. He helped them learn to apply themselves through the Protestant work ethic. Inspiring his hearers to rid themselves of those habits that stood in the way of financial success, Moody gave people the lessons of self-support they needed. But none of that got any of them to heaven. He preached providence. To save, you must proclaim grace. Moody was a great salesman and a marketing pioneer. He did not preach grace.

The church needs to show love and, as an individual Christian, you can love people in your vocation. If people are lonely, then you can start a couples' club or invite them to dinner. If people are uncertain as to how to make life work, you can give them a job placement service or send them to vocational training. If someone needs safety for their children, you can offer them daycare. But none of this ever got anyone to heaven. There is no problem with Christians responding to the felt needs of those around them. The problem arises when we define the ministry in terms of responding to felt needs. Here's what happens.

Let's say that Joe is very lonely. He has taken a job far away from home. He is single and has no friends or family nearby. So he goes to a church. The church advertises a singles' ministry, so Joe goes to the singles' ministry meeting. People are having fun. There are plenty of young men and women—potential friends. Joe joins the volleyball team sponsored by the singles' ministry. Here he makes some friends. He meets a girl. They fall in love and finally get married. Joe is happy. His life is better. He is no longer lonely. It's a happy story.

But Joe has defined faith as confidence in the providential care of God. He is, after all, an American. He is unsure that God loves him when things go wrong. He is more certain that God loves him when things go right. Things are going well, so Joe is pretty sure that God must love him. He goes to the services on Sunday and the messages tend to stress that God is taking care of us. He hears the praise songs and listens to the contemporary Christian music station that the church promotes. The message, again, focuses primarily on God's ongoing daily care. He observes the many "ministries" of the church, all of which make life go better—from AA to job searching from a Christian perspective to effective parenting to Christian time management. Through it all, Jesus has, to some extent, been relegated to "level-one faith" as C. Peter Wagner puts it. What will Joe believe? He will believe that God through the church has solved his problems.

Then God's providence turns unpleasant for Joe. His wife dies or, worse, divorces him. His friends take her side in the sordid matter. Now what will Joe conclude of God's love? Joe's problem is that he has gone to church to have his felt needs solved. He went for self-centered reasons, and his church encouraged him. That will end in tragedy.

What is happening to the congregation while Joe is a member? Keep in mind that church practice affects church doctrine. The congregation reaches out to Joe with all sorts of ministries that are responsive to his felt needs. Soon the "ministry of the congregation" is dominated by responding to felt needs. The need for forgiveness, unless it is acutely felt, recedes into the background. "Ministries" that emphasize God's providential care begin to dominate. These seem to be more effective. Joe and other new members prefer those "ministries" that respond to their need for friends, companionship, or answer the question "How can I make my life work?" When the congregation discovers those "ministries" that attract others, they accent them more. Consequently, the church's definition of her "ministry" changes. Ministry is no longer "bespeaking" people righteous in Christ. Providence has replaced grace. Practice has changed doctrine.

Bait and Switch

Joe's experience is not unusual. I had a conversation with a Church Growth advocate and asked what was the single most important strategy for growth in the church. His response was a type of "bait and switch" strategy. He suggested that we offer classes on topics that weren't particularly theological, such as parenting, marriage enrichment, handling your finances, even "how-to" courses on babysitting, job searching, or music lessons. Then he said we should offer community services, such as the use of our facilities for softball or for daycare. Once people are in the building, you can begin the various meetings or events with a prayer and a little devotion. This allows you to bring the Gospel into their lives.

I objected. "I am not trained or called to teach finances, and that is not the church's mission either. We are here to preach Christ. It seems dishonest to let people think that your goal is to help them through the week when really that is a 'front' to tell them about Christ. Why not come right out and say that we preach Christ crucified? We get people to heaven," I responded.

His answer? "That doesn't work."

The great Christian apologist John Warwick Montgomery gave a lecture many years ago called "Damned through the church." In it he said: "The church is no place for religious fellow-travelers. A man had better go to church for the right reasons—God centered not self centered—or not at all. The church can be a place of accelerated salvation. It can also be a place of accelerated damnation."[44]

If you go to church to have your felt needs met, you are going for the wrong reason. You are in danger. If you go for the forgiveness of sins, then you are safe. If a church promotes itself by its response to felt needs—if it behaves like Dwight Moody—then people could be damned through it.

Stressing Providence over Grace

The emphasis on preaching providence rather than grace has some devastating consequences for both doctrine and practice. First, the church will lose its focus on eternal life. I hope you found the quote "Monday through Friday is enough eternity for me" as chilling as I did. I have given Communion to many dying saints and preached at many of their funerals. I don't believe, even for a second, that those attending funerals really prefer messages that "get them through the week" to the message of eternal life through Christ. Apparently St. Peter felt the same because every sermon he preached in the Book of Acts had as its specific topic the resurrection of Christ from the dead. Paul does the same. Neither of these apostles said anything in any sermon that was geared specifically to "get you through the week" or to accent their view of God's providential care. They preached Christ crucified. When Christ our Lord instituted Baptism, was it "to get you through the week" or to give us entrance "into the kingdom of God" (John 3:5)? And when He instituted His Holy Communion, He did not say, "Shed for many to get them through the week." He pointed them to eternal life that is theirs through the forgiveness of sins. I'm sure that the apostles and Christ believed that the message of the cross was able to get people through the week not because it was practical but because it was eternally true.

Second, when providence trumps grace in preaching, then "witness" replaces confession. Pastors will not teach their people to confess the faith but to share their personal story. Because a man's witness must be about things that he has seen and heard, his "testimony" will take on an experiential tone. It's about him. He will talk about what God has done in his life rather than on the cross. That's providence. The result is stories of "born again" experiences of which those who deny Baptism and the Lord's Supper are so fond. Lutherans who promote change in the Lutheran church often encourage such talk.

> One reason traditional Lutherans are reluctant to give witness to their faith is that the communication modeled for us is mostly doctrinal preaching supported with Bible passages. Carefully formulated doctrine is a great strength of Lutheranism. But this specialized language is more suited to professionals and often leaves laypeople uncertain about whether they are 'saying it right.' . . . An alternative used by many other Christians over the centuries is experiential language—expressing faith in terms of personal experience. Such language has phrases like: This is what God did in my life. Here is how I found new peace in the Lord. I found new meaning in the Gospel when . . . When I am getting to know individual Lutherans better, I have found it productive to inquire about when they felt closest to God or what they remember as a mountain-top spiritual experience, or when their faith means the most to them.[45]

How sad. Yes, Lutherans are reluctant to talk about God sometimes. But just because we are reluctant to communicate through "doctrine supported by Bible passages" is simply no reason to abandon the endeavor. The advice to ape the Evangelical community by sharing religious experiences is certainly no solution to Lutheran reluctance. Rather, pastors should teach the people to confess. That's why we teach and memorize the catechism and doctrinal hymns.

The change in "style" advocated among Lutherans is like the sick patient who is taking too many pills. He takes one because he thinks he is sick. Then he takes another to counter the side effects of the first. A third, then, is required to help with all those bad things the second caused. The next pill adds to the sickness by complicating the negative effects of the first three pills, and on and on it goes. It never occurs to the patient simply to go back to health by throwing away all the pills. We tell people that they ought to learn to "speak from the heart." Then we take away the catechism because it doesn't encourage spontaneous heartfelt witnessing. Once her primary doctrinal tool is gone, the church's ability to speak doctrine is decreased. So instead of teaching people, we offer lessons and promptings on how they can share their experiences. Then we take away the doctrinal hymns and substitute songs that "capture their feelings," further impoverishing the church of her doctrine. Unable to talk doctrinally, the church now loses her ability even to pray. So we tell the people that extemporaneous prayers are best, then deprive them of the church's collects. Finally, we concede that Lutherans don't know how to talk doctrine, and we offer them the alternative, "witnessing their personal experiences." This, obviously, further reduces the need for doctrinal study. Historic collects, hymns, and the catechism, already neglected, are rendered irrelevant. The patient just gets sicker and sicker. In truth, Lutheranism needs no initial pill. We are not sick from any lack. We are diseased from an overdose of pills imported from germ-ridden sources that promise solutions to problems caused by their own germs and their own "cures." It's time to throw away all the pills and get healthy again.

Third, when preachers promote God's "Monday through Friday" providence and care rather than proclaiming forgiveness through the cross and resurrection, then the marks of the church change. In chapter 3 I showed that the true marks of the church are the Word of the Gospel and the sacraments of Baptism and the Lord's Supper. These are objective. I can easily know if your church has the Spirit. Is the pure Gospel proclaimed and taught? Are the Sacraments administered according to Christ's institution? If so, then you have the Spirit whether your congregation is being cared for providentially in a desirable manner or not. But if I constantly preach that God is taking care of my members and of the church, then the way to identify the church—the church's marks—becomes its prosperity, its growth, its excitement, or its success.

I talked to a pastor of a large Lutheran congregation employing all the techniques described in this chapter. I serve a congregation that more closely resembles your grandfather's Lutheran church. I asked this pastor, "If one of your members moved into my area and came to my church one Sunday and then went to the local Evangelical church with the 'praise services,' 'practical preaching,' 'seeker services,' and exhortational or providential preaching the next Sunday, which church would that member join?"

The pastor thought about it for more than a couple of seconds. "I don't know," was his reply. He wasn't certain that his own members would choose a Lutheran church. This was not simply another example of denominational disloyalty. The marks of the church have changed. They are no longer Word and Sacraments.

Fourth, when providence replaces grace in the church's preaching, then active faith saves and the Gospel is denied. God earned forgiveness through His Son. He bestows grace through the Gospel. We receive salvation through faith. Faith is passive as it receives because salvation is entirely and exclusively the work of God. Providence is more complex, just as "felt needs" are more complex. God's providential care is achieved by God through means, just like salvation is. But the means in this case are people working and cooperating with God. God's providential care is accomplished, to some extent, by me picking myself up by the bootstraps and acting responsibly in the situation in which I have been placed. Providential care happens through the active faith of Christians as they care for themselves and others. When this providential care becomes the message of the church, then active faith becomes dominant over passive faith. We've already shown the disastrous effects of confusing passive and active faith. Ultimately, Christ is lost.

Style of preaching is not the issue here. Whether the pastor speaks loudly or softly, with flamboyant gestures or is more subdued, using many illustrations or just a few—none of this is really the issue. I've discovered that my particular style has changed from church to church that I have served because different congregations appreciate different styles. Style is not the issue. At stake is the dominant theme of preaching. Should the pastor refuse to step down from the pulpit without proclaiming clearly that sins are forgiven solely through the life and death of Jesus? If so, grace dominates. Or should a pastor refuse to step down from the pulpit until he has assured the people that things will be okay and that God will work everything out for them in the coming week? If so, then providence dominates. The first way is Christian, apostolic, and Lutheran. The second way, quickly becoming the dominant characteristic of many sermons, is none of these.

OPTIONS AT A STEAK COOKOUT

There's nothing like a cookout. Years ago, when I was a young man and red meat was still good for you, we used to gather in my parents' backyard and eat sirloin steak by the pound. My mom would make the best potato salad in the country, and we would gobble mounds of tossed vegetable salad, always with blue cheese dressing. The level of cholesterol of the family members would increase 150 percent after each such meal. At a steak cookout there are always certain options. You ate the lettuce salad and the potato salad just the way they were served, or not. There was really no third option. But with the steak there were options. You could eat it rare, medium, or well done. You could ask the cook, Dad, to put barbeque sauce on it. But there was only one entrée on the menu. You ate steak.

One day someone brought a girlfriend to dinner. She seemed nice. We were going to give her a chance. But she did a bad, bad thing. When it came time to put the steaks on the grill, Dad asked the usual question, "How do you like your steak?" We all laughed, as if he didn't know. But the young lady answered, "Actually, I'm not able to eat steak. I was wondering if there was another option." A hushed and awkward moment followed. "You don't like steak?" was the incredulous chorus. It echoed across the patio and through the halls of the house. The birds in the trees seemed to stop their chirping. The dog tilted his head and raised his brows in that inquisitive pose, which indicates that some law of nature has been violated. The little children began to giggle with embarrassment as if they had just noticed that someone's pants were ripped in the back and the owner was still unaware. Everyone else simply gaped at the poor girl in amazement. Then, as if to add insult to injury the young lady actually said, "No. I really don't like steak." She might as well have burned the flag, yawned at baseball, and insulted our mother. It would have been somewhat acceptable had she suffered from some strange allergy to red meat. Although, who ever heard of such a thing? In that case we could have recommended an expert allergist who, perhaps, could have cured her. But to dislike steak, that was unheard of. Soon stares of inquisition began to focus upon the unlucky sibling who had actually asked this person to attend a steak cookout. What was he thinking? It was like inviting the rabbi to a pork-feed. It just isn't done.

You see, when you are at a steak cookout, your options are limited. You can have steak in all sorts of ways, but you have to eat steak. That's the way it is with the ministry of the church when it comes to the Gospel. You can teach Christ with simplicity to the young. You can challenge experienced Christians with more sophisticated nuances of the faith. You can emphasize Christ's resurrection to the dying, His rest to the tired, or His redemption to habit-ridden souls. You can promise the cross to the complacent and heaven to the weary. But you cannot ever remove Jesus and the doctrine of Christ from the ministry of the church. You can't even make it the second course. The Gospel is like steak. Your options are limited. You cannot change the primary message of the church from "You are forgiven in Christ" to "God will take care of you."

When you attempt to adjust the Gospel to the market or to adapt the Gospel to market-driven forces, you run the risk of losing it all together. It's like serving hot dogs at a steak cookout.

5. ENTHUSIASTIC, EXHORTATIONAL, AND ENTERTAINING PREACHING

Possibly the most far-reaching change initiated by Dwight Moody and the revivalists before him was the change in the style of the sermon. Moody was one in a long line of preachers whose primary goal was to get the hearer to make an immediate change.

> From the time of the revival it was no longer possible for a minister to be successful in the pulpits solely by his homiletical prowess. As a result of the revival . . . a sermon was now judged by its effect. Style was secondary to conversion; organization gave way to immediacy. No longer did a sermon direct itself to . . . a theological issue, rather the sermon called for the sinner to admit his dependence on God and repent. The minister was judged by whether or not he could bring about this experience. If the minister appealed to logic or used notes or prepared his sermon, he was standing in the way of a direct confrontation with God. . . . The method of preaching sprang logically from their concept of the doctrine of regeneration.[46]

The type of sermon that sought to effect immediate change was called "exhortational" because the speaker exhorted the people to change themselves. The preacher employed whatever rhetorical devices he could to get the people to do what he wanted.

Moody was a teacher neither by training nor by skill. But he was an amazingly effective communicator—if you measure effectiveness by his popularity or by the response of his listeners. Moody peppered his sermons with folksy anecdotes, retold Bible stories, and fervent personal appeals. All were calculated both to elicit the proper emotional response and to move the crowds to the instant choice of salvation. For example, in describing Moody's telling of the story of the Good Samaritan, one supporter described:

> His eyes would fill and his voice would tremble as he read over the description to me of the wounded man and glisten with joy as he came to the account of the kind Samaritan.[47]

This made Moody immensely popular, especially when he was contrasted with the typical parish pastor of the day who had neither Moody's flare nor his skill. Because his preaching was based upon the belief that conversion and salvation were "the deliberate act of exercising the will in a moment of decision,"[48] Moody had to work quickly and deliberately. In this style of sermonizing, the Gospel "became something not to be talked about, but to be tried and passed on."[49] The urgency of the message dominated, and people were not encouraged to analyze, understand, reflect, "read, mark, learn and inwardly digest" the Word of God but simply "either to go with it or get out of the way," as one journalist described Moody.[50]

Moody's style differed markedly from that of Jesus. Jesus taught. When He finished His Sermon on the Mount, "the crowds were astonished at His teaching, for He was teaching them as one who had authority, and not as their scribes" (Matthew 7:28–29). Christ's example has led the great preachers of history from Chrysostom to Luther, from Augustine to Walther, to evaluate their sermons in terms of their doctrine. Peter taught and the early church applied itself devotedly to the apostle's teaching (Acts 2:42). Unlike Moody's audiences, the Bereans, as told in Acts 17, when they received the message of Paul examined the Bible every day to see if the things he taught were true. The Bible teaches us to evaluate sermons not by our measure of their immediate affect but as to whether they teach Christ.

ARISTOTLE

In the study of classical rhetoric, Aristotle, who is the father of rhetoric, looms large. He says that every public speech will have elements of what he calls logos, ethos, and pathos. Logos is the thoughtful, logical content of the speech. Ethos is that aspect of speech that shows the noble character of the speaker or his right to address you—his integrity, his authority, his love, or his experience. Pathos is the emotional nature of the speech—does it move, inspire, or anger you? Early Christian preachers used these categories. Sometimes the three sides of a speech were inform, delight, and inspire.

Every sermon will have elements of all three. If pastors did nothing to delight the congregation, everyone would be asleep within minutes. So we tell stories to illustrate theological points. We quote hymns both pointed and poetic. Pastors will often say things that are humorous. We even make allusions to movies or literature.

These are to engage the congregation and help them pay attention. Pastors also employ elements of pathos in their preaching. They seek to affect the emotions of Christians or motivate for Christian living or prayer. But in proper Christian preaching, the logos dominates. People need to learn more about Jesus. This is true for communicant members of the church, for those being instructed, and for those who are still in their unbelief. Have you ever heard a sermon in which a story was told and you remember the story but not the point it made? In that sermon the ethos part of the sermon got in the way of the logos. You probably complained about the sermon, and you should have. You are not there to hear good stories but to learn about Jesus. Of Harry Emerson Fosdic, famous and flowery New England preacher of the early twentieth century, someone is reported to have said that his sermon was so great that no one had heard a better sermon since the last time he preached. In that case pathos took the front seat to logos. Obviously, sermons that are nothing more than lectures from doctrine books probably need to have more ethos or pathos within. They should delight and inspire. But the primary aspect of every good Christian sermon is to teach. Aristotle would say that logos should dominate.

WHY SHOULD YOU AVOID EXHORTATIONAL SERMONS?

Moody's enthusiastic exhortational sermons should be avoided for a number of reasons. First, because any attempt to use a sermon to motivate or entertain without information is unethical. When a sermon is exhortational, then the pathos or ethos aspects of the speech take over. The sermon is geared to motivate the hearer to a specific action without necessarily imparting the required information to do so, or it is geared to delight the hearer without any clear message of Jesus. When people are urged to commit to Jesus "without talking about it" or to "go with it or get out of the way," then there is a type of manipulation that goes on. No true Christian pastor would plan on manipulating his congregation. Probably all do so inadvertently at some time or another. The problem comes when manipulative rhetorical devices are employed.

Raymond McLaughlin wrote a book entitled *The Ethics of Persuasive Preaching*. In it he identified certain things that preachers do that are unethical. He listed such things as reading your own opinion into the Bible text, not practicing what you preach, or waiting until the last minute to prepare. No pastor would advocate these things, even though many might do them. Certain questionable practices, however, are not only common, they are often encouraged by some pastors. McLaughlin conducted an admittedly "unscientific" poll. He discovered that half of the pastors he surveyed "used entertainment rather than needful content in their sermons." Half "preached what people wanted to hear rather than what they needed to hear," and "frequently" pastors "avoided controversial subjects." The most common "unethical" practice identified by McLaughlin was "promising oversimplified solutions to complex problems."[51]

The type of sermons often advocated by Church Growth experts contain precisely those elements against which McLaughlin warns. When the congregation is told to avoid doctrinal controversies,[52] or when pastors are told not to mention doctrinal divisions because they turn people off, then the logos of a sermon—its doctrinal content—is deliberately downplayed in order to get people to become involved. People are not given all the truth they need in order to evaluate and understand the church that a given preacher represents. When the style of the service or the sermon is adjusted based on the results of marketing data or the perceived "felt needs" of the community, then the pastor is "giving people what they want rather than what they need." Billy Sunday, evangelist of the mid-twentieth century, "made preaching such a sensational event that newspaper men would cover the story." He "would tear apart a chair on stage as if striking the devil." Leading Church Growth advocate Carl George praises this strategy because Billy Sunday and others "believed passionately in the power of enthusiastic preaching."[53] Surely, "entertainment rather than needful content" has dominated.

The second reason why exhortational sermons should be avoided is that they are so often synergistic. The entire idea of getting people to make an immediate decision is based on the assumption that people can choose. Among revivalists, as cited above, the exhortational "method of preaching sprang logically from their concept of the doctrine of regeneration."[54] According to American Christianity you have to tell a person to believe and "exhort" faith. Recall, however, the words of Walther in chapter 3. He said that you don't even need to use the word *faith* to preach Christ.[55] In fact, if a pastor constantly urges his people to believe, then it is the urging rather than the Gospel that is often credited for the salvation. Jesus and His Spirit are diminished.

Third, exhortational preaching should be avoided because it spoils people. When my kids were little, they would beg, nag, whine, and otherwise abuse their parents for candy. Of course, we relented because we were weak and they were strong. We would justify our negligent parenting with the pathetic excuse, "Just this once." It was never just once. That's the way it is with candy. It becomes a habit and dulls your taste for other food so pretty soon you will only like the sweet stuff. Candy does more than rot your teeth and wreck your appetite. It spoils you. If kids have sweet things often enough, they will begin to dislike bland food, such as vegetables, milk, meat, and pasta. My kids used to go to school with a neighbor boy. His mom and I would take turns driving. One day he dropped his lunchbox and the contents spilled on the floor of my Econoline van. Out fell two candy bars, a granola bar, three fruit roll-ups, a can of Coke, two twinkies, and a banana. "What will you give me for my banana?" was his quick offer. Once you have something you like, that which is good for you will be shunned.

So it goes with preaching. It's not that pastors should avoid preaching well for fear the people will expect it from them every time. Rather, if the people "enjoy" the sermon because it moves them or entertains them, then their hearing will be tuned to "delight" rather than to the light of the Gospel. This is especially true in today's transient society. People will shop for the church with the most entertaining preacher, the preacher who tells the best stories, or the preacher who inspires them. They will employ ethos or pathos as the primary tool of evaluation rather than logos. When that happens, it may be impossible to wean them from the nonnutritious sugar of the three Es in preaching—exhortational, enthusiastic, and entertaining. It happened with Moody.

Fourth, exhortational preaching should be avoided because it is not in the Bible. You may object. Doesn't the Bible tell us to exhort one another? The Greek word for exhort is the word *parakalew*. It comes from the same root as the word *paraclete*, which Jesus uses to refer to the Holy Spirit in John 14:16 and 15:26: "When the Comforter comes whom I will send." Most often the word is used to mean "comfort." Paul says in 2 Corinthians 1 that God "comforts us in all our affliction, so that we may be able to comfort those who are in any affliction, with the comfort with which we ourselves are comforted by God" (v. 4). Jesus uses the word in His beatitudes: "Blessed are those who mourn for they shall be comforted." Admittedly, the word is used in places where a natural translation might be "exhort" or "appeal," as in Paul's missionary appeal of 2 Corinthians 5:20: "Therefore, we are ambassadors for Christ, God making His appeal [*parakalew*] through us. We implore you on behalf of Christ, be reconciled to God." In a similar passage Paul says, "For our appeal [*parakalew*] does not spring from error or impurity or any attempt to deceive" (1 Thessalonians 2:3). In both of these passages, and many others, the idea is not that we first tell people about Christ then exhort them to believe. Rather, the message of Christ is a comforting exhortation. Even when Christians are exhorted to holy living (Romans 12:1; 2 Corinthians 10:1; Ephesians 4:1; Philippians 4:2; 1 Peter 5:1), it is "the mercies of Christ," "the gentleness of Christ," or simply "the Lord" who urges and always by the Gospel itself. The word should probably be translated "urge by the comfort of the Gospel itself." That might make the English translations a bit awkward, but it would avoid the excesses that result from a wrong idea of Christian comforting and exhortation. When the first grader gets up in the Christmas program and stammers out, "A Savior has been born for you who is Christ the Lord," you have been exhorted by the simple Christmas message to trust in the Christ Child far more than when the most dynamic preacher in the world pleads passionately for you to decide for Jesus.

Preaching is best when it is a clear teaching and proclamation of the doctrine of the Gospel.

6. Converting the Churched

Thirty years ago I became interested in a certain Pentecostal denomination when I read its religious journal while at the Laundromat. Someone from the church would habitually leave the magazines behind, hoping that others might read them. It worked. I would always gravitate toward the statistics section of the magazine. Unlike our Lutheran statistics, which talk about baptisms, membership, and Sunday attendance, this journal listed the number of people who had been "saved," those who had "answered the call," and those who had "had the baptism." These were new and unusual categories for me. I puzzled over them for a while. The number of people saved in this denomination was remarkably high. There were hundreds each week. They listed the saved people by congregation. Even the local church was experiencing massive growth. I figured the church must be huge. So I found the address, and one day I drove by it. I was disappointed. It seemed rather modest. Where were all the people? One day, in the Laundromat, I watched this lady leave a couple of the magazines behind. Realizing that she was a member of the church, I approached her with my questions about what the different categories meant. It turned out, to this church, "saved" meant that you committed your life to Jesus for the first time. "Answered the call" meant that you went down in front of the church to recommit your life to Jesus. "Had the baptism" meant that you had been baptized in the Spirit and had spoken in tongues. We had a very nice chat, and she was quite forthcoming on the nuances and categories of her church. I asked her, "If I joined your church, even though I am already a Christian, would you put me into the 'saved' category or the category of 'answered the call'?"

"Oh, you would be saved," was her automatic reply, as if she had answered the question a few times before.

"But I'm already saved."

"It doesn't matter. If you have not answered the call even once, then you are saved when you answer it for the first time. Also if you've backslid."

"Backslid?" I asked. "Explain backslid."

We've all heard that there are no stupid questions. This was a stupid one, judging by her nonverbal demeanor. "If you have sinned against what you know is right, then you have backslid and you are lost. If you come and answer the call, then you are saved again."

"So you could get saved any number of times."

"Yes, that's right," she answered, "but we don't encourage that."

I was drawing analogies. I figured that getting saved any number of times was somewhat akin to the absolution you would want to receive often. So I didn't understand why you would not encourage it. "Why not encourage it?"

Again, this was a very bad question. "You would encourage people to sin and backslide? What kind of Christian are you?"

Actually, I had thought we had already concluded that I was not a Christian at all and still needed saving, but I let that go. "I'm the kind of Christian that needs to be forgiven pretty often."

"Well, you need to work on that," she said. "There's no excuse for getting saved over and over again."

I was convinced of two things. First, these ecumenical discussions were not as easy as they seemed. Second, statistics can deceive.

The woman in the Laundromat defined switching churches as "being saved" as long as her church was the recipient. This meant that anyone who joined her church was counted as saved or converted.

She and her church learned the practice from Dwight Moody. Moody would preach to a rather homogeneous audience—all white, Anglo-Saxon, middle-class Protestants in a large, economically depressed urban area. The people Moody "converted" were actually members of local Methodist and Congregationalist congregations. They really didn't need to be saved. But when they answered the altar call, they became a statistic for Moody.

THE FRUSTRATION AND IMPOSSIBILITY OF COUNTING

Many advocates of Church Growth are acutely aware of the church hopping that goes on within evangelical American Christianity. Often these advocates will claim that they seek not transfer growth but adult baptisms or conversion growth. Laudable as such growth would be, it is almost impossible to determine. Yet the system in which many Protestant churches find themselves requires growth in order to conclude that God is truly blessing the church. Earlier in the chapter I mentioned a church in my neighborhood that routinely put up a sign announcing the growth of the church. That congregation has to grow or there will be trouble. The pastor will get frustrated, the people will wonder what's going wrong, the "effectiveness" of the ministry will be questioned, and the sign will remain in storage. When that happens, the pressure to grow will increase as the congregation desperately seeks to assure itself of

God's continued providential care, measured by continued growth. The pastor will not be able to go home after church on Sunday satisfied that he proclaimed the forgiveness of sins and confident that the Gospel and Sacraments always and objectively forgive. He will have to see effects. The pressure mounts. So new measuring techniques are invented to show that God's blessings have not departed. Unfortunately, these techniques don't always tell the whole story.

Not all churches are quite so brazen in their measurements as that woman in the Laundromat. But many are equally creative. Some baptistic churches will claim large numbers of adult baptisms. The claim is often made that God is blessing these churches with unprecedented adult conversions. Remember, however, that many Baptist denominations routinely re-baptize those who join their church and have "merely" been baptized as a baby. This would mean that if a Lutheran or a Roman Catholic joined certain megachurches, they would have to be re-baptized. The statistics would indicate an adult conversion. Nothing of the kind has taken place. Lutherans recognize that to "re-baptize" anyone who has been baptized as an infant, far from church growth, is actually an insult to God. But in some baptistic churches, those already saved in Baptism are being "saved" again and counted again by those who have eroded the confidence in God's gracious washing.

Another way of achieving false growth is when a congregation deliberately situates itself to receive the disgruntled members of other churches. People sometimes simply shop for new churches. They get frustrated or indifferent with their church or pastor, denominational disloyalty sets in, they move on, and before you know it they are someone else's convert. Carl George says:

> Why do some churches grow even without being strongly evangelistic? The common explanation which fits many of the large metropolitan area churches, is that some develop a gravitational pull on the unhappy, the disillusioned and the underutilized from other churches. . . . Whenever members responded to internal congregational troubles by looking elsewhere for a new church home, they tended to drift to one or more churches that had distinguished themselves as receptor sites. These would grow large as a result of recurring trouble in the feeder churches.[56]

This practice violates the promise made by Lutherans. When they join a church, Lutherans promise to support the congregation, pray for it, be fed by the pastor, believe and confess the faith taught, and attend services regularly. These Christians should not be encouraged to break their word by the "ministry" of "receptor site" congregations. Rather, as the Ninth Commandment teaches, they should be urged to stay and do their duty. The church hopping encouraged by Carl George and practiced by many simply weakens the church.

Another way in which churches can claim conversion growth is to reach out to the "dechurched." Dechurched are those who were raised in the church but who have stopped attending and now have returned. The angels in heaven do rejoice at one sinner who repents, and there is genuine joy in the church when someone returns after a long absence. But churches need to be very cautious that their "ministry to the dechurched" is not simply taking in members of neighboring churches who may or may not have lapsed.

Dwight Moody, Billy Sunday, and Billy Graham have conducted revivals for more than a century. They have energized the Evangelical community. Growth experts have inspired their churches with endless techniques for evangelism, ideas for growth, and strategies for increase. You would expect that Christianity, and especially Evangelical Christianity, would be prospering in the United States. Sadly this is not true. William Chadwick relates a comment from C. Peter Wagner at a lecture given at Fuller Theological Seminary in 1991: "Our initial research indicates that there has been no appreciable growth in the American Evangelical population as a whole over the last ten years."[57] George Barna agrees. In 1996 he concluded that "the proportion of born again Christians in America has remained unchanged. . . . Data showed that most measures of religious activity among American adults have remained flat or are experiencing slow decline."[58]

What is happening? People are flitting from congregation to congregation playing musical churches. Some churches wax. Others wane. Christianity looses its force and credibility in an increasingly cynical world. Moody converted those who were already in churches. Today's Evangelical community does the same.

CONCLUSION

These six bad practices discussed here, based on flawed doctrine, are themselves flawed. Their effect is an impoverished church with flattened growth. The sweet Gospel is muted or it is morphed into placid promises of providential care. Worse, an invitation to synergistic decision theology replaces God's "bespeaking us righteous." Millions church hop while millions, who truly need Jesus, are ignored. Competition thrives proportionate to the church's paucity for truth. Yet sadly, Lutherans want a share in this unhappy legacy. We are tempted to follow the example of our Evangelical neighbors. The result is a compromise of the historic worship practices of the church. The gentle staff of true worship practice no longer prods toward the fire. "The Staff Is Lost."

Rather than attempt to bring growth by tampering with faithful worship, the true key to "outreach" is for Christians to confess the faith.

STUDY QUESTIONS

1. What expertise and practice did Dwight Moody apply to the revival to make it more acceptable to urban Americans?
2. George Barna contends the importance of the worship service is "bringing people to Christ" and "half of all regular church-going adults admit they have not experienced God's presence at any time during the past year." What change do dynamic pastors and congregations make to address this need?
3. Whose action do Barna and Church Growth advocates think worship is? Is this the teaching of the Lutheran church?
4. What is the false teaching promoted by the altar call?
5. What is God's providential care?
6. "Preaching providence rather than grace has devastating consequences for both doctrine and practice." What are these consequences?
7. What is the goal of "exhortational" preaching?

DISCUSSION QUESTIONS

1. What are the problems inherent for Lutheran doctrine and practice in each of Dwight Moody's new practices?

2. The author says that a word of caution is necessary because some Lutheran pastors and congregations are accepting worship principles and practices that promote the theology of altar calls. Discuss the impact of the practices that are discussed in the text on the practice and doctrine of the Lutheran church.

11

THE FIRE KINDLED

CONFESSING THE FAITH

I had a difficult time knowing exactly where to place this chapter in the book. On the one hand it belongs immediately after the chapter on Christian vocation. It is every Christian's calling to speak of Christ. On the other hand it could be seen as a corrective to the Church Growth model of evangelistic mission. Church Growth advocates want to change the church in order to save souls. The endeavor impoverishes the church and does not really bring people to faith. The proper way of evangelism is for every Christian to understand how to talk about God, actually to do so, and to have a confessional and confessing church to which the objects of evangelism can attach themselves. So we discuss here the importance of Christian confession.

One positive observation can be made of Moody's revivals. Those who participated and supported them, including Moody himself, seemed to have good intentions. They wanted people in heaven. You can't criticize Moody for his intentions. But if marketing the Gospel, reengineering the worship service, planning "seeker services" with altar calls, and preaching exhortational sermons aren't the best way to bring people to Jesus, then what is? The answer is simple. Christians have to talk to others about Christ.

The greatest good work that you can do, at least in terms of its benefits, is to tell someone of Jesus. Every single Christian can thank someone, usually many people—whether parents, grandparents, a pastor, a teacher, a spouse, or a sibling—for speaking Christ to them. Our faith does not get poured into our hearts from some mystical, extraterrestrial source, but "faith comes from hearing, and hearing through the word of Christ" (Romans 10:17). Someone talked to you about Christ—that's why you believe. In the Bible, speaking of Christ is not so much a required task placed as a duty upon Christians as it is an activity that Christians naturally do. If Christians can do what their faith instinctively and powerfully motivates them to do, then more and more people will hear, come to faith, and inherit eternal life. Tragically, the forces within our culture that have corrupted our understanding of worship have also seriously skewed the way we talk about God. God's way is simple. Just talk. But culture has rendered talk of God challenging indeed.

A particular biblical image that suggests the proper understanding of the Christian task of talking about Jesus is the image of the royal priesthood.

THE ROYAL PRIESTHOOD

The biblical designation "royal priesthood" gives all Christians great status and great comfort. It tells us that we have access to God through our Lord Jesus Christ. Through Him our prayers are heard by our heavenly Father and His name on our lips can destroy the power of the devil. We speak to one another the story of Jesus and confess the faith of Christ to the world.

The Bible says that we are a royal priesthood. The image is employed five times in the New Testament. Peter uses it in 1 Peter 2:5 and 9. John uses the expression "priests" to refer to God's people in Revelation 1:6; 5:10; and 20:6. What does God mean when He uses the idea of priesthood to describe His people? You have to know what priests did in the Old Testament. Their primary responsibility was to officiate at the sacrifices of God's people. Priests sacrifice. In the New Testament Christ did away with the need for animal sacrifices when He became the one-time sacrifice for all people on the cross. So when Jesus died, all the priests in the temple in Jerusalem were permanently unemployed. They still ignorantly slaughtered sheep and doves for a few more years in Jerusalem, much like the retiree who goes to work even after the company has said good-bye. However, God was no longer impressed or pleased with those obsolete priests performing unnecessary acts. He allowed

Jerusalem to be destroyed in A.D. 70 just to prove it. A new sacrifice—Jesus on the cross—had been made, which God accepted. God also accepts those things we offer to Him out of faith in Christ. Anyone who offers himself (1 Peter 2:5), his body (Romans 12:1), his money (Philippians 4:18), or his praise (Hebrews 13:15) to God is a priest (1 Peter 2:5) making the New Testament sacrifice. As all Christians make these sacrifices, all are called priests.

Priests in the Old Testament also talked to others when they confessed the faith. So God's people talk. The best known of the passages on the royal priesthood is probably 1 Peter 2:9 where Peter tells the church that we are, among other things, a "royal priesthood" so we can "proclaim the excellencies of Him who called you out of darkness into His marvelous light." We talk to the world. We show forth. "Show forth" means that we announce, much as the narrator of a play announces to the audience what is going on. We narrate the story of Jesus. The best way to talk about God is simply to relate the story of Jesus and explain how this story brings people into the light of God through the forgiveness of their sins. Christians need to believe that when the story of Christ is "shown forth," the power of God is at work. Talking of Christ to others effectively "bespeaks them righteous," as we learned in chapter 2. More on this below.

Christians also talk to the devil. In passages in Revelation, John is quoting from Exodus 19 where God promises that all His people will be priests and serve God. Especially notable is Revelation 20:6 where God promises that His church will reign with Christ over the devil for as long as the church endures as "priests of God and of Christ." Sometimes God's people talk to the world; here we talk to the devil. We say to the old evil foe that he has been conquered by Christ. We rub his snout in his own defeat. Every time we forgive our neighbor of sins he has committed against us or against God, we are speaking against Satan. What a privilege—to speak Christ's forgiveness to others! In chapter 3 of this book you read about absolution. Pastors pronounce it according to their vocation. "I as a called and ordained servant of the Lord forgive you all your sins." What pastors speak in their vocation all priests do as well. We forgive one another as Christ forgives us. When we do, we reign over Satan. The biblical image of "royal priesthood" is a wonderful image.

Luther, in his discussion of the word *priesthood* adds another thought. At the time of the Reformation, the Roman Church taught that the priests had special power and standing before God that others did not have. Luther realized that your vocation in this life doesn't give you special standing. Only Christ does that, and all Christians have that standing when God "bespeaks us righteous." Luther saw that the New Testament never called the ministers of the Gospel "priests." All Christians sacrifice, and we all talk about Christ. In Christ we are all priests.[1] For Luther, and all Lutherans, this means that all Christians have the command to preach—to talk about Christ. Luther quickly adds that "only a few are selected from the whole group to administer the office [of preacher] in the stead of the congregation."[2] In the presence of God we are all equally priests and preachers because we all talk about God. But "externally" before one another God chooses a few through the call of the congregation. When the pastor preaches, the whole church is preaching because the pastor functions in the stead of the people. When I baptize a baby as a pastor, the whole church is baptizing that baby. Actually, Christ is baptizing through the church that has called me. "Priesthood" means that God is working His grace through the whole church when one pastor, appointed by all, carries out the ministry.

What glorious blessings are given by the label "priest." Certain practices are derived from Peter's notion of the "royal priesthood."

First, the Bible never says that being part of the "royal priesthood" gives us rights. Exactly the opposite is true. By calling us "priests," God is telling us that we will sacrifice. We might even have to carry our cross or die for our Lord. Being a priest does not give me the right to be involved in the church anyway I want. Too often I have heard the idea of the "priesthood of all believers" invoked in such a way as if it were similar to the Bill of Rights of the U. S. Constitution. "You can't tell our church what to do. We are the royal priesthood. We have our rights. We can sing whatever songs we want in church. We are the royal priesthood. We should be allowed to decide matters in the church any way we want. After all, we are the royal priesthood." Actually, the idea of royal priesthood requires me to give up what I want, just as Christ gave up what He wanted. I don't get to decide what type of music is sung in church just because I am a priest. Rather, I should give up my rights of choice or my personal taste. According to a leading Missouri Synod Old Testament scholar, the image of the "Church as a priesthood of all believers can be very dangerous."[3] What an odd statement. Why would anyone call the biblical concept of priesthood dangerous? Because the priesthood image in the Bible has often been used to defend things that are not particularly Christian, such as "the right of laymen to baptize, the option of worshiping at home on a Sunday morning, and the personal privilege to forgive (publicly) or not forgive sins, a defense of the absolute autonomy of the local congregation."[4] In other words, some Christians have used the idea of "priesthood" to justify everyone behaving as if they are running the church. Exactly the opposite is true.

Second, priests never act independently. The "priesthood" acts together. In 1 Peter we are not called "a bunch of priests" but a "priesthood." We are collectively an order of priests. John, in Revelation, always uses the word in the plural, *priests*, and connects priests with God's kingdom, suggesting that we always function as a group. The "priesthood" never allows one priest to act independently of the others. Many times pastors or church leaders will talk about the "autonomy" of the congregation because the church is made up of "priests." Priests are simply not autonomous. Even a group of priests is not autonomous. *Autonomous* means "a law unto themselves." No Christian is autonomous, and neither is a congregation. A congregation does not have the right to make decisions about itself without any concern for the rest of the "royal priesthood." No one priest or group of priests has the right to say things differently than the entire priesthood. Above I said that the priesthood idea can be dangerous. Any idea is dangerous if it is misapplied. When a congregation adopts practices that are completely different from those of other churches or when it rejects the stated doctrine of the church, then that congregation is not acting like the royal priesthood. Rather, it is a group of renegade priests who seem to believe that they can do as they please. Confessors and priests speak with one voice what the church has been taught.

Third, when priests talk about Christ, their word is as powerful as that of Christ. Some people, even Lutheran pastors, have at times said things that gave the impression that the Word of God is not powerful unless spoken by the pastor. Such an impression is profoundly dangerous. It is dangerous, first, because it makes it seem as though the Word depends on the pastor for its power. It does not. In chapter 3 I showed that the Word is powerful because the Holy Spirit always works through it regardless of who speaks it. It is God's will that only pastors preach the Word publicly to God's people, but that does not mean that the power depends on pastors in any way. Second, such a view is dangerous because it will discourage every Christian who is not a pastor from speaking about Christ in their various vocations. To silence the "priesthood" would be tragic indeed.

There's an old saying that you hear every once in a while: "Laymen are supposed to pray, pay, and obey." That sentence has become kind of a growl phrase as if it's an old-fashioned idea. The sentence is not wrong, just incomplete. I have never met a Christian layman who had any objection to the thought that he could pray anywhere and anytime and that God both hears his prayer in Christ and regards it with the favor of a loving Father. All Christians, as priests, pray. We don't need an intermediary. Christ intercedes for us, and God hears our prayers. I have, likewise, never met a Christian who isn't happy to "pay" (assuming that the word *pay* means to give). Most Christians wish that they could give more. We give because we believe in vocation. Pastors need to be paid in their vocation. Missionaries need to be commissioned and supported in theirs. The various vendors who serve the church with office equipment, electricity, phone service, and Sunday school supplies need payment. So does the mortgage company who holds the church's loan. All Christians, as priests, pay. Christians also obey if you understand the word *obey* correctly. The Bible says, "Obey your leaders and submit to them, for they are keeping watch over your souls, as those who will have to give an account. Let them do this with joy and not with groaning, for that would be of no advantage to you" (Hebrews 13:17). The words *obey* and *submit* actually mean that Christians should allow pastors to do their jobs and Christians should listen to them with great attention as they preach the Word. So there is nothing wrong with the phrase "pray, pay, and obey." We need to add a fourth word to the formula if we are to capture what Peter means. "The church should pray, pay, obey, and say."

Christians exercise the priesthood by talking. We talk to God when we pray. We talk against the devil when we forgive. We talk when we call pastors. The pastor talks for all of us. And the priesthood talks when Christians confess Jesus to others.

Talking about Jesus is easier said than done. Many Christians are simply afraid to do so either for fear of failure or fear of rejection.

CHRISTIAN STAGE FRIGHT

Our hesitancy to talk about Christ to others can be explained largely by the general reluctance people have to communicate in contexts in which the response is unknown or feared. Researchers into stage fright have discovered that all people, to varying degrees, have fear associated with any type of communication. This fear, which experts call "communication apprehension," is defined as "an individual's fear or anxiety associated with real or anticipated communication with another person or persons."[5] There are two types of communication apprehension: trait apprehension and situational apprehension. Trait apprehension is when a person is simply fearful of communicating in general. We might conclude that such a person is shy. In such cases hereditary or cultural causes are explored. Researchers have even discovered that the size of the community in which you were raised affects your comfort with communication in general.[6] There is not much you can do about trait apprehension short of changing the culture. Situational apprehension, significantly more common, is the fear of talking in certain situations. James McCroskey, an expert and leading researcher in the field of communication apprehension, has identified five reasons why people might be fearful of talking in certain contexts. An understanding of these causes would help people overcome them, especially when they have a chance to talk to others about Christ. The first reason why people fear talking is the "degree of evaluation." This means that we are reluctant to speak if we think that people are closely scrutinizing what we say. Second is the "degree of prior success," which indicates that we will more likely talk where we think that we have done well in the past. The third reason for fear in communicating is the "degree of novelty," which means that an individual will be more apprehensive in new situations than familiar ones. The fourth reason why people fear speaking is the "degree of conspicuousness," which suggests that the more people are watching us, the more fearful we will become. You will have more butterflies when singing a solo in church than when you are part of a twenty-voice choir. Finally, a high "degree of ambiguity" exists in a situation where you are getting mixed signals as to how people might respond.[7] If someone is reluctant to talk about Jesus, one or more of these factors are probably responsible for the hesitation. Let's analyze these factors.

Degree of Evaluation

Remember those students who could answer any question in class? They impressed the teacher and the other students. But when test time came, they were so nervous that they performed poorly. They probably had a high degree of evaluation apprehension. We called it fear of tests. What was the solution? For some, a very small minority, they may just be stuck with an abnormal fear of tests. For the rest of us there was a solution. Study more. It took me a couple of years in high school, but I eventually figured out that there was direct correlation between the amount that I learned and how well I could communicate on tests. The same applies to our confession of Christ.

In the early church, when Christians gathered to hear the Word of God, they would typically listen to the Scriptures read for about an hour then listen to a sermon that lasted an hour. Many churches could not afford to purchase a single Gospel account, much less an entire Bible. When the bishop would loan a congregation one of the Gospels, it was not unusual for the minister to read the entire book each Sunday for a number of weeks. He would also request various Christians to memorize large sections of any given book. I am sometimes asked why the church doesn't grow as much as it seemed to in the earliest days of Christianity. Perhaps if Christians today would memorize huge sections of the Bible and listen to two hours of the Word each Sunday, we would not fear the degree of evaluation that often attends our current confession of faith.

If we would study the Bible and learn the catechism, we would communicate it better. Lutherans have historically been blessed with a tradition that requires them to learn the Bible doctrine. We all learned the catechism. Our problem is that we don't retain the lessons we learned, and when given an opportunity to tell someone else about Jesus, we have forgotten.

If you would spend ten minutes each day reading the catechism out loud to yourself or to your family, its contents would return to you within a month. You would have relearned the basics of the Christian faith.

ADORNING THE GOSPEL

Both the Bible and experience tell us that people will listen more carefully to our confession if they trust our integrity. We are saved by faith alone, but faith is never alone. We reach out to the lost by confession alone, but confession is never alone. If there is one reason for doing good works, it is to adorn our confession in the eyes of the world. People will not listen to a message from someone they do not trust.

STEALING BOXES

During one summer in college, I worked in Jeffersonville, Indiana, as a substitute foreman in a can factory. The workers were the salt of the earth with the saltiest tongues I ever heard. Every day after work, especially on Fridays, the guys would hit the bar across the street from the factory and carry on over a few beers, increasing the colorful nature of their discourse with each bottle. I'd been there a few days when I was invited to join them. I'd usually have a couple of beers then go home, leaving the more hardened drinkers to their own devices.

At the factory was a middle-aged, balding man named Winston who professed to be a Christian. Winston was the lay preacher at the local Congregational church and was constantly railing against his fellow workers for their swearing and drinking. He also attempted to tell the people about Jesus and invite them to church. I actually went to his church one time and heard him preach against satanism, drug addiction, and homosexuality to a congregation of people whose average age seemed in serious excess of fourscore and ten. I'm sure every one in the church that day felt comfortably smug about his misdirected, moral musings. But everyone in the factory held Winston in contempt. The other workers would roll their eyes, even when he talked on benign subjects. They would respond to him with impatience or open hostility. One day I was talking to one of the guys at the factory. His name was Red.

"Red, you really don't like Winston, do you?"

"Can't stand him."

"Is it because he refuses to drink and swear with you guys?"

"No, you don't swear, and we invite you out with us. We like you." He patronizingly put his arm around me and proudly displayed a half-toothed smile.

"Maybe it's because he gives you grief over your drinking and swearing?"

"No, we expect that. Our wives criticize us. We don't hate them. My wife asks me to come home right away on Tuesdays and Thursdays, and I do. I respect her wishes and her morals."

"I don't understand then. Why do all of you show such contempt for Winston?"

"Just watch and I'll show you," said Red.

A couple of days later, Red sidled up next to me as I was making the rounds at the factory. "Watch Winston now," he whispered, then disappeared behind a machine.

Winston was making boxes. He was working on a three-man line. At the front of the line a man was placing large sheets of metal into a machine that took the sheets and popped metal tops onto empty paper cans. We made oilcans, kitchen cleanser cans, potato chip cans, and auto parts cans. At the controls of the machine, Red, who had nimbly reappeared at his station, was making sure that the tops were lined up with the paper cans. Winston's job, at the end of the line, was to make cardboard boxes into which the completed cans were placed. He would then stack the boxes onto a large crate that was removed, when filled, by a guy running a forklift. In the factory were about seven or eight such lines, each making different cans. Sometimes two lines next to each other made the same type of can at the same time. When this happened, the guy at the end of the line, in this case Winston, could pilfer the boxes made by the person operating the line next to him. As I watched out of the corner of my eye, I saw Winston furtively ease over to the line next to his and take about a half a dozen already made boxes and bring them over to his line.

I have to admit that I am given to overanalysis at such morally ambiguous moments. I reasoned to myself that everyone was being paid by the hour, and no one would make any more or any less money. Was it, strictly speaking, thievery? Then I wondered to myself whether Winston actually knew that such an act was unacceptable to his coworkers. His furtiveness answered that unspoken question affirmatively. He knew. Maybe, I postulated, Winston had been victim of the same theft himself and was merely getting back what had been stolen from him. I even floated this theory by Red when I spoke with him at the next coffee break. "But the Bible says, 'Resist not an evil man.' Matthew 5:39," was his retort.

"Red," I replied with a grin, "you've been holding out on me. I didn't take you to be a Bible-quoting man."

"I am when I have to be," was his response. "Preacher man (they called me preacher man because I was studying to be a preacher), how can that man call himself a Christian when he steals boxes like that?"

I suppose I could have said that I have seen and heard of worse. Even back then I knew of pastors who had cheated on their wives, pilfered money from the collection plate, or slept through church because they were drunk. But at that time it occurred to me that, to Red and the rest of the factory, Winston's offense was about as offensive as could be. "He shouldn't have taken the boxes" was all I could answer.

"*&%$ right!" he barked back and returned to work.

I talked to Winston after that. "Either quit talking about Christ or quite stealing boxes" was my advice. "The two don't go together."

The same applies to every Christian. Your confession of the faith might be clear and articulate. You may have overcome every fear associated with talking about Christ. You may be the most experienced evangelist in the church. But if you give people the impression that you don't care about doing the right thing, they will not listen. If they do listen, the degree of evaluation will be raised impossibly high. People will listen only to find fault with you. "Let your light shine before others, so that they may see your good works and give glory to your Father who is in heaven" (Matthew 5:16). The Gospel is the light. We speak it to the world. Our confession invites scrutiny of its confessors. If people see your good works, they will give ear to the Gospel you confess. They will come to faith according to God's will and be able to call God "Father," which is done only through faith in Jesus, His Son. The reason we do good is to adorn our confession of the faith.

ANOTHER WORD TO PASTORS

Pastors are especially obligated to adorn their words with the fruits of faith. The more you confess Christ, the more you invite scrutiny both from the world and from other Christians. Pastors, called by God to preach and teach the Word, invite scrutiny by their very office. If you can't stand the scrutiny, then don't be a pastor.

We simply do not have the luxury of insensitivity. In the story above about Winston, the man's offense was not all that egregious. Yes, it was wrong and wrongheaded. But it's not something that would get the man thrown in jail or thrown out of the ministry. Stealing boxes did transgress a sacred trust between the workers in that can factory. Not a single person thought highly of poor Winston. His confession of faith was undermined by his own selfishness. It's not that the Word lost its power from his mouth. It's just that no one listened. I'm not altogether certain that Winston understood the offensive nature of his actions even after I talked to him. Most serious, Winston had no respect for the others in the factory. They returned the disrespect in kind.

Pastors, listen to me. If you show respect and appreciation to your people, they will return it even when they disagree with you, your patient teaching will pay off, and God will work through you. If your people get the impression that you don't care about them, they will stop listening. Christian people will forgive an awful lot from their pastors. They will forgive pastors who are forgetful, stupid, harebrained, even pastors who sin grievously. Trust me, I know. They will forgive pastors who aren't dynamic preachers if they understand the office of the ministry. They will forgive occasional lack of preparation. But they will be hard-pressed to accept a pastor if they get the impression that the pastor does not respect them.

Do you want to lose your people's respect? Then ignore them, exploit them, use them, yell at them, don't thank them, treat them like a bunch of ignorant laypeople, and complain a lot. That should just about do it. The pastor can justly claim a divine call all he wants. If his people think that he is indifferent to their tastes, their customs, their habits and traditions, their way of doing things, and their feelings, then that pastor will have a very challenging time being heard. The people, rightly or wrongly, will begin to criticize, the degree of evaluation will skyrocket, and people will not hear, no matter how orthodox their pastor might be. Pastors adorn their office by moral living. They also adorn their preaching by the charitable and respectful acceptance that Christians cherish. Christian people will return it.

Communication experts generally identify "two main variables in credibility" with any given speaker. These variables are "safety and qualification."[8] "Qualification" is a speaker's expertise—how competent a given speaker is perceived to be. If people believe that you know what you are talking about, they will think that you are a credible speaker. They will listen more. They will want to believe you. Perceptions of competence will lower the degree of evaluation.

"Safety" is the trust or the confidence a given speaker engenders. People will listen to a pastor when they perceive that he possesses certain ethical qualities. "The speaker may be perceived as a friendly, gentle, fair, ethical, and hospitable person, one who possesses those qualities in which one can *safely* place confidence."[9] The qualities identified by communication experts are remarkably similar to the qualities mentioned by Paul as necessary for the pastoral office. A pastor should be "above reproach, the husband of one wife, sober-minded, self-controlled, respectable, hospitable, able to teach, not a drunkard, not violent but gentle, not quarrelsome, not a lover of money" and other things (1 Timothy 3:2–4). God understood 2,000 years ago what researchers are realizing today. When a preacher is not perceived to possess the qualities mentioned in the Bible, he is deemed untrustworthy or "unsafe." These perceptions cause people to listen less for content and more to find fault. When faultfinding occurs, the "degree of evaluation" rises and the message of Christ is surrounded with distractions. The Word does not become less powerful in the mouth of an untrustworthy preacher. It simply is not heard.

If Christians, pastor or laity, know the doctrine and adorn their confession with love toward others, they will lower the degree of evaluation. People will listen more attentively and God's Word will be heard. Unfortunately, many Christians might still balk at talking about Jesus if they have a low degree of prior success.

Degree of Prior Success

Just as learning will lessen our fear of evaluation, so practice will increase our degree of prior success. In any endeavor of life, practice improves performance.

I used to teach a college speech class. I actually enjoyed the task immensely as it was fairly easy and renewed my confidence in the human ability to overcome fear. Fear of speaking in public is the third greatest fear in America after death and the dentist. Each term I would watch as 80 percent of the students came into class with the serious expressions of those being led to the gallows. The other 20 percent were either naïve or had taken the class in high school. The first two or three times I taught, I tried to alleviate the fears by telling the students that it wasn't that bad. I would tell them that no one had ever died or even collapsed in any of my classes, and I expected to keep that record intact. I would smile warmly, encouraging each student like a patient, doting mother. None of it did any good. Then I noticed that once the students had given their first speeches, the glazed look left their eyes and they actually engaged themselves in the learning process. But the first round of speeches was so painful, I almost felt guilty about making them do it. Then I started to ask each student to tell a sixty-second story about a sibling, friend, or acquaintance. They would get an "A" as long as they did not pass out. I didn't even care if the stories were true. I just wanted them to get up and talk. They had only a day to prepare. I discovered that the sixty-second experience gave them enough "prior success" that the first speeches improved dramatically. I have found the same when talking about Jesus. Just do it a couple of times and you will gain enough confidence to do it again. Pretty soon it will be easy.

Pastors sometimes try to give the kids in confirmation class "prior experience" by talking about Christ in class. It's a good idea. The trouble is that talking in class is such a different context than talking to friends that the experience doesn't take into consideration the "degree of novelty."

DEGREE OF NOVELTY

In our circuit the pastors exchange pulpits during Lenten evening services. That means that we not only preach for one another, we lead the services at the various churches. The first time I was involved in this "round robin," I noticed that I was a little nervous before the service. I was uncertain about some of the congregational idiosyncrasies. Did I motion the people to stand at the proper times or did they just do it? Did I hand the ushers the plates or did they just have them? Did the organist give me the tones during the portions of the liturgy that I sang or was I just supposed to have perfect pitch? Did I switch the microphone on and off or was there a sound-guy who did that? Everything was new for me. I was the only one in the church who wasn't exactly sure what was coming next, and I was the guy in charge. I was experiencing a high degree of novelty. In those situations, once I step into the pulpit I can relax. The situation is very familiar to me, and I know exactly where I am. The degree of novelty has decreased.

That's the way it is also when you tell someone about Jesus. You may be very comfortable talking about Christ in a Bible class. You share your insights freely and often. You learn how to talk about Christ. Then you find yourself with some friends at a dinner party and the topic of religion comes up. Everyone is sharing their beliefs, and you want to do the same. Unfortunately, you find that you are nervous and inhibited because the situation is new. You've talked about Christ before and you've been to dinner parties before, but you have never put the two together. You even get a bit annoyed because your personal apprehension is distracting you from doing what you know you should.

You gulp hard and throw yourself into the conversation, trusting that the words of God that you speak will not return to the Lord "empty" (Isaiah 55:11). By doing so you have overcome your fear of the degree of novelty within that situation.

What if everyone in the room stops talking and begins to look intently at you? They seem very interested in what you say. Again, you become slightly apprehensive and self-conscious. You are now experiencing an elevated "degree of conspicuousness."

Degree of Conspicuousness

Sometimes we find ourselves speaking to more people at a single time than we anticipated. In those situations you just do your best. In truth, of all the fears connected with speaking, this is the easiest to control. Most people are rarely called upon to speak to a crowd without being given an opportunity to prepare or a chance to say no. The odds of the typical Christian being asked to talk in front of kings or princes are pretty remote. It may or may not be a comfort to know that the vast majority of Christians were not born again while attending a sermon about Jesus, but through one other person talking to them. One-on-one conversations tend to be less conspicuous than talking to a group.

The degree of conspicuousness is also decreased when you are confident that the person you talk to will not think ill of you for talking about Jesus. There are two types of people that fall into this category. The first are total strangers. The second are intimate friends.

I remember when, on my vicarage as a young man, I served a church in North Dakota. There were a handful of members who would go out and make evangelism calls. We would get names from a Realtor in the church who would provide lists of those who were new to the community. We would each take two or three names, conveniently printed on index cards by the church secretary, and stop by unannounced, giving the people a little gift and some literature and asking if we could stop by sometime and talk. Every once in a while someone would be willing to listen right then and there. Those were the evenings we looked forward to. One night the names were doled out to the various members of the evangelism team. Kathy, the most experienced member of the team, casually found the addresses on her map, planned her route, and then read the names on the cards. Suddenly she gasped, "I can't visit these people! I know them."

"Well, I would think that would be better," I answered unsympathetically. "Then you won't have to spend the time getting to know them."

"You don't understand. They know me. They're from my hometown. I could never talk to them about my faith." She adamantly refused to go.

I shrugged and traded one of my cards for hers. I thought it was a bit weird, but it didn't matter to me. Later, I came to realize that Kathy's feelings were not at all weird. She was embarrassed to talk about Jesus to people she knew. They had to be total strangers or intimate family members. Why? She was willing to be awkward and self-conscious in front of someone she might never see again. But her sense of self-worth precluded such feelings in front of friends. The problem was that of all the people she visited she never saw any one of them again. None ever accepted her invitation to church.

She had it totally backward. The best way to avoid the self-consciousness that results from a high degree of conspicuousness is to talk to your intimates. Talk to those who have seen you at your worst, who have seen you fail in other contexts, whose love and acceptance of you is already assured. The worst thing that can happen is that they might not immediately agree with what you say. But you will have done a good thing.

Of the first four reasons for fear of talking, all can be alleviated either by learning the Christian doctrine better or through practice. These challenges have always confronted the church. Throughout the ages Christian people have overcome their fears and talked to others about Christ. Usually our confession becomes easier to make when we learn, practice, speak in different contexts, and talk to our closest friends. The last fear is the most difficult yet most necessary to overcome—the fear of ambiguity.

DEGREE OF AMBIGUITY

Of the five reasons for apprehension in a given situation the greatest is also probably the least understood—ambiguity.[10] If people receive mixed responses to their talking, they find themselves in an ambiguous situation. If, as a 6-year-old, you tell a story to your mother and she listens appreciatively but your father does not, you will wonder why your communication received different responses. You conclude that your father and mother are different, and you reserve your best stories for Mom. What if your mother listens on Monday but not on Wednesday? Now serious ambiguity sets in. In time, if you simply cannot understand and anticipate the results of your storytelling, you become afraid to tell stories at all. The result is what McCroskey calls "learned helplessness."[11] In "learned helplessness" a person becomes confused about talking. When this confusion remains unexplained or unresolved, communication simply stops.

Mixed Messages to Confessors of Christ

The reason why Christians are so frequently reluctant to talk about Jesus to family and friends is the persistent high degree of ambiguity over such communication both within our culture and within the church itself. We are often given mixed signals from church and world to our talking about Jesus. Our churches and our society have conspired to create a culture of Christian ambiguity. We have learned to be helpless. Let me illustrate.

Little Johnny goes to church and Sunday school. He hears about Elijah who courageously spoke to unbelievers on Mt. Carmel about the true God. What a great man Elijah is. A video of Martin Luther is shown where Luther says with conviction, "Here I stand. I cannot do otherwise." Johnny concludes that we should be like Martin Luther and tell the truth to anyone. Johnny hears Jesus call the Pharisees whitewashed sepulchers. He learns that sometimes you should not mince words. Johnny goes to vacation Bible school and sings a rousing chorus of "We Will Not Be Moved." He is resolute to confess Jesus whenever he can.

Johnny grows up and finds a contemporary Christian church. Here the watchword is "diplomacy." We don't want to offend people. Let's not turn people off or make them angry. Don't tell them no. Don't do anything in the church service people won't enjoy or understand. Don't say anything negative about others. For sure, don't say that they are wrong. Johnny is confused. Didn't Elijah poke fun at the false gods of the Philistines? Didn't Luther make the pope mad? Didn't Jesus say that people were wrong? Johnny is confused. Situations become ambiguous. Is this a time for courageous, unequivocal confession or is it a time for diplomacy? Johnny soon gives up. He is helpless.

This helplessness is compounded by a further fear felt by virtually all who would confess Christ—the fear of being marginalized by the label "intolerant."

Those Intolerant Christians

Each age has had its difficulties in the mission endeavor of the church. In the third century, Christians were often killed for confessing Christ. Fear of death would have hampered the spread of the Gospel slightly. But the church was built on the blood of the martyrs. Many of the dramatic stories of Christian confession from that era conclude with martyrdom. The world may not have appreciated such bold confessions, but the church did. Likewise in the sixteenth century, Luther's first hymn was written because two young men were killed by the papists for confessing the saving doctrine of the Lutheran church. "Still, still, tho' dead, they speak, And trumpet-tongued, proclaim To many a wak'ning land The one availing Name,"[12] sang Lutherans, proud of those young lads who had confessed Christ. The enemies of Christ didn't like Luther's song, but the emerging Lutheran church sure loved it. In early twenty-first-century America things are different. Those who confess their faith today do not generally enjoy the support of the church.

Today the temptation is not to fear or avoid the death of the martyr but the life of the marginalized. Our cultural forces are so strong that the type of Christian confession God expects of His church—to confess in doctrinal statements about Christ—inevitably results in our transgressing the one great taboo of American culture: intolerance. Intolerance by our cultural standards is not simply the hatred of people of other races, religions, or lifestyles. Such hatred is morally wrong also to Christians, whose Master told us to "love your enemies and pray for those who persecute you" (Matthew 5:44). Today's culture goes further. If you reject another lifestyle (such as couples living together without marriage or homosexuality), if you criticize the truth claims of another religion (such as the Islamic belief that the doctrine of the Trinity is a lie), or if you make exclusive claims for the Christian truth (such as Jesus is the only way to heaven), then, by cultural standards, you have grievously sinned. You have been intolerant by saying that others are wrong.

The label "intolerant" is leveled by the church as well. Years ago a friend asked me to join an organization, sponsored by the congregation, which required me to "respect the religious convictions of others." I hesitated. It seemed to me that I should have been willing to accept the right of others to hold to their religious beliefs, but actually to respect their beliefs? That seemed like a lot to ask. Should I respect the beliefs of Madelyn Murray O'Hare who claimed that the virgin mother of our Lord was impregnated by a traveling Roman soldier? Should I respect the religious beliefs of various occultists or Satanists who invoke the name of Lucifer in their gatherings? Should I respect the beliefs of synergists who deny grace alone? I respected some of the people in these religions and defended their right to hold a view different than the Christian view. But to accept the false views of these churches seemed a denial of the claims of Christ. My friend told me I was uptight. Others in the church said that I was disrespectful, another epithet that, at the time, evoked no particular guilt. What I realized later is that I had broken the first commandment of American life—I said that someone else was wrong. Yet that is exactly what a Christian confession must always say either explicitly or by inference.

In 1866 C. F. W. Walther presented an essay to the convention of the General Evangelical Lutheran Synod of Missouri, Ohio, and Other States, later known as the Missouri Synod. I hesitate even to name the essay's title as it flies so in the face of twenty-first-century sensitivities. It was entitled "The Evangelical Lutheran Church, The True Visible Church of God on Earth." In it he presented 25 theses, defended them with the Scriptures and the Lutheran Confessions, and concluded in Thesis XXV: "In short, the Evangelical Lutheran Church has all the essential marks of the true visible church of God on earth, as they are found in no known fellowship of another name; it is therefore in no need of any reformation in doctrine."[13] Can you imagine someone speaking publicly like this today? Walther was saying that the Lutheran church is the pure and true church and that he was unaware of any other churches that are. To speak like this would evoke heated reactions from many both outside and inside the church, all characterizing Walther as prideful or intolerant. He would be marginalized and unaccepted in the truly auspicious academic and religious establishments of the day. Actually, that's what happened to him a century and a half ago. Over the years we have lost the ability to talk like Walther. And with that loss we have also failed to inspire the many Johnnies in the world who admired him along with Elijah, Luther, and Jesus. The result is an ambiguous situation in which our hearers are at odds with our own expectations of ourselves. McCroskey's "helplessness" is the result. And the worst part of the ambiguity is that the church is complicit with our culture in creating it.

How did we get this way?

NOT THE REVIVALISTS AGAIN

The same forces that ultimately resulted in the rise of revivalistic Evangelicalism have also made an objective confession of faith almost impossible in the United States. Here's what happened. When America moved westward, excitement replaced doctrine as the earmark of true Christianity, as shown in chapter 8. Further, dynamism replaced orthodoxy as the primary trait of God's spokesmen, as shown in chapter 9. These two expectations—excitement and dynamism—seriously altered the way in which Christians perceive the task of talking about Jesus. When excitement and dynamism take over, a vicious cycle of evangelistic ineptitude sets in. One bad thing follows another.

First, everything becomes subjective. Because true Christianity, in revivalism, is perceived to be the possession of a particular experience, the religious talk of Christians starts to center around that Christian experience. Remember the old campfire song "It Only Takes a Spark," where we sang, "That's how it is with God's love, once you've experienced it"? Remember around the campfire when you had to share the time when Jesus was close to you or when you felt close to Him? Talking about God became somewhat threatening to those who had not "felt" the Gospel. The faith of the fathers was replaced by "your own personal faith" because who could really *feel* the faith of our fathers? How often have you been told that you are saved by "your own personal faith," as if faith could ever be impersonal, even though the expression "personal faith" never occurs in the Bible? Faith becomes so personal it turns into a private, intimate thing that only those truly in touch with their emotions are able to share.

When subjective experience replaces the objective statements of doctrine, then culture becomes impatient with statements of absolute truth. If I say, "This is the truth of the Bible that my church holds and that you must believe," well, try it with your neighbor and see what happens. You will be called prideful and intolerant. Even ostensible Christians join the disapproving chorus against any confession of the faith that it deems "prideful." You saw it in the first chapter of this book. A Lutheran church in America said that it was a symptom of human pride to claim that you possessed the truth. You saw it in chapter 8 where Lutherans of the General Synod referred to the Missouri Synod as "extremists," "selfish," "presumptuous," and "intolerant" for refusing fellowship where there was no pure doctrine. Through these labels those who confess Christ are marginalized. If Paul were to speak to the typical American audience and say, "But even if we or an angel from heaven should preach to you a gospel contrary to the one we preached to you, let him be accursed" (Galatians 1:8), he would transgress all our civil American sensitivities. You probably winced at least a little at Walther's bold words above about the Lutheran church. Yet they are essentially no different than those of Paul. Both men transgressed culture's unspoken rule against confidence in objective truth.

At least in times past the church praised the confession of her martyrs. It is recorded that the families of early Christian martyrs were often murdered in an attempt to force a recantation of their family member. Eusebius, an early Christian historian, reports that at the arrest of a young slave girl named Bladina, her mistress feared death far less than that her slave would actually succumb to the torture and deny her Lord.[14] The prayers of the church were never for God to help the martyrs learn to be more winsome. Instead, the church thanked God for the confession of these heroes and prayed that no one ever compromise, even at the pain of death. Today the church needs to pray that her marginalized martyrs, men and women who paid for their confession with loss of face rather than loss of life, be true to the Gospel that binds them to Christ. And, having seen the suffering of our modern-day martyrs, may the faithful never hold the coats (Acts 7:58) of those in the church who vilify with the labels of "intolerant" and "prideful" those who have suffered for the confession of Christ.

When the faith of the individual is measured by experience rather than doctrine, then your church also becomes relatively unimportant. We end up concluding that because there are 200 denominations in the United States your denomination is moot. What's really important is the personal heartfelt faith of the individual, we conclude. Furthermore, the cultural sin of intolerance precludes identifying Christ with your church in any meaningful way because to do so suggests that other churches might be wrong. We are taught almost to apologize for our churches. John Cuddihy, in *No Offense: Civil Religion and Protestant Taste*, states some of the stock answers to the question "What religion are you?" One is to dissociate yourself from the church of your grandfather by saying, "Oh, I was brought up Lutheran or Baptist or Catholic."[15] In this way the church becomes something like an old television show we watched with our parents when we were kids. Another "Americanized" and more insidious answer is that "people begin using the rhetoric of 'happen': 'I happen to be a Catholic.' 'I happen to be a Lutheran.' 'I happen to be a Jew.' "[16] Such an answer makes your membership in the church almost an accident. These answers, which we have heard and perhaps given, tend to downplay the importance of our church. The church is further weakened when a wedge is driven between the terms "Lutheran" and "Christian." When asked what their religion is, many Lutherans are accustomed to answer, "I'm a Lutheran Christian," as if Lutheranism is simply one of many brands of Christianity and not the church of the true confession of the faith. Or we say, "I don't call myself a Lutheran but a Christian," as if there is some shame in the label "Lutheran" or as if you could be Lutheran without being Christian. In truth, the term "Lutheran" does suggest belief in a doctrinal system that is not particularly popular these days. I've even heard Lutherans say, "Well, I'm not sure what my church holds, but I believe . . . " as if what their church holds is either untrue or not worth learning. And, of course, there is the true denying answer to questions of faith analyzed in chapter 1: "That depends on your denominational perspective." Even the very label "denomination" smacks of a kind of relativism that makes for a weak Christian confession of the faith. The word *denomination* means "name or designation." When Lutherans call their church a denomination, it's as if the Lutheran church is nothing more than a brand name, one of many varieties of Christianity from which the consumer may choose. The result is that people are tempted to see themselves as Christians apart from their church and apart from the doctrine of their church. And we wonder why our confession seems vapid.

Once talk of God is divorced from doctrine and shorn from the church, those who would confess Christ have lost their two greatest tools. A dilemma afflicts the church and renders her mute. When I attempt to tell someone about Jesus without the church or doctrine, then I am forced to begin my sentences with "in my opinion and based on my experience." But my opinion and my experience are no better than yours or those of the atheist down the street. So I find myself in a quandary where I don't know what to say. If I tell people my opinion about Jesus, I must admit that it is no better than theirs. If I tell them what God says and what the church confesses, I am labeled prideful or intolerant. The situation oozes ambiguity. The result is a profound reluctance to talk about God at all, McCroskey's "learned helplessness." Consequently, American Christianity has become "a religion of civility"[17] where the only true sin is to give offense to others by suggesting that they need the objective truth that you are speaking to them. "The fear of offending against" American civility "has made cowards of us all."[18]

Unfortunately, Americans, and Lutherans, it would seem, are more prone to irrelevance than offense. So we try the impersonal gimmicks of the Church Growth Movement. We take down our crosses and crucifixes—too gory or ritualistic. We make sure that the songs in church are heartfelt, sentimental, easy, and user-friendly with little overt doctrinal content. We invite our friends to a service with few expectations other than to enjoy the service. When we do speak about Jesus, He is not the Christ of the cross who died objectively to redeem the world, but ends up being the Christ in my heart. Osiandristic thinking runs deep in American Evangelicalism.

The revivalistic expectation of dynamism makes things worse yet. When those who speak of Christ must be dynamic, we exclude 95 percent of us from the task of talking about Jesus. Church Growth experts, for all intents and purposes, excuse 90 percent of Christians from the serious joy of confessing the faith by insisting that "in the average evangelical church, ten percent of the members have been given the gift of evangelism"[19]—an assertion about as unprovable as it is illogical and unbiblical. The Bible says that God's gift to the church is men who hold the office of evangelist, not the abstract gift of evangelism (Ephesians 4:11). When people do talk about Jesus, they are themselves convinced that the best way to do evangelism is to share their personal experience of Jesus. My experience may not offend, but it does perpetuate the problem because it continues the vicious cycle of evangelistic ineptitude. I justify my anemic confession by saying that at least people are not offended. More often than not we simply succumb to the temptation and don't talk at all.

Sadly, we are only vaguely aware of the problem we face. Frustrated, we either expect others to do what God expects of us all, namely, talk about Jesus to the world, or we just feel guilty and inadequate. When encouraged to tell others "what Jesus means to me," we are both embarrassed at the deeply personal nature of such advice and mystified about the results of the endeavor. And when we do speak of Christ, we are intimidated by our own errant expectations. All along what God wants is something altogether different. He does not want us to share what Jesus means to me but what Jesus has done for me and the world. He wants us to confess the faith.

WITNESSES FOR CHRIST OR CONFESSORS OF CHRIST

Deep down in her corporate heart the church knows that there is a problem. We want more Christians to confess the faith, especially to those who don't know Christ. But the solutions that are often offered are not always on target. One such "off-target" solution is the endless challenge that Christians need to learn the skills of effectively witnessing to Christ.

I am going to make a statement you will initially consider blasphemous: We are not "witnesses" of Christ. I know that goes against everything that you have learned, but it's true. You are not a witness of Christ. Nowhere in the Bible are we told to witness to Christ.

Every once in a while I will get something in the mail that invites me to go to a workshop, bring a couple of members with me, and learn to be a more effective "witness" for Jesus Christ. These invitations arrive so often that I decided to look up the word *witness* in the New Testament to find out what the word really means. Amazingly, I discovered that I am not a witness of Christ and neither are you. You and I never saw Jesus. To be a witness you have to see. "Were you there when they crucified your Lord?" No! In the Bible the word *witness* always refers to those who actually saw something. Sometimes witness refers to the testimony given about someone's character, assuming that the witness knows that person. At times God is called a witness. He sees everything. In the Book of John, Jesus is often called a witness. The first Epistle of John speaks of three witnesses to Christ: the Spirit, the water, and the blood, that is the Gospel and Sacraments. Never in the New Testament is the church called a witness. And never are individual Christians called witnesses unless they have actually seen something. The apostles are often called witnesses, especially in the Book of Acts, because they saw the life, death, and resurrection of the Savior. Not only did they see, they were also appointed by Christ officially to give testimony before the world to what they had seen.

Let's follow the word *witness* through the Book of Acts. In Acts 1:8 Jesus is talking to the eleven apostles: "You will be My witnesses in Jerusalem and in all Judea and Samaria, and to the ends of the earth." These men had all seen His miracles, been privy to His sermons and parables, and literally witnessed His death and resurrection. They are witnesses in the normal sense of the word, having seen something. Now they are called upon to testify to what they have seen. But there is a problem. Jesus wants twelve witnesses. Judas has killed himself so a replacement is needed. What are the criteria for such a witness? Is fervent faith in Jesus enough? No! Is an appointment by the church enough? That is not enough either. "So one of the men who have accompanied us during all the time that the Lord Jesus went in and out among us, beginning from the baptism of John until the day when He was taken up from us—one of these men must become with us a witness to His resurrection" (Acts 1:21). Then Matthias is chosen "to take over this *apostolic* ministry" because he had seen. Now he must testify—witness. Soon Pentecost arrives. Peter preaches his famous sermon concluding with this claim, "This Jesus God raised up, and of that we all are *witnesses*" (Acts 2:32, emphasis added). Peter is talking about himself and the other eleven (Acts 2:14) who are listed at the end of chapter 1 of Acts, those who were all waiting in the same place (Acts 2:1), who were all Galileans (Acts 2:7), and who all had seen the same things. A while later Peter is in the temple when, having healed a crippled man, he has attracted a crowd and begins to preach. Again, the crucifixion and resurrection are featured in his sermon with the claim, "And you killed the Author of life, whom God raised from the dead. To this we are witnesses" (Acts 3:15). Next we have the dramatic story of Peter and John getting arrested, being set free miraculously, and then getting arrested again for preaching Christ. Their defense is predictable, "The God of our fathers raised Jesus, whom you killed by hanging Him on a tree. God exalted Him at His right hand as Leader and Savior, to give repentance to Israel and forgiveness of sins. And we are witnesses to these things, and so is the Holy Spirit, whom God has given to those who obey Him" (Acts 5:30–32).

Move ahead to Acts 8. Peter and the apostles had stayed in Jerusalem while Philip the evangelist traveled to Samaria to tell the people about Jesus. Philip was not an apostle or a witness. He had not seen Jesus' ministry, death, and resurrection. So he is not called a witness. He evangelized (v. 2) and he proclaimed Christ (v. 3), but the Bible never says he witnessed. When the apostles heard that the Samaritans had believed, they sent Peter and John (v. 14). These men had seen Christ with their eyes, so "now when they had testified [witnessed] and spoken the word of the Lord, they returned to Jerusalem, preaching the gospel to many villages of the Samaritans" (v. 25). Luke, the author of Acts, is very careful to reserve the word *witness* for the apostles who had seen. Notice that the eyewitnesses have now witnessed in Jerusalem, Judea, and Samaria as Jesus told them in Acts 1:8.

For the witness to the "ends of the earth," we move to Acts 10. Peter and Cornelius have received their respective visions. Peter has preached to the Gentiles and even been convinced to fellowship with them through eating. He then tells the Gentiles about Jesus and finishes his little talk with a quadruple use of the word *witness*: "And we are witnesses of all that He did both in the country of the Jews and in Jerusalem. They put Him to death by hanging Him on a tree, but God raised Him on the third day and made Him to appear, not to all the people but to us who had been chosen by God as witnesses, who ate and drank with Him after He rose from the dead. And He commanded us to preach to the people and to testify that He is the one appointed by God to be judge of the living and the dead. To Him all the prophets bear witness that everyone who believes in Him receives forgiveness of sins through His name" (Acts 10:39–43). Notice that not every Christian is a witness. The apostles, and only the apostles, are witnesses; they saw Jesus and were appointed to report what they saw.

We aren't done with this word. Paul comes onto the scene. Paul is not a witness to Christ in exactly the way the other apostles were. He is "one untimely born" (1 Corinthians 15:8). He did not have the privilege of witnessing the miracles, death, and resurrection of Christ. At first, when speaking of the church's proclamation to Jews (Acts 13:30–31), Paul is content to report what others have witnessed: "But God raised Him from the dead, and for many days He appeared to those who had come up with Him from Galilee to Jerusalem, who are now His witnesses to the people." Toward the end of the book, having received a revelation of Christ (Galatians 1:12), Paul can assert that he also is a witness. His testimony, like that of the other apostles, is based on what he has seen with his eyes. God's servant Ananias had said to Paul, "And he said, 'The God of our fathers appointed you to know His will, to see the Righteous One and to hear a voice from His mouth; for you will be a witness for Him to everyone of what you have seen and heard" (Acts 22:14–15). In Acts 26 Paul repeats the claim that he is a witness based on what he has seen (vv. 16, 22). Paul's witness is the same as the other apostles, but he is not to speak primarily to the Jews, but to "all men," the Gentiles. To witness involves the appointment to see and report something to a specific group of people.

You and I are not witnesses. The apostles were witnesses because they saw and spoke of the things they saw. That's what witnesses do. So why the big deal over the word *witness*? There are three words in the Bible with the same root as *witness*. One is the verb. One is a noun that refers to the one who witnesses. The third is the noun that says what is witnessed. These three words, which all have the same root, are used more than 200 times in the New Testament. Never does the word refer to people who, without seeing, tell others about Jesus. Our continued wrong use of the word *witness* is a bad practice that will increase the fear of ambiguity the church already experiences. Wrong use of the word will have other negative effects on our church as well. We'll get to them below.

If you have used the word *witness* in an improper way, you have not sinned. You just have used a word incorrectly. We've all done it. Once we learn the meanings of words more precisely, then we adjust our language to reflect that precision. The church as a whole needs to start talking about the apostles as witnesses and every Christian as "confessing." By so doing we will protect the unique gift of the apostles, which is the Holy Scriptures. We will also encourage one another to measure our speech about Jesus against those Scriptures and the enduring confessions of the church.

CONFESSING THE FAITH

Much of the fear, hesitation, "helplessness," and ambiguity connected with "witnessing" can be eased simply by using the biblical language. *Confess* is a great word. The word in Greek is *homologeo*. It comes from two Greek words. *Homo* means "the same," as in homogeneous or homosexual. *Logeo* means to "say" or to "speak." We get our word *logic* from *logeo*. *Homologeo* means to "speak the same thing." Often the English translations will translate it as "confess." Sometimes they will translate it "acknowledge," which actually weakens the idea.

What does the Bible tell us about making a confession?

First, to confess means to say the same thing as someone or something else. Our confession agrees with something. When we confess our sins as in 1 John 1:9, then we are saying the same thing about our sins that God does. We agree with God when He condemns us. According to the Scriptures we are to confess Christ, (1 John 2:23) but never in some vague way. We confess agreement with the doctrine about Him: that He has come in the flesh (1 John 4:2–3), that He is our high priest who made atonement for us (Hebrews 3:1), or that He pleads for us before His Father's throne (Hebrews 4:13). Our confession agrees with the doctrine of Christ in the Scriptures. Nowhere do we confess our personal faith or our personal hope. Instead, we "confess the faith" (1 Timothy 6:12), "the hope" (Hebrews 19:23), or "the gospel" (2 Corinthians 9:13). The faith, the hope, and the Gospel are objective. They stand outside of us. Others confess the same faith, hope, and Gospel. We say the same things as God and other Christians. There is a standard against which we measure our confession.

Second, confession is always out loud before other people. Sometimes our confession is made before those who are friendly and would confess the same (1 Timothy 6:12). Other times the Bible simply says to confess before any or all men: "If you confess with your mouth that Jesus is Lord" (Romans 10:9); "Everyone who acknowledges Me before men" (Matthew 10:32). Often the confession is before unbelievers or enemies of the Gospel who will hurt you. For example, when the blind man confessed Christ in John 9, he was thrown out of the temple because "Jews had already agreed that if anyone should confess Jesus to be Christ, he was to be put out of the synagogue" (John 9:22).

Third, confession is divisive. It divides truth from error and God from the Antichrist (1 John 2:22). The word *confess* often stands in contrast to the false doctrine of those who would deceive the church by pointing away from Christ (1 John 4:2–3). We should not be surprised if confession brings friction and even divisions in the church.

Fourth, God confesses to us. When God spoke to Abraham, He confessed to him according to His own promises (Acts 7:17). Jesus promises to confess us before God in heaven. He promises to say the same thing about us as we do about Him.

Why this arduous Bible study on witness and confession? Because our misuse of important biblical terms has negatively affected our doctrine and our practice in the most important work we do as Christians.

How to Confess

Our talk of Christ repeats the church's biblical doctrine. The report of the church of Christ placed upon the ears of a needy world neither relates what we have seen and experienced nor gives our insights into Jesus. We are not simply demonstrating our faith. In confession the church is united in speaking the same thing God says and the same thing God's church has said for 2,000 years. This has some important implications for the life of the church. So how does the church confess?

1. Confess by pointing to Christ.
2. Confess by speaking back what you have learned.
3. Confess with the church.

Confess by Pointing to Christ

We are all called upon to confess the faith to others. It could be your in-laws, your neighbor, your spouse, or the people in your Bible class. A confession never starts with the words "I think" or "Let me tell you what Jesus has done for me." No one really needs to know what you think when it comes to eternal life. And we certainly will never be saved by hearing what Jesus has done for you. People need to hear what Jesus did for them through His cross and resurrection. You weren't there. Don't witness—let others hear a confession from you. They need you to speak the Gospel, the faith, and the hope of the Christian church. You can confess by echoing back to them the words of the creed you say every week. Speak by reciting the Second Article of the creed you learned in catechism class. Repeat for them the hymn "Salvation unto Us Has Come," which your dad forced you or bribed you to learn in the sixth grade. Say the things that the church has always said. They are a confession.

I once had a conversation with a woman who was at one of those church sharing sessions about how to share your faith effectively. She said that whenever she was given a chance to tell others about her faith, she just quoted the hymn "Amazing Grace." Later, in private, I asked her what she would think if someone tried to explain the Christian message without mentioning the name of Jesus, the cross, the resurrection, the Gospel, Baptism, the Lord's Supper, the

Absolution, the forgiveness of sins, the Bible, the Holy Spirit, or faith.

"Oh, that would be impossible," she correctly claimed. You can't share your faith without saying things about Jesus.

I know I shouldn't have done it. It was wrong of me to say what I did, but I couldn't help it. "Well, 'Amazing Grace' mentions none of those things."

She stared at me blankly like she was going through the lyrics in her head. "Actually, it does mention faith in the second stanza. 'How precious did that grace appear the hour I first believed.' " She accented the word *believed*, then she excused herself and walked off.

That was my mistake. The Lutheran Church—Missouri Synod had omitted the second stanza of the hymn from *Lutheran Worship* because that particular one not only said that "Grace taught my heart to fear," which confuses the Law and the Gospel, but it also pointed the Christian to "the hour I first believed" rather than to the cross of Jesus Christ. Ironically, the only reference to anything remotely Christian in the hymn (the word *faith*) had been excised by the Missouri Synod's Commission on Worship for doctrinal reasons. Yet this woman felt comfortable in using that Christless hymn as her evangelism technique.

Certainly we can do better than that. Confession of the faith must involve speaking the specific Bible truths of the Christ. I know that there may be readers who feel offended that I have insulted a hymn that means so much to them. Does the hymn contain false doctrine? The version in *Lutheran Worship* contains no doctrine. But could this hymn adequately function as a confession of the Christian faith? Be honest with yourself if you like "Amazing Grace." Is it possible that your affections toward that song are a symptom of how anemic our confession of Christ has become?

"The hour I first believed" is quintessential Revivalism. When our story of Christ becomes a "witness" to what Christ has done for me at a specific hour, then the "witness" often takes on the features of Osiandrism. We begin to talk about what Jesus has done in our lives or what He has done in our hearts. We shift away from the objective forgiveness based on the life, death, and resurrection of Christ as told by the apostolic witnesses. Instead, we shift to ecclesiastic storytelling. Chronicles surface of our congregation's successes. Stories of my own triumph over sin emerge. The effect is that my subjective experience of Jesus becomes more important than the objective, historical events witnessed by those sent specifically to report these things.

We need to be careful of testimonials. Have you ever been in church when someone got up and gave a testimonial? Sometimes people are asked to tell others what God has done in their lives. A testimonial is a witness to what God has done in your life. Remember, though, God never asks us to witness. He asks us to confess. And confess means to say the same thing as others. God does not want His church to listen to someone's witness unless they have been appointed by God to witness the life, death, and resurrection of Jesus with their own eyes. He'd rather have us confess, which we can do in the creed where we all say the same thing. Testimonials in church are a bad idea.

Confessing Christ is easier than we think. We've made it too difficult. Confession means to echo back the things you have learned.

CONFESS BY SPEAKING BACK WHAT YOU LEARNED

You probably took instruction before receiving Communion. You may have been examined before the congregation. At that time did you confess or did you witness? Keep in mind that we are not supposed to witness. Did you show that you understood and believed the doctrines of Christ by saying the same things that the church has always said? That was confession. Recall the word *catechism* from the first chapter. It is a book that instructs by having the students echo back what they learned. Did you learn the catechism and echo back the doctrines taught in it at your examination before the congregation? That was a confession. Did you speak back the exact words the church has always said by memorizing the catechism? That was confession. Or did your pastor teach you that he wanted you to say what Jesus meant to you in your own words? Did your pastor tell you that he didn't use the catechism? That was no confession. You need to find a pastor who will teach you to confess.

One of the reasons for communication apprehension is the fear of evaluation. We are afraid that people will scrutinize what we say and criticize us. If you speak of Christ with your own words, then the possibility exists that you might say something wrong. On the other hand, if your confession is simply with the words of the catechism, then you have eliminated the chance of saying things wrong. Fear of evaluation should decrease. Let me give you an example. I was talking to a college friend many years ago, before I studied theology and before I was trained to talk about Christ. We were talking about free will and fate. The conversation initially had nothing to do with Christ or the Gospel. It was one of those "deep" discussions college kids have because they can. I said that I didn't believe that everything in life was freely chosen. He responded that then I must believe in fate.

"No," I insisted, "fate is nonsense."

"Well, you can't have it both ways. It's either fate or free will," said my friend confidently.

At that point, almost impulsively, I brought God into the picture. "What about God?"

"What about God?" was his incisive reply.

"Well, if you believe in God, then you're not stuck with the choice of either free will or fate."

"No way," he said astutely.

"Yes, it's true. I believe in God, and I don't believe in free will or fate."

"Explain that," he challenged emphatically.

Now what was I going to say? I stumbled for words. How do you explain to an unbeliever that he is born without a free will, but that God determines his future not though the impersonal force of fate, nor by any other constrained influence, but rather that He, solely by His grace, changes the person, actually creating a free will when none previously existed? Explain that with easy and accurate words. Then it came to me.

"I believe that I cannot by my own reason or strength believe in Jesus Christ my Lord or come to Him, but the Holy Ghost has called me by the Gospel, enlightened me with His gifts, sanctified and kept me in the true faith. In the same way also He calls, gathers, enlightens and sanctifies the whole Christian church on earth and keeps it with Jesus Christ in the one true faith."

That, incidentally, is Luther's explanation of the Third Article, which every Lutheran memorized in confirmation instruction.

My friend looked at me, thought about it for a while, and said pensively, "I don't know about that."

I didn't convert him on the spot (which God never told me to do). I did, however, confess the faith to him right then and there. My confession was accurate, comprehensible, and simple. He understood it.

Most confession of the faith is spontaneous, unplanned, and scary. If you have memorized sections of the catechism or key Bible verses and can recite them, then you can make a confession. I am convinced that the hesitancy many Christians have in making a confession is the result of errant expectations. We think that we have to be insightful, winsome, trained, and dynamic. All we really need is to know the catechism. And if people want to hear more, then invite them to church.

CONFESS WITH THE CHURCH

Our confession of faith needs to be consistent with the confession of the church throughout the ages. We "say the same thing" as the church has always said.

Confession with the church has implications for evangelism. Many churches have evangelism programs where members of the congregation go out and visit people in the community to tell them about Christ. Those involved in this activity should view themselves as confessing Christ. They "say the same thing" as the church. Our task is to get the unchurched to hear the confession of the church again and again. Someone can hear a confession once in their living room. They can hear week after week in the Divine Service when the church confesses the faith. The goal of an "evangelism" call should never be to get the person to believe in Jesus right there. How can they believe without having heard the church's confession? You need to get the person into the Divine Services of the church regularly. When you invite someone to church, you must be completely confident that your church teaches the Word of God purely and clearly. There can be no feigned "tolerance" of false religions as mentioned earlier in this chapter. You will work at cross-purposes with God if you say or do anything that gives the impression that your church does not teach the truth of the Gospel in all of its articles.

Confession with the church has implications also for the Divine Service. The service is not intended to benefit God. Rather, through the confession of the church those present, both the instructed and the uninstructed, are blessed by God. God works through the church's confession. When you bring friends to church, they must hear the same confession that has always been made. The pastor does not use the service to make his own personal witness. Instead, the church gathers around the Word to hear and to say the same thing about Christ as she has always said. Confession with the church creates an appreciation of the church's history. When you invite a friend or family member to church, it ought to be a walk through history. Your friend needs to see that the confession of the church is as timeless as the grace of our Lord Jesus Christ. Confession involves saying the same thing as the church has said for 2,000 years. We need to learn and know the fathers, sing the hymns they composed, study the books they wrote, and pray the prayers they prayed. Our lives may be a little different than theirs, but our confession is the same.

Throughout the pages of this book, I have been critical of many of the features of American revivalism and the Church Growth Movement. These movements have attempted to find a way to save the lost, which simply is not God's way. God's way is very easy to say and extremely difficult to do. There is only one way to reach out to the lost. You must learn and confess the true doctrine of Christ. It's that simple. Be utterly confident of this Gospel doctrine and confess it. Expect to suffer. Expect to be marginalized. Expect especially to receive disapproving scowls even from the church. But never stop confessing. Confess in your home. Confess to your friends. Confess in the church. Confess. There are no programs, no styles, no techniques, no methods. The only way is through confession. The most important manner of confession is to bring your friends to church so they can hear the consistent confession of the church, receive instruction, and be blessed also with the saving sacraments of Baptism and the Lord's Supper.

Conclusion

Peter's image of the "royal priesthood" places wonderful blessings upon Christians. Christians talk. We talk, not by witnessing to the things that have happened in our hearts or even our lives, or by sharing our impressions or opinions. We talk by confessing the doctrine we have learned, faithfully speaking of Christ according to the witness of the apostles in Scripture. The response to our confession will be mixed as not even the church consistently values its confessors. Other factors as well might tempt us to temper or discontinue our confession. God grant us the grace to know Jesus and to confess His Gospel even in the face of temptations to be silent. For then the "Fire Is Kindled."

Study Questions

1. What does a Christian sacrifice to God that makes him or her a priest?
2. What does the royal priesthood talk about?
3. When priests forgive one anothers' sin, whom are they speaking against?
4. How does a Christian overcome evaluation apprehension when talking about Christ?
5. Besides knowing Scripture and the catechism better, what else improves our performance and makes us less fearful as speakers?
6. According to Scripture, can you be a witness to Christ? Why or why not?
7. What is being said when we confess our sins?
8. What is being said when we confess Christ?

Discussion Questions

1. Discuss McCroskey's five reasons for why people may be fearful of speaking in certain contexts. Do you think these initial observations are valid? Why or why not?
2. Discuss the proper and improper role of intolerance in the Christian context.
3. Establish and discuss the proper goals of an evangelism call. What could be some strategies?

12

The Fire Stoked

CHANGE IN THE CHURCH

Three bells hung in the tower of St. Mary's Parish Church when Martin Luther entered the pulpit on March 9, 1522. Only at the most auspicious occasions were these bells sounded: the death of a dignitary, the conferring of a degree, a national or city disaster. On this particular March 9, they hung mute. They should have rung, for something quite remarkable was about to happen.

Barely a year had passed since Luther, at the Diet of Worms, had heroically confessed his confidence both in the Scriptures and in the fast-moving Reformation. Emissaries of the pope had asked Luther to recant his writings. His answer had been

> unless I am convinced by the testimonies of the Holy Scriptures or evident reason . . . I am bound by the Scriptures adduced by me, and my conscience has been taken captive by the Word of God, and I am neither able nor willing to recant, since it is neither safe nor right to act against conscience. God help me. Amen.[1]

Later, Luther, granted safe travel to and from the Diet of Worms, had been "kidnapped" by soldiers under orders from Duke Frederick of Saxony, Luther's elector and protector. Frederick had comfortably "imprisoned" the young reformer at Wartburg Castle, a formidable place not more than a couple of days travel from Luther's hometown of Wittenberg. His disappearance had become the occasion for intense speculation at the gossip mills of the day. Many imagined him dead in some ditch, partially devoured by animals of prey. The mental picture of others was more gruesome, with members of the Inquisition pressing the young "heretic" as they stretched his gaunt body on some torturous wrack. The more cynical of the Wittenberg townsfolk feared he may have simply bolted to some far corner of the kingdom, caving under the relentless pressures that attend all who would effect change in the church.

What a year it had been since Luther stood in the pulpit of St. Mary's. All the leaders of the Wittenberg reformation had agreed that certain changes were necessary. The abominable teaching that the Mass was a re-sacrifice of Christ, a clear denial of the once-for-all atonement of Jesus, made the Roman Canon of the Mass impossible for any conscientious Lutheran to endure. Likewise, the Roman practice of private Masses had to be abolished because it deprived Jesus of His glory and the church of His grace. The superstitious practice of giving the Sacrament to the laypeople "in only one kind"—without the blood of Christ—took away from God's people the very blessings for which Christ died. Private confession and absolution as a precondition for receiving the Supper was consider a legalistic burden. The idolatrous Roman practice of praying to statues of saints made the statues themselves the occasion for dispute, and some wanted their immediate removal much as you might hide the cookie jar when children demonstrate an inability to resist the sweet temptation. There was no dispute on the need for change in the church.

The people wanted change. Any number of "reformers" preceded the Lutheran attempt at change, including the well-known Bohemian reformer, Jan Hus, whose aborted attempt at reform resulted in his own execution. The label "Saxon Hus" had been placed upon Luther, thanks to his Czech predecessor. Even Roman Catholic historians have recognized the incredible forces for change that existed in Germany in the century preceding Luther.

> By the end of the fifteenth century the world was filled with impatient or furious, sadly revolutionary, defiant outcries against the rule of Rome and the clergy, against their suppression and exploitation, against their arbitrary action, and against their all too sensualist existence.[2]

The sleepy town of Wittenberg did not slumber during the half decade preceding the eventful winter of 1522. The citizens ardently embraced any suggestion that would free them from the bonds of Roman oppression. Luther's own agitation two years earlier against the financial tyranny of Rome did not go unnoticed by the warlike nobility of Germany.

> How is it that we Germans must put up with such robbery and extortion of our goods at the hands of the pope? If the kingdom of France has prevented it, why do we Germans let them make such fools and apes of us? . . . And we still go on wondering why princes and nobles, cities and endowments, land and people grow poor. We ought to marvel that we have anything left to eat![3]

Change was in the air, and Duke Frederick sensed it. He called for a disputation, a discussion among the theologians of the day. Like all politicians, he urged that change be initiated slowly and cautiously. His advice was not heeded by all. Some young students forcibly entered the parish church, the same church whose pulpit Luther would ascend six short months later. They drove out the priests, tore down the altar, and destroyed many of the prayer books. It seemed they opposed church rituals and any prayers that were not spoken extemporaneously. Frederick, calm and patient, called for another disputation. He agreed, guardedly, with the winds of change but wanted the pastors to see what sometimes eludes them; change must be initiated slowly. The disputation determined that no innovations would take place at Wittenberg until things had calmed down in the aftermath of the student looting. This time Frederick was ignored.

Andreas Bodenstein von Karlstadt assumed the reigns of leadership in the absence of Luther. On Christmas Day 1521, he celebrated the "first Protestant Communion." The changes were not particularly radical from the perspective of twenty-first-century Lutherans. According to Karlstadt, the people did not have to go to private confession before they communed. Karlstadt offered people both the bread and the wine in the Sacrament, also instructing the people to take the bread in their hands during Communion because Jesus had said, "take and eat." Advocating marriage of the priests, he followed his own matrimonial advice and was wed to a young woman from the town. Karlstadt urged that the statues in the churches be removed. They were simply the occasion for too much idolatry. Finally, he celebrated the Sacrament in street clothes because he could find no section of Scripture that said that pastors should "vest" when they celebrated the Sacrament.[4]

Observe that every single change advocated and initiated by Karlstadt, except his preference for street clothing, has been the custom of Lutherans in the United States for at least a hundred years. These were mostly good changes. We might justifiably consider Karlstadt a pioneer if not a hero.

Frederick was less than thrilled. His response was predictable.

> We have gone too fast. The common man has been incited to frivolity, and no one has been edified. We should have consideration for the weak. Images should be left until further notice. No essential portion of the mass should be omitted. Moot points should be discussed. Carlstadt should not preach any more.[5]

The Wittenberg city council, jealous of their power and frustrated that Frederick was imposing his will upon them, sent a letter to Luther. Hoping that he could withstand the significant pressure of Frederick, they pleaded with him to come back to Wittenberg.

Luther, understandably, was eager for any excuse to return to his home and church. He informed the duke of his acceptance of the invitation, even though Frederick disapproved. At great risk to his safety, his prestige, and the benevolent support of Frederick, Luther announced his intentions "to speak on these matters" in the Parish Church beginning March 9, 1522.

The bells remained quiet during all of his eight sermons. He preached from Sunday to Sunday, March 9–16. Later called "Luther's Eight Wittenberg Sermons," or his "Invocavit Sermons," because they were preached on Invocavit Sunday, these homilies have provided Lutherans a manual on the proper attitude and approach to the question of change in the church for almost 500 years.

Never in the history of the church was a situation so primed and ready for change. Luther was confronted with a state of affairs in which the Gospel of salvation demanded change, the people were eager for change, necessary changes had already begun, Luther was both an agent and an ardent advocate for change, and he had been invited specifically to make the changes. The occasion was the kind of opportunity for which most pastors only dare to dream.

What did Luther say to those he loved and had taught? What did the great reformer preach at his first foray into the pulpit for more than a year? In his very first sermon, with loud resonant voice and piercing falconlike eyes,[6] he stared at his people and declared:

> I would not have gone so far as you have done, if I had been here. . . . All those have erred who have helped and consented to abolish the mass. . . . I cannot defend your action. . . . One can see that you do not have Spirit, even though you do have a deep knowledge of the Scriptures.[7]

With that, Luther pretty much ended the changes in Wittenberg, at least for a while.

What would possess the man to throw away the chance of a millennium?

Five fundamental principles of change in the church are apparent in Luther's Wittenberg Sermons. The church should follow them today.

1. Change must be required by the Gospel.
2. The Word, not force, should effect change.
3. If it isn't broken, don't fix it.
4. Don't let yourself get pushed around.
5. Always yield to the weak.

Let's examine these basic Lutheran principles of change.

1. Change Must Be Required by the Gospel

In his first sermon Luther laid down the most basic and fundamental principle of change in the church. "Take note of these two things, 'must' and 'free.' "[8] Faith is a must. You can never let that be taken away. Every Christian should be unyielding when it comes to the "musts" of the Christian faith. This is doctrine. Doctrine and faith can never change. "But 'free' is that in which I have a choice, and may use or not, yet in such a way that it profit my brother and not me."[9]

Some things in the church must change. In his second sermon Luther said, "The mass is an evil thing, and God is displeased with it, because it is performed as if it were a sacrifice and work of merit. Therefore it must be abolished."[10] Private Masses were big business at Luther's time. In the Sacrifice of the Mass a priest would go through the liturgy of the Mass privately. The church taught that the liturgical action of the priest gained merit before God. According to Roman Catholic doctrine, the death of Christ had only taken away original sin. The sacrifice of Christ by the priest in the Mass took away daily sins. The Roman Church also believed that this merit before God could be transferred from the priests to those who had paid for the Masses to be performed. So countless wealthy patrons of the church paid for Masses to be performed by the priests and believed that they were completing what was lacking in the atoning work of Jesus. The various monasteries throughout Europe would often authorize priests to perform Masses almost endlessly, storing up the merits of these Masses to be doled out for profit to those who wanted some years shaved off of their stay in purgatory. At Luther's time one of the monasteries near Cologne had "banked" more than 6,000 Masses.[11] The body and blood of Jesus in the Supper were never consumed by anyone except the priests. In fact, rarely did anyone but the priest even see the Mass performed. No wonder Luther opposed the Mass. To this day Lutherans have wisely chosen not to use the word *Mass* for fear people will be subjected again to the Christ-denying spiritual and theological atrocities encountered by the early Lutherans. So the abolition of the Mass was never debated. The Mass had to go.

Note the reason for changing the Mass. Change was not necessary simply because of the felt needs of those who attended the services. These Masses were done in private and really did not affect most people because they were too costly for the peasant class to procure. The Mass was not changed simply because it was culturally irrelevant. Actually, the Sacrifice of the Mass lent itself well to the social structure of late Medieval Europe. The rich and privileged could afford salvation while the peasants could not and had to depend on others. Everyone knew their place. Change was not urged by the Lutherans simply because the ritual of the Mass had lost its meaning. Never in their criticism of the Mass did the Lutherans disparage the liturgical rituals simply because they were rituals. Quite the contrary. In their celebrations of the Sacrament,

Lutherans were quick to say, "People are drawn to Communion and to the Mass. At the same time, they are also instructed about other, false teaching concerning the sacrament. Moreover, no noticeable changes have been made in the public celebration of the Mass. . . . For after all, all ceremonies should serve the purpose of teaching the people what they need to know about Christ."[12] Change was required because the saving work of Christ was denied in the private sacrifices of the Mass. Change is always required when Christ is denied.

2. THE WORD, NOT FORCE, SHOULD EFFECT CHANGE

In Luther's second sermon he introduced, through another distinction, a second principle of change in the church. Even when the Gospel makes change necessary, it should never be forced. "In the things which are 'musts' and are matters of necessity, such as believing in Christ, love nevertheless never uses force or undue constraint."[13] Luther offers two examples of things that must change but should never be changed by force. First, the Mass was a terrible thing. It still is. But Luther insisted that no one should be forced to do away with it. Rather, change "should be left to God, and his Word should be allowed to work alone, without our work or interference."[14]

A second example of necessary change was Luther's insistence that Communion be given in both kinds. In his fifth sermon Luther agrees that "it is necessary that the sacrament should be received in both kinds." But he quickly adds that it "must not be made compulsory nor a general law. We must rather promote and practice and preach the Word, and then afterwards leave the result and execution of it entirely to the Word, giving everyone his freedom in this matter."[15] Never force change. Let the Word do it.

Even the novice student of Luther knows how he began his rollercoaster Reformation role. In 1517 he nailed 95 theses to the Castle Church door in Wittenberg. The Castle Church, incidentally, was the other, smaller church in Wittenberg. Those 95 theses, which rocked both pope and world, attacked the Roman custom of allowing people to buy indulgences, little pieces of paper that purportedly released the souls of dear departed relatives from the protracted and painful problem of purgatory. How did Luther view his heroics of five years earlier? He comments on his opposition to indulgences in his second sermon. "I opposed indulgences and all the papists, but never with force. I simply taught, preached, and wrote God's Word; otherwise I did nothing . . . the Word did everything."[16]

The same confidence that Luther placed in the Word during his fight against indulgences he placed again upon God's strong Word in his fight against the Mass. Luther's desire to offer Communion in both kinds showed the same confidence. Allow God to work change through His Word.

A SAD STORY

Many well-meaning pastors attempt to make changes in their congregations that are justifiable and even necessary. The manner in which change is initiated can result in exactly the opposite of what is intended, especially if the change is forced rather than taught.

Pastor Johnson was called to St. John's Lutheran Church. He came into a congregation pretty happy with how things were going. Their previous pastor, Hank, had initiated gradual changes during the previous nine years. He had introduced the practice of lay readers and had recruited musicians for a praise band during the second service. But he had taken the time for the people to get used to the ideas before they became institutionalized. Hank had been patient and had taught the people that these things would get more people involved and would enliven the worship service. When he preached, he would not use the pulpit but would walk back and forth in the chancel area. Hank did not wear the traditional vestments. Instead, he preached wearing a nice suit or a sports-coat. He explained that such vestments created a "distance" between the speaker and the audience. Besides, "Jesus never wore clothes different than the people." Finally, Hank, "for hygienic reasons," had discontinued the use of the chalice during Holy Communion. Instead, he served the blood of Christ in individual cups. All these changes had been implemented with patience. Hank was well liked and trusted by the people. They went along with his ideas because they trusted him.

Pastor Johnson was extremely uncomfortable with the changes. They were unwise and wrong.

The first Sunday Pastor Johnson put on his clerical collar and his robes. He preached from the pulpit. In fact, he decided that he would wear the clerical collar whenever he went to work as it was a symbol of his call in the ministry. A couple of people asked him why he didn't roam the chancel as had Hank. He said he didn't think it was appropriate. On the anniversary of his third month, Pastor Johnson told the praise band that their services would no longer be needed. "Hymns were better than praise songs." Besides, he insisted, even if the church did have a band, it belonged in the back of the church. In the fifth month, Pastor Johnson told the lay readers that he felt it was inappropriate for them to read the lessons because he had been called to do so. They silently complied. But they were not happy. At the one-year mark, Pastor Johnson decided it was time to bring back the chalice. So he instructed the altar guild to store the individual cups in one of the closets and reintroduced the common cup. A short while later he asked the elders to support his decision to offer the Sacrament every Sunday. They refused.

Fifteen months after his installation, Pastor Johnson was approached by three elders and asked to resign from the pastoral ministry at St. John's. Stunned, hurt, and angry, he wondered why he would be asked to do such a thing.

"Because you have lost both the affection and trust of the people," was the answer. "Everyone in the church is wound up like a yo-yo guessing what you will do next. We were not consulted about your changes, and we feel as though you don't approve of anything we were doing. You have insulted our previous pastor. You have taken people's jobs away from them. These people were using the gifts God had given them. Now they are frustrated. They don't accept you as their pastor. You act 'holier than thou' with that collar everywhere you go. People think you don't care about them at all. You are perceived as being self-serving. We hate having to say this, but you have failed as our pastor."

Pastor Johnson was completely baffled. He had done nothing differently than at his previous parish where the people loved and accepted him. The church of his youth practiced all the things he had initiated and that was a happy congregation. The seminary had taught him the salutary rationale behind every change. Yet he was on the verge of being rejected.

His first response was predictable. "I have a divine call. I can't resign. It would be wrong. And it is wrong for you to ask me." Pastor Johnson was correct, but the elders were adamant and didn't seem to care. If he did not resign, he would be fired. So the conversation shifted from challenges regarding the proper way to bring about change in the church to questions about the propriety of firing a called servant of the Word. But no matter the question, these people had been poorly served by God's servant.

Pastor Johnson did not realize that he had broken some rules regarding change in the church. To be sure, the changes initiated by Pastor Johnson were right and proper. But he had forced change when he should have used the Word to effect change. The result was a frustrated congregation about to sin against God and fire its pastor without cause or due process. And Pastor Johnson would have to share the responsibility for their sin.

What should Pastor Johnson have done? He should have made it immediately clear that, while the changes initiated by his predecessor were not necessary, he would not change them back until the people had been prepared by the teaching of the Word. Pastor Johnson had a wonderful opportunity and responsibility to teach the various articles of the faith, the office of the ministry, the direction of the communication in the Divine Service, the importance of the teaching nature of hymns, Christian vocation, and the unity of the church at the Sacrament. Christian people love pastors who teach them Christian things. These people of God, if they were of God, would love him if he taught them. The practices would have been changed, perhaps not quickly, but eventually by both the pastor and the congregation. Pastor Johnson should have trusted God, who is long-suffering. God would never hold a servant guilty who taught change even if he did not quickly initiate it.

Jesus taught massive change. He abolished the Law and founded the church. His teaching was so powerful that the church was able, by the Word alone, to establish wonderful and permanent practices and customs that, for two millennia, have withstood the challenge of His enemies. And Jesus had confidence enough in His teaching that

He didn't feel constrained to dictate the precise practices that they impied. Virtually every synagogue in Galilee enjoyed the teaching of the Rabbi of Nazareth, yet not once did Jesus actually initiate change in any local congregation. Jesus was murdered for His doctrine. Pastors today should risk the same. Change will always take place because of doctrine. When it comes to change, pastors should be like Jesus.

3. IF IT ISN'T BROKEN, DON'T FIX IT

Some of the reformers were, at times, just as prone to the imposition of new laws as were the papists from whom they sought to free the German people. Luther's return from hiding was occasioned chiefly because Karlstadt, in his absence, had imposed new laws upon the Christians. He was just as bad as the papists, complained Luther. One law that Luther found particularly galling was the rule that you had to take the Communion bread into your hand and then into your mouth. "You become as foolish as the pope, in that you think that a person must touch the sacrament with his hands."[17] Admittedly, Luther was convinced that the first disciples "took it with their hands," but that certainly did not justify making a law out of the matter. In fact, it was wrong to introduce this custom because you cannot accept laws in matters of freedom. So Luther, while admitting that the people committed no sin when touching the Sacrament with the hands, still begged them to "give up this practice."[18]

Luther always preferred to retain an old custom unless it conflicted with the Gospel. The new law about handling the bread, while not sinful, should be revoked. The church should go back to the old way of receiving the bread in the mouth because "the universal custom is to receive the blessed sacrament from the hands of the priest."[19] Luther figured if it isn't broken, don't fix it.

ANOTHER SAD STORY

Often pastors violate the rules laid down in Luther's sermons. The following is an example of a pastor who tried to force change. He didn't teach. Most sadly he tried to fix something that simply wasn't broken. The results were disastrous. It is one of the saddest church stories I have ever shared.

I attended a banquet in the mid-1990s and was privileged to sit next to a gentleman named Gene, who has since gone to heaven. Gene and his wife had been members of a Lutheran congregation for more than 40 years. He saw his children baptized, confirmed, and married at his church. Half a dozen faithful pastors had come and gone during his tenure. Through the years Gene had supported his church with prayers, offerings, and thousands of hours of time. One extended family in the church owed their faith to Gene as he had helped them during some tough times and had taken the opportunity to confess Christ to them. When they had responded with interest, he had brought them to his pastor and to his church. Gene loved his church. It was his life. One day a new pastor was called, Pastor Bill. And within five years, 150 members of the congregation had left, Gene among them. What happened?

Pastor Bill had zeal to save the lost. He was convinced that the church was not doing everything it could to save those people who lived in the community. So the pastor initiated changes. First, he convinced the elders that the Divine Service in the congregation simply was not able to speak to the unchurched in a meaningful way. The liturgy is German, he claimed, while we are Americans. If we want to speak in the "heart language" of the community, then we will have to offer them a service in their own language. Because many of the members were used to the liturgy, Pastor Bill retained it at the 8 A.M. service. But the 10:30 service was changed to a praise service. A band with guitars, drums, and keyboard positioned itself in the chancel in front of the pulpit. This would get the young people involved, insisted Pastor Bill. Hymns were employed sparingly. Instead, praise songs with a strong beat were used. Pastor Bill reasoned that most people were familiar with the type of music in praise songs because it was what they listened to all day. A screen was placed in the front of the chancel upon which was projected the words of the songs. This way people could sing without having to look at their hymnal or their bulletins. Their hands were then free to hold in the air—a prayer posture Pastor Bill advocated. The screen covered the large cross that had adorned the chancel for forty years, a cross Gene and his wife had helped purchase, at significant personal sacrifice, when they were young and struggling. Gene told me, with tears, how he had loved to sing certain hymn stanzas that asked him to look to the cross and how he would look at that cross and think of Christ upon a similar piece of wood.

"Do we pass that cross unheeding, Breathing no repentant vow?"[20]

"When I survey the wondrous cross, On which the prince of glory died, My richest gain I count but loss And pour contempt on all my pride."[21]

"Stricken, smitten, and afflicted, See Him dying on the tree."[22]

"Upon the cross extended See, world, your Lord suspended."[23]

"Hold thou thy cross, before my closing eyes."[24]

These hymns were no longer sung. The cross was no longer visible.

Creeds were discarded by Pastor Bill in favor of "a weekly thematic faith statement" written by the pastor himself, which carried the theme of the service. The rationale was that people could not relate to statements written so long ago and that were laden with theological jargon. Both the pastor's traditional vestments and the paraments on the altar and pulpit went unused during the 10:30 praise service. Instead, Pastor Bill would sit on a stool in the middle of the chancel with slacks and a sweater. His preaching posture varied, now sitting and now walking around the chancel area. He would often sing solos, occasionally using his boom box as accompaniment.

Gene told me of the changes to his church, and I listened with rapt attention. At one point he blurted out, "I know that all these things are adiaphora. Maybe it's not worth being particularly contentious. But they have taken away my church, and I don't know where to find it."

I asked Gene where he had learned the word *adiaphora*. He told me that Pastor Bill had taught it to the church. I wryly wondered to myself if pastors teach the word *adiaphora* as nothing more than a prelude to taking from God's people the things they treasure.

I asked Gene a few more questions. "Why didn't you just go to the 8 A.M. service?"

"I did, but the church was divided. It's not just that we were personally inconvenienced and could no longer flit from one service to the other. We were divided by music preference or worship preference, and it was obvious the pastor favored the praise service. He was doing the traditional service only to placate us. Even the words *praise* or *contemporary* sound so much more exciting than *traditional* or *liturgical*. We never called them *traditional* or *liturgical* until they started the new ones. Before that they were simply worship services. I don't want to be identified by the type of service I like. I want to be identified by what God gives me in the service."

"Did others think like you did?"

"Yeah, we lost 150 members. Some, like me, found other Lutheran churches. Others found Protestant churches. Many just quit. They didn't like the new services, and they didn't like the controversy. They don't go to church for the most recent fad. They go for eternal food. They go because they are weak and they need strength."

"Did you talk to the pastor?"

"Yes, but his mind was made up. He politely listened, but he did not hear."

"Did he explain the changes?"

"Well, yes and no. He was convinced that this would bring in the unchurched. So the reason behind the changes was noble. He was convinced the changes would help us keep the young people in our church. Again, that's noble. But when we pressed him, he gave answers that I really questioned. I asked him why the creeds had to be taken out along with hymns and liturgical parts of the service that had been used for over a thousand years. I wondered if the unchurched and the young people of the previous 40 generations had been poorly served by these parts of the worship service. I wondered why this particular generation was so different from all previous generations. But I never got any good answers. I don't think there are good answers."

"What did the pastor say when you left the church?"

Gene's face grew hard, his eyes began to water, and he responded with a sentence that was, in my mind, both heartrending and church-rending. "Pastor Bill said to me, 'You are already going to heaven. I don't need to worry so much about you. I need to get people to heaven who might not get there. You will find another church. But for the lost, this might be the only chance they have.' "

So Gene and his wife left, heartbroken.

Pastor Bill broke some rules. He made changes that were not necessary. The Gospel required nothing he had done. He forced change upon resistant people. He did not teach the changes and let the Word effect change. If he had simply stuck to the Word, he probably would have come to realize himself that his changes were unnecessary for the proclamation of the Gospel in his congregation. Especially, Pastor Bill insisted on fixing something that was not broken.

Pastor Bill, in Gene's estimation, was well intentioned. He wanted more people in heaven. But he made the mistake many Church Growth pastors make. He thought that he was responsible for getting people to heaven. The Great Commission does not say that pastors are supposed to get people to heaven. It says that they are to make disciples by baptizing and teaching. Gene's church was baptizing both children and adults and teaching the doctrine of Christ long before Pastor Bill was born. Pastor Bill should have just let God get the people to heaven. He didn't mean to do so, but Pastor Bill greatly weakened the church. He hurt Christians unnecessarily. He did wrong.

I asked Gene one final question. "Did the church grow?"

"Well, there might have actually been a net gain. I don't know. We lost 150 members as I said, but 150 joined during the same time period. So I guess it grew. It seemed like we were transferring members from other Lutheran churches and bringing in converts from the Pentecostal and Evangelical churches in the area all the time. But you know, in the five years of Pastor Bill's leadership, I think that we baptized only one adult."

Gene's congregation had experienced a phenomenon that has become increasingly obvious to Church Growth observers in the past years. People are simply playing musical churches, flitting from here to there and "rearranging the ecclesiastical furniture." Meanwhile, the number of Christians in America actually decreases.[25] For all his noble motives, Pastor Bill was simply rearranging the human furniture of the church. He had traded 150 Lutherans for 150 Baptists and Pentecostals. By so doing he changed the church from Lutheran to the Protestant Evangelical style that so dominates the American ecclesiastical landscape. People were not changed. The church was. The result was frustration, anger, disillusionment, and a weakened church.

He could have avoided all the fuss by understanding the principles of change in the church from Luther's Eight Wittenberg Sermons. The church was not broken. The Gospel was proclaimed, people were saved by grace, yet the pastor felt he needed to fix things.

A PLEA TO FELLOW PASTORS

When Jesus gave His Great Commission to the first pastors on the mountain in Galilee, He promised to be with them. His presence was not based upon the fact that they were nice guys, change agents, or especially dynamic. Jesus was with them because they were teachers. God does not want nice, creative, and dynamic pastors. He wants pastors who can teach.

There have been too many damaged churches and tortured souls. Pastors can be deaf to their cries no longer. Please, pastors, don't make change your goal. Don't take the first year of your ministry to determine what changes need to be made. Don't choose your elders so they will support you in change. Just teach. If you can't get it changed by teaching, then you won't get it changed.

The beauty of teaching the doctrine is this: Even if you are not able to change the things you want, the people will learn to love God more. And by extension they will love you more. God will be pleased with you. You will probably be happier. And, most important, faith will grow as God blesses the people with the forgiveness of sins, which comes only through the Word.

4. DON'T LET YOURSELF GET PUSHED AROUND

The fourth principle of change involves making rules in matters of freedom. Luther was a stubborn man, not simply because he was German, though that certainly must have contributed. He was a Christian, and there is a time for Christians to be stubborn. We are stubborn in our refusal to be saddled with human laws that God does not intend. Paul said, "Stand firm therefore, and do not submit again to a yoke of slavery" (Galatians 5:1). Any time a church rule burdens Christians beyond what Christ has placed upon them, then the church is being made a slave. She must resist. She must disobey. She must be stubborn.

The situation of Paul, recounted in chapter 4 of this book, was simple. You are free to get circumcised or not. So there really should not be any laws about circumcision. People at his time were saying that you must get circumcised in order to be a complete Christian. So Paul did more than tell the people they were free to do as they wished. He said that they were obligated to disobey the imposition of a new rule. “I, Paul, say to you that if you accept circumcision, Christ will be of no advantage to you” (Galatians 5:2). Paul reasoned that if you caved into the pressure of accepting a new law, then you were obligated to be saved by observing the Law and Christ died for nothing.

Luther confronted the same type of situation. During his day the Roman Church had imposed all sorts of laws upon the people. One example was the law that you could not eat meat on Friday. Luther’s response was simple and stubborn.

> If you should be pressed to eat fish instead of meat on Friday, and to eat fish and abstain from eggs and butter during Lent, etc., as the pope has done with his fool’s laws, then you must in no wise allow yourself to be drawn away from the liberty in which God has placed you, but do just the contrary to spite him, and say: Because you forbid me to eat meat and presume to turn my liberty into law, I will eat meat in spite of you.[26]

Luther insisted that it was not enough simply to assert your freedom. You were obligated, in the case of a false law, to disobey. When it comes to the Gospel, don’t let yourself get pushed around.

Buddha in the Garden

Joan called me up one afternoon with a problem. She had a Buddha statue in her garden. The statue of the false god sat under a beautiful bonsai tree with a little stream of water flowing around the little fat man’s tummy. I’d seen it before and thought that it looked nice off in the corner.

The garden was Joan’s pride and joy. She spent much of her free time there, pruning, planting, and harvesting the flowers that grace the foothills of Mount Diablo in the eastern suburbs of the San Francisco Bay area. People admired her garden and congregational social events were hosted by Joan simply because she had such a beautiful backyard. No one had ever suggested that the Buddha was inappropriate.

On this particular afternoon all that changed. Joan had invited some friends over and was showing her garden to them. A certain woman had demanded of Joan, "How can you, who call yourself a Christian, display an image of a false god? The Bible says, 'Thou shalt not make unto thyself any graven images.' And here you have violated the Second Commandment by actually displaying this idol in your backyard." Joan had hemmed and hawed in response to this confrontation. After her friend left, she called me and asked if she was sinning.

The first order of business, I felt, was to reaffirm the Lutheran way of numbering the commandments. We consider the graven images reference to be an explanation of the First Commandment rather than a separate commandment. My brief lecture on legal numeration gave me time to gather my thoughts and respond to the fundamental problem. Should Joan take the Buddha down?

For years no one had even considered the possibility that Joan might be an idolater. We knew that she was a God-fearing, faithful Christian woman. Many members of the church had seen the Buddha statue and it never occurred to us that she was breaking any command. It is not the statue itself that is wrong, but the worship of the statue. We figured that Joan was not sneaking out to her backyard when no one was looking and lighting incense bars to the pudgy and long dead founder of a false religion. The existence of the Buddha statue in her backyard was not wrong. Luther himself insisted that images are wrong when they are abused, but we should never reject something just because others abuse it. "Wine and women bring many a man to misery and make a fool of him; so we kill all the women and pour out all the wine?"[27]

Further, I thought, this "friend" of hers was trying to impose a law upon Joan that not only forced unwanted compliance upon her but also implied that she had been breaking the First Commandment for the last dozen years. In addition, if Joan took down her statue, it would suggest that every Christian in the world who had art pieces depicting false gods was sinning. From statues of Buddha to pictures of Confucius, from icons of the blessed Virgin, who is prayed to idolatrously by millions, to depictions of the Hindu Brahman bull, all would have to be removed. The thought was staggering.

So I said, "Did you feel intimidated and judged by your friend?" When Joan acknowledged affirmatively, I said. "Leave the Buddha there. Your friend is wrong. She is trying to judge you when Jesus does not." Then I explained all the reasons.

Joan happily complied.

Whether the law involves circumcision, Buddha statues, eating only fish on Friday, drinking gin and tonic on a hot afternoon, the color of wine in the Sacrament, or a host of other man-made requirements, Christians need to DARE. Dare to say no to drugs, alcohol abuse, and the imposition of any new laws.

5. ALWAYS YIELD TO THE WEAK

The fifth principle of change, and clearly the most important to Luther, is the principle of love. "Love, therefore, demands that you have compassion on the weak."[28] Luther's return from Wartburg was motivated by a concern that the changes in Wittenberg had not been initiated out of concern and love for the weak.

Love is patient. It does not expect others to understand change more quickly than is realistic. Even if mature Christians know the need for change, that does not justify change. They have had the time to learn. Give others the same time. Luther gives the example, drawn from the Scriptures, of a mother feeding her children. "First she gives it milk, then gruel, then eggs and soft food."[29] So we should be patient with our neighbor and allow him to move slowly toward solid food. "Dear brother, if you have suckled long enough, do not at once cut off the breast, but let your brother be suckled as you were suckled."[30] Even when change is necessary for the sake of the Gospel, it must be initiated slowly in deference to the weak.

Love is orderly. When change is implemented recklessly without the approval of authorities, then it violates the law of love.

> All those have erred who have helped and consented to abolish the mass; not that it was not a good thing, but that it was not done in an orderly way. You say it was right according to the Scriptures. I agree, but what becomes of order? For it was done

> in wantonness, with no regard for proper order and with offense to your neighbor. If, beforehand, you had called upon God in earnest prayer, and had obtained the aid of the authorities, one could be certain that it had come from God.[31]

At Luther's time the authority was the duke and the city council.

Love is a fruit of the Gospel. "We shall now speak of the fruit of this sacrament, which is love; that is, that we should treat our neighbor as God has treated us."[32] God does not drive us away from Himself. He especially does not do so through the Divine Service of Word and Sacrament. So we dare not drive away Christ's sheep by making changes in the administration of the Sacrament or the Gospel, even if the changes are good. If such changes antagonize the weak and they leave, then you effectively deprive them of the Sacrament. When the Sacrament is ignored, then the power of God is lost and the fruit of the Sacrament, love, cannot be achieved. "You are willing to take all of God's goods in the sacrament, but you are not willing to pour them out again in love . . . nobody seriously considers the other person, but everyone looks out for himself and his own gain, insists on his own way, and lets everything else go hang."[33]

THE REST OF THE BUDDHA STORY

Remarkably, the story of Joan and the Buddha did not end there, even though Joan's friend never broached the subject again. It so happened that Mary, another member in the congregation, completely ignorant of the discussion about the Buddha, called me about a year later with a similar concern. She had been invited to Joan's house along with a friend who was visiting from China. This friend was a new Christian who had previously been a Buddhist. Her family still prayed in front of the Buddha statue. Mary was concerned that her friend would not understand the presence of a Buddha in the garden of a Christian. Mary knew that the statue was not wrong, but a new Christian, formerly a Buddhist, might not. I told her I would talk to Joan.

I called Joan and explained the situation. Immediately, she understood. "Pastor, don't worry. I'll take the Buddha down. I don't want to make Mary's friend uncomfortable."

I couldn't resist mentioning her contrasting responses to similar requests. "Why didn't you just remove the Buddha when your friend asked you to a year ago?"

Joan's reply was quick and decisive. "Oh, her. *She's* the one who needed to feel uncomfortable. She was trying to push me around."

Joan was able to distinguish the strong from the weak. To the strong she did not submit. To the weak she did. She showed strength against those who would force their will. She showed love to those who were immature in the faith. Joan, I do not believe, had ever read Luther's Wittenberg Sermons. She simply knew people, the freedom of the Gospel, and God.

Much of the Lutheran doctrine and many Lutheran practices are foreign to others. For the sake of the weak any Christian should be willing to sacrifice his or her prerogatives so as not to alarm someone unnecessarily.

THE CONFLICT BETWEEN STRENGTH AND LOVE

Love distinguishes. Possibly the most difficult thing to do in the church is to distinguish between those people who are weak and those who are strong. The ability to tell the difference is vital for pastoral leadership, especially when change is needed. Consider, for example, the Reformation change in Friday dietary practices.

Luther was commanded not to eat meat on Friday. Those commanding him were strong and stubborn. In response he defiantly ate meat. You must resist the strong who would impede the freedom of the Gospel. At the same time, Luther did not eat meat in front of those who were weak. "If we use our liberty unnecessarily, and deliberately cause offense to our neighbor, we drive away the very one who in time would come to our faith."[34] Luther explains his double practice of both eating and not eating. "Toward such well-meaning [weak in faith] people we must assume an entirely different attitude from that which we assume toward the stubborn."[35]

Luther's double advice merits further examination.

THE MATRIX OF CHANGE

Change can be required of individuals or churches. Similarly, change can affect individuals or the church. The principles that govern change are radically different when applied to individuals than when applied to the church. We can divide the challenge to change into four categories.

1. Individuals changing for the sake of others.
2. Individuals changing for the sake of the church.
3. Churches changing for the sake of the individual.
4. Churches changing for the sake of the church.

INDIVIDUALS CHANGING FOR OTHERS

A Christian should, for the sake of the Gospel and because of love for others, be willing to change. We should inconvenience ourselves, give up our rights, sacrifice, give in, suffer the cross, even die, that we might show Christian love and patience to another for whom Christ has died. Joan willingly took down the Buddha, changed her style, and inconvenienced herself for the sake of a weak individual Christian.

The apostle Paul adamantly asserted his dietary freedom in 1 Corinthians 8–10. "All things are lawful" (10:23). He was free to "eat whatever is sold in the meat market without raising any question on the ground of conscience" (10:25). But some of the people in the Corinthian church strongly associated the eating of certain meats with idol worship, especially because the meat may have been purchased at a market that procured its meat from pagan temples. These former idol worshipers were reminded of their former way of life when they ate meat that had been used in pagan temples. In such cases, even though he was free, Paul's concern was for "the weak person . . . the brother for whom Christ died" (8:11). "Therefore, if food makes my brother stumble, I will never eat meat, lest I make my brother stumble" (8:13).

The Bible is full of people who made serious personal adjustments for the sake of their confession. Esther, with fear and trepidation, violated monarchical protocol and endangered herself in order to influence her husband, the king, not to persecute her people unjustly. Peter risked severe criticism and ate with the Gentile Cornelius. Jonah, at great risk and with serious reservation, preached to murderous pagans. Jesus healed on the Sabbath and got Himself killed for it. All these people made individual changes for the sake of their confession.

One of the proudest moments in my ministry was given to me by a sports team willing to change and sacrifice for the sake of others. It happened when I was on an intramural basketball team. Year after year our team, The Wittenberg Lutheran Chapel Net Prophets, ended its season without making the playoffs. Our only annual consolation was the hearty conviction that we were going to heaven some day, an eschatological if unrelated hope. One year, and one year only, providentially, we managed to put together a good team. Our winning season was the crowning sports achievement of the orthodox in that corner of the world. Better, we soared through the first couple of playoff rounds and found ourselves in the semifinals. Two more victories and we would be the University of North Dakota class B intramural champions, a coveted, if local, honor. The last games were scheduled and we were ready. Ours was a finely tuned athletic machine with experience and divine guidance. On Sunday, after services, a couple of days before the game, I was informed by Rich, our captain, that the intramural powers that be had been forced to reschedule the game from a Tuesday night at 7:30 to Thursday night. I stared at him as, in anguish, he told me what I already knew. We had the choice of Maundy Thursday services or a chance at basketball fame. This was a time that tried men's souls. Phone calls were made. Quid pro quo deals were proffered. Prayers ascended with ardor that betrayed more flesh than spirit. The inescapable truth finally set in. The conflict was set in concrete. I told Rich that I could not play because I would be leading the Divine Service. I didn't add that the loss of its aging second-string point guard probably enhanced the team's chances, and he graciously offered no comment on the matter. I was profoundly disappointed, but went back to Holy Week preparations.

That evening a knock on the study door revealed a dour Rich and a handful of equally disheartened Lutheran basketball players. "We decided that we couldn't win without you," he said, "so we forfeited the game."

I knew he was lying. These guys simply could not bring themselves to play basketball "on the night He was betrayed." I smiled. "Is that what you really said?"

"No, we told them it is a Christian holiday and we will honor it."

The team was comprised of young men with varying degrees of Christian maturity. They were all free in Christ, but not all fully understood their freedom. They could have played ball on Maundy Thursday evening without jeopardizing their faith. One of the local Lutheran churches even had a service early in the day that our team could have attended and still played in the game. So why did they forfeit something they had wanted for so long?

There were a couple of guys on the team who would have viewed playing ball as a compromise of the faith. For the sake of these players the more mature decided that they did not want to give the appearance of capitulating to the values of the world. Rather than insist on their rights in Christ, those team members who were secure in their faith showed a willingness to change their habits, their desires, their dreams, for the sake of "someone else's conscience" (1 Corinthians 10:29). I was extremely proud. This bunch of Lutheran basketball players was more Lutheran than they were basketball players.

Our team was in the same category as Luther who, for the weak, gave up roast beef on Fridays, Paul who circumcised Titus, Joan who put away the Buddha for the former Buddhist visitor, and countless other individuals whose confession of Christ is adorned with a willingness to give in to the weak.

Against the strong, on the other hand, we must never give in. Recall the story of drinking gin and tonic with Judith. There we did not give in even for a minute. Or think of Joan refusing to remove the Buddha when pushy, legalistic, judgmental forces were brought to bear.

(Oh, incidentally, the opposing team refused to accept our forfeiture, rescheduled the game for the week after Easter, and beat us by 23 points. But that is not the point of the story.)

Individuals Changing for the Church

Individual Christians often find it necessary to change and sacrifice for the sake of the church.

Paul's willingness to yield to the weak is captured by the famous phrase "I have become all things to all people, that by all means I might save some" (1 Corinthians 9:22). What exactly was he saying?

Paul writes these words to the congregation in Corinth. A casual reading of 1 Corinthians reveals that the church in that corner of the world suffered serious divisions over doctrinal, moral, financial, and practical matters. Paul's ministry was rendered even more challenging because he was criticized and abused by some of the people in the church and by competitors outside the congregation. In chapter 9 Paul asserts clearly that ministers of the Gospel have the right to expect their livelihood to be rendered from the work of the ministry.

> Do we not have the right to eat and drink? Do we not have the right to take along a believing wife, as do the other apostles and the brothers of the Lord and Cephas? Or is it only Barnabas and I who have no right to refrain from working for a living? . . . If we have sown spiritual things among you, is it too much if we reap material things from you? If others share this rightful claim on you, do not we even more? Nevertheless, we have not made use of this right, but we endure anything rather than put an obstacle in the way of the gospel of Christ. . . . The Lord commanded that those who proclaim the gospel should get their living by the gospel. But I have made no use of any of these rights. . . . For I would rather die than have anyone deprive me of my ground for boasting. I have become all things to all people. (1 Corinthians 9:4–6,11–12, 14–15, 22)

Paul is expressing a willingness to make a personal sacrifice on behalf of a congregation. He sets an example for both individual pastors and individual laypeople. Sacrifice your wants for the sake of the church. Paul changed his personal expectations, his comforts, even his needs so as to proclaim Christ. But Paul never expected anyone else to do the same, whether the Lord's brothers, Cephas, or even Sosthenes, with whom he authored and sent the letter.

Simply put, Paul did not advocate corporate change—change within the church—with his dramatic words in 1 Corinthians. Rather, he promoted a willingness on the part of pastors to sacrifice. When this passage is used to justify changing the practices of a congregation, such as liturgical practices or Communion practices, then the passage is being misused and misapplied. Don't use "all things to all people" to justify change in the church. It's unbiblical. Use it to encourage yourself in your personal sacrifice.

Churches Changing for Individuals

I have presented many examples of change within the church from the Scriptures, from the pages of other historical documents, or from my own personal experience. I cannot bring to mind a single example of the church initiating change of its practices for the sake of individuals. That's a bold statement. It's also true.

Individuals make changes for the sake of the weak. It happens all the time. But churches don't make changes for the sake of individuals. Churches delay or put off change for the sake of the weak. But the church simply does not initiate change, especially changes to her historic and cherished practices, in order to give in to individuals, no matter how weak. Lutheran churches especially don't change good, Gospel-centered, Christ-promoting, confessional practices for the sake of the unchurched or for individuals from other churches who don't understand or appreciate them.

Luther made his comments about considering the weak because the church, though desperately needing change, was moving too fast. Every change he advocated was necessary for the sake of the pure doctrine of the Gospel. God wanted change. But, in Wittenberg, the changes had been initiated too quickly and without the proper teaching. The principle that we must consider the weak applies to the slow initiation of necessary change, never the quick initiation of unnecessary change. Review the changes Luther initiated. Some were required: the abolition of the Canon of the Mass and private Masses, Communion in both kinds, private confession as a precondition for the Lord's Supper. There is no suggestion that these changes be made for the sake of the weak. On the contrary, they were decelerated for the sake of the weak. Some proposed changes were matters of indifference: pastors preaching in street clothes, taking the bread in hands, getting rid of icons. All of these indifferent customs were retained. None were changed. The only change Luther strongly advocated was eating meat on Friday, and that was an individual matter, not a church matter. Even then Luther said that you shouldn't do so in front of the weak.

Let me say again that true Christian churches do not change their customs or practices for the sake of individuals, no matter how weak. Instead, for the weak, the church willingly slows necessary change.

Today we hear many voices that advocate change in the church. "We need to become all things to all men. For the sake of the weak or for those who do not understand we should change or update the liturgy (whatever that means). We need to change our idea of the church if we are to reach out to the lost. If Americans are to relate to our message, then we must change our church style and make it more American." If those who make such comments are willing, like the apostle Paul, to work for no wages, then I agree with their advocacy of change. Unfortunately, the church's customs are targeted by many of today's "change agents" more than the personal comforts that Christlike individuals have sacrificed since the time of their master. Such sentiments are unLutheran. If the German Christians at the time of Luther became confused over necessary changes in the Divine Service, how much more should the church avoid any unnecessary changes?

THE GIFT OF THE CRUCIFIX

Often pastors are forced to change their hopes or expectations for the sake of those in the church who are weak. At the same time congregations themselves are often required, for the sake of love, to defer necessary change. A pastor friend of mine named Jim shared the following conundrum.

Jim owned a cherished and beautiful processional crucifix. A crucifix is a cross with the body, or "corpus," of Christ on it. In many congregations the pastor, the worship assistants, the acolyte, and perhaps the choir, will process into the church on a Sunday morning. Jim's church had occasional processions on Reformation Sunday, Easter, Confirmation Sunday, Pentecost, and other special holidays. Many churches add to the procession a crucifer, someone who carries the processional cross or crucifix. The cross, which is typically mounted on the top of a six-foot pole, is placed into a stand near the pulpit, where it will stay during the service. The processional cross or crucifix adds a visual reminder to the congregation that the center of our worship is Christ crucified. The pastor also is reminded that he is to "know nothing among you except Christ and Him crucified" (1 Corinthians 2:2). Jim's crucifix was about 20-

inches high. After he had served his congregation for a couple of years, Jim, out of generous and affectionate motives, gave the crucifix to the church because it had been a gift to him. When he gave it, he recited the words from Paul to the Galatians: "It was before your eyes that Jesus Christ was publicly portrayed as crucified" (Galatians 3:1). Then he proceeded to use it in the service processionals.

Many churches ask the people to face the crucifix as it enters the nave (the sanctuary) and makes its way down the center aisle. As the crucifix processes past each, he will turn and follow the cross with his eyes. The idea is that we should "fix our eyes" on Jesus (Hebrews 12:2). Jim didn't teach his church this practice, as he wanted to do one thing at a time. He simply made a gift to the church and enhanced their worship. He did not ask anyone to do anything except to see a beautiful Christ-centered piece of art and to be reminded of the great sacrifice God made.

Unfortunately, Jim's gift was not received with thanks by all.

The first Sunday that the people saw the crucifix there was some grumbling. Jim did not hear it because not everyone in the congregation had been apprised of the unhappiness, and as everyone knows, the pastor is always the last one to know things. The grumbling continued until Jim first introduced the crucifix into the processional a couple of weeks later. At that point the complaining was directed specifically at the unwary minister. "Pastor, this is just too Catholic for us," griped one. Another said something about graven images. A third reminded the pastor that Jesus was no longer upon the cross and that Lutherans have always believed in the empty cross.

Jim saw his problem. He had not taught the people yet. So he developed a Bible class on church art and customs using the Bible and history to teach his people how God's people have used art through the centuries to proclaim and confess Christ.

In the first part of the class, Jim patiently explained that there will always be an overlap in customs between the Lutherans and the Roman Catholics. The Christian church had depictions of Christ upon the cross long before there was a Roman Catholic Church. Crucifixes are not a Roman Catholic invention. Besides, taught Jim, just because something is Roman Catholic that doesn't mean it is wrong. We also inherited from the Roman Catholics many things no one seriously questions—church buildings, pastors who are educated, altars, pulpits, choirs, the liturgy, many hymns, such as "Of the Father's Love Begotten," "Jesus Christ Is Risen Today," "Come, Holy Ghost, Our Souls Inspire," "Jesus Christ, Our Blessed Savior," and "Silent Night." Along with "Silent Night" we also inherited from the Roman Church the use of the guitar in the worship service. Jim asserted that he had never heard anyone complain about the guitar because it was "too Catholic." He also taught that we should accept or reject church practices not on the basis of where they come from but on whether they promote Christ's Gospel. Certainly a depiction of the crucified Savior advances the teaching of forgiveness through Christ's death.

In the second part of the class, Jim taught about graven images. He explained that the Law against graven images was given by God before He Himself had taken on the form of humanity in Christ. Now that God was Himself flesh with a body we could perfectly well attempt to depict that body in the various activities the Gospels teach. He again cited Paul who claimed to have "publicly portrayed Jesus Christ as crucified before your eyes." Paul was not content to present Jesus to the ears. He presented Him also to the eyes. Jim showed the people art from Christian churches around the world that showed Jesus, often in woodcarvings or stone statues. "These are not wrong," he said. Even the cross without Jesus upon it is a graven image. Jim furthered explained that the Christian church has been blessed throughout the centuries with pictures and statues that have depicted our Lord upon the cross, dead and being taken from the cross, whipped and beaten before Pilate, full of anguish in prayer in the Garden, or as a tiny baby in the manger. Jim showed a replica of the *Pieta*, a beautiful statue by Michelangelo that shows the body of Christ being held by His mother, Mary. He showed the congregation photographs of woodcarvings made by the earliest Lutherans. These were graven images of Jesus in various stages of His passion and death. Certainly, concluded Jim, there is nothing wrong with a statue of Jesus. Every children's Christmas program has a baby doll in the manger. Certainly no one would complain that the children are involved in idolatrous worship of images by depicting Jesus through a three-dimensional likeness.

In the third part of the class, Jim taught the people the importance of placing the crucifixion of Jesus at the center of their theology and life. He rehearsed for the people the basics of Luther's theology of the cross, presented briefly in chapter 1 of this book, and showed them that the death of Christ is the single most important event in the history of the world. Reminding them of the importance of reflecting and meditating upon Christ's death, Jim taught his church the many beautiful Lenten hymns written by the great Lutheran hymnist Paul Gerhardt. These hymns depict the death of Christ in particularly vivid, even disturbing, lyrics.

O sacred head, now wounded,
With grief and shame weighed down,
Now scornfully surrounded
With thorns, your only crown.
O sacred head, what glory
And bliss did once combine;
Though now despised and gory,
I joy to call you mine!

How pale you are with anguish,
With sore abuse and scorn!
Your face, your eyes now languish,
Which once were bright as morn.
Now from your cheeks has vanished
Their color once so fair;
From loving lips is banished
The splendor that was there.[36]

Upon the cross extended
See, world, your Lord suspended.
Your Savior yields his breath.
The Prince of Life from heaven
Himself has freely given
To shame and blows and bitter death.

Come, see these things and ponder,
Your soul will fill with wonder
As blood streams from each pore.
Through grief beyond all knowing
From His great heart came flowing
Sighs welling from its deepest core.[37]

Paul Gerhardt did not create a mental image of the empty cross with these words. He wanted us to picture the cross with the dying and dead Christ upon it. In our mind's eye Paul Gerhardt made us see the Savior of the world gory, tortured, bloody, abused, helpless, feeble, weak, dead, and rejected by God. In one of the final stanzas of the second hymn quoted above, the church sings:

Your cross I place before me;
Its saving pow'r restore me,
Sustain me in the test.
It will, when life is ending,
Be guiding and attending
My way to your eternal rest.[38]

Certainly the cross guides us, not because we see it as empty. It guides, sustains, convicts, forgives, challenges, comforts, and transports us to heaven because Jesus died upon it. We need to hear, picture, and see His gruesome death.

Further, Jim taught his people that crucifixes in the church were not initially removed by Lutherans. Lutherans place the crucifixion in the center of their Gospel and correspondingly they placed the crucifix upon their altars and in their chancels. Historically, crucifixes were taken down by those who opposed the Lutheran Reformation. They were removed by the same people who wanted to rid the church of all pictures. It was precisely against these people that Luther preached his famous Eight Wittenberg Sermons. Jim explained to his people that the reason the crucifixes were originally removed was that people had changed the central doctrine of the church from the death of Christ to the decision of the believer. Jim insisted that the church simply must return to the proper Lutheran practice.

When Jim finished teaching, a curious and confusing thing happened. Most of the members of the congregation had initially been a bit ambivalent about the whole affair. They didn't care one way or another. But as they learned they embraced the idea. They saw the importance of picturing Christ crucified in a variety of ways. Maybe they didn't like the crucifix, but they valued it. Worship is more about what is valuable than what is likable. The people saw the crucifix as helpful to their faith and to their Christian faith and life. They needed it.

Regrettably, those who had opposed the crucifix grew more adamant in their opposition. They simply were not going to give in. They saw the crucifix as an idea being imposed upon them from without. This was their church, and they were not going to let anyone, not even the pastor, tell them, or even instruct them, on how to decorate it. So they called a special voters' meeting with the stated agenda that there be a decision as to whether there would be a crucifix in the church or not.

Jim saw what was happening. The gift he had intended was depicted as the imposition of his will. A wonderful, ancient, and beautiful custom had become the occasion for controversy. Jim decided to back away from the crucifix idea. He was profoundly disappointed. But it was not worth dividing the church.

The night before the voters' meeting, Jim was in his office preparing his sermon when Ann stopped by. She had been a member of the congregation for 38 years and had served on the altar guild for every one of them. "Pastor, I want to talk to you, but I guess this is not a good time." Jim told her to sit down and asked her what was on her mind. She taught him a lesson that night and the next afternoon at the voters' meeting.

"Pastor, I know how much you want that crucifix. I know that you want it not for yourself but for us, and I think we need it. I want it really badly too. But there are a handful of people in our church who will raise a big stink. They already have. I know them. I love them. They have been doing this for years. They're bullies. If this matter comes to vote, they will probably lose, which will make them furious, and they will continue to raise a stink. Or they might win, which will embolden them. Either result is bad."

Jim interrupted, "I know, Ann, that's why I've decided not to push the issue. I don't want winners and losers. We'll let this one go at least for now. I really appreciate you coming in and sharing."

"I'm not done, Pastor," she said abruptly. "This is not your issue to drop. This is the church's issue. Your job is to teach. This you have done. I want to speak tomorrow before you do. I want you to trust me." The pastor was not in a trusting mood, but he decided that Ann was worth it.

The next day right after the meeting had begun, a motion was made to instruct the pastor to take the crucifix out of the church.

Cries of protest were heard throughout the crowd. Ann raised her hand and was acknowledged by the chairman. She said, "The Bible tells us that sometimes changes in the church can be very upsetting, especially to weak Christians. This change that the pastor suggested and implemented is a very good change. The crucifix is a good thing. But it is a change which is solid food. Some of the people in the church are still on milk. I think we should wait a couple of years and hold off on the crucifix for now. Then we can give these weak Christians time to get used to solid food. We don't want to drive away any weak Christians by doing things that they are not mature enough to understand. I think we should give in to the weak on this matter. I don't want to hurt the weak. Sometimes we need to think of our members as little children. We need to let them grow up before we make things too hard for them. So for the sake of the weak I think we should respectfully ask the pastor not to use the crucifix in the service until even the weakest of our members is ready. The Bible says that we should not offend these little ones." While Ann spoke, she looked squarely at those who had opposed the crucifix. Her tone and demeanor were soft and gentle, but her eyes did not waver. When she was done, she stayed standing for at least another five seconds and then slowly sat down.

Jim observed how Ann had characterized those who opposed the crucifix. They were weak, on milk, immature, children. Jim liked Ann's little talk.

After Ann spoke her sister got up and said, "Pastor, would it be okay if we did not have the crucifix in the church for a while to give some of the members a chance to learn more about it?"

Jim, seizing his chance, rose and said, "That would be fine." The meeting was adjourned, and everyone went home a little stunned and a lot confused.

Jim learned what Ann had long since known. Bullies are weak. Some people oppose good ideas and good changes simply because they are in power. Bullies just want to have their way. But bullies also create a quandary for pastors and congregations. Should you treat them as strong and oppose them? Or should you treat them as weak and give in to them? Weak people acting strong are a dilemma. If you oppose them because they are bullies, you are not giving in to the weak. If you yield to them because they are weak, then you are letting yourself be pushed around.

Jim was in a no-win situation. Churches are often afflicted with leaders who, in weakness, try to act with power. What the churches need are leaders, both pastors and laity, who in strength act with weakness. Unfortunately, many pastors try to act with their own strength, which is usually a sign of weakness. Instead, pastors need to be like Jesus and follow the example of Luther. Entrust your case to Jesus. Be strong in the Word. Be forceful in the Word. With the Word you are in a position of awesome power and responsibility. Preach and teach with strength. Act with weakness. Too bad all pastors don't have someone like Ann around. She was able to give in to bullies precisely because they were weak.

How did the story end? About a month later an "anonymous" member donated a beautiful processional robe for the crucifer to wear. It was delivered to Jim with a note that said, "Pastor, go ahead. I don't think anyone will give you any more hassles over the crucifix." And no one ever did.

Jim worked for a good and praiseworthy change in the worship customs of his congregation. His gift of a crucifix indicated a willingness to change his own needs for the sake of the congregation. His willingness to sacrifice his plans demonstrated a compliant and long-suffering attitude toward the needs of individuals. The congregation itself could slow down Gospel-centered change for those individual members who needed more time.

Should the church as a whole ever change because of another church?

CHURCHES CHANGING FOR OTHER CHURCHES

There are two types of congregations in the world. Some churches are orthodox and some are heterodox. For the sake of an orthodox congregation a sister church should always be willing to initiate, delay, postpone, or renounce change.

Historically, congregations of The Lutheran Church—Missouri Synod have valued the common practice shared between them. We followed the same church year, wore the same vestments, used the same hymnal, employed the same Divine Service, confirmed the young people at roughly the same age, held the same Communion practice, expected the same education of pastors, expected the same from their pastors both during the service and elsewhere—basically tried to do things the same way. We were uniform in practice, not because the way we did things was always the best way, but because we recognized that uniformity was good. For the sake of one another and the unity they shared, individual pastors and congregations gave up their quest for uniqueness. Unity of practice reflected unity of doctrine in Christ. Today things are different.

About fifteen years ago I lost a family to another church. I had said to the sixth-grade catechumens at the beginning of the school year that I expected them to be in church—so did God. If they did not come to church regularly, then they would not be confirmed. You can't promise to be faithful in your use of the means of grace if you chronically are unfaithful in their use. About three weeks later one of the mothers called me up. "Matt will no longer be coming to confirmation class," she announced. "We've decided to join St. Andrew's Church. We've been shopping around for the last three weeks and we have found the church for us. At St. Andrew's they don't require Matt to go to church in order to be confirmed. Besides that, they only ask for one year of instruction instead of three like you do. Frankly, Pastor, it's a better deal."

Orthodox congregations or church bodies do not allow weak and immature Christians to shop for the best deal. We do not encourage Christians to identify themselves either by their worship style or their felt needs. Uniformity between the churches communicates the importance of peace and unity. It avoids needless competition. And it requires that churches be willing to change for the sake of other congregations they love and treasure in Christ.

As differences between orthodox churches should be discouraged, so different practices between orthodox and heterodox churches should be encouraged. If you are not similar to a false church, then don't act like you are. For the sake of the heterodox no truly Christian church would ever, even if it meant outward peace or the appearance of unity, even if it seemed practical, even if the whole world was doing it, even if it was advocated by famous leaders, no orthodox church would ever initiate change.

Paul refused to yield to the Judaizers on the matter of circumcision. At the time of the adiaphoristic controversy, the Lutherans simply refused to change. When the Missouri Lutherans came to the United States, they refused to modify their liturgy for the sake of peace or the appearance of unity. In fact, they made it a rule that you could not change the liturgy to make it appear like their Evangelical neighbors. Today, Lutheran churches, if they wish to follow in the train of Paul, Luther, and the Saxon immigrants—all spiritual fathers—will refuse to change the historic Lutheran practices simply because of the recommendation of Protestant Evangelicalism. Protestant Evangelicalism is heterodox, contrary to the Gospel, to the Scriptures, and to the Lutheran Confessions. It is a false expression of Christianity and something not worthy of our emulation. Lutheran must do more than assert the indifferent nature of change. We must, with the Lutheran Confessions, say that any change in practice or style rendered under the influence of American Evangelicalism, is wrong.

The matrix for change is easy:

1. Individuals, for the sake of the Gospel, will always show a willingness to change, adapt, or sacrifice for the sake of weak Christians. But to the strong and self-righteous they yield not an inch.
2. Individual pastors and leaders, likewise, will change their needs and wants for the sake of the church.
3. Congregations will never initiate change for the sake of individuals. Nor will congregations bring about change too quickly, even when the Gospel requires it.
4. Congregations will change for the sake of unity between faithful congregations. But no true Christian church will ever initiate change, even in matters of indifference, which give the impression that we are similar to false and heterodox churches.

Conclusion

From his sermons Luther teaches us five principles of change in the church.

1. Change must be required by the Gospel.
2. The Word, not force, should effect change.
3. If it isn't broken, don't fix it.

4. Don't let yourself get pushed around.
5. Always yield to the weak.

While the first three principles concern both individuals and churches, principles four and five apply differently to individuals and congregations. Individual Christians should be willing to change themselves for the benefit of other people or for the church. Congregations should never change for the sake of individuals or heterodox congregations. But to show unity and peace with other orthodox churches a Christian congregation should always be willing to change.

Luther was a change agent. He initiated more changes in the church than any other person since the time of the apostles. Most of the changes were necessary for the purity of the precious Gospel of Christ. Many were changes in practice flowing out of the evangelical doctrine. Luther changed the way the church believes, worships, thinks, learns, and even feels.

We need to follow Dr. Luther. His changes affected the fire of the Gospel. Through his patient and salutary teaching of change, "The Fire Was Stoked."

STUDY QUESTIONS

1. What principles of change did Martin Luther outline in his Eight Wittenberg Sermons?
2. Why was the abolition of the Mass a change required by the Gospel?
3. Even when the Gospel requires change, no one should ever force change. Let the Word do it. How did Luther say this should be done?
4. For what reason should an individual be willing to change?
5. Should congregations make changes for individuals?
6. For what reason should a congregation be slow about making necessary changes?

DISCUSSION QUESTIONS

1. Why do Lutherans historically refrain from using the term "Mass" in reference to the Divine Service?

2. Discuss the necessity and the challenge of teaching for change but not instituting that change immediately. What are some local examples of how this has been done well? How could this have been done better?
3. Consider and discuss the author's statement, "I wryly wondered to myself if pastors teach the word *adiaphora* as nothing more than a prelude to taking from God's people the things they treasure."

CONCLUSION

A PLEA

CHARLES PORTERFIELD KRAUTH

In 1859 a pastor by the name of Simeon Harkey was embroiled in a bitter battle over church practice. His chief opponent was the redoubtable Charles Porterfield Krauth. Krauth insisted that the Lutheran doctrine must be pure and that church practices reflect the doctrine of Christ. We need not change our practices or adapt them to American sensitivities, he claimed. Why should we shuffle our feet and murmur when accused of being too European in our teachings? We are neither European nor American. We are Lutheran, asserted Krauth. We can teach our doctrine and promote our historic practices without compromise and for all the world to hear and see. Krauth opposed the same type of radical "New Measures" that have occupied the attentions of Lutherans in our day. Harkey, on the other hand, favored a more "American" understanding of the Gospel. God's Word needs to be "adapted." We need to change our practices, thought Harkey. Certainly, he claimed, the basics of the faith should remain. But we should not get too bogged down in the incessant attempts to purify our doctrine. In a sermon preached in 1859 Harkey said:

> O! If I had a voice like an angel's trumpet, I would make this truth sound and resound throughout the whole church. Cease. Oh, cease from your controversies and disputes about non-essential points of doctrine and practice, and labor with all your might for the conversion and salvation of mortal souls! Give up your mistrust of each other, your hard feelings and bitter

> speeches against each other, and come let us strive together to bring a lost world to Christ. Let us lift high the banner of vital piety and true holiness, and spend all our energies to marshal all our people under it. Then our church will be safe.[1]

Does this sound familiar? Times haven't changed much it seems. For your information, Harkey listed as among "non-essential points of doctrine" the bodily presence of Christ in the Sacrament and baptismal regeneration. He rejected out of hand the practice of private confession and absolution. He disdained the historic Lutheran ceremonies connected with the celebration of the Lord's Supper.

In response Krauth called upon the church to be true to herself and return to an emphasis on pure doctrine. The pure, Lutheran, Christ-centered doctrine must characterize our mission and form our practice. The desire for the pure doctrine must never be sacrificed on the altar of American expediency. "Purity in the faith," said Krauth, "is first of all, such a first, that without it there can be no true second."[2] Krauth sensed a loss of pride in the Lutheran doctrine and her corresponding practice. Why did Lutherans visit Methodistic churches, study at revivalistic (Krauth called them "sectarian") schools, and steal baptistic practices when the Lutherans had so much to offer? He was puzzled that all the "Evangelicals" of his day didn't rush to the Lutheran churches and Lutheran seminaries to learn about true Church Growth. I would suspect that many Lutherans today wonder the same. Krauth perceived in many of his contemporaries a keenness to adjust the Lutheran practices to the expectations of the Protestant communities around them. He told the Lutheran church to admire and respect the "Evangelical" community, to "pray for the increase of its labors of love, to acknowledge that it has some of the truth and powerfully sets it forth." But he warned "in the midst of sectarianism . . . not lightly to consent to swell that destructive torrent of separatism that threatens the welfare of pure Christianity on our shores more than all other causes combined."[3] Then Krauth issued a stern warning to the Lutheran church of his day. If Lutherans want to be respected by those around us, then

> we must begin by knowing ourselves, and being true to that knowledge. Let us not, with our rich coffers, play the part of beggars, and ask favors where we have every ability to impart

> them. No Church can maintain her self-respect or inspire respect in others, which is afraid or ashamed of her own history, and which rears a dubious fabric on the ignorance of her ministry and of her members.[4]

Krauth pleaded with his church to count her blessings. God has "preserved to us" the true faith and proper practice of the church. Why should we covet the "flickerings of success" among the Evangelicals around us when honesty compels us rather to give freely to others that which any true Christian would desire: The pure doctrine, proper administration of the Sacraments, and practice consistent with the Gospel and Sacraments? Why should we bear the noble name "Lutheran" and then apologize for what we are by God's grace or hang our heads in shame in our dealings with those churches that should be learning from us?

Krauth understood that sometimes Lutheran pastors change the historic practices of the church because of "a want of information or the pressure of surrounding denominations."[5] Every pastor and congregation in America today feels the pressures. We all understand. Still, Krauth tells his fellow Lutherans to return to the historic Lutheran doctrine and practice that has preserved the Lutheran communion in this country. Better to have a dead church, says Krauth, and a deserved death it would be, if we do not seek to impart with liberality that of which we are too prone to show shame—our doctrine and practice.

The pages of history tell us that even as he spoke Krauth saw his beloved Lutheran church turn around. Ever so slowly she recovered from her faithless love affair with American Evangelicalism. A time of confessional Lutheranism was beginning, and the church of the Reformation would thrive, at least for another century and a half on American shores.

RETURN TO THE LUTHERAN DOCTRINE AND PRACTICE

The theme of this book is that doctrine and practice have a reciprocal relationship. If you change one, you will change the other. This is happening with Lutherans in America who blithely copy the practices of the Evangelical community around us. We need to understand the influence of novel, uncritically accepted practices. They gradually change our doctrine. And we should equally understand what happens when the historic practices of Lutheranism are discarded. We will loose our Christ-centered doctrine. Charles Porterfield Krauth understood the importance of preserving doctrine through preserving practice. So must we. Christ's mission is endangered and souls of sinners jeopardized when we throw away the treasures of our Lutheran heritage through disuse.

WORD, SACRAMENT, AND MISSION

Saving souls cannot be separated from the pure Word and Sacraments. Pure Word and Sacraments cannot be separated from the practices of the church.

The Bible says that the way in which sins are forgiven, hearts are comforted, and people are made Christians, in short the saving of souls, is through teaching the Word and administering the sacraments of Baptism and the Lord's Supper. These means "bespeak us righteous" (1 Peter 1:22–25; Romans 10:17; 1 Corinthians 10:16; John 17:17; 1 Timothy 3:15).

Our Lutheran Confessions use three terms to talk about the way in which God blesses people through the Word and Sacraments. Sometimes the Lutheran Confessions will refer to the Word and Sacraments as the "means of grace." In doing so Lutherans confess the way in which the Holy Spirit gives us the forgiveness of sins. "[W]e should and must insist that God does not want to deal with us human beings, except by means of his external Word and sacrament."[6]

The same Word and Sacraments are the marks of the church. We recognize Christ's church by the same means He employs to create the church. "It nevertheless has its external marks so that it can be recognized, namely, the pure teaching of the gospel and the administration of the sacraments in harmony with the gospel of Christ. Moreover, this church alone is called the body of Christ."[7] God does not give to us the prerogative to define the church any way we want, "because, God be praised, a seven-year-old child knows what the church is: holy believers and 'the little sheep who hear the voice of their shepherd.' "[8] We know God's people, for they gather around God's pure Word and His Sacraments.

The means or marks are also the "ministry." "So that we may obtain this faith, the ministry of teaching the gospel and administering the sacraments was instituted. For through the Word and the sacraments as through instruments the Holy Spirit is given, who effects faith where and when it pleases God in those who hear the gospel."[9] By calling the Gospel the "ministry," the Lutherans are teaching what the church should do. God has not left us with a command to make disciples in the best way we can. Nor has He given us complex or hazy directions in the endeavor. The Holy Spirit is neither tired of using the Gospel nor vague about whom He expects will function as His instruments in the task. Until Christ comes again, His church saves souls through the Word and Sacrament (Matthew 9:1–8; 26:26–29; 28:16–20).

The church is to proclaim and teach the Word and administer the Sacraments. By these—means, marks, and ministry—souls are saved, the church is identified, and the mission of the church is accomplished. The means, the marks, and the ministry are all the same thing. Luther says:

> For creation is now behind us, and redemption has also taken place, but the Holy Spirit continues his work without ceasing until the Last Day, and for this purpose he has appointed a community on earth, through which he speaks and does all his work. For he has not yet gathered together all of this Christian community, nor has he completed the granting of forgiveness. Therefore we believe in him who daily brings us into this community through the Word, and imparts, increases, and strengthens faith through the same Word and the forgiveness of sins. Then when his work has been finished and we abide in it, having died to the world and all misfortune, he will finally make us perfectly and eternally holy. Now we wait in faith for this to be accomplished through the Word.[10]

No chasm exists between speaking the pure doctrine and properly administering the Sacraments, on the one hand, and the saving of souls, on the other, as if the church must decide between the two. Rather, we save souls only by purely teaching the Word and properly administering the Sacraments. It's not even helpful to talk about a "balance" between true doctrine and missionary zeal. You do one by doing the other. You cannot have pure teaching that is not taught. And you cannot have missionaries who don't know what to say. Missionary zeal without doctrinal purity leads to crass enthusiasm where people are passionately spreading a message that may or may not be true or even comprehensible. And true doctrine without missionary zeal leads to a type of "ivory towerism" in which doctrine is no longer taught. Instead, it is hoarded and analyzed to the peril of the world. The forming document of The Lutheran Church—Missouri Synod listed as reasons for forming a synod both "the preservation of the unity of the pure confession" and "the unified spread of the kingdom of God."[11] God has always saved souls by the Word and Sacraments. What other way is there?

WORD, SACRAMENT, AND PRACTICE

Unity and purity of doctrine and proper administration of the Sacraments are threatened when historic practices of the church are discarded or ignored. Someone once said, "It's easier to change a doctrine than a tradition."[12] That may be true. It would be just as correct to say, "The best way to change a doctrine is to change tradition." I have shown in these pages the close, even inseparable, bond between the traditions or practices of the church and the doctrine of the Gospel of Christ. Once the practices of the church are made vulnerable to change or, worse, disposal, then the blessed Gospel itself is at risk. Conversely, if our theology changes, adapts to the culture, or undergoes reform either negatively or positively, then practice soon follows. The two simply cannot be separated.

When practice is treated indifferently or thoughtlessly changed, then doctrine suffers. When doctrine suffers, the mission of the church suffers and souls are lost. It's really that simple. Lutherans should love the doctrine and practice of their church not simply because we are used to them and comfortable with them. We love the Lutheran doctrine and practice because through them God reaches out to souls longing for salvation. It's all about saving souls.

THE PLEA TO LUTHERANS TODAY

In Christ's parable the prodigal son "came to his senses." Literally, he "came to himself" and went home (Luke 15:17). His father welcomed him with open arms. Many Lutherans today need to come to themselves. Those Lutheran pastors, congregations, and individuals who have found themselves in a foreign place, doing foreign and often unsavory things, having sacrificed their heritage for things as fleeting as those gained by the hapless young man in Jesus' parable, also need to come home. Come back to the old ways that have characterized Lutheranism and much of Christendom for centuries.

Have you dismissed the importance or even the possibility of pure doctrine? Come back. Have you exchanged the pure Gospel of justification for an Osiandristic "Jesus is in my heart" notion of salvation? Come back. Have you traded the Gospel and Sacraments for the uncertain feelings of the heart? Come back. Have you replaced the grace of the Holy Spirit with the decision of the sinner? Come back. Have you imposed unnecessary changes on the church or impetuously forced change? Come back. Have you discarded the historic liturgy? Come back. Have you exchanged the Christ-centered, Lutheran, hymnic heritage and birthright for the "red pottage" of popular praise songs? Come back. Have you modeled your worship services after the synergism of Dwight Moody? Come back. Have you relented under the pressure of our pluralistic age and sacrificed the ancient practice of closed Communion? Come back. Have you blurred the distinctions between men and women by encouraging women to assume pastoral roles? Come back. Have you deprived Christians of the joy of their vocation by touting "church involvement" as more noble? Come back. Have you preferred the emotion of the camp church over the "peaceful quiet course of God in accordance with the written Word" as reflected in the catechism, liturgy, and creeds of the village church? Come back. Have you despised the office of the pastor because its occupant was not "dynamic" enough? Come back. Have you compromised the work of the church by preferring subjective testimony to a clear confession of Christ? Come back. Have you simply lost your heart and cynically concluded that the differences between churches are unimportant? Come back.

The Lutheran doctrine is precious because it centers in the forgiveness of your sins earned by Christ on the cross and bespoken to you in Word and Sacraments. The Lutheran practice is vital because it supports and guards the precious Gospel. The two belong together and are mutually supportive, much like a shepherd's staff and his fire. Hopefully this book has helped explain the relationship between the two. If you lose one, you will lose the other. If you love the one, you must protect the other.

BIG NIGHT

In the movie *Big Night*, recounted at the end of chapter 1, Secondo, the brother who craves success in America even if it means compromising the purity of his brother, Primo's, culinary feats, sadly returns to the restaurant after his skirmish with Primo. He is ruined. The man he had thought was his friend had promised that Louie Prima would come to the dinner, a promise never made and certainly never realized. Secondo had depended on a man who did not love him, who was untrustworthy, and who had dubious motives. As Secondo enters the restaurant, he notices his unscrupulous rival playing the piano. The man stands up. Awkwardly they face each other. Secondo takes a threatening step but thinks better of striking out. Instead, he asks a simple question, "Why?" Why had the man intentionally ruined him? Why had he been so shamelessly exploited? Unstated are a hundred "whys" asked of himself. Why had he trusted such a man? Why was he drawn to him? Why had he not trusted his brother? Why had he craved success to the point of destruction? Why was he willing to compromise when, deep in his heart, he knew the purity and beauty his brother tried to teach? Why?

In broad and beautiful Italian accents the exchange between the two is played out.

The businessman answers with calculated precision, "What I did, I did out of respect. He's a great investment—your brother. You, too, of course."

Secondo understands. He has been bankrupted so that he would be forced, along with his brother, to work for this despicable man. What a profound irony. He who possesses rich coffers must play the part of beggar to a man whose only concern is the profit margin.

He bristles with controlled rage. "You will never have my brother. He lives in a world above you. What he has and what he is, is rare. You are nothing."

Alas, his passion is wasted. He doesn't even gain the meager satisfaction of speaking the last word. The man replies, "I am a businessman. I am anything I need to be at any time. Tell me, what exactly are you?" He walks away, leaving Secondo alone with his thoughts.

So Secondo learned, painfully, the value of what was his all along. He realized the duplicitous and fleeting nature of success and the price he could not pay to have it. He came to know what Lutherans must understand. The Lutheran doctrine cannot be adapted to Protestant revivalism that has learned to be "anything it needs to be at any time." Those Lutherans who cannot resist the practices of American Protestantism must choose between the fleeting and vulgar success of the churches around them and the "Big Night" of word and feast. Lutherans in America today must hear and answer the question, "Tell me, what exactly are you?" My prayer is that every Lutheran pastor and congregation will learn to defend, and actually to become, his older brother, "Primo." We must say of our heritage, our doctrine, and our practice those words of rueful admiration a wayward brother finally realized. "He lives in a world above you. What he has and what he is, is rare."

God grant it for the sake of Christ.

Answers to Study Questions

Introduction

1. Biblical doctrine points to Jesus Christ and saves sinners through faith in Him.
2. The central article of Christian doctrine is "justification by grace through faith." It is the article of doctrine upon which the church stands or falls.
3. The means of grace are the Gospel of Christ and the sacraments of Baptism and the Lord's Supper. The Holy Spirit has committed Himself to these means of grace and to no others. The Word and Sacraments alone are the power of God unto salvation.
4. The theme of this book is that doctrine and practice are so intricately woven together that when one changes, the other changes as well.

Chapter 1

1. The marks of the church—the Gospel of forgiveness in Christ that pronounces us right with God and absolves us; Baptism that washes us of our sins through Jesus Christ; and the body and blood of Christ in the Lord's Supper, which carried and washed our sins.
2. What you believe about Jesus—His life and death and their meaning to you, His gifts of Baptism and Holy Communion, the end times, about all sorts of things—this is the doctrine you hold.
3. Doctrine is God's, not ours.

4. First, doctrinal statements show the whole church and the world what the church believes, showing the world and Lutherans alike what it means to be called Lutheran. Second, doctrinal statements unite the church by exposing disunity. Third, unity around doctrinal statements unites the church in its mission. If we are to "teach whatsoever I have commanded," then we must agree on what the Lord has commanded before we can work toward the same goals.
5. Christ. The Bible witnesses to Christ. The Gospel is the good news of Christ. Doctrine is the teaching of Christ. Whether we speak of faithfulness to the Gospel of Christ, to the Bible, or to the doctrine of Christ—we speak of the same thing.
6. Yes. The powerful Word of God actually accomplishes what it announces. It creates the faith it requires.
7. Our salvation. Because the doctrine of Christ saves you, you cannot be saved without it. "Everyone who goes on ahead and does not abide in the teaching of Christ, does not have God. Whoever abides in the teaching has both the Father and the Son" (2 John 9). Without Christian doctrine you cannot be saved. Notice what is at stake in the discussion and debate about doctrine: the honor of Christ, the consolation of consciences, the forgiveness of sins, faith, grace, righteousness, the glory and benefits of Christ.
8. Our success is measured only by whether we consistently and purely teach this Word and rightly administer Baptism and the Lord's Supper.
9. You cannot have the true and loving God without the bloody death of Christ. God will not love you without the gruesome spectacle of His Son's corpse. God cannot accept you except through the naked, bloody, dead Savior on Golgotha.
10. Law and Gospel. The Law points to what we do. The Gospel points to the cross of Jesus Christ. The Law tells us what to do and that we have not done what God expects. The Gospel tells us of the Savior who has done everything for us. The Law says, "I fail." The Gospel says, "I am forgiven."

Chapter 2

1. Osiander taught that the righteousness that counts before God is not that which Christ earned. Rather, "Christ dwelling in us

by faith is our righteousness." According to Osiander, you did not look exclusively to the life and death of Jesus for the basis for God's verdict of "not guilty." Instead, you looked into your heart where Jesus dwells.

2. Righteousness is from outside of you, from Jesus. "God imputes to us the righteousness of the obedience and death of Christ without works or merits, alone by faith that apprehends the grace of God the Father and the merits of Christ."
3. "Justify" is used in a judicial way to mean "to absolve a guilty man and to pronounce him righteous" and to do so on account of someone else's righteousness, namely, Christ's, which is communicated to us through faith.
4. "Objective" means that something is analyzed and evaluated apart from its effect on you.
5. "Subjective" means that something is analyzed and evaluated only as it affects you. Subjective always depends on objective.
6. God has justified all people through the death of His Son. Remember that the Lutheran Confessions treated forgiveness and justification as the same. If your sins have been taken away, then you have been justified before God. So the Bible says, "Behold, the Lamb of God, who takes away the sin of the world!" (John 1:29). "In Christ God was reconciling the world to Himself" (2 Corinthians 5:19). These passages mean that all people have been justified. We are objectively justified.
7. No. The Bible is the Word of God objectively apart from our understanding. It is the Word of God whether you believe it, understand it, or even know that it exists. The Bible is inspired and inerrant because that's the way God made it.
8. When you don't have it, you are lost. When you do have it, all you think about is what's in it. When a person does not have faith, we say, "They are lost. You can't get to heaven without faith. Faith is necessary." But when a person believes, you stop talking about faith and talk only about Jesus.
9. Faith simply receives all the gracious promises and blessings of God. Faith is passive. It does nothing. It offers nothing. It contributes nothing. It's like the bag of the trick-or-treater. Our

confessions say, "To have faith is to desire and to receive the offered promise of the forgiveness of sins and justification."

10. Faith always produces works. Faith is always active. Luther says that faith is always "a living, busy, active, mighty thing, this faith. It is impossible for it not to be doing good works incessantly."
11. The doctrine of justification is the Gospel that has always been taught and will last until Christ comes again. Justification is the doctrine upon which the whole Christian church on earth stands.

CHAPTER 3

1. The Holy Spirit is active wherever the word of forgiveness in Christ is spoken. The Holy Spirit can be found only and always through the Word of Christ.
2. If the Gospel of Christ is proclaimed, then the Holy Spirit is active. And if the Holy Spirit is active, then there must be the proclamation of the Christ. There can be no Wordless Spirit and there can be no Spiritless Word.
3. Acts 4:12—"And there is salvation in no one else, for there is no other name under heaven given among men by which we must be saved."
4. God pronounced you forgiven. You were washed clean of your sins. You were made radiant in the eyes of God, without blemish—stainless, pure, and holy. The name of God was placed upon you. You were born again and given faith. You were justified by grace. The Holy Spirit came into your life.
5. Holy Communion is the true body and blood of our Lord Jesus Christ, under the bread and wine, given to us Christians to eat and to drink, instituted by Christ Himself.
6. Absolution is the announcement of an accomplished fact—the forgiveness of Christ earned on the cross and pronounced in the resurrection. In Absolution, Christ's verdict of justification is bestowed, imparted, conferred, and given truly, personally, intimately, and powerfully.
7. To feed the church of God with the true, pure, and salutory

doctrine of the divine Word. To administer and dispense the Sacraments of Christ according to His institution. To administer rightly the use of the keys of the church, or of the kingdom of heaven, by either remitting or retaining sins.

8. The minister's tools are the same tools that the Holy Spirit uses to declare us righteous in Christ: the proclamation of Christ, Baptism, Holy Communion, and Absolution.
9. No. Faith is the conviction that our loving Lord has met all requirements.
10. The Gospel is powerful for us and in us. It is powerful for us by forgiving our sins. It is powerful in us by creating faith. You are always talking about two blessings: forgiveness and faith.

CHAPTER 4

1. "Practice" refers to the churchly acts carried out by pastors or other leaders acting on behalf of the church.
2. If the doctrine of the Gospel is at stake, then a church's practice has significance.
3. One is grace alone. Sinners are brought into the hands of a loving God by grace alone. The second is "universal grace." The Gospel applies to all people. "Universal grace" is the expression used by the church to show that Christ died for all and that Christ wants all to believe.
4. When something is a matter of indifference, it is called an adiaphoron.
5. In the case of confession, nothing is indifferent. "We believe, teach, and confess that in a time of persecution, when an unequivocal confession of the faith is demanded of us, we dare not yield to the opponents in indifferent matters. . . . For in such a situation it is no longer indifferent matters that are at stake. The truths of the Gospel and Christian freedom are at stake."
6. "Catholic" means "a qualitative wholeness or integrity." It also means universal. "Roman Catholic" refers to the church that pledges loyalty to the bishop of Rome.

7. The Kyrie (Lord, have mercy), the Gloria in Excelsis (Glory to God in the highest), the Creed (I believe), the Sanctus (Holy, Holy, Holy), and the Agnus Dei (Lamb of God).
8. The parts that change each week are called the Propers. They are proper because they correspond to a specific season or Sunday. The service varies week to week because of the Propers: the hymns, the readings, the prayers, and the sermon.
9. An important aspect of catholicity is that the creeds and the Ordinaries do not belong to any individual or even to the congregation. They are catholic. They are blessings that belong to the entire church of all times and from all over the world. When pastors or churches misuse, abuse, or don't use these catholic blessings, they are depriving themselves and their children of the undivided heritage that is ours by the grace and guidance of God.

CHAPTER 5

1. The service should teach people about Jesus Christ.
2. The greatest way to praise God is to tell everyone what He has done. The praise of God is neither in the use of verbs to describe me nor is it in the use of verbs to describe Him. Praise of God is using verbs to tell what He did for us in Christ.
3. It is indelibly linked in our minds to something profane. We associate it with things of this world. The beat tends to define and dominate the music. Pop music by definition cannot be catholic. It is in today, out tomorrow.
4. The sermon is the primary way in which God, through the pastor, teaches you.
5. The purpose of the liturgy is the same as the purpose of hymns and sermons. It is to teach or to show us Jesus. Of course, the liturgy moves, transforms, edifies, illuminates, and inspires God's people, but only if it teaches and shows Jesus.
6. The word *liturgy* is a Bible word that refers to religious ceremonies and services rendered by God through His people to His people.
7. Christ and His forgiveness are proclaimed and pronounced

nowhere more clearly and directly. We are taught (1) that a man needs a call to proclaim Christ publicly in the church; (2) that God has given men the right to forgive sins; (3) that the announcement of grace entails the forgiveness of sins; (4) that forgiveness can only be given by and through Christ, who is our Savior; (5) that forgiveness is bestowed upon those who are baptized; and (6) that God's grace is received by humble faith.

8. You don't go to church primarily to pray, praise, and sing. You go to hear and learn and receive. If the Divine Service is understood as God giving us the forgiveness of sins, then you go to be there.
9. The Gospel makes us all the same. When I am serving my neighbor, then I am different and unique. But when I am being served by the Gospel, then I am just like every other sinner. I am equally as sinful as you. And I am equally as forgiven as you. We are the same. We are identical. Of course, my sins might be more profound, more heinous, and more creative than yours. But in Christ both you and I are bespoken righteous, clothed and covered in the righteousness of the heavenly Bridegroom, and cleansed in the blood of the Lamb. Sin, which makes us different and divides, is forgiven. Good works, which distinguish and divide us, are irrelevant when it comes to salvation. So we are the same. The Divine Service reflects this.

Chapter 6

1. Good works require action. Good works are done according to our vocation. God does not need our good works. Good works help other people. Good works are done whether we want to do them or not. Good works done in faith are valued by Jesus Christ.
2. Faith is passive when it comes to salvation. Faith is like the bag of the trick-or-treater. It simply receives. The Gospel tells me what I receive. The Gospel directs me toward God and His Son. The Gospel tells me that we are equally redeemed from the Law and equally righteous before God through the death of Christ. Jesus is equally our Lord and our God. We are equally "bespoken" righteous. Finally, the Gospel both

promises a heavenly rest and gives us that rest in Christ. All this we are passively receiving from God.

3. Faith, when it is active, is directed toward my neighbor. When my faith is active, I am not thinking of heaven. I'm thinking of others and their needs. I'm aware of how my love is needed throughout the world. In my activities my faith is different than yours, just as it is identical to yours in what it receives. I have different abilities, gifts, inclinations, and especially a different station in life than you. So the actions of my faith will be different than the actions of your faith.
4. First, you cannot have active faith without passive faith. Second, God feeds faith through the Gospel. He feeds passive faith and that faith becomes active. Lots of people believe that you can strengthen your faith by doing good works. That would make active faith foundational. No, you feed active faith by forcing it to stop, rest, do nothing, and be completely passive. God is then able to feed us with His Word and Sacraments.
5. For example: Family—mother, father, sister, brother; World or society—farmer, craftsperson, doctor; Church—pastor, hearer, prayer, giver, singer.
6. There are many right ways to carry out your vocation. Just act in love and do what the job requires. When asked, "What good works should you do for your neighbor?" Luther responded, "They cannot be named." The person should use the wisdom God gave and exercise love. After that, people are free.
7. We do our good works for our neighbor.
8. They are descriptions of those people whom God controls.
9. Every single blessing of God comes to us through someone else, acting in their vocation according to the Ten Commandments. God uses other people to shower His blessings on us.
10. False. Jesus values every work done in faith.

CHAPTER 7

1. Experience replaces faith and the Holy Spirit becomes unpredictable; uncertainty results; and divisions occur. Jesus and jus-

tification end up taking a backseat to the Holy Spirit and sanctification.

2. Wesley believed that the Word of God had no power of its own but that God added His power to it whenever He decided. The work of the Spirit became rather unpredictable in Wesley's system of theology.
3. According to Wesley, it is not enough to be forgiven and to be justified before God. You must also be restored to the way things were in the Garden of Eden, your "first estate." How do you achieve this? You must experience complete holiness, a type of sinlessness in your life.
4. The revival or tent meeting.
5. Speaking in tongues.
6. The Charismatic Movement.
7. Justification by grace through faith in Jesus Christ.
8. They make us think that (1) Christ is mere, (2) experience transcends faith, (3) God's grace is uncertain or unpredictable, and (4) there are different levels of Christianity.
9. *Synergism* literally means "work together." It is the notion that we cooperate with the Holy Spirit in our own conversion.
10. God. The Scriptures teach that God brings us to faith not by our own act of will, or our own decision, but because of His own grace in the Gospel.
11. Evangelism is any time or occasion in which the Gospel is proclaimed or taught.

CHAPTER 8

1. Intense feeling.
2. Osiander believed that it was Jesus in your heart that made you righteous and acceptable before God.
3. The village church recognizes parish boundaries, looks to creeds and Scripture for guidance, emphasizes infant Baptism, expects the Holy Spirit to come through God's Word and Sacraments, and stresses instruction and confirmation. The camp church has boundaries determined by the member's

"self-professed personal relationship with Jesus" and a "born again" experience; uses only the Bible and the people "make up their identity as they go along"; emphasizes initiation through "intense religious experiences"; expects the Spirit to come through the Word unpredictably; and stresses the importance of people being "ready to open up their feelings for Him to move them in spontaneous ways."

4. Closed Communion is the practice of restricting participation in the Sacrament of the Altar to full members of the congregation.
5. A church that holds a doctrine that goes against the Bible or the creeds, specifically the Nicene Creed.
6. Orthodox churches believe and worship in the proper manner. *Ortho* is the Greek word for "straight and proper."
7. The Nicene Creed was written so the Church could be assured that her members confessed the true doctrine.
8. A church body will declare fellowship with another based on mutual acceptance of creeds and confessions.
9. To encourage the confirmands to learn, to know, to speak, and to confess.
10. The Synod opposed worship and sharing the Sacrament with those who were part of the new Union church.
11. (1) It is possible to know the truth unequivocally. (2) Confessions and creeds contain the truth without any doubt. (3) Confession and doctrinal statements of other churches are false and unbiblical. (4) The church's doctrine is followed by those partaking in Communion. (5) The confession of the church is a matter more urgent than life. (6) Indifference about confession is a sin against God.

CHAPTER 9

1. People become "dynamic" by expecting the Spirit to come upon them in new and unpredictable ways.
2. Salvation will no longer be viewed as passive. The Divine Service will no longer be seen primarily as the place in which forgiveness is imparted.

3. If a pastor is openly and scandalously immoral, he should be dismissed. And if a pastor is unable or refuses to teach the true doctrine, he should be dismissed.
4. He is different because God has called him through the church to speak on His behalf and forgive sins.
5. Original sin condemms us. We have no free will to choose or believe. We will die even if we have never committed an actual sin. We must rely 100 percent on the grace of God both for our redemption and for our new birth.
6. Such churches or pastors will deny that infants are sinful, teach free will in conversion, deny both objective condemnation and objective justification, and sooner or later they will ordain women into the pastoral ministry or at least allow them to preach and teach.

Chapter 10

1. Business and marketing.
2. The use of music to affect the people and ready them for worship. The use of popular music to be relevant to the visitor. The decreased use of historical liturgies, creeds, and rituals. The increased involvement of laypeople in worship leadership roles. The practice of open Communion.
3. Our action toward God. No—worship is God's action toward us.
4. Synergism—the false teaching that the sinner works with God and cooperates with his or her own conversion.
5. God is taking care of us. He provides when He showers prosperity upon us and when He sends incredible hardships. He prospers us when our kids are born and when they die in our arms. He takes care of us when we are promoted in our careers and when we lose our jobs.
6. The church will lose its focus on eternal life, witness replaces confession, the marks of the church change, active faith saves, and the Gospel is denied.
7. The preacher employs whatever rhetorical devices he can to get the people to do what he wants, which is to change themselves.

Chapter 11

1. Body, money, praise—all Christians make these sacrifices; all are called priests.
2. The royal priesthood proclaims the excellence of Him who called you out of darkness into His marvelous light. We narrate the story of Jesus.
3. We speak against the devil.
4. Study more. If we would study the Bible and learn the catechism, we would communicate it better.
5. Practice.
6. No. Being a witness is tied directly to those who personally saw Jesus or were there for His earthly ministry. We are not witnesses, but we can confess what we have heard and learned and believe.
7. We are saying the same thing about ourselves that God says about our sin, i.e., we agree with God that our sins merit His anger and wrath.
8. We say about God the same thing that He says about Himself in His Word—that He has come in the flesh, that He is our high priest who made atonement for us, and so on.

Chapter 12

1. Change must be required by the Gospel. The Word, not force, should effect change. If it isn't broken, don't fix it. Don't let yourself get pushed around. Always yield to the weak.
2. The Mass is an evil thing, and God is displeased with it because it is performed as if it were a sacrifice and work of merit. Therefore it must be abolished.
3. We must promote and practice and preach the Word, and then afterward leave the result and execution of it entirely to the Word, giving everyone his or her freedom in this matter.
4. Individuals should be willing to change for the sake of the Gospel and because of love for others.
5. No. Churches simple do not initiate change, especially change in her historic and cherished practices, in order to give in to individuals, no matter how weak.

6. True Christian churches do not change their customs or practices for the sake of individuals, no matter how weak. Instead, for the weak, the church willingly slows necessary change.

Abbreviations

AC	Augsburg Confession
Ap.	Apology of the Augsburg Confession
Ep.	Epitome of the Formula of Concord
K-W	Kolb, Robert, and Timothy J. Wengert, eds. *The Book of Concord*. Translated by Charles P. Arand et al. Minneapolis: Fortress, 2000.
LW	Luther, Martin. *Luther's Works*. American Edition. General editors Jaroslav Pelikan and Helmut T. Lehmann. 56 vols. St. Louis: Concordia; Philadelphia: Muhlenberg and Fortress, 1955–1986.
SA	Schmalkald Articles
SD	Solid Declaration
Tappert	Tappert, Theodore G., ed. *The Book of Concord*. Philadelphia: Fortress, 1959.

Notes

Introduction

1. "Abide with Me," *Lutheran Worship*, 490.

Chapter 1

1. Small Catechism, "The Lord's Prayer," 5 (K-W, 356).
2. LW 26:59.
3. Cited in Preus, "Fellowship Reconsidered," 7.
4. LW 27:41–42.
5. *Lutheran Worship: Agenda*, 111–12.
6. Cited in Pieper, *Christian Dogmatics*, 1:55–56.
7. SA II, 1–4 (K-W, 301).
8. LW 27:38.
9. LW 40:213–14.
10. SD III, 6 (K-W, 563).
11. Kolb, "Forms and Facets of Faith," 323.
12. Ap. IV, 2–3 (K-W, 120–21).
13. LW 27:41.
14. Schaller, *44 Ways to Increase Church Attendance*, 23.
15. Hunter, *Moving the Church into Action*, 17–22.
16. Callahan, *Twelve Keys to an Effective Church*.
17. Galloway, *20/20 Vision*, 16–18.
18. George, *Prepare Your Church for the Future*.
19. AC V, 3 (K-W, 40).
20. Hunter, *Confessions of a Church Growth Enthusiast*, 98.
21. AC V, 2–3 (K-W, 40).
22. Hunter, *Confessions of a Church Growth Enthusiast*, 236–37.
23. Wagner, *Strategies for Church Growth*, 39–40.
24. *The Lutheran Hymnal*, 473.
25. LW 31:39–41.
26. Schwiebert, *Luther and His Times*, 329.
27. LW 31:40.

28. LW 27:38.
29. LW 31:41.
30. Preus, *Preaching to Young Theologians*, 73, 74.

CHAPTER 2

1. SD III, 6 (K-W, 563).
2. Krauth, *Conservative Reformation and Its Theology*, 203.
3. Krauth, *Conservative Reformation and Its Theology*, 203.
4. Cited in Pieper, *Christian Dogmatics*, 2:515.
5. LW 26:10, 29.
6. Ep. III, 4 (K-W, 495).
7. Ep. III, 16 (K-W, 497).
8. Chemnitz, *Ministry, Word, and Sacraments*, 72.
9. Bente, *Historical Introductions to the Book of Concord*, 156.
10. Bente, *Historical Introductions to the Book of Concord*, 157.
11. Bente, *Historical Introductions to the Book of Concord*, 157.
12. Bente, *Historical Introductions to the Book of Concord*, 156.
13. Bente, *Historical Introductions to the Book of Concord*, 152.
14. Ap. IV, 305 (Tappert, 154).
15. Graham Kendrick, "Heaven Is in My Heart," in *Maranatha! Music Praise Chorus Book*, 118.
16. *The Other Songbook*, 150.
17. A. H. Ackley, "He Lives," in *The Other Songbook*, 61.
18. "I Am a 'C'," in *The Other Songbook*, 156.
19. John Barbour, "Make Your Presence Known," in *Maranatha! Music Praise Chorus Book*, 49.
20. Chemnitz, *Ministry, Word, and Sacraments*, 72.
21. Ylvisaker, *Grace for Grace*, 156–99.
22. *Faithful to Our Calling, Faithful to Our Lord*, 1:36; 2:20; 89, 98.
23. *The Lutheran Hymnal*, 143:4.
24. Ap. IV, 48 (K-W, 128).
25. Walther, *Law and Gospel*, 269.
26. Walther, *Law and Gospel*, 272.
27. LW 26:4–5.
28. SD IV, 11 (K-W, 576).
29. Plass, *What Luther Says*, 503.
30. Ep. IV, 16 (K-W, 499).
31. *Small Catechism with Explanation*, "The Third Article," 144.

CHAPTER 3

1. Theologians use the expression "the analogy of faith." It means that all the articles of the Gospel should point to Jesus Christ who died for you. Jesus and His sacrificial life and death for us are the central and unifying teaching

of the Bible. Everything relates to this central point.

2. *Lutheran Worship*, 328:3.
3. Brinkley, *Thy Strong Word*, 35.
4. SA III, 10 (K-W, 323).
5. LW 31:40.
6. *Luther's Small Catechism with Explanation*, 197.
7. *Lutheran Worship*, 505.
8. Small Catechism, "Sacraments," 10 (K-W, 359).
9. Small Catechism, "Sacraments," 2 (K-W, 362).
10. Walther, *Law and Gospel*, 171, 173.
11. Small Catechism, "Sacraments," 16 (K-W, 360).
12. *The Lutheran Hymnal* 171:7.
13. One word that Lutherans have always been reluctant to use of pastors is *clergy*. See Preus, *Doctrine of the Call*, 18.
14. Chemnitz, *Ministry, Word, and Sacraments*, 26.
15. AC V, 1–3 (K-W, 41).
16. Chemnitz, *Ministry, Word, and Sacraments*, 26.
17. Feucht, *Everyone a Minister*.
18. Large Catechism, 91–92 (K-W, 399).
19. Christenson, "Perspective on the Charismatic Renewal in the Lutheran Church," 11.
20. Large Catechism, 41–43 (K-W, 461).
21. Krispin, "Philip Jacob Spener," 10–11.
22. Calvin, *Institutes of the Christian Religion*, 1:463.
23. The Westminster Confession of Faith, chapter XVIII, 6.098, in *The Constitution of the Presbyterian Church (U.S.A.)*.

CHAPTER 4

1. Bainton, *Here I Stand*, 202.
2. Scaer, "Relationship between Doctrine and Practice," 1.
3. Kittel, *Theological Dictionary of the New Testament*, 4:9.
4. Nelson, *Lutherans in North America*, 132.
5. Forster, *Zion on the Mississippi*, 16–17.
6. Nelson, *Lutherans in North America*, 132.
7. Bente, *Historical Introductions to the Book of Concord*, 107.
8. Actually the ringing of the bells may have been the most offensive Roman practice. The Roman Church taught that at the precise moment the bell was rung the Holy Spirit came into the Sacrament and made Christ's body and blood present. This gave the impression that it was not the Word alone that brought the Spirit, but the Word plus the bells.
9. Ep. X, 6 (K-W, 516).
10. AC XXIII, 24 (K-W, 67).
11. *Lutheran Worship*, p. 199.

12. Marquart, *Church and Her Fellowship, Ministry and Governance*, 26.
13. Ap. XV, 38 (K-W, 229).

Chapter 5

1. Pittelko, "Worship and the Community of Faith," 44–45.
2. Ap. IV, 49 (K-W, 128).
3. Ap. IV, 154 (K-W, 144).
4. Ap. IV, 301 (Tappert, 155).
5. Grime, "Lutheran Hymnody," 8.
6. *The Lutheran Hymnal*, 387; *Lutheran Worship*, 353.
7. *The Lutheran Hymnal*, 377; *Lutheran Worship*, 355.
8. Westermeyer, *Te Deum*, 142.
9. *The Lutheran Hymnal*, 387:5.
10. Polack, *Handbook to the Lutheran Hymnal*, 278.
11. *The Lutheran Hymnary*, 205.
12. *The Lutheran Hymnary*, 205:10.
13. *The Best of the Best*, 108.
14. *The Best of the Best*, 120.
15. *The Best of the Best*, 87.
16. *The Best of the Best*, 107.
17. *The Best of the Best*, 12.
18. *The Best of the Best*, 118.
19. *The Best of the Best*, 186.
20. *The Best of the Best*, 154.
21. Day, *Why Catholics Can't Sing*, 51.
22. Day, *Why Catholics Can't Sing*, 2.
23. Plass, *What Luther Says*, 2:980.
24. Resch, "Music," 33–34.
25. Zager, "Popular Music," 20.
26. Muren, *The Baby Boomerang*, 194.
27. Zager, "Popular Music," 20.
28. Zager, "Popular Music," 24.
29. Zager, "Popular Music," 21.
30. Zager, "Popular Music," 23.
31. Grime, "Lutheran Hymnody," 8.
32. *Webster's New World Dictionary*.
33. *Lutheran Worship*, 294.
34. Resch, "Music," 36.
35. Resch, "Music," 36; Zager, "Popular Music," 22.
36. St. Augustine, *Confessions*, Book X: 239.
37. Strawn, "Role of Music," (lecture).

38. Grout and Palisca, *History of Western Music*, 35.
39. Lischer, *Theories of Preaching*, 44.
40. Kittel, *Theological Dictionary of the New Testament*, 4:216.
41. *The Lutheran Hymnal*, p. 16.
42. LW 53:61.
43. LW 53:21.
44. LW 53:61.
45. LW 53:47.
46. LW 40:141.
47. Most of the church's ancient songs are named for the Latin words that begin them. So the words "Te Deum Laudamus" are Latin for "We praise You, O God."
48. Pless, "Daily Prayer," 448.
49. Lischer, "Cross and Craft," 7–8.
50. Dorough, *Bible Belt Mystique*, 50.
51. Dorough, *Bible Belt Mystique*, 53.
52. Dorough, *Bible Belt Mystique*, 52.
53. Dorough, *Bible Belt Mystique*, 50.
54. Seilhamer, "New Measure Movement among Lutherans," lists the New Measures: protracted meetings, animated, fiery, heart-searching preaching, calling out of sinner for private prayer, anxious or inquiry meeting, and the mourner's bench.
55. Nelson, *Lutherans in North America*, 216.
56. Gustafson, *Lutherans in Crisis*, 92.
57. Gustafson, *Lutherans in Crisis*, 93.
58. Gustafson, *Lutherans in Crisis*, 93.
59. Gustafson, *Lutherans in Crisis*, 112.
60. *Luther's Small Catechism with Explanation*, 213.
61. Nelson, *Lutherans in North America*, 224.
62. Nelson, *Lutherans in North America*, 220.
63. Arand, *Testing the Boundaries*, 26.

CHAPTER 6

1. SD II, 89 (Tappert, 538).
2. SD IV, 11–12 (K-W, 576).
3. Wingren, *Luther on Vocation*, 13.
4. AC XIV (K-W, 47).
5. LW 21:237.
6. Wingren, *Luther on Vocation*, 48.
7. Wingren, *Luther on Vocation*, 25.
8. Wingren, *Luther on Vocation*, 120.
9. LW 4:181.
10. Large Catechism, "Ten Commandments," 100 (K-W, 400).

11. Large Catechism, "Ten Commandments," 47 (K-W, 392).
12. Large Catechism, "Ten Commandments," 70 (K-W, 395).
13. Large Catechism, "Ten Commandments," 84 (K-W, 397).
14. Large Catechism, "Ten Commandments," 89 (K-W, 398).
15. Wingren, *Luther on Vocation*, 6.
16. LW 31:39–40.

CHAPTER 7

1. SA III, "Concerning Confession," 10 (K-W, 323).
2. SA III, "Concerning Confession," 5, 9 (K-W, 322–23).
3. Frost, *Aglow with the Spirit*, 13.
4. Borgen, *John Wesley*, 33.
5. Wesley, *Works*, 5:187, 188.
6. Wesley, *Works*, 7:512.
7. Wesley, *Plain Account of Christian Perfection*, 55–56.
8. Charles Grandison Finney, "What a Revival of Religion Is" (1864), in McLoughlin, *American Evangelicals*, 87.
9. Finney, *Memoirs of Charles G. Finney*, 20.
10. Campbell, *Pentecostal Holiness Church*, 247.
11. Robinson, *I Once Spoke in Tongues*, 79.
12. Lensch, *My Personal Pentecost*, 20.
13. *The Other Songbook*, 65.
14. *The Other Songbook*, 178.
15. *Greatest Hymns and Praise Choruses*, 9.
16. *The Best of the Best*, 39.
17. *Greatest Hymns and Praise Choruses*, 181.
18. *The Other Songbook*, 16.
19. SD II, 12 (K-W, 545).
20. Small Catechism, "The Creed," 6 (K-W, 355).
21. *The Lutheran Hymnal*, 37.
22. Bruner, *Theology of the Holy Spirit*, 327, 328.
23. Finney, *Sermons on Important Subjects*, 18.
24. Finney, *Sermons on Important Subjects*, 18.
25. Bloch-Hoell, *Pentecostal Movement*, 122.
26. Hollenweger, *Pentecostals*, 316.
27. Hunter, *Two Sides of a Coin*, 75.
28. Christenson, *Speaking in Tongues*, 128.
29. Bright, *Ten Steps to Christian Maturity*, 16, 17.
30. Graham, *How to Be Born Again*, 160.
31. Walther, *Law and Gospel*, 260.
32. LCMS Department of Evangelism, *Do You Know the Four Steps to Success?*

CHAPTER 8

1. Luecke, *Evangelical Style and Lutheran Substance*, 54.
2. McLoughlin, *Revivals, Awakenings, and Reform*, xiii.
3. Gustafson, *Lutherans in Crisis*, 16.
4. Marsden, "From Fundamentalism to Evangelicalism," 135.
5. Marsden, *Fundamentalism and American Culture*, 45.
6. Bosley, "Role of Preaching in American History," 25–26.
7. Luecke, *Evangelical Style and Lutheran Substance*, 53–56.
8. Luecke, *Evangelical Style and Lutheran Substance*, 54, 55, 56.
9. Ahlstrom, "From Puritanism to Evangelicalism," 179.
10. Hatch, *Democratization of American Christianity*, 64.
11. Hatch, *Democratization of American Christianity*, 64.
12. Cross, *Burned-Over District*, 7–8.
13. Klaas, *In Search of the Unchurched*, 6.
14. Hunter, *Confessions of a Church Growth Enthusiast*, 236.
15. Elert, *Eucharist and Church Fellowship*, 75.
16. Elert, *Eucharist and Church Fellowship*, 75.
17. Elert, *Eucharist and Church Fellowship*, 76.
18. Roberts and Donaldson, *Ante-Nicene Fathers*, 7:442.
19. Elert, *Eucharist and Church Fellowship*, 143.
20. Elert, *Eucharist and Church Fellowship*, 131.
21. Elert, *Eucharist and Church Fellowship*, 132.
22. Ap. XXIV, 1 (K-W, 258).
23. Sasse, *This Is My Body*, 213–14.
24. LW 27:39.
25. Luecke, *Apostolic Style and Lutheran Substance*, 28.
26. Luecke, *Apostolic Style and Lutheran Substance*, 28.
27. LW 27:36–37.
28. Walther, *Selected Writings: Editorial from "Lehre und Wehre,"* 74–75.
29. Wells, *God in the Wasteland*, 99.
30. Wells, *God in the Wasteland*, 226.

CHAPTER 9

1. Wagner, *Leading Your Church to Growth*, 22, 21.
2. Wagner, *Look Out!* 39–40.
3. Dornfield, *Have You Received the Holy Spirit?* 4.
4. Du Plessis, *The Spirit Bade Me Go*, 43.
5. Ervin, *And Forbid Not to Speak with Tongues*, 34.
6. Cockburn, *Baptism in the Holy Spirit*, 46.
7. Hunter, *Confessions of a Church Growth Enthusiast*, 174.
8. Hunter, *Confessions of a Church Growth Enthusiast*, 247.
9. Hunter, *Confessions of a Church Growth Enthusiast*, 188.

10. Hunter, *Confessions of a Church Growth Enthusiast*, 184.
11. Luecke, *Evangelical Style and Lutheran Substance*, 67.
12. Luecke, *Evangelical Style and Lutheran Substance*, 67.
13. See Heinecke, *Courageous Churches*.
14. Hunter, *Confessions of a Church Growth Enthusiast*, 173.
15. LW 26:375.
16. LW 31:40.
17. Hatch, *Democratization of American Christianity*, 9.
18. McLoughlin, *Revivals, Awakenings, and Reform*, 182.
19. McLoughlin, *Revivals, Awakenings, and Reform*, 183.
20. Hatch, *Democratization of American Christianity*, 13.
21. Hatch, *Democratization of American Christianity*, 13.
22. Hatch, *Democratization of American Christianity*, 20.
23. Hatch, *Democratization of American Christianity*, 45.
24. Hatch, *Democratization of American Christianity*, 20.
25. Hunter, *Confessions of a Church Growth Enthusiast*, 174.
26. Koehneke, "Call into the Ministry," 380.
27. Marquart, *Church and Her Fellowship, Ministry and Governance*, 159n32.
28. Koehenke, "Call into the Ministry," 381.
29. Fritz, *Pastoral Theology*, 45.
30. Fritz, *Pastoral Theology*, 45–46.
31. Preus, *Doctrine of the Call*, 58–59.
32. Marquart, *Church and Her Fellowship, Ministry and Governance*, 158.
33. Pragman, *Traditions of Ministry*, 113–14.
34. Hatch, *Democratization of American Christianity*, 78.
35. Nichols, *Pentecostalism*, 63.
36. Synan, *Holiness-Pentecostal Movement in the United States*, 188.
37. AC II, 1 (K-W 28).
38. Kersten, *Lutheran Ethic*, 153. In the same survey 75 percent of LCMS pastors agreed with the statement. At the same time three-fourths of the pastors from the LCMS disagreed.
39. Strommen, *Study of Generations*, 367.
40. Marsden, "From Fundamentalism to Evangelicalism," 129,
41. McGavran, *Bridges of God*.
42. McGavran, *Understanding Church Growth*.
43. McGavran, *Understanding Church Growth*, 394–96.
44. McGavran, *Understanding Church Growth*, 69.

CHAPTER 10

1. Quebedeaux, *By What Authority*, 22.
2. Quebedeaux, *By What Authority*, 26.
3. Findlay, *Dwight Moody*, 229.

4. Findlay, *Dwight Moody*, 229.
5. McLoughlin, *Revivals, Awakenings, and Reform*, 144.
6. McLoughlin, *Revivals, Awakenings, and Reform*, 144.
7. Marsden, *Fundamentalism and American Culture*, 45.
8. Quebedeaux, *By What Authority*, 27.
9. Considine, *Marketing Your Church*, 69.
10. Callahan, *Twelve Keys to an Effective Church*, 24.
11. Barna, *Habits of Highly Effective Churches*, 83.
12. Barna, *Habits of Highly Effective Churches*, 87–88.
13. Barna, *Habits of Highly Effective Churches*, 87.
14. Barna, *Habits of Highly Effective Churches*, 99.
15. Zager, "Popular Music and Music for the Church," 24.
16. Barna, *Habits of Highly Effective Churches*, 99.
17. Hunter, *Confessions of a Church Growth Enthusiast*, 175.
18. Barna, *Habits of Highly Effective Churches*, 99.
19. Barna, *Habits of Highly Effective Churches*, 90.
20. Heinecke, *Courageous Churches*, 82.
21. Lassman, "Church Growth Movement and Lutheran Worship," 52.
22. McGavran and Arn, *Back to Basics in Church Growth*, 52.
23. McGavran and Arn, *How to Grow a Church*, 41.
24. McGavran and Arn, *How to Grow a Church*, 32.
25. Luecke, *Evangelical Style and Lutheran Substance*, 21.
26. Luecke, *Evangelical Style and Lutheran Substance*, 73.
27. Luecke, *Evangelical Style and Lutheran Substance*, 78.
28. Hunter, *Confessions of a Church Growth Enthusiast*, 196. See also Hunter, *Launching Growth in the Local Congregation*, 36.
29. George, *Prepare Your Church for the Future*, 48.
30. Kelly, "Successful or Justified?" 244–45.
31. McGavran, *Bridges of God*, 144–45.
32. Hunter, *Confessions of a Church Growth Enthusiast*, 45.
33. *Religious News Service* (16 July 1991).
34. Chadwick, *Stealing Sheep*, 79.
35. Chadwick, *Stealing Sheep*, 89–90, 181.
36. Wagner, *Your Church Can Grow*, 53.
37. Wagner, *Leading Your Church to Growth*, 199–200.
38. Muren, *The Baby Boomerang*, 96.
39. Muren, *The Baby Boomerang*, 96.
40. Klaas, *In Search of the Unchurched*, 51.
41. Considine, *Marketing Your Church*, 70.
42. Klaas, *In Search of the Unchurched*, 51.
43. Hunter, *Confessions of a Church Growth Enthusiast*, 178.

44. Montgomery, *Damned through the Church*, 24.
45. Luecke, *Apostolic Style and Lutheran Substance*, 92–93.
46. Collins, "Rhetoric of Sensation," 115–16.
47. Findlay, *Dwight Moody*, 223.
48. Heisey, "On Entering the Kingdom," 152.
49. Findlay, *Dwight Moody*, 225.
50. Findlay, *Dwight Moody*, 223.
51. McLaughlin, *Ethics of Persuasive Preaching*, 25.
52. Wagner, *Leading Your Church to Growth*, 217.
53. George, *Prepare Your Church for the Future*, 27.
54. Collins, "Rhetoric of Sensation," 115.
55. Walther, *Proper Distinction between Law and Gospel*, 260.
56. Chadwick, *Stealing Sheep*, 25.
57. Chadwick, *Stealing Sheep*, 64.
58. Chadwick, *Stealing Sheep*, 64.

Chapter 11

1. LW 30:52–54.
2. LW 30:55.
3. Meyer, "Priest and Priesthood," 133.
4. Meyer, "Priest and Priesthood," 132.
5. Richmond, "Relationship between Trait and State Communication Apprehension," 338.
6. McCroskey and Richmond, "Community Size as a Predictor of Development of Communication Apprehension," 212–19.
7. McCroskey, *Introduction to Rhetorical Communication*, 33–35.
8. Bettinghaus, *Persuasive Communication*, 85; Brembeck and Howell, *Persuasion*, 256.
9. Brembeck and Howell, *Persuasion*, 257.
10. McCroskey, "Relationship between Trait and State Communication Apprehension."
11. McCroskey, "Relationship between Trait and State Communication Apprehension," 19.
12. *The Lutheran Hymnal*, 259:2.
13. Walther, *Selected Writings: Walther on the Church*, 192.
14. Green, *Evangelism in the Early Church*, 177.
15. Cuddihy, *No Offense*, 12.
16. Cuddihy, *No Offense*, 16.
17. Cuddihy, *No Offense*, 5.
18. Cuddihy, *No Offense*, 8.
19. Wagner, *Your Church Can Grow*, 77.

Chapter 12

1. Schwiebert, *Luther and His Times*, 505.
2. Lortz, *Reformation in Germany*, 124.
3. Spitz, *Renaissance and Reformation Movements*, 2:326.
4. Sider, *Karlstadt's Battle with Luther*, 148; Bainton, *Here I Stand*, 206; Schwiebert, *Luther and His Times*, 535.
5. Bainton, *Here I Stand*, 210.
6. Schwiebert, *Luther and His Times*, 576.
7. LW 51:72–74.
8. LW 51:74.
9. LW 51:74.
10. LW 51:75.
11. Spitz, *Renaissance and Reformation Movements*, 2:308.
12. AC XXIV, 1–3 (K-W, 68).
13. LW 51:75.
14. LW 51:76.
15. LW 51:90.
16. LW 51:77.
17. LW 51:89.
18. LW 51:90.
19. LW 51:90.
20. *Lutheran Worship*, 90:2.
21. *Lutheran Worship*, 114:1.
22. *Lutheran Worship*, 116:1.
23. *Lutheran Worship*, 120:1.
24. *Lutheran Worship*, 490:1.
25. Chadwick, *Stealing Sheep*, 70.
26. LW 51:87.
27. LW 51:85.
28. LW 51:77.
29. LW 51:72.
30. LW 51:72.
31. LW 51:73.
32. LW 51:95.
33. LW 51:96.
34. LW 51:87.
35. LW 51:87.
36. *Lutheran Worship* 113:1, 2.
37. *Lutheran Worship* 121:1, 2.
38. *Lutheran Worship* 120:7.

Conclusion

1. Gustafson, *Lutherans in Crisis*, 145.
2. Krauth, *Conservative Reformation and Its Theology*, 200.
3. Krauth, *Conservative Reformation and Its Theology*, 202.
4. Krauth, *Conservative Reformation and Its Theology*, 205.
5. Krauth, *Conservative Reformation and Its Theology*, 208.
6. SA, 10 (K-W, 323).
7. Ap. VII, 5 (K-W, 174).
8. SA, 2 (K-W, 325).
9. AC V, 1–2 (K-W, 41).
10. Large Catechism, "The Creed," 61–62 (K-W, 439).
11. *Concordia Historical Institute Quarterly*, 2.
12. von Schenk, "Confirmation and First Communion," 3.

Bibliography

Ahlstrom, Sydney. "From Puritanism to Evangelicalism: A Critical Perspective." In *The Evangelicals, What They Believe, Who They Are, Where They Are Changing*, edited by David F. Wells and John D. Woodbridge. Nashville: Abingdon, 1975.

Arand, Charles P. *Testing the Boundaries: Windows to Lutheran Identity*. St. Louis: Concordia, 1995.

Bainton, Roland H. *Here I Stand: A Life of Martin Luther*. New York: Abingdon-Cokesbury Press, 1950.

Barna, George. *The Habits of Highly Effective Churches*. Ventura, Calif.: Regal Books, 1999.

Bente, F. *Historical Introductions to the Book of Concord*. St. Louis: Concordia, 1965.

Bettinghaus, Erwin P., and Michael J. Cody. *Persuasive Communication*. New York: Holt, Rinehart, and Winston, 1987.

Bloch-Hoell, Nils. *The Pentecostal Movement*. Oslo, Norway: Universitetsforlaget, 1964.

Borgen, Ole E., ed. *John Wesley: An Autobiographical Sketch of the Man and His Thought, Chiefly from His Letters*. Leiden, Netherlands: E. J. Brill, 1966.

Bosley, Harold. "The Role of Preaching in American History." In *Preaching in American History*, edited by DeWitte Holland. Nashville: Abingdon, 1969.

Brembeck Winston L., and William S. Howell. *Persuasion: A Means of Social Influence*. Englewood Cliffs, N.J.: Prentice-Hall, 1976.

Bright, Bill. *Ten Steps to Christian Maturity*. San Bernardino, Calif.: Campus Crusade for Christ International, 1968.

Brinkley, Richard N. *Thy Strong Word: The Enduring Legacy of Martin Franzmann*. St. Louis: Concordia, 1993.

Bruner, Frederick Dale. *A Theology of the Holy Spirit: The Pentecostal Experience and the New Testament Witness*. Grand Rapids: Eerdmans, 1970.

Callahan, Kennon L. *Twelve Keys to an Effective Church*. San Francisco: Harper & Row, 1983.

Calvin, John. *The Institutes of the Christian Religion*. Translated by Henry Beveridge. 2 vols. Grand Rapids: Eerdmans, 1975.

Campbell, Joseph E. *The Pentecostal Holiness Church, 1898–1948*. Franklin Springs, Ga.: Publishing House of the Pentecostal Holiness Church, 1951.

Chadwick, William. *Stealing Sheep*. Downers Grove: InterVarsity, 2001.

Chemnitz, Martin. *Ministry, Word, and Sacraments: An Enchiridion*. Translated by Luther Poellot. St. Louis: Concordia, 1981.

Christenson, Larry. "A Theological and Pastoral Perspective on the Charismatic Renewal in the Lutheran Church." Essay presented at the LCUSA Conference on the Holy Spirit, Dubuque, Iowa. 1976.

———. *Speaking in Tongues*. Minneapolis: Dimension Books, 1968.

Cockburn, Ian. *Baptism in the Holy Spirit*. Plainfield, N.J.: Logos International, 1971.

Collins, Edward. "The Rhetoric of Sensation Challenges the Rhetoric of the Intellect: An Eighteenth–Century Controversy." In *Preaching in American History*, edited by DeWitte Holland. Nashville: Abingdon, 1969.

Commission on Worship, the LCMS. *Lutheran Worship*. St. Louis: Concordia, 1982.

———. *Lutheran Worship: Agenda*. St. Louis: Concordia, 1984.

Concordia Historical Institute Quarterly, vol. 16, no. 1 (April 1943).

Considine, John. *Marketing Your Church, Concept and Strategies*. Kansas City: Sheed and Ward, 1995.

Cross, Whitney. *The Burned-Over District: The Social and Intellectual History of Enthusiastic Religion in Western New York, 1800–1850*. Ithaca: Cornell University Press, 1950.

Cuddihy, John Murray. *No Offense: Civil Religion and Protestant Taste*. New York: Seabury Press, 1978.

Day, Thomas. *Why Catholics Can't Sing: The Culture of Catholicism and the Triumph of Bad Taste*. New York: Crossroads, 1990.

Dornfield, A. G. *Have You Received the Holy Spirit?* Plainfield, N.J.: Logos International, 1971.

Dorough, C. Dwight. *The Bible Belt Mystique*. Philadelphia: Westminster, 1974.

Du Plessis, David J. *The Spirit Bade Me Go*. Plainfield, N.J.: Logos International, 1970.

Elert, Werner. *Eucharist and Church Fellowship in the First Four Centuries*, St. Louis: Concordia, 1966.

Ervin, Howard. *And Forbid Not to Speak with Tongues*. Plainfield, N.J.: Logos International, 1971.

Faculty of Concordia Seminary, St. Louis, Missouri, The. *Faithful to Our Calling, Faithful to Our Lord: An Affirmation in Two Parts*. 2 vols. St. Louis, 1973.

Feucht, Oscar. *Everyone a Minister*. St. Louis: Concordia, 1974.

Findlay, James. *Dwight Moody*. Chicago: University of Chicago Press, 1696.

Finney, Charles G. *Memoirs of Charles G. Finney*. New York: Fleming H. Revell, 1903.

———. *Sermons on Important Subjects*. New York: John Taylor, 1836.

Fritz, John. *Pastoral Theology*. St. Louis: Concordia, 1932.

Frost, Robert. *Aglow with the Spirit*. Plainfield, N.J.: Logos International, 1965.

Forster, Walter. *Zion on the Mississippi*. St. Louis: Concordia, 1953.

Galloway, Dale E. *20/20 Vision: How to Create a Successful Church*. Portland: Scott Publishing Company, 1986.

George, Carl F. *Prepare Your Church for the Future*. Grand Rapids: Fleming H. Revell, 1991.

Graham, Billy. *How to Be Born Again*. Dallas: Word Publishing, 1977.

Greatest Hymns and Praise Choruses of Yesterday and Today, The. Laguna Hills, Calif.: Maranatha! Music, 1987.

Green, Michael. *Evangelism in the Early Church*. Grand Rapids: Eerdmans, 1970.

Grime, Paul. "Lutheran Hymnody, Is It Possible or Even Necessary Anymore?" *Logia* 3, no. 2 (April 1994).

Grout, Donald Jay, and Claude V. Palisca. *A History of Western Music*. 4th ed. New York: Norton, 1988.

Gustafson, David. *Lutherans in Crisis: The Question of Identity in the American Republic*. Minneapolis: Fortress, 1993.

Hatch, Nathan O. *The Democratization of American Christianity*. New Haven: Yale University Press, 1989.

Heinecke, Paul, Kent Hunter, and David Luecke. *Courageous Churches: Refusing Decline, Inviting Growth*. St. Louis: Concordia, 1991.

Heisey, Ray. "On Entering the Kingdom: New Birth or Nurture." In *Preaching in American History*, edited by DeWitte Holland. Nashville: Abingdon, 1969.

Hollenweger, Walter J. *The Pentecostals: The Charismatic Movement in the Churches*. Minneapolis: Augsburg, 1972.

Hunter, Francis, and Charles Hunter. *The Two Sides of a Coin*. Old Tappan, N.J.: Logos International, 1970.

Hunter, Kent R. *Confessions of a Church Growth Enthusiast*. Corunna, Ind.: Kent Hunter, 1997.

———. *Launching Growth in the Local Congregation*. Corunna, Ind.: Kent Hunter, 1981.

———. *Moving the Church into Action*. St. Louis: Concordia, 1989.

Kelly, Robert. "Successful or Justified? The North American Doctrine of Salvation by Works," *Concordia Theological Quarterly* 65, no. 3 (July 2001).

Kersten, Lawrence. *The Lutheran Ethic*. Detroit: Wayne State University Press, 1970.

Kittel, Gerhard, ed. *Theological Dictionary of the New Testament*. 10 vols. Grand Rapids: Eerdmans, 1967.

Klaas, Alan C. *In Search of the Unchurched*. Bethesda, Md.: Alban Institute, 1996.

Koehneke, P. F. "The Call into the Ministry." In *The Abiding Word*, edited by Theodore Laetsch, Vol. 1. St. Louis: Concordia, 1946.

Kolb, Robert. "Forms and Facets of Faith: Factors in Witness and Assimilation." *Concordia Journal* 24, no. 4 (October 1998).

———, and Timothy J. Wengert, eds. *The Book of Concord*. Translated by Charles Arand et al. Minneapolis: Augsburg Fortress, 2000.

Krauth, Charles Porterfield. *The Conservative Reformation and Its Theology*. Minneapolis: Augsburg, 1963.

Krispin, Gerald S. "Philip Jacob Spener and the Demise of the Practice of Holy Absolution in the Lutheran Church." *Logia* 8, no. 4 (Reformation 1999).

Lassman, Ernie. "The Church Growth Movement and Lutheran Worship." *Concordia Theological Monthly* 62, no. 1 (January 1998).

Lensch, Rodney. *My Personal Pentecost.* Kirkwood, Mo.: Impact Books, 1972.

Lischer, Richard. "Cross and Craft: Two Elements of the Lutheran Homiletic." *Concordia Journal* 25, no. 1 (January 1999): 4–13.

———, ed. *Theories of Preaching: Selected Readings in the Homiletical Tradition.* Durham, N. C.: The Labyrinth Press, 1987.

Lortz, Joseph. *The Reformation in Germany*. London, 1964.

Luecke, David. *Apostolic Style and Lutheran Substance: Ten Years of Controversy over What Can Change*. Lima, Ohio: Fairway Press, 1999.

———. *Evangelical Style and Lutheran Substance*. St. Louis: Concordia, 1988.

Luther, Martin. *Luther's Works*. American Edition. General editors Jaroslav Pelikan and Helmut T. Lehmann. 56 vols. St. Louis: Concordia; Philadelphia: Muhlenberg and Fortress, 1955–1986.

Lutheran Church—Missouri Synod Department of Evangelism, The. *Do You Know the Four Steps to Success?* St. Louis: Concordia, n.d.

Lutheran Hymnal, The. St. Louis: Concordia, 1941.

Lutheran Hymnary, The. Minneapolis: Augsburg, 1913.

Luther's Small Catechism with Explanation. St: Louis: Concordia, 1986.

Maranatha! Music Praise Chorus Book. Laguna Hills, Cal.: Maranatha! Music, 1993.

Marquart, Kurt. *The Church and Her Fellowship, Ministry and Governance*. Ft. Wayne, Ind.: International Foundation for Lutheran Confessional Research, 1990.

Marsden, George. "From Fundamentalism to Evangelicalism: A Historical Analysis." In *The Evangelicals, What They Believe, Who They Are, Where They Are Changing*, edited by David Wells and John Woodbridge. Nashville: Abingdon, 1975.

———. *Fundamentalism and American Culture, The Shaping of Twentieth Century Evangelicalism 1870–1925*. New York: Oxford University Press, 1980.

McCroskey, James. *An Introduction to Rhetorical Communication*. Englewood Cliffs, N.J.: Prentice Hall, 1982.

———. "Communication Apprehension: Reconceptialization and a New Look at Measurement." Paper presented at the Central State Speech Association Convention, Chicago, April. 1981.

———, and Virginian Richmond. "Community Size as a Predictor of Development of Communication Apprehension: Replication and Extension." *Communication Education*, no. 27 (1978).

McGavran, Donald. *The Bridges of God: A Study in the Strategy of Missions*. London: World Dominion Press, 1955.

———. *Understanding Church Growth*. Grand Rapids: Eerdmans, 1970.

———. *How to Grow a Church*. Glendale, Calif.: Regal Books, 1973.

———, and Win Arn. *Back to Basics in Church Growth*. Wheaton: Tyndale, 1981.

McLaughlin, Raymond. *The Ethics of Persuasive Preaching*. Grand Rapids: Baker Book House, 1979.

McLoughlin, William. *The American Evangelicals, 1800–1900: An Anthology*. New York: Harper and Row, 1968.

———. *Revivals, Awakenings, and Reform*. Chicago: University of Chicago Press, 1978.

Meyer, William. "Priest and Priesthood: Image of Christ and His Church." *The Springfielder* 36, no. 2 (September 1972).

Montgomery, John Warwick. *Damned through the Church*. Minneapolis: Dimension Books, 1970.

Muren, Doug. *The Baby Boomerang*. Ventura, Calif.: Regal Books, 1990.

Nelson, E. Clifford. *The Lutherans in North America*. Philadelphia: Fortress, 1975.

Nichols, John. *Pentecostalism*. New York: Harper & Row, 1966.

Other Songbook, The. Phoenix: The Fellowship Publication, 1984.

Pieper, Francis. *Christian Dogmatics*. 4 vols. St. Louis: Concordia, 1950–57.

Pine-Coffin, R. S., trans. *Confessions*. New York: Penguin Books, 1961.

Pittelko, Roger. "Worship and the Community of Faith." In *Lutheran Worship: History and Practice*, edited by Fred L. Precht, 44–57. St. Louis: Concordia, 1993.

Plass, Ewald M., comp. *What Luther Says*. St. Louis: Concordia, 1959.

Pless, John. "Daily Prayer." In *Lutheran Worship: History and Practice*, edited by Fred L. Precht, 440–70. St. Louis: Concordia, 1993.

Polack, W. G. *The Handbook to the Lutheran Hymnal*. St. Louis: Concordia, 1942.

Pragman, James. *Traditions of Ministry*. St. Louis: Concordia, 1983.

Presbyterian Church (U.S.A.). *The Constitution of the Presbyterian Church*. Louisville, Ky.: The Office of the General Assembly, 1991.

Preus, Robert D. *The Doctrine of the Call in the Confessions and Lutheran Orthodoxy*. St. Louis: Luther Academy, 1991.

———. "Fellowship Reconsidered." Casper, Wyo.: Mount Hope Lutheran Church, 1971.

———. *Preaching to Young Theologians: Sermons of Robert Preus*. St. Louis: Luther Academy, 1999.

Quebedeaux, Richard. *By What Authority: The Rise of Personality Cults in American Christianity*. San Francisco: Harper and Row, 1982.

Resch, Richard. "Music: Gift of God or Tool of the Devil?" *Logia* 3, no. 2 (April 1994).

Richmond, Virginian. "The Relationship between Trait and State Communication Apprehension and Interpersonal Perceptions during Acquaintance Stages." *Human Communication Research*, no. 4 (1978).

Roberts, Alexander, and James Donaldson, eds. *Ante-Nicene Fathers*. 10 vols. Peabody, Mass: Hendrickson, 1994.

Robinson, Wayne. *I Once Spoke in Tongues*. Wheaton, Ill.: Tyndale, 1973.

Sasse, Herman. *This Is My Body: Luther's Contention for the Real Presence in the Sacrament of the Altar*. Adelaide, South Australia: Lutheran Publishing House, 1977.

Scaer, David P. "The Relationship between Doctrine and Practice." Paper given to the joint faculties of Concordia Theological Seminary, Ft. Wayne and Concordia Seminary, St. Louis, 2002.

Schaller, Lyle E. *44 Ways to Increase Church Attendance*. Nashville: Abingdon, 1988.

Schwiebert, E. G. *Luther and His Times*. St. Louis: Concordia, 1950.

Seilhamer, Frank H. "The New Measure Movement among Lutherans." *Lutheran Quarterly* 12 (May 1960): 121–43.

Sider, Ronald. *Karlstadt's Battle with Luther*. Philadelphia: Fortress, 1978.

Spitz, Lewis. *The Renaissance and Reformation Movements*. Vol. 2, *The Reformation*. Chicago: Rand McNally, 1972.

Strawn, Paul. "The Role of Music within the Worship Services of the Congregations of The Lutheran Church—Missouri Synod." Lectures given at University Lutheran Chapel, Minneapolis, 2003.

Strommen, Merton, Milo Brekke, Ralph Underwager, and Arthur Johnson. *A Study of Generations*. Minneapolis: Augsburg, 1972.

Synan, Vinson. *The Holiness-Pentecostal Movement in the United States*. Grand Rapids: Eerdmans, 1971.

Tappert, Theodore G. *The Book of Concord*. Philadelphia: Fortress, 1959.

von Schenk, Berthold. "Confirmation and First Communion," *Una Sancta* 14, no. 3 (Pentecost 1957). Cited by Donald Deffner in *Lutheran Worship: History and Practice*, edited by Fred L. Precht. St. Louis: Concordia, 1993.

Wagner, C. Peter. *Leading Your Church to Growth*. Ventura Calif.: Regal Books, 1984.

———. *Look Out! The Pentecostals are Coming*. Carol Stream, Ill.: Creation House, 1973.

———. *Strategies for Church Growth: Tools for Effective Mission and Evangelism*. Ventura, Calif.: Regal Books, 1987.

———. *Your Church Can Grow*. Ventura, Calif.: Regal Books, 1976.

Walther, C. F. W. *The Proper Distinction between Law and Gospel*. Translated by W. H. T. Dau. St. Louis: Concordia, 1929.

———. *Selected Writings of C. F. W. Walther: Editorials from "Lehre und Wehre."* Translated by Herbert J. A. Bouman. Edited by Aug. R. Suelflow. St. Louis: Concordia, 1981.

———. *Selected Writings of C. F. W. Walther: Walther on the Church*. Translated by John Drickamer. St. Louis: Concordia, 1981.

Webster's New World Dictionary of the American Language. New York: Simon and Schuster, 1982.

Wells, David F. *God in the Wasteland: The Reality of Truth in a World of Fading Dreams*. Grand Rapids: Eerdmans, 1994.

Wesley, John. *A Plain Account of Christian Perfection*. London: Epworth Press, n.d.

———. *The Works of John Wesley*. 14 vols. Grand Rapids: Zondervan, 1958.

Westermeyer, Paul. *Te Deum, The Church and Music*. Minneapolis: Fortress, 1998.

Wingren, Gustaf. *Luther on Vocation*. Translated by Carl C. Rasmussen. Evansville, Ind.: Ballast Press, 1999.

Ylvisaker, S. C. *Grace for Grace*. Mankato, Minn.: Lutheran Synod Book Company, 1943.

Zager, Daniel. "Popular Music and Music for the Church." *Lutheran Forum* 36, no. 3 (Fall 2002): 20–27.

Zehnder, Mike, ed. *The Best of the Best in Contemporary Praise and Worship*. Phoenix, Ariz.: Fellowship Publications, 2000.